SHOWING THE FLAG

SHOWING THE FLAG

The Civil War Naval Diary
of Moses Safford,
USS Constellation

LAWRENCE J. BOPP
STEPHEN R. BOCKMILLER

CHARLESTON   LONDON
History
PRESS

Published by The History Press
18 Percy Street
Charleston, SC 29403
866.223.5778
www.historypress.net

First published 2004
Manufactured in the United Kingdom

ISBN 1-59629-014-5

Library of Congress CIP data applied for.

Front cover: In 1856, Italian artist, Tomaso de Simone painted this image while the ship was in Naples. *USS* Constellation *Museum, Baltimore, MD*
Back cover: Moses Safford as he appeared at the height of his career in 1880 as a local attorney in Kittery, Maine. *Courtesy of Joseph Frost*

Dedicated to Joseph Frost, World War II veteran, historian and a good friend, without whose efforts much of the history of Moses Safford, the USS Constellation *and Kittery, Maine, would have been lost forever.*

January 1, 1865
Off Fortress Monroe

Another year has overtaken me in my prison-house—how soon it has arrived. This is the third "New Year's Day" that I have spent on board this ship and during this time war has caused the land to mourn the loss of many of its bravest and best and has brought affliction and sadness to every home. Although as it has happened I have not been exposed to the shots of an enemy on the field of battle nevertheless I have reason to be thankful to Him "who marks the sparrow's fall" for my preservation from the dangers of the sea and from disease in the many unhealthy places that we have visited.

Contents

Acknowledgements

L ittle did we know that working on this diary about the USS *Constellation*'s three-year Civil War cruise would lead us onto a journey just as long. Our voyage, like Safford's was a welcome mix of good and bad experiences always coupled with hard work and interesting research. Fortunately, we did not have to make this journey alone. Our great thanks goes to those who supported us in many ways.

First of all, we are greatly indebted to the staff of the USS *Constellation* Museum. Former director Lou Linden put us in charge of this project and current director Chris Rowsom has continued that support and encouragement. Ship historians Glenn Williams and Ken Hickman were instrumental in providing historical background information. Director of Operations Stan Berry has always given us time from his busy schedule to assist us with practical knowledge in regard to running the ship. Ship's Manager Paul Powichroski was always willing to enlighten us as to the 1860s configuration of the ship.

We are also fortunate to belong to a group of excellent naval historians known as Ship's Company who stand ever willing to share their knowledge with their fellow members and the public at large. Of particular note is Myron Peterson who put his time and computer skills to work on our behalf to reproduce the archived images. Karl Feldmeyer did a great job of creating the maps for the project. Dave Nelson lent his past experience in the navy to compare our notes on the 1860s with the modern age to see how tradition continues to be carried on.

We thank the staff of the Office of the Historian, U.S. State Department, for their assistance in identifying many of the diplomats and consuls who appeared unnamed throughout the diary.

One of the great joys learned through our research was the welcome and helpful assistance we always received from libraries and librarians. Research librarian, author and close friend Lee Hadden ably assisted us in postproduction efforts. Numerous jaunts to the Nimitz Library at the United States Naval Academy were always productive thanks to its helpful staff. We thank Larry Clemens who introduced us to the staff and gave us the inside track as to the resources that exist at this fine facility. Pat Redfearn and Gary O'Shea of the George Hail Free Library in Warren, Rhode Island, unquestionably answered our inquiries in a most cordial manner. Hope Neilson at the Rice Library in Kittery, Maine, not only went out of her way to assist us in gaining local information about Moses Safford but put us onto our greatest asset when she introduced us to Joseph Frost.

Joe seemed to recognize us as fellow historians right from the start and welcomed us into his fold with strikingly warm hospitality. His bust, that is displayed prominently at the Athenaeum in Portsmouth, New Hampshire, rightfully honors this man. He has dedicated his long life to the preservation of the history surrounding his family, his community and the great state of Maine. We are greatly indebted to him and are proud to list him as one of our good friends.

Most importantly, we thank our wives, Katie A. Bopp and Stefania G. Bockmiller. Given the expense, both in time and money associated with accomplishing a project like this, the level of support, encouragement and particularly tolerance of a good and loving wife can make or break a married man's ability to achieve his goals. Katie and Stefania have always assisted and encouraged us in our pursuits in history education, and we thank them most heartedly for their love and support. They prove the adage that behind every strong man there is an even stronger woman.

Finally, we thank Moses Safford, the old sailor who not only served his country but also had the foresight to preserve his Civil War naval experience. Without the sacrifice and dedication of Americans like him, the United States of America would not be the great country it is today. We only hope that our efforts, in some small way, contribute to the proud heritage of the country we hold so dear. Thank you, Moses, for allowing us, as well as many others, to learn that the journey was well worth the taking.

Lawrence J. Bopp
Stephen R. Bockmiller

A Ship, A Man and a Legacy: Part One

Mention the Civil War navy and one with even a basic knowledge of the war will immediately call to mind stories of the *Monitor* and the *Merrimac* (CSS *Virginia*) or the *Alabama* and the *Kearsarge*. This is rightfully so, since these ships participated in two of the key battles that marked naval history during this era. The wheel of Dame Fortune spun in favor of these vessels as circumstances brought them to fame and glory. And yet, what of all the other ships and crews who risked their lives going to sea in search of victory? Are their efforts any less heroic despite the fact that they were not thrown into similar epic contests testing their bravery and skill? Was their participation any less important in the overall grand plans of war in blockading the Confederacy, seeking out enemy warships or protecting American commerce? Dispatched to the Mediterranean in 1862 to "show the flag" or defend American merchant shipping, the ship USS *Constellation* seemed to be far removed from the seat of war with slim hopes, or fears, of encountering an enemy vessel.

This last U.S. Navy all-sail-powered ship was to venture from an age of sail into an age of steam in a daring effort to take on ships not only capable of steam power, but also equipped with ironclad hulls and advanced rifled guns. The *Constellation*'s three hundred young males would be willing to stake their lives in any contest with any enemy. Risking the very real dangers of sea and weather, this vessel and her crew waited only for the call of opportunity to perform—to do their duty for their country. Indeed, during this three-year voyage, ten men would lose their lives. Just as with the thousands of young men and women today who serve on numerous unknown ships, patrolling perilous seas, awaiting opportunity through monotonous days of routine tedium and ever alert to serve in time of danger, *Constellation*'s crew nevertheless carried out her small assignment in the highest tradition of the U.S. Navy.

The USS *Constellation* had been completed and launched in 1797 from Baltimore, Maryland, as one of the first warships of the newly authorized United States Navy, approved by a Congressional act of 1794. She came to glory in 1799 and again in 1800 when she single-handedly won the very first victories of the U.S. Navy against French frigates *L'Insurgente* and *La Vengeance* in the so-called "Quasi-War" with France. The *Constellation* continued in service, performing numerous non-combative naval activities until 1853, when she was deemed unfit by naval authorities and was condemned. Efforts to build a new ship with the same name were at first rejected, but allowance was given to refurbish the old ship. (There remains the debate as to what can actually be considered "rebuilding"—simply making a change to the original ship or building a new vessel. The *Constellation* has been embroiled in this controversy since its own rebuilding.) Although some timbers from the original vessel were used in the building of the new ship, an entirely different vessel emerged from Gosport Navy Yard in Virginia. This new twenty-gun sloop of war was broader and longer than her predecessor and fated to be the last all-sail-powered vessel to be built by the U.S. Navy.

Launched in 1854, the newly created *Constellation* was sent in 1855 to protect American commerce in the Mediterranean. The U.S. Constitution had called for the abolishment of the slave trade to take effect in 1808. In compliance with this law, *Constellation* was appointed the flagship of the U.S. African Squadron, seeking out slavers, from 1859 to 1861. Several vessels were captured, including the *Cora*, which was carrying seven hundred newly acquired slaves. These captives were freed in Monrovia, Liberia, and the ship hoped to repeat her success with more prizes. In 1861, the ship *Triton* was taken. This ship turned out not to be carrying slaves but did reveal shocking news. The United States was now torn in two by a civil war that had begun the previous April with the firing by southerners upon the Federal Fort Sumter in Charleston Harbor. Inadvertently, *Constellation* had made the very first capture of a Confederate vessel. Upon the ship's return to New York, she was ordered to Portsmouth Navy Yard in Kittery, Maine, for refitting for future service in protecting American shipping in the Mediterranean. It was here that she would be joined by our diarist, Moses Safford.

Moses Atwood Safford was born on September 28, 1833, the second child of Edward Deering Safford (1806–1856) and the former Mary R. Lewis (1808–1860), at Kittery Point, Maine, near Pepperell Cove. His father was a master mariner and a fishing boat captain with a long past of seagoing experience, and Moses was not long in following his father's interests. This countered the desires of his mother who, seeing the intellectual ability of the boy, hoped that education would lead him to a far more lucrative and safer career than going to sea like the rest of the family. His grandfather, Moses Safford, was a Baptist minister who had died at the age of forty-five, leaving a widow with three children surviving from the eight they had brought into this world. Roger Mitchell Safford, the eldest child, was captured from the privateer *Harlequin* by the British in the War of 1812 and died in Dartmoor Prison in 1814. Edward's second eldest brother, Moses B. Safford, died of yellow fever while on a voyage in 1816. Mary Lewis's father, a shipmaster, had also died of yellow fever on a return voyage from the West Indies when she was just a girl. Thus, Mary's fears for her son were well founded.

Home-schooling, supplemented by church lessons, provided Moses with his early education. Edward joined Mary in discouraging their son from the sea but it came to naught. Being surrounded by nautical men and stories, Moses kept his eyes always to the sea. He took his first sea voyage at the age of eight on his brother's schooner, with his mother, on a trip to visit Boston. He fell victim to seasickness but it failed to discourage him from enjoying the trip. Later, as a teenager, Moses overcame his bouts of seasickness to ably perform his duties as a ship's cook. The allure of the sea continually called him back again and again every summer between winter school sessions.

At age sixteen his mother added to his private studies of geometry, trigonometry and navigation, with a tutor in French. Moses and a friend contracted a private instructor of their own by the name of "Peg-Leg" Griffin, a cobbler, pensioned marine and former London prizefighter. Griffin had lost his right leg when it was crushed by a loose gun during a storm at sea. Moses struggled with French but enjoyed becoming proficient in the lessons of fisticuffs.

When he was seventeen, Moses served aboard his first square-rigged vessel, the brig *Juniata*. He was disappointed that the West Indies did not live up to its exotic reputation. However, it was during this trip that he acquired all the skills of seamanship that he would need if he were to continue his dream of being a real sailor.

That winter Moses began private instruction under the direction of the attorney Stillman B. Allen, who would later head the esteemed law firm of Allen, Long, and Hommaway. Partner John D. Long later became governor of Massachusetts and was the secretary of war during the Spanish-American War. Mr. Allen also taught at the local public school, which allowed Moses to get a double dose of learning.

By 1851, Moses's father was ready to leave the sea and had become elected to the Maine legislature. Yet the owners of the ship *Memmon* approached him to take charge of their vessel to run charters to Liverpool. When he accepted, Moses soon begged to join him on that summer voyage. By this time Mary had become resigned to the fact that Moses was determined to be a mariner and declared that Moses should at least be taught "to run a ship properly" and that his father was the best man fit for this duty. Thus it came to pass that Moses became a crewmember and would learn to serve his father in a new discipline.

Edward Safford was a pious man and a strict disciplinarian. He tolerated no nonsense and was fair but firm in his dealings with his crew. He believed in keeping men busy, and everything aboard came under his close and watchful eye. He taught Moses the art of dealing with the complaints of his crew in private and showed him the importance of taking away their bravado before an audience. He warned Moses to avoid profanity, which "is not only sinful, but in bad taste." With a stroke of humor he also added, "Besides if men become accustomed to hearing you swearing at them all the time it will do no good on some occasion when it might possibly be useful." Another surprise to young Moses was his father's ability to deal with the medical ailments of his crew by referring to a local medical book, *Family Physician: Designed to Assist Heads of Families, Travellers and Sea-Faring People* by Dr. John Frisbee.

The toughness of his father in the first three weeks of the voyage set a pattern of behavior and conditioned the men in such a way as to avoid problems in handling the ship for the rest of the voyage. Such pressure was necessary and (as Safford would describe in his diary), the boatswain remarked when asked about it, "It didn't kill any of you, and would have been worse in winter. If a man can't stand getting ready for a summer cruise he had better enlist in the Marines, or stay on shore and keep store, or teach school and help educated fools to raise h—l trying to turn the world upside down to make it suit 'loafers' like themselves."

Upon his return, Moses signed aboard the schooner *Otis* to earn money fishing for mackerel in the Gulf of Saint Lawrence. Fortunately he was in a safe harbor when the great gale of 1851 swept the eastern seaboard. Nearly a hundred vessels were destroyed and hundreds of lives were lost when a two-day devastating windstorm bulled its way through New England on the third and fourth days of October.

The following spring Moses signed aboard the hermaphrodite brig *Cocheco* with twenty-three-year-old Captain Thomas Waldron, master. Carrying a cargo of "shooks" (bundled staves of molasses casks or hogsheads, of which those made of Maine ash were highly favored in Cuba) they sailed for Matanzas, Cuba. On the return voyage, when only three days out of port, Captain Waldron took sick and retired to his cabin leaving Moses in charge of navigating the ship. Hot, feeble winds slowed their progress and prevented them from entering Hatteras to get needed medical attention for the captain. Suddenly, a storm came up and they were caught in a severe squall. After fighting the storm successfully, the crew discovered that the captain had died in his cabin. To compound the men's grief, they were informed that sixteen-year-old crewman William Matthews was missing after last seen trying to unfoul the jib downhaul from the bowsprit. His body was never found.

Strong northerly winds prevented the ship from making port, so they were forced to give the captain a burial at sea. Upon arrival in Portland, public sentiment rose against the young crew and they were blamed for the loss of the two men. Although the voyage had been made in decent time and crowned a profitable trip, Moses suffered the bitter lesson that leadership bears heavy responsibility—and sometimes, blame.

Moses's need for funds caused him to take an apprenticeship in Massachusetts to learn to make shoes, and he was surprised to find that in only two months he had mastered the craft. However, his newly learned skills were temporarily put on hold when he was invited to go with his father to the legislature in Augusta, Maine. While there, he became a page for the House of Representatives. Moses became familiar with the members of the legislature and the manner of transacting governmental business. He spent a great deal of time in the Maine State Library, which added to his new experience as well as to his enjoyment of reading. However, the best part of the trip was the time he spent with his father, getting to know him more personally than ever before.

In the spring of 1853 Moses returned home and began his shoe business, sewing together parts sent to him from Lynn, Massachusetts. When his supplier went out of business, Moses easily returned to the sea. Hired as a first mate, he soon regretted his decision when he discovered that the captain who hired him was under the influence of alcohol. The captain's drunken habits put the entire crew on edge and the heavy responsibility of running the ship again fell upon Moses. On arrival at St. Pierre, France, Moses used his knowledge of French to learn from a French mariner of a good place to pick up a cargo. While the captain slept off a drunken spree, Moses ordered the ship to St. Thomas where they picked up a cargo of sugar and molasses to take to New York.

During this trip the captain fell into a sullen stupor that suddenly broke when they were only an hour out of port. His seeming insanity was well displayed when he inexplicably leaped overboard. Somehow the dunking returned his senses long enough for him to grab hold of a thrown grating. Although he had safely brought his captain back this time, Moses was filled with apprehension as to the portents of his future.

While anchored in the harbor, Safford's ship was accidentally struck and damaged severely by a towing steamer. Fortunately for Safford, he discovered the captain of this vessel was a relative, Captain Edward Parker, and he was offered a job aboard as second mate. Anxious to leave his present perilous situation, he accepted the offer and was off to Europe to drop off cargo and to pick up new goods and emigrants for the return voyage. While in Antwerp, Belgium, the first mate fell and broke his leg and was put in hospital, which thrust Moses back again into the position of first mate. He performed his duties well but he did not like hauling passengers. On the return trip he recorded his opinion in his diary, "I doubt a more objectionable cargo than human beings can be found for a ship." On his journey back Moses weathered a hurricane and the disagreeableness of the passengers, and returned safely home.

School at Dartmouth College, where Moses not only took courses but also taught navigation and surveying, was cut short when he was called home to take care of his father who had suffered a fall. With both his brothers at sea, his father's poor condition and severe suffering took its toll on the young man. Moses could not bear to see a man who had been such a symbol of strength now declining rapidly and losing courage to continue life. When a chance to become an assistant clerk in the House of Representatives came his way in December of 1855, he accepted only after his father had given him his blessing.

Politics was distasteful to Moses for what he described as its deceitfulness, and yet he managed to not only make his first political speeches, but also to gain a position in the secretary of state's office. He was also appointed a delegate to the Democratic State Convention at Bangor, Maine, the following April.

Politics was left behind when Moses returned home to find his father fighting futilely for his last moments of life. Regardless of the pain he was suffering, Edward asked Moses to tell his brothers to follow his example and remain ever faithful to God. With a firm reliance upon the mercy of the Almighty, Edward Safford passed away on August 19, 1856, at the age of fifty.

In February of 1857, Moses was elected captain of Company B, Maine Light Infantry, in a group organized by his law teacher and friend, Stillman B. Allen. Differences between Moses and Stillman, who had expected to be elected captain, were reconciled when Moses retained his rank but also agreed to continue study under Mr. Allen by way of apprenticeship for the practice of law. An agreement to pay Moses $100 for the first year was made and soon Moses was engrossed in his efforts to pursue his newly chosen profession.

Political and legal success came his way as a succession of appointments were given to him. He was appointed justice of the peace and quorum for York County. He taught school in district 6 of Kittery for a short while. In 1858 Moses was elected one of the selectmen and assessors for the town of Kittery. But the most influential appointment of his life came when Stillman Allen was appointed clerk of the U.S. Navy Yard at Kittery and Moses was asked to become assistant clerk.

However, the need to devote full time to his job as selectman and chairman of the board, as well as to finish his legal studies, forced him to resign his position at the navy yard in 1860. During this time Moses became actively involved in the court system and had an appellate case upheld in his favor for a trespass case known as *Frisbee v. Cutts*. Further involvement with his community came when his appointment as deputy United States marshal allowed him to take the census of the town of Kittery and the Isles of Shoals within Maine.

In September of 1860, tragedy struck again. Moses's mother had grievously suffered from the loss of her husband and her strength steadily declined. Finally, on September 2, she passed away. At the time only Moses was there with her, since Edward was in the Gulf of Saint Lawrence as the master of a fishing vessel and his brother John was settling a new home in Massachusetts after his recent marriage.

Always a staunch Unionist, Moses was upset with fellow Democrats who showed lackluster enthusiasm for the Union government and its operations to maintain the union of states. Such poor support by his party pushed Safford to the Republicans, the party which he reservedly supported throughout the rest of his life. When war broke out in 1861, Moses believed that if it were not a short affair, then he would most likely be conscripted. Desiring to make his own choice, he enlisted in the navy in November with hopes that his seafaring experience would eventually lead to his placement as a master's mate. While he awaited his desired appointment, he took a position as clerk at the navy yard where his talents were greatly needed and applied. Now the Fates took a hand in bringing a man and a ship together.

At that time, USS *Constellation* was in the yard undergoing extensive repairs after her work with the African Squadron. One day a summons from the commandant of the yard brought Moses before Commodore Henry Knox Thatcher. The commodore used his former friendship with Moses's father to make an appeal to Moses. Thatcher was to take command of *Constellation* when she was ready and he needed a worthy and accomplished man for a position in which he felt Moses was best qualified. He offered Moses the position of ship's yeoman. In those days this was a directly appointed rank, instead of an advancement to a clerical position for an enlisted man as it is today. It required a well-trained seaman who was also intimately acquainted with all operations necessary to the performance of a sailing ship. To add to the enticement, Thatcher offered Moses an opportunity to serve as his legal representative on board to handle some of his personal affairs. Knowing full well that taking this position would end all hopes of a future commission, Moses nonetheless accepted. In his reasoning, such a request was more of a command and, therefore, as a loyal subordinate to the commodore, he could not refuse.

Thus it was that the man and the ship were joined. To help pass the time aboard, Moses began keeping a diary. He wrote on sheets of foolscap and carefully inscribed his thoughts in ink using a steel pen. In his seafarer's way, he recorded the wind changes and setting of sails much like as in a ship's logbook. That he desired this voyage to be a chance to see the world became most obvious as he meticulously documented his numerous excursions.

His position of yeoman was ideal for observing life aboard ship since he was considered an enlisted man but served in the capacity of a warrant officer. His views of life around him were open and honest as he recorded his personal opinions of those with whom he served, from the lowest enlisted stewards and bandsmen to all of the commissioned officers, including the two captains he served. Moses was proud to be in what he believed was the original frigate and yet he lamented being aboard a vessel he described as being "archaic, obsolete, or at least beyond its time."

He was truly a man wishing to keep in touch with the happenings at home while serving abroad, as revealed by his close following of accounts given by newspapers both domestic and foreign. The lapses of time from the occurrence of the event and his recording of the same combine with the sketchy quality of journalism of the era to provide a skewed recording of history on his part. For a man who later became a renowned historian, he must be forgiven his mistakes with the understanding that he was only recounting what he was reading as the truth.

Regardless of his own misgivings with his command of the written English language, Moses Safford was quite literate and often poetic in his entries. Personal emotion colored his writing with a full palette of feeling and understanding. The losses of war were balanced with the full activities of his life both on and off ship. Although the diary was strictly for his own edification and personal remembrance, his writing brings the reader back in time and place and opens a window to the past, allowing a view of Civil War naval life through the eyes of a literate and master seaman.

Moses referred to his life aboard ship as a "confinement" and often counted the days of his "imprisonment." Although he feared dire results from any encounter with a superior steam-powered or ironclad vessel, Safford was united with the crew in their desire for action, if for no other reason than to break up their days of routine sea duty. Insulated from combat, serving aboard an outdated vessel, and completely naive about the horrors of warfare, Safford, along with the rest of the crew, believed he had been assigned the worst duty station in the war. Yet, despite the regrets of his decision to serve this ship, Moses nonetheless very capably performed his duties as assigned. He grievously lamented when illness took him away from his work and he deplored poor performance by others. Diary entries show his empathy for crewmembers even when they were in the wrong. His complaints about sea life are often belied by entries that reveal his honest love of the sea and his enjoyment of life aboard a man-of-war ship.

The editors have maintained the integrity of the diary as much as possible. Safford's abundant use of capitalization has been retained. Endnotes address most misspellings, particularly of names of people and places. The reader is informed as to the true nature of the events Safford reports from newspapers and colleagues. Assistance is also provided to give understanding of events well known to Safford's contemporaries but vague to modern readers. Explanations of nautical terms, customs and regulations of the time appear to assist the reader's understanding and knowledge. The excursions Moses took to "see the world" will serve to relieve the reader of sea life much as they did for Moses and his compatriots, as well as to give the reader a glimpse of the foreign world during this time of American crisis.

Now let the vision of Moses Safford become yours as the diary unfolds. This narrative of the ship, the man and the legacy will be completed at the end of the diary. But for now, go back to 1862 and relive life aboard a warship seeking to "show the flag," or demonstrate to foreign nations that American commerce still remained under the protection of American might despite the ravages of a civil war at home. Share in the thrill of seeking out enemy raiding vessels while defying the cruel elements of nature. Join the men of this crew as they risk their lives while trying to preserve the noble idea of maintaining the *United* States of America.

The Civil War Naval Diary of
Moses Safford

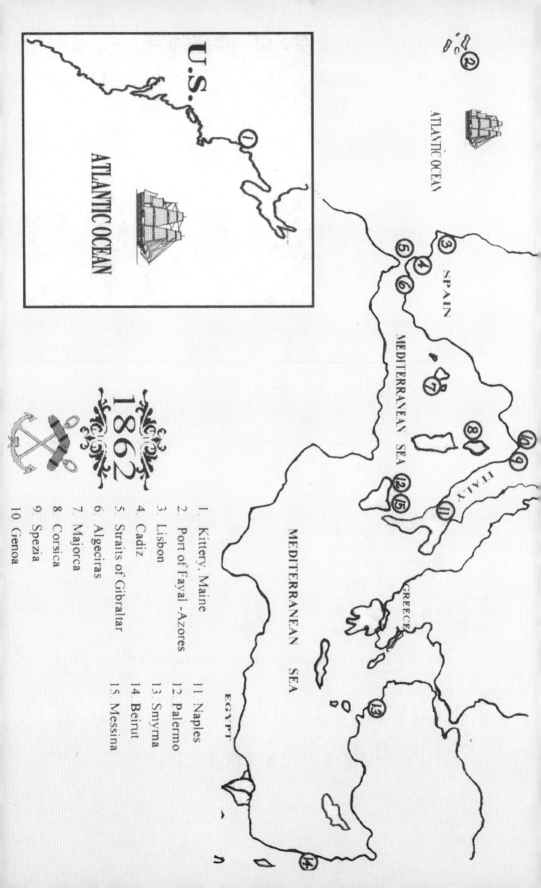

U.S.

ATLANTIC OCEAN

ATLANTIC OCEAN

ATLANTIC OCEAN

SPAIN

MEDITERRANEAN SEA

ITALY

GREECE

MEDITERRANEAN SEA

EGYPT

1862

1. Kittery, Maine
2. Port of Fayal -Azores
3. Lisbon
4. Cadiz
5. Straits of Gibraltar
6. Algeciras
7. Majorca
8. Corsica
9. Spezia
10. Genoa

11. Naples
12. Palermo
13. Smyrna
14. Beirut
15. Messina

Chapter One
March 1862 to June 1862

March 11, 1862
On board U.S. Ship Constellation.

This day at three o'clock, P.M. the topsails are hoisted at masthead and fasts singled, all ready to sail from the Kittery Navy Yard. Half an hour later we are coming down the Piscataqua with a breeze from the West. Upon approaching forts McClary and Constitution, the usual salutes are fired and the compliment was returned by our ship by hearty cheers from the men in the rigging.[1]

The breeze freshens and soon we are free from the harbor at Portsmouth, out upon the broad Atlantic. It is a pleasant night and as our ship sails on her way some are singing songs, some are playing upon the viol, guitar and tambourine, and many looking sad, at the idea of leaving the comforts and associations of home for a cruise of three years. Nobody knows where. We are sailing under sealed orders.

March 12
Atlantic Ocean

This morning on coming on deck the sails are to be seen trimmed closer to the wind but our ship is going along finely at the rate of ten knots. We are steering an ESE course. The weather is fine. Some of my mess are sick—sea-sick. I am not although I have not been on a voyage at sea for eight years.

Some say that we are to go to the Azores and there receive orders, but no one knows with certainty whither we are sailing.

This day I have been in the Store Room quite busy all day securing and delivering stores.[2]

It is more rough and the ship rolls quite heavily at times. I find myself nearly used up with a cold on my lungs. I am so hoarse that I can scarcely speak aloud. Nearly all the ship's company are affected in the same manner. I hope that we shall soon change the atmosphere, for with it I look for a cure.

March 13
Atlantic

The ship rolls deeply, the wind has changed more to the Northwest and we are flying before the wind at a fast rate. The sun shines and it is very pleasant. As much wind as we want.

As the night approaches the sea grows rougher and the increasing wind forebodes a storm. I have been in the storeroom all day—have not been on deck an hour.

March 14

During the night the wind died away and lower studding sails have been gotten out. The morning is mild and the weather has that peculiar characteristic to be observed in the Gulf Stream. I find my cold much better. During the past twenty four hours our ship has sailed twelve and fourteen knots per hour. Could we have such a wind for a week longer we should reach Fayal by the end of that time. At noon the wind changed to the Eastward. It looks like a storm. I am very busy in the Store Room. Sometimes six men are in at a time—some for blocks, one for a piece of leather, another for a piece of seizing; one for spikes, one for a piece of lead—and everybody for something—if he can get it. Flying from one place to another tends to make me cross and the waiting men find short answers and rough invitations to leave the room as soon as may be consistent with the object of their visit. I have always had an unreasonable prejudice against shop-keeping and I fear that this experience may make me rough and morose in my manner. One can find good use for all patience which he may be fortunate enough to possess.

I was at Quarters two hours today. A marine was "triced up"[3] in the Brig for being found asleep on post at the Spirit Room[4] when Fire Quarters was called. Here we find discipline and inconsistency combined. The poor fellow who, I presume, was frightened made a loud noise.

March 15
At sea

Last night it rained and the wind blew from the East. The ship was put under single reefed top sails and headed to the South. This morning the wind changed to the West and now we have a fine breeze and we are making good speed on our course. The sea is a little rough but the weather has changed to summer warmth.

This forenoon we made a ship, hove to and waited for her to come up. At 1½ o'clock she sent a boat to us. She proved to be an American ship from England to New York, sixty days out. Her captain was on board about an hour. I sent a letter to my brother Edward by her. Her name was the *Helena*. The day has been quite warm, tonight it is foggy.

March 16, Sunday
At sea

This morning there is a gentle breeze from the Southwest with the occasional showers. Last evening it was very pleasant. The moon shone brightly and the weather was warm. I remained on deck until three bells.

I am constantly impressed with the stupidity and irresponsible character of many of our crew. Without supervision and restraint they would be wasteful and lax in all duty. There <u>are</u> however men of true thrift and business capacity in our crew.

All hands were mustered on the Quarter Deck as is customary on Sabbath forenoons. The ship is damp in every part. My Store Room is like a damp cellar. I do not consider any part of such a ship healthy below the Spar Deck[5] with so many men on board. The wind has changed and blows heavy from the South and we are under reefed top-sails.

Since I finished my last period, as I supposed for today, while sitting forward near the Fore Hatchway while the Forecastle crew were hauling up the bight of the Port chain the ship gave a sudden heavy plunge and the cry of "Man overboard" suddenly rang fore and aft. It was the Captain of the Forecastle, John Campbell, a good natured benevolent looking man with whom I had been conversing only a short time before. I had previously known him for several years under the name of John Alexander. He was a sober reliable man and why he changed his name I do not know.

A boat was lowered, the life buoys dropped, and the ship stayed; we ran in the direction of the man while the boat had gone to the buoys. We came so near to him that we could look down upon him and see him floating with his head under water. The boat found him. The Doctor tried to resuscitate him but life was extinct. The poor fellow is shrouded in his white linen suit with his black hdkf. on his neck and laid on the Gun Deck.

How uncertain is life—a few minutes he was a strong man in the vigor of manhood—now he lies cold and dead.

March 17
At sea
Rough all night and rough now. The ship is on her course but in the heavy sea under double reefed top-sails she does not make much headway. Great quantities of water come on the Berth Deck and settle to the leeward. Weather warm.

Seven bells. All hands are called to "bury the dead."

I went on deck to the Port Gangway and around the dead sailor who was drowned yesterday were congregated his shipmates with uncovered heads. They listened to reading from the Testament by the First Lieutenant and the corpse was lifted to an inclined position to slide with the lurch of the ship to leeward into the sea. It is an impressive sight to witness.

The good ship is driving along under reefed top-sails, the storm pouring upon us, while every roll she makes puts in motion everything unsecured. Decks are full of water. A disagreeable day.

March 18
At sea
A dull stormy morning. The wind is the same as yesterday—ship under the same sail—quite rough and wet. The ship is on her course and making good headway. Everything aboard is in a mixed up state. Surely life on a crowded warship in such weather is disagreeable, everything so damp, decks so slippery with slime and water that one cannot stand, much less can he walk, without holding onto something.

Fair weather commences and one of the finest of days follows the storm. By Friday, March 21, I expect to see the Western Islands if the wind continues fair.

March 19
A pleasant morning with the wind fair but light. Conditions aboard are more comfortable. I am busy all day in the Store Room, writing.

It is strange and rather disgusting to hear so many who have been long in the Service expressing a wish to be out of it and asserting positively that if on shore nothing could induce them to return. I know how sailors talk and growl, but men who are in different capacities should keep quiet for the present and carry out their resolves when free to do so. A man-of-war is not a very agreeable place for a man to enjoy life, I must admit, but it will be well to <u>remember</u> it in the future rather than <u>talk</u> of it now.

March 20
At sea

This morning commences with good weather. A fine breeze from the same quarter continues to propel us along on our course. All hands are washing clothes and cleaning ship. The ceaseless motion of the ship rocks me from side to side down in my small cavern apart from the little world in which I live. Here I can muse alone, but like a plant screened from the rays of the sun I fear that I shall not grow stronger physically or mentally. This store keeping is a new experience for me. No responsibility for the ship nor for the crew. No watch to stand. It is like being a passenger.

March 21
At sea

Still fair wind and fair weather. The old ship is on her course, but, <u>how</u> she rolls. She is better for performing this part of her motions than anything I was ever on or ever saw. Our mess came near going into the main hold, table, chairs and all.[6]

I saved myself by dropping on my face and bracing my feet against the hatch coaming, being back to the hatch. Our Paymaster's Steward, who is one of our mess, thinks that this is a "hard life." He is seasick and has been so for ten days. Poor fellow, Cox, he cannot see the fun in going to sea. According to my mental reckoning since leaving home we should see the Azores today. They are not in sight yet.

March 22
At sea

This morning the wind is fair with a smoother sea. No land in sight yet. I surmise that we will run past the Azores without seeing them. I should judge that we had already run more than two thousand miles.

There can be little enjoyment on board so long as the ship labors so heavily. I consider her one of the <u>greatest</u> of rollers. We have really had a good wind to cross the ocean, if ten dollars worth of dishes have been broken in the Ward Room.

This afternoon we have a strong breeze and a reef in the top-sails. At night the ship was hove to under close reefed top-sails. Evidently we are supposed to be near land and are waiting for daylight.

March 23

This is a fine morning and land is to be seen, a very high mountain which the men call "Peak of Pico." If so, the outlying Flores, 150 miles northwest, which I reckoned on making the 21st must have been passed without being sighted. Pico is now to the East of us and looks fifty miles away, but it may not be a quarter of that distance. In a clear day I am told that it can be seen a day's sail at sea. The twelfth day from home with a fair wind nearly all the time and a good breeze too, we have just come to the Western Islands. Surely the Atlantic is something more than a mere mill pond.

Last night a man fell from the main topsail yard while reefing the main topsail. One of the nettles[7] drew through the sail . He was not seriously injured although he fell backward some twenty feet.

At twelve o'clock, M. we hove to close in to the Port of Fayal. The land is lofty, the middle of the island rises in a high cliff, the top of which is seldom seen at this season on account of the dense clouds which overhang it. The land slopes gradually to the water where it terminates in a steep rugged shore. Numerous ravines traverse the vineyards and wind their way to the sea from the mountains. The vineyards look like regularly formed beds, from the sea, as we sail along the coast. A boat is lowered to go ashore but is stove alongside and again taken to the davits. No pilot answers the signal from our ship and as the wind increases the topsails are close reefed and the ship headed to sea again. How it blows. The ship labors heavily and is very wet. Tonight will be a tough one—the roughest since we came out. I have been in my Store Room twelve times since eight bells—four times while completing my supper.

March 24
At sea

Last night the wind blew a gale. The ship was run under close reefed topsails and main storm staysail. The decks were flooded, the cabin was nearly filled and it required a large crew to clear it from the water which rushed through the ports. The ship lurched fearfully, throwing mess chests from their beds across the deck, and every now and then a shot from the racks would fly across the deck with lightning speed. It is a little ludicrous to see the Captain's mattress, bed clothes, trunk and everything movable vanishing across the Cabin, right and left, with the water two feet above the floor.[8]

His clerk is wedged firmly under a 32 Pdr. gun and the First Lieutenant is dashed headlong between the gun and ship's side on the other side of the Cabin just in time to escape a large trunk which follows him and jambs him in with no more regard for a First Lieutenant's head than the ship's cook's. Water is coming through the chain pipes onto the berth deck by the bucketful. On such an occasion surely one may sit and philosophize— learn to be content wherever he may be, and more than all, appreciate the comforts of a home on the sod.

But somebody must "plough the waves" and I am content for the present. This a disagreeable ship in rough water—wet and uneasy—but a very good sailor. Last night she ran 14 knots per hour.

Towards noon the sea becomes smoother and the ship runs along much easier. This has been a very quiet day with the exception of the cries of a poor fellow who was "triced up" for about two hours.

March 25
At sea

This morning is fine—a fair wind and a smooth one—the sun shines bright and our good ship is heading on her course. It is reported that we are to proceed directly to Lisbon. If so we have more than nine hundred miles to sail before we see the land again.

March 26
At sea

Last night all hands were called to reef topsails. It blew heavy and rained hard. This morning it is fine again and the wind still fair. During the forenoon the reefs are shaken out of the topsails and the topgallant sails are set. We have been under easy sail since we left. We are evidently not in a hurry on this cruise. I have been accustomed to crowding sail on a vessel and I feel impatient when fair winds prevail to make this ship travel. Had all the sail been kept on her which would have been prudent we would be in Lisbon now. Yesterday afternoon we ran thirteen knots per hour. The two last days have been the finest since we have been at sea.

Saw a ship south of us standing to the westward on the wind. It is the fourth or fifth, only, which we have seen since we sailed.

March 27
At sea

This morning finds us with the same fair wind. How we have been favored. Had it been desired to accept true favor we could have been in Lisbon today. A man-of-war is not often in a hurry.

The wind increases to a gale. The mizzen topsail is furled, the fore and main topsails close reefed and the foresail reefed and these with the jib are driving her along from ten to twelve knots per hour. I have been very busy in the Store Room all day. Our corned beef is the worst kind of "horse."[9]

Our mackerel, labeled "Mess," are "poor threes." Both beef and mackerel were furnished by Moulton & Blaisdell, Portsmouth, N.H. at high prices. I wish that they had to eat the rusty fish and drink such quantities of our water as is required to freshen them sufficiently for digestion to function after they are eaten. Our water comes from iron tanks and looks like some liquor for coloring red.[10]

The cloth on our table has been saturated with coffee, grease and everything else during our entire rough passage from the United States and now it refuses to part from the hand which may happen to rest on it during a meal. It smells like a fish cart in mid-summer. It won't do to say much to the mess cook for one has left us since we started on the voyage and the trouble that they have in catering for the mess is not all in our favor. However I will leave this subject for the present as I shall doubtless say something more particular hereafter.

As night approached the wind increased to a gale and we being only about 100 miles from Lisbon the ship was hove-to under close reefed main topsail and main spencer. The sea was quite rough during the night.

March 29
At sea

This morning our ship lies in the same position. Three ships are in sight—hove-to—and probably waiting for the gale to subside that they may run on to land. I found the Store Room blockaded with all kinds of stores, the result of rolling last night. This ship cannot be beaten for that thing.

We have remained all day in the position as we were this morning. The wind has subsided and the sun shines beautifully. A lovely day but still at sea with a fair wind. Perhaps we may be lying for the *Sumter*, that privateer which has eluded the grasp of the Federal Navy thus far.[11]

March 30
At sea

The wind increases and rain comes. The ship is still hove-to. I suppose that it was considered too rough to go over the bar at Lisbon yesterday, hence the delay. Now it is thick weather and the storm prevents. About four bells more sail was put on the ship to keep her to the windward. A dull day in many respects. Sometimes it rains and then the sun shines. This is Sunday—a Sunday on a man-of-war.

March 31
At sea

We have "kept off" at last for port. A fine morning with a fair wind give assurance that we shall see the coast of Portugal before night.

At twelve o'clock M. The high land off Lisbon is in view. What a fine day. A gentle breeze fans us toward the shore whence Columbus nearly four hundred years ago departed for an unknown land across the Atlantic. My home is in that land. Today I see the headland on which the eye of that adventurous navigator last rested as he sailed upon his momentous voyage. How the world has changed since then. For many years now America has been sending its ships to the land whence Columbus came. I am sailing under the flag of one of the nations which has grown up in Columbus' New World. I am on a war ship representing the Navy of the United States, still important and still formidable even though a dark cloud of political strife hangs over my once happy country. What if some features of the passage across the Atlantic have been unpleasant, today I feel emotions which I never felt before as I approach this part of Europe associated in my mind with so many historical events.

The wind did not permit us to go in tonight. A gun was fired for a pilot, but none appeared until we had hauled off, then the flash of a torch showed in the distance that a pilot was approaching. He put back again soon afterward and we lay until morning with the main topsail aback.

April 1
Lisbon

A calm morning, not a ripple on the water. We have drifted a little out from the land. All hands are busy in cleaning the ship. One of the men slipped and fell on the ladder to the gun deck and broke his arm and dislocated the bones of his wrist.

Afternoon. We are entering the port of Lisbon. On the left inland from Cape Roque [Cape Roca] the land is high and rises in numerous little cone-like hills. I am informed that these prominences were caused by the great earthquake which destroyed so much of the city of Lisbon.[12] As we come nearer there appears a castle like fortress against the base of which the waves dash and foam. In the distance upon a high hill is to be seen what is said to be the largest convent in the country. Then comes the Castle of Belem, famous for its political prisoners in times past. We hoisted the Portuguese standard and fired a salute of 21 guns. Soon afterward the guns of the Castle of Belem belched from beneath its lofty turrets clouds of smoke which were followed by the barks of its black-muzzled war-dogs and echoes from the recesses of the fortress. Beyond there comes in view the Palace of Don Juan taken by the British in the Peninsular War and used as soldiers' barracks. These buildings are of a yellowish grey color and around them are smaller structures of an ashy hue, like dirty whitewash.

The slopes along the river are a spring-time green in which almond trees are recognizable by their purple blossoms. Here and there are houses built of stone, some of a pinkish and light brown color. Scores of windmills are to be seen in every direction on the hills. They are fitted with sails which are in motion. The houses are square and without chimneys above the roof. Small outlets are made on either side of the roof and sheltered by a portion of the roof as a window would be in a similar situation. I am told that one or the other of these openings are used to let out smoke, according to the direction of the wind. Numerous pretentious residences with verandas and gardens are seen along the margin of the river. These houses of different colors, as white or pink or blue, stand out in striking contrast to the green about them. The land on the south side rises from the water as a steep bank of yellow sand on the top of which the grass grows green and houses are to be seen. Along the city water front the land is level, but soon rises in hills and cliff-like eminences. Some of the streets are very steep and narrow.

April 2
Lisbon

We are at anchor a short distance below the city. The outgoing current is very strong. Last evening a boat came alongside with figs, oranges, cherries and other fruit which the men eagerly bought and ate.

April 3
Lisbon

Last night a man fell overboard from the gig at the stern. The current carried him a long distance but he was finally recovered.

All hands labored late making ready to clean the ship this morning in order to be in shape to receive official visitors. The cleaning began at an early hour this morning. The decks have been holystoned[13] and in other respects the ship begins to look clean and shipshape for the first time since she has been in commission. She has hither to looked more like an emigrant ship than a man-of-war.

The American[14] and British Ministers were on board today. The Store Room was illuminated for them. I have been very busy with my men all day putting things in order.

April 4
Lisbon

A fine day. The crew was put early at work cleaning hammocks and clothes. Two salutes were fired yesterday for Ministers and one today for the King of Portugal[15] who boarded a Portuguese man-of-war. Yards were manned and the Portuguese ship was decorated with flags. The King was rowed in a large barge followed by two smaller boats. A lively day.

April 5
Lisbon

The crew complains of the work which they have to perform in cleaning ship and in the exercise of yards and sails than they can do now.

I am told that Lisbon is a dear place for foreigners. Nothing but fruit can be bought for a reasonable price.

April 6
Lisbon

The bells sound forth their morning chorus which denotes the Sabbath in New England, but here a day of pleasure and pastimes—a holiday. Bull fights and theaters are among the regular local amusements of the Sabbath.

This afternoon I went on shore with John M. Glenn, the Master-at-Arms and one of my mess mates. He is a very jolly, good natured man although he has the reputation of having been "on his muscle," and some of the crew declare that he still is. He is a young man from Troy, New York. He has fought in the ring as a broken nose and other evidence of pugilistic encounters indicate. Physically he is a good specimen of manhood.

The day is as warm as July at home. We reached the landing at Lisbon about 1½ o'clock P.M. There was a crowd about the landing place, including fishermen, boatmen and beggars. The buildings nearby are of stone and ancient in appearance, four stories high and square. The streets are paved with stone of a dark blue color, like our slate, together with a white free-stone so arranged as to represent stars and other figures in the public squares.

The inhabitants regard Americans as easy money. A glass of English ale takes all of one's half dollar. A luncheon takes a dollar. At a place of amusement a poor seat costs an American a price above the best to a native.

We saw the famous Black-Horse Square[16] in the center of which is a massive bronze statue of Joseph Ist, King of Portugal. He is on horseback with his face turned to look toward the west. On the base of the statue, in bas relief, a Hercules like figure is represented as struggling with an elephant and a horse. Beyond the statue is a high archway leading into one of the principal streets of the city not yet finished. The buildings under construction are of better appearance than the buildings generally. The shops are small dark apartments and the markets are not worthy of the name.

We visited the King's Garden, so called, a kind of museum and picture gallery. It is a rough place in some respects. I presume that the king must have other "gardens." In it are numerous works of art, both of sculpture and paintings. One of the best examples of sculpture was an immense Hercules in a reclining position. The face is most life-like in expression. Many statues bore marks of time and were broken, suggesting that they went through the earthquake more than a century ago. Some of the paintings were lifelike and beautiful. One in particular, that of a lady with a youth by her side, impressed me. A silk dress with many trimmings was so skillfully pictured that the very luster of the silk was shown. So real did it seem that I could almost fancy that I could hear the silk rustle.

Glenn and I were glad that we changed our original intention of going to a bull fight. We will have other opportunities to see bull fights, but we may not get another chance to see Lisbon. Our afternoon's ramble was very satisfactory, considering our lack of a guide and our inability to speak Portuguese. The guides have the reputation of being untrustworthy, dishonest and treacherous.

In the evening we took a guide and visited some places of amusement. We also went into an eating saloon for a luncheon. They brought us beef steak cut in thin slices and smothered in garlic. The first taste was not bad, it reminded me of Canada, but I got a surprise after I had swallowed some. I have always claimed that a person who would eat onions should not object to garlic, but even a good thing may not be over done. I was hungry and managed to get this Portuguese culinary product down with the help of liberal gulps of wine and half a loaf of bread, for which we succeeded in getting the waiter to bring us some butter after considerable pantomime. Glenn could not eat his portion and ordered fish.

April 7
Lisbon

Came on board this morning at seven o'clock. Found all hands busy cleaning ship. During the day they started breaking out and re-stowing the hold. This work was not completed until midnight. The crew complain loudly of the hours which they are compelled to labor. They are "worked up" pretty well and get little sleep.

April 8
Lisbon

The day is lovely. Everybody is busy and nearly everybody is cross. There may be such a thing as too much work, even for sailors. Tonight I am glad to turn into my hammock.

April 9
Lisbon

The crew is busy "rattling down"[17] the ship's rigging. Stores went out rapidly today and I have had as much as I could do in the Store Room.

I hope that this busy time may end the <u>drive</u> for labor for many months.

The Captain and the First Lieutenant went on shore today to visit the King, by invitation.

April 10
Lisbon

Business on shipboard continues brisk but by the end of the week much which now employs the men will be completed.

The American Minister was again on board today.

The weather is like a hot summer day at home. Everybody on board is now thoroughly thawed out.

April 11
Lisbon

A lovely morning again appears. How unlike our New England Spring. The crew is still "rattling down" and painting.

The U.S. Sloop-of-War *St. Louis* has arrived below from Cadiz.

April 12
Lisbon

A sunny morning. Less work is being done today than for some days.

The *St. Louis* has come up near the city. She is twelve days from Cadiz.

Tonight Glenn, the Master-at-Arms, punished a Negro by "tricing up" until he came near his end. He was carried on deck unconscious but was revived. Four boys were also "triced up" unmercifully. Glenn unfortunately was intoxicated and acted without his usual care. I am sorry for Glenn. He is now in the brig in double irons. "Tricing up" is a bad custom and should not be allowed at all. The whole crew are aroused and are indignant and reckless over the affair.

April 13
Lisbon

The Sabbath has come again. It is showery, but the sun shines most of the time—really a fine day. There were general quarters and inspection of the ship's company. The ship now looks clean and quite creditable in other respects.

In the afternoon I went on shore alone. I visited another "King's Garden." It is a beautiful place. There is a profusion of plants and flowers. There are ponds shaded by numerous trees, iron fountains sustained by sculptured marble figures, swans and fishes and seats for visitors. A good band added music. Men and women in groups are sitting about. Everybody looks comfortable and happy.

From this garden I strolled through the city to the Market which was open, though the day was Sunday. Men and old women of all sorts and kinds, some grotesque in appearance were offering for sale vegetables of all kinds, poultry, cheeses, curds and other articles. Fowls were being killed and dressed on the spot, a proceeding which tended to make the market offensive. One old woman was burned out the night before and was mourning over a pile of ill smelling feathers, all that remained of her stock of fowls. It was doubtless a serious loss to her.

Along Gold Street I had an opportunity to see in the balconies the women of the upper social classes. In appearance the women of Lisbon will compare favorably with those of any place. Some are dark in complexion but many might be mistaken for English women.

At sunset I went to the landing to take our boat to return to the ship, but the boat was overloaded and the Boatswain whom I met there and I decided to return uptown and hire a boat later to take us back to the ship after the tide had turned. The Boatswain, a jolly fellow townsman of mine, had been in Lisbon before in merchant ships and we called on a family with whom he was acquainted. Before we left a considerable company had gathered there only one of whom a man, the Boatswain's friend, spoke English. Several of the women spoke French of about the same kind as mine, which has suffered badly from lack of practice in recent years. Nevertheless we all managed to have a really enjoyable time.

Lisbon houses as a rule are not occupied on the first floor except for storage purposes. Heavy entrance doors are attached to stone side posts by massive butts. The latches are also large and clumsy. It seems like entering a warehouse from the street. The living rooms are however high, neatly furnished and attractive.

Outside in the street beggars lie sleeping in the sun or annoying passersby in demanding alms. Poverty and vice, wealth and refinement offer striking contrasts in Lisbon.

April 14
Lisbon

There are indications that the ship is about to sail. The American Minister and his family are making a farewell visit. By orders my Store Room is lighted for inspection, as usual when distinguished visitors are aboard. My exhibits more useful than ornamental, but everybody is invited down to take a look.

I am content to leave old Lisbon and go to a new place. We go to Cadiz.

April 15

All hands are called at eight bells to weigh anchor. The sails are set and we rapidly glide out of the harbor. Farewell to Lisbon. I have seen your streets, your gardens and your buildings and have enjoyed your entertainments for which I have paid at an exorbitant rate. I am ready to go. The hill slopes—how green; everything—how beautiful. Castles, towers, palaces and ruins fade rapidly in the distance and we soon feel the Atlantic's swells. Clouds grow heavy and light sails come in. We are running into a storm.

April 16
Atlantic Ocean

Topsails were reefed last night but the wind is not so heavy this morning. Twenty-five sails are in sight, ships and other square rigged vessels going toward and from the Strait and Spanish ports.

April 17
At sea

Off Cape St. Vincent with a good breeze, but with the wind ahead and making little headway. Run to the leeward or heave to with a fair wind, and beat when the wind comes ahead—that is the way they do in a man-of-war.

Last night at seven bells all hands were called to Quarters. This was the first time that I was ever turned out for Quarters at night, but I was the first man to report to the officer of my Division, and I took my hammock up to the nettings, whereas some left theirs on the berth deck behind the mess chests. The whole affair was discreditable to us. Some guns were fired in their breechings and boarders responded after a fashion when called away, but even when retreat was beaten we were not in readiness for action. We demonstrated the lack of drilling but there was also too much confusion to suit my idea of doing things at such a time.

Probably the reports of our guns will give rise to rumors that an engagement has taken place off Cape St. Vincent between some Federal vessel and a Rebel cruiser. It will be quite as true as hundreds of rumors which are being spread by the newspapers in these times of excitement.

April 18
Cadiz

The sea is smoother this morning than we have seen it since we sailed from Portsmouth. I estimate that we are about forty miles from Cadiz, towards which we are moving under a light breeze. At twelve o'clock land and the city of Cadiz are in view. The buildings and high walls of Cadiz stand out distinct from the surrounding land and give an impression of a city on the sea. As we approach nearer a lighthouse is seen to the southwest of the city and the dome of a cathedral in the center. Near the water, all around the city as far as we can see, there are high walls or fortifications built of a dark colored stone. The buildings of the city to be seen are large, square and very white.

For some reason on which I do not know, we are quarantined and not permitted to communicate with the shore.

April 19
Spain

Summer warmth with a gentle breeze. Cadiz looks like a miniature city on a glass surface. We are permitted no communication with the shore except through the health officer. I am busy on some personal work for the Captain trying to straighten out some badly tangled accounts. He got into the habit of using me for such work before the ship went into commission, while she was fitting out.

April 20
Cadiz

A summer-like day with a strong breeze. All hands are mustered in white frocks. Captain Pickering of the USS *Kearsarge* was on board with other officers of his ship.

April 22
Cadiz

An American ship leaves tomorrow for New York and word is passed that letters may be sent by her. We are all taking advantage of this opportunity to write to our families and friends.

News has just reached us that a great battle has been fought in Mississippi in which the Confederates lost thirty five thousand and the Federals twenty five thousand men. The Rebels were led by Beauregard and Johnston and the Federals by Grant and Buell. Johnston is reported killed and Beauregard severely wounded. Manassas, Clarksville, Leesburg and Big Bethel all are ours and the army is advancing "on to Richmond." Whether this be all true may be with safety questioned, but if so, it seems that the Rebel cause must be a hopeless one. The account, if true, tells of a slaughter of human beings unequaled in the history of our country.[18]

April 23
Cadiz

Today I visited the city. It is a fortified city surrounded on all sides by a wall, not of stone as I thought from a distance, but of concrete in which are to be seen shells, stones and brick bats. The sea washes against the base of the wall. In shore there is outside the wall a deep moat which may be flooded. The city in parts is built on filled O [?- illegible] in land so that in places its level is thirty feet above the level of the base of the wall. The defenses include large and smaller guns and mortars. Some of the guns and mortars are of brass and of an ancient style. Where guns are not mounted along the walls there are apertures for muskets.

Work is now in progress with view to making the fortifications more modern.

There is in the city a large academy for naval and military instruction.[19] The cathedral is of inspiring appearance.

To go on shore makes one appreciate more his home on the ship and it relieves the monotony.

April 24
Cadiz

I desired to go on shore again today but Mr. Low, the Executive, thought that I would be needed on the ship until Sunday. I have more leisure in my department but the ship's business is likely to require the Store Room to be open until late evenings.

Little contentment seems to be found by anybody on this ship. The Surgeon, the Lieutenant of Marines and the Purser have almost nothing to do, but even they are harassed by personal differences among themselves and with their fellow officers.[20] It would appear that this ship is a marvel. If one would believe the sailors no such ship ever sailed from America, so far as regulations, orders and management on board are concerned. In short, everybody is misused and deprived of "rights" customarily recognized on ships of war. My experience on such ships is limited, but whatever cause for complaint there may be, the mere fact that the sailors "growl" and find fault is to me no evidence of the truth of what they say, for I have had enough acquaintance with this class of men to know that fault finding and maltreatment are not convertible terms. Nevertheless I think that there is good opportunity for improvement in present methods of managing the ship and handling the men. Mr. Low, the Executive, is naturally blamed by the men, but some hold that it is the fault of Commodore Thatcher, our Captain, who would, of course, have to bear the responsibility if serious trouble should develop.

It seems to me that some of the discontent arises from the monotony and purposeless character of much of the duties with which the men are kept occupied. A successful engagement with another ship would probably clear the atmosphere. Competitive target practice with another ship, if practicable would, I believe, have beneficial effects not merely on present conditions aboard, but in case we are called on to fight unexpectedly.

During the salute on entering Lisbon I saw one gun captain so nervous that he could not pull the lanyard with sufficient force to explode the primer. The officer of the Division had to run up and pull it.

I have seen my father make a very satisfactory ship's crew in a comparatively short time out of a most unpromising collection of beings. I, myself, in a limited way have had to meet difficulties with men on vessels with little experience to guide me, but I can see that a ship of war presents larger, different and more complicated problems than a merchant ship. On a man-of-war there is a military organization to consider as well as the matter of satisfactory seamen. Then too, in the Navy certain customs, privileges or prerogatives have developed, which it may be unwise for an Executive or a Captain to disregard, whether they may approve or not. Enough of this. It is one of the compensations of my position on this ship that I do not have to worry about the management of the ship or the crew. Furthermore, I am going to find other forms of mental exercise than criticizing those who are responsible for such matters.

April 26
Cadiz

Warm and beautiful weather. News came by telegraph from Gibraltar that we are to proceed there immediately and consequently everybody is hurrying to get the ship ready to sail within twenty four hours. What is up?

April 27
Cadiz

The wind blows a gale—dead ahead for proceeding to Gibraltar and we do not attempt to sail.

April 28
At sea

The wind still blows hard, but in response to the signal gun the pilot has come aboard and we are preparing to sail.

Just as we were starting out the U.S. Gunboat *Ino* came in. We hove-to and she sent a boat aboard. She is from Gibraltar and they say that no reason was known by the Captain the day before, when she left, to require our presence there.

The *Ino* has been to Spezia with stores. She is a fast sailor. She came from Gibraltar to Cadiz in four hours. She was thirteen days from Boston to Gibraltar. While there the Captain took from Tangier on the African side an ex-consul of the United States and others, agents of the Confederates and sent them to the United States. The *Ino* was a New York clipper and has been bought by the Navy to carry stores. She is commanded by Josiah Cressey formerly Captain of the *Flying Cloud*.

April 29
At sea

Yesterday the wind was first against us and then died out so that we made little progress toward Gibraltar. Today the weather is delightful, but a dead calm prevailed until afternoon when a light breeze sprang up.

At four a.m. we were off Trafalgar Bay where the deservedly famous Nelson lost his life in his most memorable fight. Where this battle took place we hove to and engaged in target practice with the crew at General Quarters. The Parrott guns were tried out. They throw the 20 pr. shell a distance of five miles. All the shots were very good for the first trial, I am told. I could not witness the practice, being in the 5th Division at the Starboard Shell Room.

The target practice prevented us from getting into port tonight. This place is noted for sudden showers accompanied with lightning and heavy squalls.

April 30
Gibraltar, Strait and Bay

This morning the wind is fair to enter the Strait and when I came on deck we were bearing down for the opening between Spain and Africa. The high land on the African side suggests that a Gibraltar might exist there also.

The Rock of Gibraltar does not show itself until you are well within Cape Spartel. The outer and lowermost point first presents itself beyond the main land on the Spanish side and after passing a little further on the highest part appears and then the whole rock which stands out like an island. We pass to the left of the Rock and enter a bay, on the left of which is the town of Algeciras.

On the right and near the Rock lie numerous vessels in the British waters or harbor of Gibraltar. The Rock itself does not give indications of being a fortification so far as visible guns, artillery or sheltering breastworks are concerned. Its military value lies in its strategic position rather than in its armament.

The U.S. Steam Sloop *Tuscarora* is here watching the Confederate Cruiser *Sumter* which has annoyed our commerce for some months past. A Spanish Line-of-Battle Ship is also here. The Spanish regard the *Sumter* as a pirate and would seize her as such in their own ports, but the British are more partial in their attitude toward her.

A few nights ago the *Sumter* attempted to leave the port but the approach of the *Tuscarora* and the Spanish war ship caused her to make a quick return.

May 1
Algeciras

The date reminds me of the May Day festivities back in New England and the hunting there for the first flowers of the spring. They came here long ago and now are "faded and gone."

This evening I gave letters for home to a young man who with several others is being "invalided" to New York by the surgeon.

Boats were exercised today.

May 2
Algeciras

The Assistant Surgeon, Carpenter, and a midshipman were on shore today and were hissed at and hooted by some of the *Sumter's* officers and crew, in the presence of British officers who appeared to enjoy the proceeding. The crew of this troublesome Rebel pirate have taken occasion to insult men belonging to the *Tuscarora* when on shore and if their number has seemed to warrant, have endeavored to provoke a quarrel with the *Tuscarora's* men and have usually succeeded. In these affairs the *Sumter's* bullies from New Orleans and other Southern seaports by reason of superior numbers have generally come out the winners.

We hear today the news of a battle on the Potomac in which the Federals gained a victory with great loss of life on both sides.[21]

George Lucianda who was born and whose parents reside in Algeciras was refused permission to go on shore to see his mother whom he has not seen for more than twelve years, although his father who begged the Captain to let the son go offered to pay three hundred dollars for the privilege. The poor fellow with his father wept like children and as they separated the young man's shipmates gathered about him and expressed their sympathy. No reason was offered to the father for the refusal of his request, nor can a good reason be imagined. This incident has had a bad effect on the crew. They say that this is an illustration of the kind of inducements that are offered men to join or remain in the Service.

May 3
Algiciras

Thirty of the Port Watch were triced up today for not being present at muster when, under orders, they were doing something else.

Men's boots and clothing are thrown overboard because they are not allowed to take them on the Berth deck nor leave them on the spar deck.

Some of the men went on the *Tuscarora* to see a theatrical performance which the ship's company of that ship are presenting. Before the performance was half over, Mr. Low sent for them and had them brought back because of some alleged informality in leaving. Such is Naval life on our ship.

May 4
Algeciras

Another Sabbath. A beautiful day. The sun sparkles on the bay as Glenn, Cox and I in company with the Paymaster, Lieutenant and Sergeant of Marines[22] and the Gunner and sailed to Gibraltar, passing on the way close to the *Sumter* with the Rebel flag flying.

On landing at the Rock one enters the city through a gateway in the walls called the "Water Port." One encounters soldiers at the landing and does not lose them from sight while ashore. Before leaving the ship we were cautioned by our officers who had been ashore and had been insulted by the *Sumter's* crew, to avoid trouble with them. We were told that we would be insulted frequently and in the event of a fight the British would help the *Sumter's* men if help appeared to be needed.

I found the place to be larger than it appeared from the harbor. The streets are good.

Public houses are more numerous than anywhere I have ever been, in Europe or elsewhere. All along the water front are fortifications made of finished stone, and the Rock towers in the rear.

After waiting for the Town Major to come from church we obtained a pass to visit the Rock and see the galleries. It was so late however that the ascent would leave us no time to see anything after we arrived and therefore we gave up the idea. We went up some distance however and inspected some batteries in which Armstrong guns were mounted. These famous guns are not handsome and their general appearance does not indicate great superiority.[23]

During our stay on shore we met and talked with various people, men from ships of war, soldiers and others. We talked freely and were not insulted by anyone, contrary to what we had been led to expect. When we were ready to leave no permit could be obtained to return to our ship although we would be allowed to go to Algeciras. We decided to stay in Gibraltar all night.

We took lodgings at the Kings Arms Hotel. Here an incident occurred which for a moment promised to be unpleasant. We met some men in citizens clothes and our sergeant of Marines who was in uniform invited one to have a glass of beer with him. The man refused saying something which our sergeant resented. We moved to the support of our sergeant and the man's friends did the same. The man however apologized gracefully saying that he and his friends were British officers, that he forgot that he was not in uniform and was disconcerted by being asked to drink with a sergeant in uniform, thereupon our sergeant also apologized.[24]

Morning came at last and we found the boatmen whom we had engaged waiting for us. After rowing two hours we arrived at Algeciras. The boatmen were required to return to the authorities at Gibraltar a certificate that we had been landed at Algeciras. On my way to the office of the officer of the port for this purpose I passed along the principal street and through the Market Place. The streets are poorly paved and do not in other respects compare favorably with those of Gibraltar. In the market I saw fruit, vegetables and other products in profusion. The potatoes were the smallest which I have ever seen offered for sale.

We noticed in the eastern part of Gibraltar an ancient castle which shows numerous well defined indentations made by shots when the place was besieged for six weeks by the combined fleets of France and Spain. It is said that for day and night during the whole time the guns of the rock did not cease firing except when necessary to cool them off.

May 5
Algeciras
The ship is prepared for the visit and inspection of the resident Governor at Algeciras. Among other preparations the awnings are spread and my Store Room ordered to be lighted.

Our guests arrived shortly after noon. The Governor is a white headed robust old man. He was attended by his Secretary and several cavalry officers on whose brilliant uniforms were to be seen pinned numerous decorations. The American Consul was also with them.[25] He spoke Spanish during the ceremony as did also our Captain. When the Governor and his suite left a salute of seventeen guns was fired.

Word is passed that we sail tomorrow. This news with the incidents of the past week is causing much speculation on board. Why were we hurried to Gibraltar? Why are we now being sent away? Is the *Sumter* concerned? Was it feared that we could not take care of ourselves if attacked by the *Sumter*? Could she not easily rake us with her fire in a calm or light wind, since we have no guns which can be fired directly fore or aft? Is it probable that her crew are able to shoot any better than ours? Is she going to get away from the *Tuscorora* as she has from our other Naval ships before? Do our Naval officers want to fight anyway?

May 6
The *Tuscorora* came alongside and took our lines and we were soon outside the Rock where a fine breeze caused us to run away from our escort which left us to return to her duty of watching the *Sumter*.

As we sail out we see the land on the African side like that of Spain reaching almost to the clouds. We keep to the Spanish coast and as we sail along the breech between Europe and Africa gradually widens and the lofty summits of the Sierra Nevada mountains come into view. We pass Malaga and keep on with the hills of Old Spain still in sight. A glorious sunset.

May 7
The Mediterranean
A fair wind is sending us along 9½ knots an hour. The Sierra Nevada range is now higher and is snow capped. It seems very near, but large ships are hull down between us and the shore. As we approach Cape Gata we see on the headlands small towers which form a part of the telegraphic system to prevent smuggling.

This is the pleasantest sail I ever had in my life. Smooth as a lake—a gentle breeze and a warm sun—all sails set and land on the port so beautiful and attractive as to be unreal. If I live, no doubt I will think at some future time of this day's sail and wish for it again forgetting the much which I now have to make me unhappy. Such is man. We passed the ancient Cartegena before sunset. The evening is light and beautiful, the most pleasant that I have ever experienced. The wind has died away until only enough is left to fill the sails.

May 8
The Mediterranean
The wind has changed to the East, ahead but the sea is smooth and with all sail set we are making fair progress. One hears the men say that they wish that we may be kept at sea a month because they have more peace and comfort than when in port. To be frank I am well pleased to be at sea, especially to be having such a pleasant sail on a sea which possesses for me almost a sacred character. Still I would like to see all the adjacent countries even at a sacrifice of comfort.

Moffatt, the Carpenter's mate, was "triced up" last night for asking for and taking a glass of water in the Ward Room while at work there to quench his thirst while doing work intended for the personal comfort of the Ward Room officers. This unreasonable and tyrannical exercise of authority is a fair sample of the kind of encouragement which this ship offers for a self-respecting man to enter or remain in the Navy. Officers, like our Executive, do the Navy incalculable harm. Mr. Low has the misfortune to have been born unfit to command men. Instances of mean cruelty on the part of a ship-master or an officer usually arise, as on our ship, from personal fear inspired by the officer's realization of his own natural shortcomings and inability to secure the confidence and respect of men. He hopes to prevent consequences that he fears by acts of terrorism which do not promote, but demoralize discipline. Discipline may call for harsh methods, but they must be directed to the accomplishment of a recognizable purpose. Discipline can never have a personal objective.

May 9
The Mediterranean
With all sails set we are going along at a splendid rate. Today I had one of my regular exercises or drills with "single sticks"[26] on the quarter deck. Some of my grade dislike this practice, but I like it and never ask to be excused.

May 11
The Mediterranean
Last night we made the Balearic Islands, but stood off to wait for morning. We have been off the islands with light variable winds all day. I have not been well for nearly a week and today I am nearly used up. I am injured by confinement to the Store Room where the air is bad—none at all.

May 12
The Mediterranean
A fine wind today and the ship is going along at a good rate. At 5 pm we passed in sight of Island of Majorca and, kept on to the eastward. I feel better than for three days.

May 13
The ship is going thirteen knots an hour with a fair wind and all sail set. Towards night as the wind dies down land is seen, the Island of Corsica. Tonight for the third time, by orders of the First Lieutenant, Mr. Low, I have had to have the equipment boxes for the boats brought up on deck and see that they were inspected, etc. and properly stowed in the boats. I do not understand why Mr. Low wants me to attend to this duty which properly belongs to those in charge of the boats and their crews. He evidently has, however, some distrust or suspicion, whether justifiable or not, which makes him prefer to have me do it.

May 14
Spezia
Variable winds, calms and showers. General Quarters and single stick exercise. We are about sixty miles from port—in the Gulf of Genoa. It is hard for me to realize that I am now in the place which I first heard of as a little boy when my teacher made me point it out to her on the map. I felt that she was unreasonably fussy since it was so far away.

May 15
Spezia
The mountains of Italy are just ahead and the rugged shore of the peninsula stretches far to the seaward. The sight of this historical land not only thrills me but its character in itself is imposing.

Our ship was heading for Genoa but for some reason the Captain has changed his mind and we are running down the coast to Spezia. Numerous cottages, apparently not accessible by roads, appear on the sides of the mountains which tower above the sea. As we near the port of Spezia there appears at the entrance an island, a high, steep rock with a light house on it. On the other side is an old tower which, as the orderly sergeant tells me, is known as the Porto Vellire[27] and is more than a thousand years old.

At seven bells we are entering Spezia. On a high eminence which overlooks the town are the ruins of a fort erected by Napoleon I, and near it a dilapidated castle. Spezia is at the head of a little bay and except towards the water is surrounded by mountains. The United States Navy Store House is on the port side as we enter and about a mile below the town. The Sardinian flag is flying in front on the battery. At 5 pm we drop anchor on Sardinian bottom.

May 16
Spezia
Last night we had a heavy shower and the sailors indulged in the luxury of fresh water for bathing purposes.[28]

The day is delightful and the gentle breeze from the mountains is refreshing.

As soon as the ship anchored "Boy Jack," "Boy Tom," "Boy Bill," "Boy Jim," all women and the mother of them all, whom we may safely call "Old Boy" came aboard to secure the "bumboat" privilege of selling provisions, fruit and other articles to the crew. They are one family and the daughters have been trading with American ships since they were old enough to accompany the mother who, I should judge, has passed her three score and ten. The daughters received their "nicknames" in their childhood from the sailors and though now women well along in life are still known by these names and answer to them. Most sailors who have visited Spezia have become known to the "boys" and as "Boy Jack," the leading spirit among them and a real business character, came over the gangway she greeted her former acquaintances on board and seemed highly elated over the arrival of our ship.

May 17
Spezia
We hear that New Orleans is taken by the Federal forces, also Memphis and other large places in the South.[29] If this be true the Confederate cause is hopeless.

May 18
Spezia
A beautiful serene Sabbath morning. A Sabbath in Italy. I suspect that it will not remind one of a New England Sabbath ashore.

After muster I landed on the shore of Italy for the first time, near the U.S. Naval Store House, and in company with two of my shipmates walked to town. The roads for half the distance were narrow and rocky, but the olive trees and green foliage made up for their shortcomings.

The terraced wheat patches on the hillsides attested the industry of the natives. Beyond the Lazarette, about two and a half miles from the town, the road is very circuitous and walled up, reminding one in places of a drain. We passed ancient solemn appearing stone churches whose bells are tolling. We came out on a splendid road lined with locust trees which furnished us with a grateful shade from the hot sun. On entering the town the Hotel D'Odessa is the first building of importance which we see. It was here that Victor Emmanuel and the Queen stayed a few years ago. We went through the Public Garden where hundreds of people were sitting on the benches and enjoying the shade. We next went to a public house kept by a Swiss who spoke English very well and had a rest and a bottle of wine preparatory to exploring the old castle in the vicinity. On our way I tried to buy some food to take with us. My French enabled me to get what we wanted, but when we attempted to pay for it we were told that our money, "Americana" or "Spanuela" was "non Buona." We obtained as a guide a little lad who offered to lead us when we appeared in his mother's garden after going through several alleys and arches and up a flight of stone steps.

After half an hour's walk of a gradual ascent up a road and pathway bordered by vineyards and wheat patches we came to the castle, overlooking the town.[30] The castle is about forty feet high. Its walls are pierced for guns and muskets. We entered the castle through an underground passage and noted the well which once supplied its people with water.

On returning from the castle we passed again through the Public Garden and went to the Restaurant kept by the Swiss, where I had an omelette, a fried steak, a roll of bread and a bottle of wine. At tables out of doors, outside the restaurant, people were sitting, singly and in family groups, eating or drinking wine, chatting and reading newspapers, as is the pleasant custom of the country. Another party from our ship, the boys, in charge of the Master-at-Arms passed by and the little fellows seemed to be enjoying themselves very much.

I see some good looking women here, but on the whole I do not consider them remarkable for their beauty and they appear to age earlier than American or English women. The older women look dried up—smoked, as it were. Fourteen years ago today I sailed on my first voyage alone for any distance, away from home, on the schooner *Lady* for the Gulf of St. Lawrence. I recalled the date as I came down the road today from Spezia. How far I was then from dreaming that I would today be walking the streets of this ancient place under the genial sun of Italy. How little did I imagine the experiences through which I have passed since that day, the scenes which I have witnessed and the associations which I have enjoyed, especially those of my dear father and mother who lived the greater part of this time to comfort and benefit me. Here today as I roam about in this foreign land far from home, amid scenes new and strange, memory takes me back into the past and it is hard to realize that the present is not a dream.

One sees Sardinian army soldiers everywhere, many of whom have fought beside Garibaldi and Victor Emmanuel in the recent wars. They are a good looking well dressed set of men and as soldiers none anywhere have a better reputation.

The people here are so accustomed to war that its threat does not disturb them. Even the children exhibit a warlike spirit. On my way to the landing I met a company of little boys from five to ten years of age with their faces painted to imitate ferocious looking mustaches. They were led by a little fellow who showed himself a real captain and the privates exhibited a commendable proficiency in drill. As we approached they were ordered by their captain, in Italian, to salute by company. They opened ranks and counter-marched through the center with the precision of veterans. At the command, "avanti," they marched to our rear. We all lined up and returned their salute. Who knows that we may not have met in this little captain another Napoleon in wars to come.

A pleasant walk in the cool of the evening brought us to the U.S. Store House. We met on the way long robed priests with broad rimmed hats strolling leisurely along and heard the voices of men and women singing and saw the beautiful background of mountains and terraced hills adorned by the luxuriant green of olive and fig trees—all in keeping with what I had read and heard of Italy. I contrasted the scene with the hills and pines of my native state which seemed as dear as ever to me, but I could not help thinking that had I been reared on this Italian coast I could never be contented with the somber woodlands of Maine.

May 19
Spezia

This afternoon Charles Lever, the author of *Chas. O'Mallory, the Irish Dragoon*, etc., etc., an Englishman of much literary ability and possessed of a large fund of good humor, visited the ship and as a matter of course the Store Room.[31] He was accompanied by Mr. Low.

I had on my desk the Bible, Tupper's Poems and the well known Helper Book on *Impending Crises*,[32] all of which Mr. Lever examined. He said, "I see that you have Mr. Tupper." "How do you like his book," I replied, "as it contains many good things." Thereupon he remarked, "I do not like him." Mr. Low, the First Lieutenant, then joined in with, "he is out of date."

Tupper's *Proverbial Philosophy* contains many things that will not go out of date because they must ever be true—they ever have been—and facts, although they be unfashionable, will still remain true even if unpleasant.

The Governor's daughter and her brother were also on board today. She is a fine looking young lady.

May 20
Spezia

The Store Room was turned upside down to get out the falls for sending down all the spars above the lower masts and in the midst of this work the Governor came aboard accompanied by the American Consul[33] and everything had to be dropped for a salute of seventeen guns.

The Governor is a stout robust man with bright eyes and a short turned-up nose. He speaks French but not English.

May 23
Spezia

Spars and yards have been overhauled and sent up again and today is devoted to painting. Painting on a man-of-war has to be repeated because of what seems to be an established custom, doing it simultaneously with the scraping of spars. The shavings which fall from aloft onto the fresh paint make it necessary to do the painting again, but eventually guns and everything shine out in the spotless glory of new paint and varnish. It also is an inviolable practice on a man-of-war for the crew to do painting in white clothes.[34]

General Quarters and target practice. Target practice makes some mess on the gun deck but it is too bad that we cannot have it oftener. It not only teaches the men to handle the guns and shoot, but the competition is good for them.

May 24
Spezia

All hands in white frocks, Boat drill. All our boats are put over and completely armed and equipped are landed through the surf. Everybody gets wet, but the imitation of landing an armed expedition was really very creditably done as the return to the ship and the restoration of everything to its usual place.

May 25
Spezia

After muster and inspection I went ashore with W.G. Smith, the Surgeon's Steward. We wanted to visit Porto Venere, an old town built at the time of the Crusades on the site of a temple dating from the days of Julius Caesar and dedicated to Venus.

A delightful walk over a smooth hard road winding around the mountains brings us to our destination. The town is crowded on a narrow shelf between the base of a mountain and the water. Above it on the mountain side is a fort. One principal street winds through the town a little back from the water front. Other streets are little better than narrow stone stairways leading up the mountain. At the southern point, overlooking the sea, are the ruins of the ancient temple, the walls of which have crumbled and fallen in many places. The north side is built of white and dark colored marble in alternate layers. A tower stands at one corner extending far above the main building and containing openings in the sides like a belfry. We went to a public house where I had some bread and cheese and wine. We had a pleasant walk back to Spezia in the cool of the early evening.

May 26
Spezia

We are taking water aboard and making other preparations for sailing. "Boy Tom" came on board to settle our mess bill which is $23. We are living a little too extravagantly for poor people. We must curtail.

May 27
The Mediterranean

We are sailing for Genoa with a fine breeze but nearly ahead. How beautiful the coast is—blue water and on shore a mingling of sunshine clouds and mountains. The evening comes calm and serene.

May 28

Morning comes with the City of Genoa and towns along the coast in sight, but no wind. A steamboat approaches and offers to tow us in for 300 francs, but our warships are not allowed to hire tow-boats except when necessary in emergencies. A pilot comes aboard, but it is night before we are able by trimming the sails for every breath of air to enter the harbor under the guidance of a light house, the lantern of which shines high in the air above the city like a comet.

May 29
Genoa

Morning finds us within a basin snugly secured by stone piers. Here are vessels of all nations, American, Italian and even Greek. Among them are Sardinian men-of-war, good examples of naval architecture and very effective.

The ship *Governor Langdon* of Portsmouth is here and her second mate was killed yesterday by one of the crew. I find that I did not know him.

The salute which we fired for the Sardinian flag must have broken glass ashore as we are so near the buildings.

May 31
Genoa

The crew are looking forward to liberty tomorrow. The ship is in good condition to receive visitors. Tomorrow is an anniversary of the battle of Solferino, a great Sardinian holiday and the celebration is starting tonight with the ringing of bells and fireworks.

The captain of the American ship *Ocean Romp* came on board today and claimed a man belonged to him, a seaman whom we shipped yesterday.

June 1
Genoa

Rain falls in torrents and the wind blows almost a gale thus putting a bad damper on the holiday celebrations.

The crew is mustered on the gun deck, the Articles of War read and formalities closed by "tricing up" sixteen of the men for not having all their clothes marked. Why are men so careless as to let their clothes get into the "lucky bag" as it is so ironically called?[35]

Italians are certainly a musical people. A party of four women and one man came aboard at eight bells last night and sang to the accompaniment of a guitar and viol and gave us a really enjoyable musical entertainment. They had superior musical talent and could fill a theater in America.

In the afternoon I visited the city. It impresses one that with the ancient appearance of its buildings, arches and columns. The streets are well paved with large flat stones, are rather narrow and arched or crowned toward the center to form channels or drains for the flow of water along the curb stones.

The weather improved toward night and this Italian Fourth-of-July celebration became livelier.

The streets are thronged with soldiers, sailors and marines dressed in many varieties of uniforms. One thing that I admire in this country is the good looking uniforms of the soldiers.

This evening there is a great display of fireworks, all public buildings are illuminated and the ships of war in the harbor are dressed with lanterns from their decks to royal yards.

June 3
Genoa

The hold is being emptied and the contents put on the Berth and Gun decks. In goes pig iron—I am glad to observe.[36]

The Captain has an idea that the ship is not stiff enough for rough weather, as I had also after watching her roll in the Atlantic. The putting in of this ballast comes just as the men thought that they would have a respite from hard work. It is strange how much work there may be found to do on a ship. I received letters from my brother Edward and others at home today.

I have been busy all day as I have been for several days past making out a new station bill for Mr. Low. We are trying to take into account better the personal capabilities of the men than in the present bill.

June 4
Genoa

A lovely day. The minstrels who were aboard a few days ago came again to sing and play. Their music is so good that I am sorry when they leave. A Sardinian Admiral visited the ship.

June 5
Genoa

The Sardinian war vessels are dressed with flags preparatory to sailing. The king's son is rowed down the harbor in a barge and as he passes our yards are manned and a salute is fired. Two steamboats loaded with troops follow. Later two frigates sail. The Duke of Genoa[37] was on one of them. I suspect that this movement is connected with doings at Rome.

The Governor visited our ship and is received with a salute. What a quantity of powder courtesy demands.

June 6
Genoa

Liberty for twenty four hours is being given to the crew beginning today—a quarter watch at a time.

June 7
Genoa

When liberty expired at seven bells today most of the men had returned in good condition. The few who have not returned are delaying liberty for those waiting to go. Tonight two of the liberty party came aboard showing signs of having been on a "hard time," but they had waited until they could go straight.

June 8
Genoa

All men who were over time are "triced up." Some twenty meet this fate and hang like fowls by the wings for from two to twelve hours. It seems very strict to thus deal with men who are in the habit of getting drunk and go on shore for this purpose. Would some of those who live further aft have done much better under similar circumstances?[38]

The second quarter watch started on liberty. The Surgeon's Steward and I also went ashore at the same time. Burns, the Boatswain's Mate, who said he wanted a quiet time joined us. We went first to the "Cafe Italie," a beautiful garden patronized by the fashionable people of the city. After visiting the City water works and an attractive park we came to the "Grand Caire" and took dinner there, after which we hired horses and started for the "Grotto," but our directions landed us into a German "Beer Garden" on the roof of a building. Then, four of us, Glenn, the Master-at-Arms, "Buck" Burns, the Boatswain's mate, the Surgeon's Steward and myself remounted our steeds and rode through the city to the westward. After meeting with various annoyances we reached the outskirts of the city. Here Burns who is a heavy man and who rode with a list to port parted the strap to the port stirrup and stopped at a nearby confectioner's for assistance in making repairs. These being completed the rest of the party proceeded to patronize the confectioner's establishment to compensate him for his trouble, but I did not dismount. When they came out a considerable crowd had collected. I do not know whether they were unaccustomed to the sight of mounted men or whether they expected Americans to give them an exhibition of the wild horsemanship of the Western Plains, but if it was an exhibition of wild riding that they were expecting they were not disappointed. The horse in the lead was urged into a gallop and the rest followed at the same gait. We bore to the right over a bridge and up near a railroad station where an incoming train frightened all the horses beyond control and mine which proved to be the fastest passed all the others and nearly brought my head in contact with an iron lamp post in doing so. I cleared everybody out of the streets as I went along and finally managed to stop my horse by steering him into a high stone wall. A small boy fell in the street in front of me, but fortunately my horse jumped over his body. Why I did not go off I do not know. The language which excited people sent after us sounded abusive, but not understanding Italian I missed the finer shades of meaning of their remarks. Our horses had taken us in the wrong direction and therefore we retraced the more recent part of our course, with the help of two accommodating Italians, one pulling and the other pushing. I finally persuaded my horse to pass the place where he had been frightened, but he went through all sorts of evolutions before I succeeded.

We were all soon outside a gate of the old city. My horse seemed somewhat overcome by his exertions and as we went along I fell behind the others who galloped off on the wrong road. After waiting some time for them to discover their mistake and return I started slowly alone on the right road to the seacoast. Everything along the route was beautiful. I passed through two considerable villages, saw some pretentious dwellings with magnificent grounds and as I made my way back into the City I viewed a most gorgeous sunset. On arriving at the place where we had hired the horses I found that the Surgeon's Steward only had arrived. Without waiting I immediately made my way to the ship.

June 9
Genoa
Our sailor's horseback ride of yesterday ended as I supposed it would. All our party had not returned aboard until noon today. I am so stiff and sore that I can scarcely move. If I am over the ride in a week I will do well.

Most of the crew who went on liberty are returning in good shape for sailors—one expects them to get drunk, but only five thus far have come aboard showing signs of drunkenness.

One man, Giles, returned dressed like a potato peddlar. A felt slouch hat, a dark waist coat, too short, a pair of light trousers—six inches too long, a shirt which perhaps once was white, and without shoes or stockings. All who arrive "over time" are "triced up" as usual.

June 10
Genoa
Another liberty party starts today. Two men of the previous parties who have not returned have probably deserted.

We hear that General Banks' army has been badly cut up near Richmond,[39] but the report is lacking certain indications that it is true. Every rumor in favor of the Rebellion is received here with eager glee.

June 12
Genoa
Among those who have not returned from liberty and presumably have deserted is the ship's painter who has been in the Store Room as an assistant to me. He was a man who was much out of place in his position on this ship, but was very quiet and told me nothing about himself and gave me no intimation that he would desert. I fear that he will have a hard time before he reaches home even if he should succeed in evading capture.[40]

June 13
Genoa

The last part of the crew to go on liberty returned tonight. They do not return in as good condition as the others. Many have come aboard drunk. Two have been brought back, handcuffed, by policemen and four others in charge of an officer of the ship. One drunk immediately on reaching the deck threw a spit-kid [wooden spittoon] at one of the boatmen who had brought him off and laid the boatsman's head open with a bad wound. The "Brig" contains a full complement tonight.

June 17
At sea

With a pilot aboard we have been waiting for three days for the wind to change in order to get out of the harbor and on our way to Leghorn. Today, towards evening the wind came northwest and we started with a good breeze.

This is the anniversary of the battle of Bunker's Hill and celebrated in Charlestown where I happened to be a year ago on this date. How quickly the year has passed, and what changes.

June 18
Leghorn

At two pm today we anchor at Leghorn. Many ships and other vessels are lying here. The water is comparatively shoal. An artificial breakwater makes the harbor safe for shipping. The country about here is less mountainous. The land looks sandy where there is no vegetation.

June 19
Leghorn

It is some time since an American man-of-war has been here and we have numerous visitors including many ladies. The women of this place are good looking. This place does not impress me. I suspect that European ports are losing their novelty.

June 20
Leghorn

A fine day. Many visitors on board.

Last night news reached us that the Federal forces had opened the James River, taken Memphis, Fort Wright on the Mississippi and marched on Mobile; that seven thousand of our troops were killed in ambuscade and that General Pope had captured ten thousand of the Rebels, completely routing their entire force which was scattering in all directions.[41]

One of our crew, Giles, an Englishman, is being severely punished for uttering while drunk in the presence of the officers disrespectful language against our flag.

Several others keep him company for offences connected with their recent liberty. D. Gallagher who committed an assault upon one of the boatmen, received as the sentence of the Court Martial called to try him, loss of three months pay, thirty days solitary confinement in double irons and four days a week on bread and water.

June 22
Leghorn

A dull day. One unacquainted with a man-of-war would be astonished at the quiet which prevails among so many men on the Sabbath.

June 23
Leghorn—Pisa

This morning Cox, Robbins and I started on the morning train, first class, for Pisa. Here an official punches your ticket before you board your train and another takes it up when you leave. I regard this an improvement on the American practice since it does away with our "conductor," saves the passengers annoyance and keeps all money in the hands of the agents at the stations. The cars are very comfortable and their arrangement prevents disagreeable crowding as in America.

The country is beautiful and the wayside is adorned with trees. The roads are perfect and in many places shaded with a kind of pine trees of uniform height and having large spreading tops. The people are making hay and the yield indicates that it must be highly cultivated.

A ride of forty minutes brings us to Pisa. We are greeted by an annoying crowd of coachmen and guides proclaiming their ability to speak English and their historical knowledge of the city. The others feared that we might need a Guide to find the "Leaning Tower," but I told them that if we could not discover it without assistance it was not worth the visit. A short walk from the station over the Arno brought us in sight of the "Tower." Here I was before the actual structure with which I had been familiar since childhood from the impressive picture in my geography. Its vicinity was deserted but a man who said in broken English that he was guardian of the Cathedral soon appeared and we accepted his services as a guide.

The massive bronze doors of the Cathedral with their scriptural scenes in bas-relief became even more impressive as we are told of their ancient history. On being admitted by the porter my eyes rested on the most magnificent interior that I ever saw and its artistic features acquire even greater interest by reason of the history-mementoes of ancient Jerusalem and of the Crusades, of Constantinople and of Rome and paintings from the hands of famous ancient Italian artists.

What impressed me most in the neighboring Baptistry was a pulpit in the construction of which iron and marble were combined with striking effect to picture Biblical scenes. We entered the "Tower" through a small door and ascended a spiral staircase of well worn marble steps—274 in all. The "Tower" is 190 feet high. It was built in 1174. At the top hang seven bells, five of which are very large. One notices the inclination of the tower as he passes around the stairway and as one approaches the part on the outside which overhangs the base he feels that he is about to be pitched headlong below.

After having at a good French restaurant a good dinner for which we pay a good price we start out to see the rest of the sights of the city.

After returning to Leghorn we stroll about this City. The streets are wider than those of Genoa and the buildings and the city generally have a more modern appearance.

Near the landing are figures of pirates chained to a pump. I am told that this monument commemorates the final suppression of a company of famous ancient pirates who had a rendezvous on an island off the coast and for a long time committed depredations on Italian commerce.

June 24

This morning after the usual amount of bustle and noise of chains and blocks strained by the muscles of three hundred men we are again sailing upon the Mediterranean. We are bound for Naples.

June 25
At sea

This morning we are between the two islands which will always recall Napoleon's career, Corsica to starboard and Elba to port. A delightful day, a smooth sea and a grand breeze, but dead ahead. General Quarters, as is customary every Wednesday. The clothing of the eight men who deserted at Genoa was sold today as is the practice also when one of the crew dies. The money is supposed to go to the established relief fund for sailors.

June 26
At sea

This has been as fine a day's sail as I ever had. It is not too warm. The sun feels good.

Our ship has come to look as a man-of-war ought to look. Our contact with foreign men-of-war at Genoa and Leghorn was also beneficial. Our men are becoming more inclined to take a pride in the ship's appearance. I observed an amusing incident in this connection today.

The quarter gunner, known as "Cocky" to distinguish him from the two other Andersons, is extremely solicitous that nothing shall happen to mar the dazzling splendor of his big Parrott gun. As he was with a group of men in another part of the ship one of the boys, feigning alarm, ran up and called out, "Cocky, there's a fly on your gun." The men laughed and Anderson took the joke good naturedly and told the boy that he need not worry about the fly, but that he might properly worry about what would happen to him if he ever touched the gun with one of his dirty fingers.

June 27
At sea

It is night but owing to light unfavorable winds we are still about thirty five miles from Naples. Mount Vesuvius is to be seen from aloft. We can see the extremity of the bay from the deck. A delightful day and one of the most beautiful sunsets that I ever saw.

I have more leisure time now than formerly. In fact, save for "these bonds" I would be very happy, but I cannot expect enough freedom while in port to see all that I desire.

June 28
Naples

Finally the high summit of Vesuvius has come in sight—far up in the clouds. The castles and fortifications of the island of Gaeta appear on our left. As we enter the Bay a large town appears on the seashore close under Vesuvius while Naples remains hidden from view. At the head of the Bay are the famous barracks built by Napoleon I, and said to be capable of accommodating thirty thousand soldiers, with room to drill them on the flat roofs. As Naples, now a city of about 4,000,000 inhabitants, comes into view there stands out prominently on an eminence to the westward the Royal Palace in which Queen Joanna hung her husband.

June 29
Naples

After inspection I went on shore with Cox, the Paymaster's Steward and in fifteen minutes after landing we were in a carriage with a guide on our way to Pompei and Herculaneum, about sixteen miles distant.

We passed the palace of a former King and many pretentious residences in the rear of which I caught glimpses of beautiful gardens containing statuary and frescoes, besides trees, shrubs and flowers in profusion. It is Sunday and the streets are thronged with people and carriages.

At the landing our attention was first drawn to the sight of men and boys playing cards on the quay with copper coins stacked up on the stone posts which served as card tables, and all the way to Pompei we saw groups similarly engaged in games of chance. A ride of less than two hours brought us to Pompei and its ancient amphitheater. I saw much that I cannot describe and was inspired to thoughts which I cannot express.

June 30
Naples

The day starts with a sad casualty, Albert Dyer, a native of Maine, fell from the mizzen topmast rigging while engaged in loosing sails. He struck one of the quarter davits and was instantly killed. How uncertain life. How quickly his was snuffed out and his messmates lose one of their numbers. Last night at supper he sat around the mess-cloth,[42] before breakfast is "piped" he is lifeless in the Bay.

His body was soon recovered and this afternoon was taken ashore to be buried.

On arrival at the landing place the common bond of language and the sea led the burial party to join with another company of sailors who were bringing ashore the bodies of fifteen shipmates, likewise to be borne to a final resting place in a foreign land. These dead were from a British ship-of-the-line just arrived from Palermo where they had been shot by soldiers. Many more had been wounded. In some way trouble arose ashore between men from the ship and the inhabitants and it is claimed that the sailors had to be shot to stop them from maltreating the natives.

The news of poor Dyer's death will be a heavy blow for his widowed mother who has several younger children. He was about eighteen years old. His father also died a violent death, being killed for his money by a robber.

Chapter Two
July 1862 to December 1862

July 3
Naples

We hear that 50,000 of general Beauregard's army have deserted. Certainly bad for the Rebels, if true.[1]

"Ration money" is being served out today in order that the men may have extra for the "Fourth of July," and to trade with. This is duly appreciated by the peddlers of jewelry, pictures and curios who have been swarming aboard. Their prices immediately go up.

When sailors get hold of money they believe in putting it into circulation immediately. If they can find no other way of getting rid of it they will pay their debts with it.

"Fourth of July"
Naples

The ship is dressed with flags and the gangways and gun deck trimmed with shrubbery brought aboard for the purpose.

I go ashore alone, hire a carriage and a guide and proceed to the Museum. I find this a most interesting place, a museum, an art gallery, a library and an artist's studio combined. It is here, rather than to Pompeii itself, that one should come to see how the people of that ancient city really lived. It is here that one finds the mosaics, frescoes, household utensils and other movable articles which were collected when the buried cities were excavated. Here too are Roman antiques and the originals of famous Italian artists.

From the Museum I go down to the Catacombs of the Greeks, dating from before the Christian era and largely cut from solid rock.

After a day of sight-seeing I return to my home on the *Constellation*. It is amusing to hear others who have been ashore today recount their experiences on their return. Most of them started for Pompeii and Herculaneum, but in many instances their passion for the ancient and historical succumbed to the temptations of modern life. Even those who kept on had interesting experiences with overloaded vehicles and avaricious guides and coachmen with persistent beggars. These certainly exasperate the foreign visitor.

July 5
Naples

The "Fourth of July" has passed. Both officers and men seemed to have enjoyed it very much. The men who remained on board had as good a time as if they had been on shore—perhaps better. Dinners for the several messes were prepared by caterers ashore and brought on board and served by them. The men evidently managed to get stuff which both "cheers and inebriates" as they were very merry when I returned. Everything is quiet today and the conduct of the ship's company shows no perceptible effects of yesterday's indulgences.

July 6
Naples

A Sabbath has come again. On going ashore I meet the Doctor's Steward, W. G. Smith. John Hunter, Acting Boatswain and Gaven Moffatt, Carpenter's Mate who want to go to Pompeii. I am ready to visit Pompeii again and volunteer to go with them as guide. After the usual fuss with coachmen and guides we finally get started. The driver of our carriage takes us through the town of Resina. The roads are dirty and the dust suffocating. Standing or lying on the stone pavements we see lead colored pigs without a sign of food near them. One end of a chain is fastened around the middle of the body, the other to the wall at the side of the street. A piece of coarse cloth laid across two sticks projecting from the wall serves as a shade to protect them from the sun.

The drive is tedious and near old Pompeii we stop for refreshments. The food is miserable and the wine vile. When we complain the Proprietor refers to the wine as "Vino di Vesuvio." Being asked if he meant that it was something which was thrown out by the volcano during an eruption, he protested that he made it himself from grapes grown on the sunny slopes of the mountain. I suggested that the grapes might have been affected by the fumes from the crater. Thereupon my companions good naturedly declared that it was astonishing to see how quickly I had adopted the ways of other Neapolitan guides; that evidently I was in collusion with the proprietor whom I was trying to defend; that the dirty route over which we had come had already proclaimed me to be a failure and a fraud as a guide and that I would have to pay the proprietor's bill. This I insisted on doing in spite of their protests.

We spent several hours rambling about the ruins. I saw many things which I had previously seen. We got along very well with the aid of a guide book.

July 7
Naples

I was ashore all day waiting for the expected arrival of the French Mail Boat due with official mail for the Captain in care of the Consul. The Master-at-Arms came ashore with me to look for a boatswain's mate who was overstaying his liberty.

July 11
Naples

We hear that our store ship has arrived at Spezia and that we are to sail in a few days to meet her at Palermo. Vesuvius has been showing considerable activity for several days, sending out large quantity of smoke part of the time. Fruit has been freely purchased by the men until yesterday when the selling of certain kinds aboard was forbidden. The peddlers of pictures and curios and other wares have been prohibited from coming aboard altogether. It requires a stream of water from the gun deck hose to keep them away from the side of the ship.

July 12
Naples

I go again to the consul's for mail. Our Consulate here is a disgrace to the United States. It is dirty and in a dirty place. One enters it through a back yard and passage way to a stable, up five flights of dirty stairs and then through dirty corridors and past dirty entries to dirty tenements. On my first visit I turned back after climbing several flights of stairs, thinking that I must have made a mistake even though the American Coat of Arms was at the entrance on the street.[2]

I hope that all the Naples tailors are not like the one recommended to me and from whom I ordered two pairs of duck trousers a week ago. He has made four sets for me and not a pair which I could wear—too short, too long, too tight or too loose in the wrong place. Tonight I took back his last attempt and told him to keep them and that I would try again in some other port. I will have to borrow a pair for Muster tomorrow.

July 13
Last night at eight bells, "All hands—Up all hammocks"[3] greeted the ears of the ship's company who had scarcely fallen asleep. Sails were loosed but the anchor was not weighed as there was not enough wind to move the ship. It was not until nine o'clock this morning that the anchor broke ground and we stood out of the Bay.

July 16
Little wind and hot, as for the past three days. The metal gun tracks on the deck are so hot that one cannot touch them. Stromboli is looming up not far off. Like many of the ship's company I have been sick with a diarrhoea for three days and barely able to move, but feel somewhat better today. I hope that I shall not be sick here. It is a poor place for a sick hen.

July 17
Palermo

Today we entered Palermo. Like other Italian ports which I have seen this is open to the sea and has a <u>mole</u> or sea wall to protect the shipping. The land is high on both sides of the harbor, forming a sort of basin. The city is pleasantly located and from the water the buildings look substantial and neat. A large mail came aboard. Among the letters one to me from Houston, the ship's painter who deserted at Genoa. He was in Marseilles, well and on a ship bound for the United States. He evidently got discouraged here. I notice one American bark in port.

July 19
Palermo

This is called the garden of Italy and the appearance of the country from the ship would seem to justify the name. Palermo itself is attractive from this distance. Conspicuous on the right near the entrance to the harbor is a fine residence formerly occupied by Lord Nelson and Lady Hamilton.

Last night the Captain told the crew that he was going to give them liberty here, small parties at a time. One party started today, to be aboard tomorrow morning at eight bells.

July 20
Palermo

After church services Cox, the Purser's Steward and I went ashore. On landing one has to contend with persistent guides who can only be stopped from following one by summary measures. If a visitor is not careful he will find that one of these pests has followed the visitor into a restaurant and ordered something which the proprietor has put on the visitor's bill.

Among the city's attractions which we saw were the King's Garden and the catacombs. In these habitations of the dead are to be seen thousands of men, women and children placed in a standing position in niches along the walks which are lighted from above. A futile effort has been made to preserve these once human forms but only a skull with a little skin attached protrudes from the coarse mantle which covers the rest of what now remains of a living body. Similar forms attired in gaudy robes or plain mantles may also be seen through the glass sides of coffins. Here and there a human relic is marked by an emblem suggestive of noble birth or military rank. In the floor of stone and tiles are frequent marble slabs inscribed to indicate the tomb which lies beneath. The bodies are all numbered and most of them bear a card giving the name of the deceased and the time of death.

On our return through the city we stopped two hours to see a Circus performance, a strictly Italian affair and very good. I was especially impressed by a twelve year old rider. Two good looking little girls about the same age were almost as proficient. Before coming off to the ship we took a walk on the promenade which is brilliantly lighted by gas lamps for about a mile along the front of the city by the water. The equipages passing up and down were more elegant and more numerous than I have ever seen anywhere else.

July 21
Palermo

News comes today of a defeat of Gen. McClellan before Richmond with a loss of a siege train and 2000 men killed and 1200 taken prisoners. This is bad if true but I do not credit it without confirmation.[4]

July 22
Palermo

A report comes from the Consul[5] that the French have recognized the Southern Confederacy.[6] This coming from an official source and immediately after our reported defeat at Richmond brings sadness to the hearts of many of the officers and men. Nothing else is being talked about on the ship.

July 23
Palermo

Insufferably hot, as for two weeks. The men continue to go on liberty. Two of the last party have apparently deserted.

The reported defeat of our troops at Richmond is confirmed.

July 24
Palermo

This morning the two men supposed to have deserted were brought aboard dressed in a comical rig. Some of the men who returned from liberty this morning on time were very noisy. Several were put in double irons. It calls for much patience to give a ship's crew liberty. General Quarters. Hot as ever.

This day nothing is transpiring except the punishment of some men who were ordered triced up for offenses resulting from their liberty. Their outcries are very annoying to me as I am very near them. This practice of "tricing up" is in my opinion worse than of flogging in the old way, as it is more freely and more unreasonably invoked and is more likely to be carried to excess.

July 30
Palermo

This morning a marine, Young by name, who was punished yesterday rather severely was missing. The ship was searched and he was not found. A reward was then offered ashore for his apprehension. Towards evening he crawled out of the main hold and went to the mast to plead for release from the further punishment which awaited him. By his act he has committed a new offense and will receive more punishment.

July 31
Palermo

July is gone. How rapidly the time passes even pent up as I am in a ship. A ship is really a little world in itself with its own peculiar annoyances or troubles and its unpleasant sights, but they are made endurable by frequent changes of scene.

Four more Italian men-of-war arrived today, making eight in all in port. The last have some twelve hundred boys on board, in training. Trouble is evidently expected here. Another man, an Italian shipped at Genoa was declared a deserter today.

August 4
Palermo

Hot as ever. This afternoon Cox and I went ashore after I had written letters to Miss B. and my brother Edward and to others. We enjoyed a ride about the city and in the evening we witnessed a great demonstration which included a torch light procession led by a band. The cause we were unable to learn. On arriving on board we found that considerable excitement had prevailed in the harbor and that the Italian war ships near the city had moved further out, fearing an attack from shore.

It appears that the government is jealous of Garibaldi who has a considerable force in the interior. Victor Emanuel is not very popular here. Trouble will soon start.

August 6
Palermo

Receiving stores today from the store ship, *Release*. Every part of the ship is in confusion—made worse because the men have managed to get hold of liquor in some way in considerable quantities.

One of my numerous fellow townsmen on this ship, Mr. Langdon, the Boatswain, who has been off duty for several months, being removed for alleged incompetency, is detached and ordered to join the *Release* and report to the Navy Department on arrival in the United States. Among other things, Mr. Langdon was blamed for the death of John Campbell, a neighbor of his, whom we lost in the Atlantic while trying to secure the port chain in rough weather, it being claimed that Mr. Langdon should have had it properly secured before. I feel very sorry for Mr. Langdon. He lacked the experience to assume the duties of Boatswain on a ship like this—then too, as my father used to say, "a seaman is born, not made." I really think that Mr. Langdon would be better off if he would give up the sea and go back to his father's prosperous farm in the backwoods of our town. His chief boatswain's mate "Jack" Hunter has succeeded to the position as "acting" boatswain, and if there is no question about Hunter's ability to fill it.

August 7

Stores are aboard and we are getting ready to sail. I am not sorry for I have seen enough of this place. We have been here three weeks. Our destination is Smyrna, and in anticipation of a tedious passage our mess has provided a supply of vegetables for three weeks.[7]

As we were coming out this evening a Negro by the name of Hubbard made an unsuccessful attempt to swim ashore from the ship. He went over the bows and was not seen until in the water. Then some one cried, "man overboard," that horrible sound on ship-board. All was great excitement for a few moments. The Negro started yelling loudly and made a great splash. Several men jumped into the water to his rescue. When they reached the Negro they found that he had a bundle of clothes lashed to his back. This was cast loose by the men while in the water, but was seen and picked up by the boat which fished everybody out of the water and so the Negro's game was exposed. His excuse was that he had been thinking long about leaving the ship in this way and finally was unable to resist the impulse to do so. The punishment which awaits the poor Negro may give him some training in self control.

August 11
Strait of Messina

For three days we have been drifting through the sea battleground of ancient Roman times but the peaceful sea and calm summer days furnish no suggestion of former warlike scenes. It is intensely hot. Stromboli is now far astern. Mount Etna looms up back from the Sicilian shore and near its summit patches of snow are seen in striking contrast to the verdure on its lower slopes. We have passed the cities of Messina on the one side and smaller Reggio on the other. The highly cultivated Calabrian shore is no less beautiful than the mountainous Sicilian coast. Why is it that this part of the world so appeals to us when God has so made us that it does not destroy our high regard for a most dismal landscape—if <u>there</u> be our home.

A pilot from a Sardinian brig brought us to the entrance of the Strait where the regular pilot came aboard. It seemed hardly more than a mile wide in places and reminded me of the passage translated from "Ovid!"

(?) To the Italian earth was tied,
And men walked where ships at anchor ride,
Till Neptune overlooked the narrow way,
And in disdain poured in the conquering sea.[8]

A good breeze sprang up to carry us through the Strait and the log showed a speed of thirteen knots as we passed Cape Spartivento.

August 15
The Grecian Archipelago
For three days we have been having one of the finest sails that I ever had in my life. The weather has been delightful and somewhat cooler, and with all sails set—studding sails most of the time—we have been running thirteen and sometimes fourteen knots a part of every day.

This morning the island of Millelos was just ahead and off the harbor we took aboard a Greek pilot for Smyrna. The islands about here look barren and desolate but a boat came alongside with grapes to sell. This was formerly a great rendezvous for pirates but since steam vessels are now so common the old local industry has become so difficult as to be unprofitable.

August 16
The Grecian Archipelago
The wind blows hard from the northeast and while beating between two large islands under double reefed topsails the mainsail, which was an old one, was blown away. Another was soon bent. These islands look barren from the water, but some settlements are to be seen and a large castle on one of them.

In the afternoon the leech rope of the fore top-sail parted and the sail was somewhat torn before it could be furled. It was replaced by another sail. Our sails are very poor. All of them are old ones and I fear that we may feel serious need of better ones before we reach winter quarters.

August 17
Last night those in charge of the ship had plenty of excitement beating through the "Dark" passage with the wind blowing strong against us. Today the ship is being kept under a good press of sail with the mainland of Asia in sight. Our pilot is very attentive to his duty and has not slept for two nights. He has however not neglected eating and as the result of unsolicited attention on the part of some of our officers his long and unsightly hair has been cut, his beard trimmed and to some extent he has been washed. With these embellishments and in a complete new outfit of clothes furnished by the officers he makes a much more youthful appearance than when he came aboard, and whether his social standing in the Levant may have suffered by the change he certainly has become more nearly fitted to grace Western society. I wonder if his family will recognize him when he returns to them.

August 18
Smyrna
This morning we are entering the Bay with a fine breeze. The land on both sides has that rough and dull appearance peculiar to this country. The high hills are stony and bare and the ravines are filled with shrubbery. Little villages come into sight which are at first not discerned because of the color of the buildings. As we approach the head of the bay the scenery grows beautiful. Close to the water are little villages with flourishing gardens and groves. Camels are feeding in the tall luxuriant grass. The land and water blend in coloring to make this the prettiest picture from our ship that I have yet seen in the Mediterranean.

We come to anchor off the city. It is built on the lower slope of Mount Pegus, on which, in the rear of the city are to be seen the ruins of ancient temples. The buildings are mostly small and low and one notices their roofs from the ship. Scattered among them are numerous slender minarets.

Many English and French steamships are here. Enormous quantities of fruit are exported. We have already been well supplied by boats from shore. The American Consul came aboard accompanied by an attendant or bodyguard, a Greek dressed in the ancient Greek costume, with side arms.

August 19
Smyrna

Armenians, Jews, Maltese, Turks and Greeks have been identified among the peddlers who have come aboard peddling small wares, including perfumery, slippers, beads, and pipes all of which many of our crew saw fit to buy. Smyrna has a great variety of people. It is said that there are seven distinct quarters for as many nationalities.

August 20
Smyrna

The Captain in company with the American Consul[9] visited the Pasha, who, at eight bells received an appropriate salute from our guns. The Greeks here are large athletic men and in trade are notorious cheats.

August 22
Smyrna

We are living well here. Plenty of fresh meat and an abundance of fruit. We are painting ship. In my Store Room I am overhauling iron-work and having it blacked. This I do mostly myself, as I usually do such things in preference to having a half a dozen of the crew about it, whom I could have for the asking. Most sailors are such loafers and so careless and irresponsible that I prefer not to have them for a job of this sort. While I was engaged in this work the Captain brought down several English gentlemen to visit the Store Room.

August 23
Smyrna

This afternoon the Governor with two Turkish officers and two attendants visited the ship.[10] The American Consul accompanied them through the ship. With the officers of the ship who showed the party about they spent some time in my Store Room where the Governor exhibited considerable curiosity with respect to its contents. One of his attendants acted as interpreter.

The Governor is about fifty years old, of medium height and rather stout. His head is inclined slightly forward and there are gray hairs in his beard. His nose is very prominent and decidedly Jewish. His eye suggests an easy going man who likes congenial company.

He complimented our Marine Guard and through the interpreter told them that he did not expect to see soldiers so clean and neat on a ship and said that he was once a soldier in the ranks and had risen to his present position by his own exertions. He spoke of being with Sir F. Williams at the siege of Sebastopol in the Russian War.

I went ashore and with Sergeant Robbins mounted donkeys, hired a guide and started to see the sights of the city. On our road we passed many neat residences approached through yards or courts with figured pavements made of shiny varicolored small round stones.

We passed the "Meles" of Homer, once a river, but now an insignificant stream and by two Turkish cemeteries shaded by handsome tall conical shaped trees resembling our poplars. The graves are marked by marble slabs on the tops of which are carved the Turkish turban.

Still following along the valley which shows the former size of the "Meles" we passed from streets and roads to a rough steep trail over which our donkeys are kept going at a good gait by a man who follows, striking them with a long stick and shouting, "ha-a, a-ah." I enjoyed the ride, but Robbins at first was afraid of being thrown and tried to stop the driver from beating his animal. He soon gained confidence however and did better.

We crossed the deep bed of the "Meles" over a double arched caravan bridge, met numerous camels with huge baskets on their backs and approached a high masonry wall with a gateway in its eastern side. This is our destination. Within is one of the "Seven Churches." We dismount and enter.

We find the space inside largely devoted to garden purposes. There is a small comparatively modern Greek Catholic church which we inspect. It contains numerous paintings, images, etc, but nothing of special interest.

This is sacred ground. Both St. John and St. Paul here preached the gospel of Christ, but long since the torch of the Turk lighted the walls of the edifice in which they stood and the cold forms of Muhammadanism supplanted the simple worship of Christ.

South of the site of the church, water, as it comes from several sources in the rocks above, is collected in a pipe and allowed to fall on the concave surface of a rock below whence it runs off over the ground. This is pointed out to us and an ancient well whose water still possesses miraculous power to cure the sick as of old. In proof of its efficacy we saw strings and various articles of wearing apparel fastened to a nearby tree by invalids who had recently tested its power to heal.

We next visited a cafe for refreshments and sat down at a table out of doors, but within a walled enclosure shaded by trees. We ordered eggs, wine and bread. The eggs were cooked in the true Eastern way out of doors over a small collection of twigs which were lighted for the occasion.

Here as in every place where I have been about the Mediterranean attempts were made to overcharge and cheat us. This propensity on the part of guides and everybody else with whom a visitor comes in contact is very annoying.

On our way back we saw everywhere Turks smoking their "hubble-bubbles"[11] and Armenians, Jews, Greeks, Arabs and representatives of various other elements of the land population chatting, bargaining, or singing to the accompaniment of musical instruments.

The Greek and Armenian women whose features I was able to see were very good looking.

August 26
Smyrna

I have never met in a responsible position a man so small and mean as our Executive Officer. I asked him for permission to go ashore again today. After hesitating he grudgingly said that I might go for two hours. Apparently however he became somewhat ashamed of his attitude because when I came on deck to go he told me that I need not come back until sunset.

He is constantly asking me to do something for him, often help in some purely personal matter, and he has aroused comment among the men by reason of the character of duties which he has occasionally called upon me to perform on the ship, but I have never received from him any consideration in the way of a favor or a sign of gratitude. The more I do for him the more unwilling he seems to be to allow me out of his reach, probably lest he might want me for something.

Perhaps I ought to be more charitable toward him. I wonder how I might become if I had our crew on my hands, most of them ready to take any advantage of me, and I found a petty officer who might seem to me especially useful and dependable? Still the exercise of authority without a recognizable objective is not conducive to discipline, absolutely essential on any ship. After all what an existence if a man's life is determined by the tyrannical whims and caprices of somebody else.

I wanted to get a general view of the city this time and therefore I set out on foot to do it. The streets generally are dirty and narrow. Water and drainage flows along a depression in the center of the street. Streets are further narrowed by the custom of store keepers of exposing wares outside of their shops. Rapid progress is impossible even for a pedestrian and the meeting of a dozen loaded camels strung together or a train of pack horses presents a traffic problem of considerable difficulty.

As I came to the higher slopes on which part of the city is built I noticed the habitations of the lower classes, small low flat-roofed one story structures of stone and wood. In the western part of the city the Turks are especially to be seen lounging lazily in their places of business, or bazaars, smoking and watching the people passing in the street. Mixed with them are Greeks, Moors, Arabs, Jews and Armenians, for the Turks do not live exclusively in a quarter by themselves as I was at first led to suppose. The southern portion of the city, largely populated by the Greeks and Armenians, is superior to the western part. The streets are wider and more regular and the dwellings neatly built and comfortable. I saw no large public squares and no public buildings of any pretensions in the city. I met many women in Western European dress who were very handsome and attractive.

There are no wagons. Everything is carried on the backs of men or beasts. It is astonishing to see what loads the men can carry. On their backs there is a wedge like pad with the thick part downward to ease the burden off their shoulders. The population of the city is about 170,000 of whom about 70,000 are Turks.

August 29

We are leaving ancient Smyrna, but are becalmed in the bay opposite the fort. Here the scenery is beautiful. Nature's coloring of the mountains and their green ravines and the water of the bay with the varied shades of the green of the trees and luxuriant vegetation which cover the intervening table land makes a rare picture. Among the trees back from the shore some handsome residences are to be seen. At two embrasures of the fort we can make out two large brass cannon and piled near their muzzles large stacks of solid shot of <u>Marble</u> which the Turks use in their guns.

August 30
Vourlah Bay

Here about fifteen miles from Smyrna, good water, which has become a luxury with us, may be obtained and today we are watering ship. It is being brought off in casks. All our boats are being used for the purpose, but it is a tedious affair.

Two natives of the vicinity came aboard. They look fierce and are equipped with various weapons useful for self defense—and other purposes. They carry a metallic box hung from the neck, a bag at the shoulder and another at the waist, in front. They acted as though they had been on a ship before.

August 31

A quiet Sabbath in the Bay of Smyrna. After dinner I went ashore with the Gunner, the Master's mate, a Midshipman and the Purser's Steward. We strolled into the interior, sat down in the shade and had a drink of water from a nearby spring or fountain. What a refreshing change to drink water from its source and not from a rusty iron tank.

It is near here that we obtained our water yesterday for the ship. This is a general watering place for cattle. Numerous Turks sitting on stones from an ancient building were watching their herds of camels, asses, cattle and horses. Some of the bulls took offense at our boat's crew in their white duck suits and charged them. One bull more furious then the others caught one fellow, Fortune, in the back and threw him some distance and almost in the water. The manner in which it was done caused a roar of laughter among our company. Fortunately the man was not injured. Had the bull's horn struck Fortune it would have been no laughing matter.

Grapes, figs and pomegranates were growing in great profusion. The figs were green but quite palatable. Our company went among the grape vines from which the crop had been and gathered as many as they could conveniently carry of the most delicious grapes which I have ever tasted.

The natives were villainous looking, of a dark swarthy complexion. They dressed in a Turkish costume with the legs bare to the knees. All were armed with pistols, knives and swords. They exhibited astonishment and wonder at the revolvers carried by our men. As the natives increased in numbers their actions seemed to make it advisable to give them a demonstration of revolver shooting which was done with view to making them believe that a revolver would shoot indefinitely without reloading.[12] As I sat alone with three of them waiting for the return of my comrades I could observe that every movement which I made was regarded with suspicion. Next to cupidity, fear of one whom they regard as their superior appears to be their predominant trait.

September 1

Today the whiskey ration in the Navy is stopped by an Act of Congress.[13] This has caused a great volume of talk among some of the old sailors who have long been in the Service. They declare that it will be the death of the Navy; that all the inducement the Navy offered to lead a man to prefer it to the merchant service was the whiskey. They denounce the officials supposed to be responsible for the enactment of this measure and call them a set of psalm-singing old fools, but mostly other hard names too bad for me to record.

They die hard, but it will soon be over. This talk must be expected. The abolition of the whiskey ration is a good step in the right direction. Rum-serving by the Government was a poor example to men of such habits as seamen and "boys." Some say that since they cannot have spirit on shipboard they will leave it off entirely. This will be so undoubtedly in many instances.

Today the ship is supplied with a full amount of water.

Two men, Lemmon and Giles, Englishmen, ran away while on shore on duty. Search was made but they could not be found.

Antonio the Greek who sold supplies to us at Smyrna came down to us here today. While he turned his back upon his goods some of the crew stole six boxes of sardines, some cheeses and ten francs in money. Such thieves as are here can only be found on a man-of-war. How <u>mad</u> the Greek looked. He was black with rage.

September 2

We are standing out of the Bay of Smyrna under a strong cold wind from the north.

In the afternoon the cry, "<u>Man Overboard</u>," again strikes our ears. In tacking ship the main sheet took "boy" Stevens from the deck when the main yard was swung and threw him into the sea. He caught the "Jacob's Ladder"[14] at the stern and saved himself.

This is the second accident which has happened to him since we came out. Once before he was nearly killed by falling down the fore hatchway.

This last accident to him resulted in the fore top-sail being split and the jib "busted." The sails were old and rotten and we were making short tacks in a narrow passageway under a stiff wind.

September 3
Grecian Archipelago

We are bound for Beirut, Syria and are having a splendid sail in a blue sea under a good breeze, passing barren desolate looking islands.

The men bear the deprivation of their whiskey much better than I expected. I did however happen today to overhear a quartermaster say at his mess that now "the Navy has lost all its <u>charms</u>." Whatever attractions the Navy may have possessed for anybody I had never before heard them characterized as "charms."

September 4
The Mediterranean

Two years ago today I followed my dear mother to her last resting place. How rapidly have these two years passed. It was a lovely day and a gentle zephyr fanned the passenger on her way. In the pleasant evening twilight I sat with a few relatives and friends in the room which now seemed so strangely vacant as I realized that my mother like my father was gone forever.

What changes have come to me and to that home in these two brief years. How little then I imagined that this anniversary would find me far away amid the scenes in which I find myself today. Last night I paced the deck in the pleasant moonlight of the Aegean Sea with my mind full of memories which this day recalls, and probably will do the same tonight. I hope that those who tonight remain in that distant home are well and happy.

Boxes are being fitted up in the "brig" in which to confine men who are being punished. I hear that "tricing up" as a form of punishment has been abolished by the Department. I hope this is true for, as applied, the effect is demoralizing besides being conducive to physical injury.

September 6
Mediterranean

Light winds, otherwise we would have made port tonight. The usual pre-Sunday preparations are being made. Saturday afternoon being a sort of overhauling day for sailors on a man-of-war. They have their clothes bags on deck—a privilege not often accorded. The sun is hot and flies from land to the windward annoy us very much.

September 8
Beirut

Yesterday we made a landfall evidently close to our destination, but we stood off and ran down the coast to the leeward. After we had gone about forty miles somebody discovered that we were going astray. Whether the pilot was responsible for the error or not I do not know, but he was blamed and sent below in disgrace. At noon today we had succeeded in beating back about fifty miles to the windward and then a meridian altitude evidently showed that we had passed our destination in the other direction for we squared our yards and after running some distance to the leeward turned and came into Beirut, where we now are, practically an open bay or roadstead unprotected from the sea. We find here a British line-of-battle ship and a French war ship.

September 9
Beirut

It is much warmer here than at Smyrna. The heat is oppressive, especially at night.

Among the many visitors[15] today were a native missionary Mr. Larkees, and four pupils of his school, two of whom Moustafa Ameen and Abdullah Bydocen, are Muhammadans, the latter being the son of a former Governor or Pasha of this place. They all visited the Store Room. Mr. Larkees and one of his pupils, Abraham Dibe, spoke English fluently.

Mr. Larkees asked me to go ashore with him and visit the school. I was glad to avail myself of this invitation and I was soon on the rude stone landing place at Beirut. I was then taken through the city, visiting first a bookstore conducted by the missionaries and where books in English are sold. We then passed through the market place and some of the principal streets, which are narrow, dirty, crowded with people who exhibit remarkable skill in avoiding the laden donkeys as they pass along.

The manner of trading is as at Smyrna. A room six feet by eight with the front open to the street makes a comfortable shop for a dry goods merchant. The floor is elevated and on it the wares are exposed so that they can be conveniently seen from the street. The Turk, Arab or Syrian proprietor stays inside. The customer stands in the street and blocks traffic.

The women here wear a white sheet-like outer garment which covers them from head to feet. A separate piece of gauze of a different color veils the face. If a veil be not worn the white robe is arranged to cover the face. While the Turkish women thus conceal their faces from the gaze of a man and expose their ankles to everybody, voluptuous looking Armenian and Syrian women stare brazenly at men with uncovered faces but cover their lower extremities.

A Turk is not supposed to see the face of his bride until after the marriage and the unveiling is a matter of some formality. There is a story of a Pasha who was asked before whom of his relatives a newly acquired wife should unveil and he replied that he did not care, provided that she did not do it before him.

After having a glass of lemonade with some real ice in it from Mount Lebanon and smoking a "hubble-bubble" we boarded an omnibus for a ride out into the country. A French company has the monopoly of passenger transportation over a good turnpike road between Beirut and Damascus. We went out on this road. We stopped at a sort of park and smoked "hubble-bubbles" and cigarettes and watched the mustering of soldiers nearby. The soldiers are to be used by the Pasha or Governor to enforce the collection of a tobacco tax against which the people in a neighboring district have rebelled. Music from a band was supposed to stimulate the military ardor of the recruits. On our return we passed the Governor riding a horse with the attendants running alongside on feet.

The population of Beirut is about 150,000. The scenery on the outskirts of the city is grand. From the water the city and its surroundings make a beautiful picture.

September 11
Beirut
British officers are visiting the ship. The pilot was discharged last night and another engaged. Giles and Lemmon, the two men who deserted at Boulong bay have been caught at Smyrna.

I supposed that we would go to Genoa from here, but we may go to ——— [illegible] on this coast as another missionary has been killed there.

September 13
Beirut
British naval officers have been aboard today, but our most important visitor was the pasha of Beirut. He did not look over the ship.

We took on two more pilots and weighed anchor and sailed at four p.m.

September 14
At sea
As we sailed along the coast last night the numerous lights from the dwellings on the mountain sides shown very brightly and made the shore look like the "Milky Way."

It is a beautiful day and as we sail along the coast of Syria we are near enough to shore to see something of the country. We pass one town of considerable size and can see the minarets of several mosques.

At noon the old Turkish pilot who has been put at our mess tells us that we are eighty miles from Beirut and have a hundred more to go.

The modified law for the government of the Navy[16] was read at muster.

I love to see the Sabbath on shipboard. Everything moves, but moves quietly and the men seem to enjoy themselves. They sleep on deck, read old papers and letters and overhaul their "ditty" bags—that interesting receptacle in which a sailor keeps not only needles and other gear for repairing his clothes, but every trinket and treasure which he owns.

September 15
This morning a high mountain is just abeam of us and the sun rising above its lofty summit as heavy clouds were rolling up made a magnificent sight. At the same time to the seaward numerous waterspouts were in process of formation and wild dark clouds told us that we were in for a violent squall. It soon struck us ahead but we were prepared for it and the ship was kept off before the wind. After many changes in the weather the good ship had fair wind again and brought us into Iskenderun Bay and a good spacious harbor.

September 16
The guide of the Consul was sent to communicate with the pasha of the town last evening.

It appears that the object of our visit to this place is to obtain redress for wrongs done to persons entitled to the protection of our government. There are bands of robbers here who make a practice of robbing caravans, or other persons who may tempt them. A boat came alongside with fish. The natives in it were naked and very rude in their manners.

September 17
Exercise at general quarters nearly all day. We also had target practice with the big guns and

with small arms. More than sixty shells and numerous solid shot were used.

The messenger sent to the Pasha of the town in the interior has not yet returned, nor to my knowledge has any communication been received from him.

September 18

The messenger sent by the Consul to Edna has returned bringing word that the Pasha declines to visit the ship, but says that he has two prisoners in his custody who may be seen, should the officers of the ship or the consul wish to visit them. This seems to me quite cool and dignified and indicative of some diplomatic instinct, if not training.

The various Divisions have been engaged in target practice with pistols all day.

September 19

The monotony of existence at this place was relieved only by the departure of the Consul, with his guide, the purser, the Lieutenant of Marines and the Captain's Clerk for the inland town where lives the Pasha of the Edna District.

The country is practically a deserted waste. There are no houses and the only living creature that one sees is an occasional wild boar roaming undisturbed near the shore. The harbor is good and would seem to favor some sort of a settlement near but this once famous region now seems abandoned except for marauding bands of Arabs in search of plunder.

September 20

Saturday is here again with its regular pre-Sabbath preparations, cleaning ship, overhauling clothes bags, etc.

Some of the officers went ashore to hunt for game.

For some reason which I do not know the ship chandler who came with us from Beirut to keep us supplied with fresh provisions has been put ashore by the Captain to find his way back to Beirut as best he can. I do not like to contemplate his journey through this wild country with the money which he must have on his person.

September 21

Another Sabbath with soft wind and hot sunshine. The ship looks very clean. The Captain used more than his usual scrutiny in his inspection this morning than is usual. He asked me if I thought that, "a lady could enter the paint room with a silk dress on and not spoil it?"

During the past week I have, in spite of myself, been quite reflective and apprehensive regarding my friends and affairs at home, but I hope that my fears may be due to a disordered imagination resulting from too much concern for what is beyond my control. It is better to try to be happy under all circumstances, since we have so little time for enjoyment in this life, if we stop to picture its ills no time will remain for aught else.

September 22

Last night we had a violent squall with thunder and lightning and had to let go a second anchor.

My head aches usually in the morning. I presume that it is from lack of air on the berth deck. So many men make the air very impure and when the ship lies at anchor, head to the wind, but little air comes on the berth deck. I wonder that with the little exercise which I have in the open air, I am so well as I am. I am certainly tired of this wild lonesome place.

September 23
This morning a boat with the Second Lieutenant, Assistant Surgeon and a crew of men left the ship with provisions for a week to meet the Embassage sent to the Pasha. The Captain is evidently disturbed by their failure to return. Chains, shot, shells, etc. were taken on deck today for their periodical overhauling. I have been reading Pope's *Essay on Man* and sleeping most of the day. No prospect of leaving this place.

September 24
At noon the boat that went to Alexandretta returned without news of the party which went with the Consul. Except when at General Quarters I have been reading Pope's *Essay* and sleeping.

September 25
This morning the First Lieutenant, Mr. Low, visited the Store room in my absence and found two towels hanging there. This he decided to be a direct infraction of the regulations of the ship. I made no excuse save to remark that it was not my practice and that I would see that it did not occur again. This however was enough to cause him to yield to his mean instinct and testify in rebuttal that he himself seen it "fifty times before." In my associations with men he has no precedent. Long may he live—so long as he keeps at sea. Pope says, "that the proper study of mankind is man," and I have one rare specimen for this purpose.

September 26
At last we are sailing away from this place. We are going back to Beirut.

The Consul and his party returned yesterday. With them was the Pasha's chief Captain who was responsible for their safety. They were assured by the pasha that if any of them were killed or injured by robbers the Captain's life would be sacrificed. On the way back a band of thirteen robbers were met, but they did not attack our party which numbered sixteen.

The Captain and the natives who came with him were fine physical specimens. Two of them were Circassians. All were well armed. They carried carbines or rifles, side arms and pistols. They were shown all over the ship and the guns were shotted and fired for their benefit.

According to the Pasha's promise the two prisoners in his custody are to be executed today.

September 27
Ten months ago today I was attached to this ship. How rapidly the time has passed.

A report reached us yesterday that a battle had taken place between the Federal forces and the Confederates resulting in the defeat of the former. The report adds that Gen. McClellan has been superseded by Gen. Pope.[17] Affairs look bad and I am much concerned about the outcome of this unusual war. I fear that there is no prospect now of a union with the Confederacy. It looks as though the time in which the North might have conquered has passed. Of course I am forming a judgement on uncertain premisses,—news which reaches us through European channels,—yet I fear that it may be too true.

September 28
Twenty nine years ago today I first saw the light. One year ago today I was examined, passed and proposed for admission to the York County Bar.

September 29
Beirut
After a tedious passage we are back again at Beirut. We have been short of provisions and everybody is half starved. As soon as we dropped anchor a boat was sent ashore for bread and vegetables. Word of our needs must have been passed ashore for we are being surrounded with boats bringing bread and fruit to sell. Arrangements are being made for the sailors to keep potatoes onboard, a privilege not before allowed.

September 30
Great quantities of fowls have been tumbled aboard and scores of bags of potatoes have been piled on the booms on the spar deck and now we are for the Straits of Messina.

I hope that the passage will be short as I am anxious for news from the United States. The Confederates seem to be gaining. I read the following in a French newspaper dated Paris, September 14, 1862, which I have obtained at Beirut:

New York, 1st, September. —The Federals have been defeated near Richmond and have lost most of their artillery.

Paris, 5th September. —The news from America is generally very favorable to the Confederates. Cotton is wanting in New York.

Paris, 8th September. —Confederates menace an attack on Washington. Cotton 58 cts.

New York, 9th September. —5,000 Confederates have crossed the Potomac and occupy Fredericksburg.[18]

New York. 10th September. —The Confederates occupy Maryland. Gen. McClellan has marched against them. The Federal Corps d'Armee is encamped near Baltimore. They will destroy the town if the Confederates should take possession of it. The Federals have enrolled 5,000 Negroes in their ranks.

I am disposed to give this news more credit than I could wish.

October 1
At sea
A good breeze becoming strong. Royals and topgallant-sails taken in. The wind is too nearly ahead to permit us to keep on our course.

October 2
At sea
Light head winds. The Gunner is getting shells ready for use. Exercise in drills and serving our clothing. A busy day for all hands.

The Orderly Sergeant has been "to the mast" several times with marines. There is a general row in the Marine Guard. The old man is nervous and on such occasions as the serving out of clothing he meets with a good deal of what he calls, "disrespect," "mutiny," or "sedition," in the ranks. It is amusing to hear the old man talk to the men on such occasions. He turns quickly from whatever he may be doing and berates the man before him and then as abruptly stops and turns his attention to whatever he may have been doing.

October 3
At sea

The ship is close hauled with a moderate breeze.

A Court martial was held to try Geo. W. Phelps, charged with smuggling spirits into the ship's boat at Beirut, and Moses E. Handren for bringing liquor on the ship and being drunk on duty. I was asked to act as counsel for both men and left my work and appeared before the Court without any preparation.[19]

The facts in Handren's case were so well established and the evidence against him so conclusive that I advised him to make no defense. He pleaded guilty.

Phelps had no witnesses, but trusted to the inability of the Judge Advocate to make out a case against him.

The first witness, Brown, a Negro, testified that Phelps bought a bottle and placed it in his market basket, but could not tell what it contained or whether it was carried to the ship's boat. Phelps was a steerage steward and was on duty as such on shore.

Crosby a boatman testified that he saw Phelps' basket come on board the boat and saw the basket passed over the ship's side, but failed to show how he identified this basket from the others which were passed over the ship's side. He testified further that he saw Handren take a bottle from the basket to which Phelps referred and saw Handren bring a bottle back to the boat.

The boat went again to the shore and after it had returned to the ship the second time, a bottle of <u>something</u>, the corporal on duty could not tell what, was found on Handren's person and another bottle was found in the boat, which bottle the corporal was pretty sure contained spirit.

Brown was being cross-examined by me when Mr. Wallace, the Second Lieutenant, who was President of the Court, squirmed in his seat and interrupted me by saying that he did not believe that I had any right to ask such questions. I did not insist although the questions were quite simple and proper, and passed to another line of questioning intended to test the witness's recollection about the covering of the bottle by Phelps which he bought with view to concealing it. This served to bring out on the part of the President an evident desire to convict regardless of the rights of the accused, as set forth in the articles for the government of the Navy, and a determination to do so which would be considered very indiscreet in a judge of a court of law. The outcome was that I was ordered out of the cabin with my client and the witness, and the court went into a conference.

Mr. Wallace who is inclined to make trouble for himself on the ship because of his high handed methods was evidently brought back to his senses and his alarm about a failure to convict quieted by the other members, especially Mr. Hinckley, the Recorder, who is familiar with legal proceedings. At any rate when I was recalled I was allowed to proceed with the examination of the witnesses without further interruptions. Before noon the Court was adjourned until 2 p.m. to allow the Master to take and work up his noonday observations.

At 2 p.m. I was notified by the Court's orderly that they were ready to proceed. I had no witnesses to present and began with my argument on the Government's evidence. After the case was closed Handren was brought before the Court and the orderly sent to request my attendance with the prisoner, Phelps. The Court stated that although it was contrary to the usual practice they wished to examine Handren.

He was questioned as to where he obtained his liquor, but nothing was elicited tending to show that it came from Phelps' basket. I attempted to make some suggestions to the

Court as counsel for Handren, based on facts learned by <u>me</u> after the trial, but I was promptly choked off by Mr. Wallace, the President. I put in however a plain statement of my rights in the matter as Handren's counsel and then withdrew. What disgusted me with the proceedings of the Court Martial was not so much the failure to observe conventional procedure of a court of law as the disregard of the rights of enlisted men of the Navy stipulated and supposed to be guaranteed by the Articles of War and the Regulations of the Navy.

October 4
At sea
Very rough. Strong head wind and heavy sea.

All hands were mustered on the Quarter Deck to hear the judgement of the Court Martial in the cases of Phelps and Handren. Handren was sentenced to loss of pay for two months and of liberty for six months. Phelps was acquitted.

October 5
At sea
This Sabbath comes with a strong gale from the north. Under reefed topsails the ship is plunging heavily into a head sea. This is one of the most trying days since we have left home. Everything is in confusion. Many are seasick. Poor Cox is quite used up. For a while today I myself felt a little disagreeable in the stomach. The forecastle is very wet. So is the gun deck. The guns on the lee side are housed. This is not a dry ship in rough weather anyway.

The Captain's goat, poor little thing, looks friendless and sick as she stands on the deck trying to keep her balance.

October 7
At sea
We are still under double reefed topsails.

I am reading Pope's *Homer's Iliad* and this lends added interest to the view which I have had of the Island of Candia, in close proximity to which we passed today. It is monotonous at sea but things are constantly happening on a man-of-war to make one feel gay as well as sad.

October 8
At sea
This morning our ship was flying like a thing of life before a northeast gale and now a few hours after we are under all sail with studding sails alow and aloft.

Although it has been quite rough general quarters took place and the men were drilled at small arms and in the sword exercise when under double reefed topsails.

October 10
At sea
Calm drifting about. Six ships in sight. I am reading Macaulay's *History of England*. Have also been drilled at small arms. What a bore to be drilled by one like the Midshipman in command of our Division whose proficiency is acquired entirely from reading a book just prior to the drill.

October 11
At sea

Last night Mount Aetna was sighted and today we are entering the Strait of Messina with light variable winds.

October 12
Messina

After slow progress through the Strait we enter the harbor of Messina at noon. Sunshine, scenery and coloring of land and sea make the Strait the most beautiful place which I have seen in the Mediterranean.

October 13
Messina

The harbor is protected by a breakwater and opposite there are strong fortifications. Two Americal barks and a brig are lying here. Vessels moor here head or stern on to the quays as they do in Havana.

A large mail for the ship was sent aboard by the Consul.[20] Letters from home bring more of anxiety than of pleasure and many of them tell of the deaths of relatives and friends in the war. The general tenor of the news indicates a desperate feeling in the North. A draft has gone into effect and men are prohibited from leaving for foreign countries.

There are no letters for me.[21] My last was dated May 12. My failure to hear from home is giving me considerable anxiety both regarding my brother Edward who is supposed to have gone to war[22] and on account of my personal affairs which were left in his hands. It is reported here that 100 guns were captured by the Federals near Baltimore and that another battle has taken place near Bull Run, favorable to the Federals, but I never liked the words "Bull Run" in connection with a battle.[23]

Salutes were fired for the Italian flag, the United States Consul and minute guns for Martin Van Buren who has died.

It would seem that the Navy might better be using some of this powder on Confederate privateers. It is reported here that several merchant ships have been destroyed by these privateers in the Mediterranean and also on the coast of Spain outside the Strait. A marine by the name of Smith while on duty at the port gangway in full dress uniform walked off— musket, accouterments and all—into the water alongside. His rescue, minus the musket, furnished a diversion which everybody enjoyed except the marine.

All hands busy tarring and repairing the rigging.

October 14
Messina

This morning on a large parade ground visible from the ship several regiments of infantry and one of cavalry met and formed a hollow square and executed by shooting a soldier who had deserted and joined Garibaldi and had been recaptured. Others of his force captured at the same time were released from the prison where they have been confined.

News is received of a Federal victory in which the Confederate Army has been badly cut up.[24] There is also a report of a capture of a Confederate cruiser by a British man-of-war.

October 16
Messina

Watering ship, painting and taking on provisions. Liberty is being given in small parties.

I asked for permission to go ashore in the afternoon, but Mr. Low gratified his natural instinct by saying that he might need me. This is his acknowledgment of all I have done for him the past two weeks in the way of personal help properly outside of the scope of my duties. I content myself with the fact that this is not an eternal existence.

October 17
Messina

The Governor of Messina visited the ship and received an appropriate salute on his departure.

All the marines who went on shore on liberty two days ago have been arrested by order of the Captain and are being kept prisoners on shore. Many of the sailors have overstayed their liberty and others have returned intoxicated. Last night one man got over the bows and started to swim ashore but was caught and brought back. He was drunk. Some of the men who went on liberty last night have been arrested, among them our mess cook.

October 18
Messina

The usual pre-Sunday preparations. More men go on liberty tonight. None went yesterday. All were put in irons still remain.

News comes of the surrender of Gen. John C. Breckenridge with 2,000 men and that Gen. S. Jackson has been intercepted in Maryland and his retreat cut off.[25]

October 19
Messina

After muster and religious services I went on shore accompanied by Mr. Wilson, Master's Mate, and Cox and Smith, my mess mates.

We first visited the "Mother Church," a building 1300 years old with a high dome conspicuous from the harbor. One of its many objects of interest is a sun-dial in the floor upon which sunlight falls through an aperture in the roof. Mass was being said when we entered. Some people were seated in the spacious area near the altar and others stood in groups around them. People were coming and going as they might in a market or place of business without any ceremony, except respectful decorum.

The galleries are supported by two rows of remarkable pillars obtained from the ancient city of Cataria whose site is now marked by a beautiful lake near the Strait.

We took a carriage to drive to an eminence which overlooks the city. A steep winding smooth macadamized road bordered by orchards of lemon and other fruit trees and chestnuts brought us to a sugar-loaf hill which we climbed of foot by a circuitous path. From this vantage point we could see for miles around, inland the rugged Sicilian landscape out of which Mount Aetna arose and to the north across the sparkling blue sea the smoky summit of Stromboli. Below us lay the city of Messina, the ships in the harbor looking like children's toys in a basin and beyond, glistening in the rays of the sinking sun, the hazy coast of Calabria.

On our return to the city we stopped to examine in a mountain gorge the ruins of an old monastery built at the time of the Crusades and used on various occasions as a place of refuge and defense.

October 20, 1862
Messina

I am still enjoying the recollection of yesterday's trip ashore.

Recent liberty for the men has resulted in courts martial and in imprisonment ashore. It would seem that they had taken this occasion to settle all their grudges. Several men were injured by fighting. A sergeant of marines was set upon and to escape jumped overboard and swam to the ship where he arrived minus his best coat and his shoes. Geyer, the coxswain of the Captain's gig, was badly beaten by a number of his shipmates. He is in the fort ashore with one other seaman and the marines who broke their liberty.

Geyer is a native of Maine, quick tempered and handy with his fists, and has been a "fighting" first mate on merchant ships, but apparently he has met his match on this ship. The men say that he was in prison in Massachusetts for killing a man on his ship and that his family, who are influential, secured his pardon on condition that he enlisted in the Navy. However, this may be he is a man of good appearance and can talk intelligently on almost any subject, and, as captain of the After Guard he is always to be seen at the right place in any emergency and taking leadership in doing the right thing. He is said to be of the family to which the mother of Captain Marryat of the British Navy belonged.

October 21
Messina

It is reported that the Confederates have two ironclad steam cruisers in these waters and that they are looking for us; also that Confederate privateers have hoisted the black flag. These two reports are about equally unworthy of credence.[26]

This is a busy port. Five steamships arrived yesterday and seven today. Seven departed today. Enormous quantities of fruit are expected from here.

October 22
Messina

We have been standing by all day to man the yards and fire a salute in honor of the Prince of Wales and a Prince of Prussia who are expected here on a pleasure trip. They did not arrive.

It is reported that Fort Sumter has been taken by the Federals and that the great part of the Confederate Army has retreated to Richmond where they are hemmed in by the Federal forces.[27]

October 23
Messina

A boat drill—the arming and equipping of all of our seven boats. The ship is turned upside down by the boat crews in their search for the necessary articles. The drill was useful in demonstrating the need of arrangements for obviating such confusion.

Three of the crew received today Court Martial sentences for various offenses. One man, Rooney, who attempted to swim ashore had forfeited three months pay. He was charged with attempting to desert. The facts did not justify such a charge, but his punishment may serve as a useful warning to others.

October 24
Messina

Rumor reaches us of a battle near Harrisburg, Pa. in which the Federals were victorious with a great loss on both sides. It is said that we have lost 30,000 and the Confederates 20,000.[28]

There is also a report that two Confederate ironclads are lying outside waiting for us to come out. I do not know what we could do against two ironclad steam warships, but if I know Commodore Thatcher they will have a fight on their hands and we will have to take our chances.

October 26
Messina

While dressing to go ashore I was suddenly taken sick with severe pains in my body which soon made me extremely weak. I made my way as best I could to the Sick Bay, was put on the "sick-list" and remained in a hammock all day. This the first time I have been under the Doctor's care during the cruise. I could not attend General Muster so there was no alternative. Here one is either sick or well, and unless officially pronounced sick you could be excused from nothing that a well man may do. This is better however than the merchant ship custom which seemed to be that a man was either well enough to work or sick enough to take calomel and jalap.

After keeping quiet in the hammock I soon became more comfortable.

October 27

At 4 a.m. while I was lying quietly in my hammock in the Sick Bay all hands were called to unmoor ship. After the usual noise and commotion the ship was under way, passing out of the Strait of Messina. After quarters I left the Bay and resumed my duties. The wind died out and during the afternoon and at night Mount Stromboli was close by. Clouds of smoke arise from the crater, but no flame is seen.

October 29
At sea

We are opposite Naples and the coast can be seen. There is a strong breeze. All sail is set and the ship is running along splendidly. During the evening heavy showers with lighting of the sharpest character come on. The light sails are taken in and top-sails are reefed. The ship rolls heavily, water comes in through the gun deck ports and rushes over the hatch coamings down into the berth deck. Every part of the ship is flooded; even the cabin requires attention to free it from water. Dishes and everything movable circulate among the men. The Orderly Sergeant's mess table makes a leap to the leeward and broken dishes come flying over towards our mess. We eat and hold on.

October 30
At sea

This morning finds us under full canvas with a fine breeze between the islands of Corsica and Elba with Monte Christo also in sight.

I have taken a cold and most of the ship's company are similarly affected. The nights are growing cool, yet the days are sufficiently warm for comfort.

Many of the men are afflicted with disease as the result of their last liberty at Messina, and some of the officers likewise if I can judge from their complaints. It is a sad thing for sailors that they cannot forgo liquor which impels them to rush headlong into the arms of prostitutes. The Captain's practice of giving night liberty is, in my opinion, ill advised, since the men arrive on shore too late to go about by themselves and see the sights and thus find diversion and so fall into the hands of "guides" who exploit them to get their money.

Those who drink too much do not have time to become sober before they have overstayed their liberty. A reward is offered of ten dollars, or more, which eager local police officials collect without losing any time. The practice of allowing men thus arrested to remain in a foreign prison with injury to their health and among criminals of the basest sort is, in my opinion highly reprehensible on the part of an American who has American seamen in his charge. It is properly regarded by our men as an unjustifiable indignity and a breech of trust on the part of an American Naval Officer.

October 31
Spezia
After an absence of five months we sail into Spezia amid showers but with a fair wind. Spezia seems more like home to me than any place visited since we came to the Mediterranean. Of all the places we have seen none has such attractions for me as this little bay, with its beautiful surroundings, its terraced hills, its fertile ravines, its mountain peaks, its neat villas and garden-like shores. I love to look upon its old ruined castles and steep shores.

Garibaldi the Italian patriot is here, a prisoner, suffering from a wound in his ankle. A large part of the Italian fleet is here. The improvements in the fortifications of the harbor are still progressing. This place is well adapted for defensive purposes which the King is not failing to improve.

A large mail came on board but no letters or papers for me. I feel considerably disturbed at not hearing from home as I counted on receiving several letters here. I cannot understand why I do not hear from my brother Edward. News from home received by one of my fellow-townsmen on the ship would indicate that Edward is in the Navy also and a Master's Mate on the *Colorado* on the blockade. My anxiety is doubtless increased by the letters which my shipmates are receiving bringing news of the deaths of relatives and friends who have fallen in battle and by disease. Hunter (Acting Boatswain) received the news of the death of his brother in the battle of Bull Run, August 29, by a ball passing through his head just above the eyes.

It is reported now that the *Colorado* is at Gibraltar, and is to come up to Genoa for the winter. If my brother Edward is on her, as reported, this means that I will see him soon. Possibly I may receive my long awaited mail by this ship.

November 1
Scrubbing and holystoning decks. The Consul came aboard. It seems evident now that the Confederates have two cruisers just outside the Strait, if not within the Mediterranean. Their presence there is apparently bringing our warships into that region. It seems quite certain that we will spend the winter in Genoa. There is plenty of beef, pork and whiskey in the Store House here but no cordage.

November 2 & 3
I went ashore with the Doctor's Steward Smith and the Master-of-Arms, Glenn. After spending a short time in Spezia we took a carriage for Sarzana, a town about ten miles

distant on the north side of the bay. I was not inclined to go on the ride but I yielded to the wishes of my companions. The road is the route to Leghorn and passes through a most picturesque country. On arrival at Sarzana we went to the "New York" Hotel, a very good house, where we hired a room and after admiring the views from our windows we ordered refreshments. When ready to return to Spezia Glenn went to the stable to find our coachman. On hearing a hub-bub outside shortly after we found Glenn standing off our driver and five other men armed with clubs. It seemed that our driver was too slow in making our carriage ready to suit Glenn and to accelerate his movements Glenn took such measures as naturally suggest themselves to the Master-at-Arms of a man-of-war and at the same time expressed his opinion of the driver in French using language which Glenn thought the driver might understand and which he evidently did. The other Italians about the stable picked up cudgels and came to the driver's help, but Glenn retreated to the hotel in good order facing his opponents. When we came out as reinforcements to Glenn, armed with fireplace accessories which we had grabbed on the way from our room and Glenn's opponents saw that we meant business they stopped, and there was a truce. The driver was very indignant at his treatment by Glenn and while he showed no ill-will toward Smith or myself he refused to take us back to Spezia unless paid an "indemnity," in advance. As we were so far from Spezia and the time when we were due back on the ship was not far off Smith and I decided to pay the man his price and I did so.

By this time some Gens d'armes appeared on the scene, presumably called by the hotel proprietor. Their arrival assured the cessation of hostilities and the affair seemed to be settled. The three of us seated ourselves in the carriage and the driver mounted his seat and we started off, when to our astonishment Glenn stood up, faced the people who were watching our departure, and commenced to sing Garibaldi's Hymn, which is regarded as treasonable here in Italy today as the Marseillaise ever was in France.

Then things began to happen. Our carriage was quickly stopped, we were arrested and our passports demanded. We had none. We then found ourselves being marched to the military barracks with an escort of Gens d'armes, who handled us rather roughly from an American point of view. They were half drunk. They brought us to a dark prison house, pushed us in, followed us, swung the heavy iron door to, and then they drew their swords and started in to beat us up. We thought that they were going to kill Glenn who came in for the greater part of their attention. He had been giving them his opinion of them in French and they probably understood some of it. We were then rushed into a smaller room where the lights were extinguished and they gave us some more beating with their swords, Glenn coming in for more than his share. He was beaten unmercifully.

We were then put into "stocks" and compelled to lie on a platform covered with straw. I protested as well as I was able and through the intercession of one of our guards who appeared to be the most nearly sober Smith and I were released from our stocks in a short time. We were then ordered out and I called for my money which had been taken from me supposing that we were to be released, but we were merely moved to another part of the building. Here we were placed in a room which had as a bed for us a platform covered with some straw. I finally however induced them to bring us a mattress and blanket and we were left to reflect on our situation and go to sleep, which we did.

We presumed that our inability to produce passports was regarded as sufficient evidence that we were Garibaldeans. Anyway we were in an Italian prison as enemies of King Victor Emanuel and old Garibaldi himself also a wounded prisoner in Spezia a few miles away.

I awoke at an early hour. It was dark, I could hear the rain falling in torrents in the courtyard. I had considerable curiosity to know the state of my companion's spirits but I waited until daylight appeared through our iron barred window before I moved or spoke. I was cold and I moved. Then I heard Smith laugh. Glenn did not feel quite as good natured. He got a worse mauling than we, and besides he had lost about half of his heavy long moustache of which he was rather proud. He was not only "sore" about this, but his lip was sore on the side where his tormentors had pulled the hair out and it hurt him to laugh. However after hearing us laugh he did some chuckling.

It was late in the morning when an officer accompanied by some soldiers came to our room and with the help of a French writer whom we pretended not to understand tried to get information about us, our names, the names of our parents, our birth places etc. When after a good deal of circumlocution our questioner would ask us if we did not understand we would reply "sacraments" with all the dignity and politeness which we could muster, an answer which never failed to make our questioners appear disconcerted and perplexed.

This confab ended the officer and the soldiers went out and closed the door without our being able to learn from them what charge, if any, they had against us, or when we should change our quarters, for freedom or trial. After a while however, we succeeded in obtaining some water to wash our faces and hands, and a towel.

At eleven o'clock a plate of boiled rice and vegetables with a small loaf of bread was brought us. As we sat upon the bed and partook of this frugal repast we noticed that we were being watched by people in the windows of adjacent buildings who could look down and see us through the window of our room. Their faces bore expressions of pity and sympathy.

At noon we were informed that we were to be taken to Spezia. This was good news for we supposed that no information had reached the ship or the Consul at Spezia regarding our whereabouts. Our duties on board required our attention and we feared that in one of his freaky moments Commodore Thatcher would offer a reward for our apprehension as deserters. This thought especially disturbed us but we kept cool.

At one p.m. Smith and I ironed together and Glenn behind also ironed were marched into the street and put into a waiting vehicle. Two Gens d'armes with muskets and otherwise armed to the teeth followed us as an escort through the streets.

It began to rain soon after we started. Smith and I had an old blanket which we put over our heads while the great cloak of one of the Gens d'armes on the seat with Glenn served to protect the owner and Glenn. Streets and balconies were thronged with men and women who watched our departure as that of important state prisoners.

When out of town our escort came into the carriage with us, making six of us besides the driver in our two wheeled, one horse, open carriage. The rain soon stopped and n spite of our uncomfortable crowding we had the benefit of the scenery along the route. The news of our "capture" had evidently preceded us. Peasants working in the fields, men and women with their skirts clewed up, came running to the road where they stood and watched us until reminded by some absent minded movement that it was water which they had balanced aloft.

It was five p.m. when we reached Spezia and as we passed through the principal street people appeared at the doors and windows to catch a glimpse of the now famous Garibaldean prisoners. We were taken to the prison and delivered over to the local authorities in charge of that institution.

In the apartment where we were lodged was an Englishman who had been incarcerated the night before for some trivial offense. He was an intelligent expert mechanic who was employed on the government works and it was something of a solace to find some one who could sympathize with us in English in our predicament and who shared our views regarding Italian police procedure and methods. It appeared to be the regular practice to take a man's money and every article of value from him and return what they please. Our knives were not returned, nor was all of our money.

Our guards promised to send for the American Consul but they did not and had it not been for some gentlemen who came to visit the Englishman we would have remained in prison another night. They kindly promised to inform the Consul and soon we had a message from him. Meanwhile we had ordered a real supper to be brought in from the outside. When it came it was dark and we had some trouble in inducing our guards to bring in a light so that we could see to eat it. We had beef cooked in different ways, baked chicken, fried potatoes, bread, wine, apples and other fruit. We had no table, but napkins were spread on the straw which covered the platform intended to serve us as a bed. The Englishman was invited to join us and we did eat.

This "couch" was like the one to which we were first introduced at Sarzana, with stocks at the foot. This attachment the Englishman with the help of a fellow prisoner had succeeded in rendering useless the night before. Our prison walls were of stone three feet thick and through a grated aperture one and a half feet square the air of sunny Italy was allowed to intrude itself into our room. Here we sat, cross legged, Turkish fashion, and enjoyed our supper while the iron door admitted a score of people, prison guards and friends of the Englishman who stood watching us. After eating, Glenn who had a splendid voice started up some old songs, including those which Robby Burns and Tom Moore have given us and we all joined in. We heard afterward that the Gens d'armes had to clear the street of the crowd which collected outside to hear the "Garibaldeans" sing, but the guards did not attempt to stop our hilarity. There were signs that the authorities were becoming nervous on account of our treatment. We, however, did not attempt Garabaldi's Hymn again.

A messenger arrived from the Consul to tell us that we would be taken to the Prefect of Police and then to the Consulate where we would be released. We took time to finish our supper and our singing and then said good bye to our fellow prisoner whom we had cheered by our company. He had a family and felt quite blue over his imprisonment. He promised to visit the ship when set free.

We were ironed again. This time Glenn and I together and Smith behind. A walk of five minutes at full military step in the rain with an imposing military escort brought us to the Prefecture of Police. Our irons were removed and an official came from the interior of the building with instructions to take us to the Consulate, where we proceeded free from irons. The Consul greeted us with a smile, as did also our Paymaster Pangborn and Lieutenant of Marines who were with him. Then they all burst into laughter. They considered it a great joke. An official order for our release was written and with it a statement for our Executive Officer exculpating us from all blame for our absence from the ship.

On our arrival at the ship we were met by Mr. Low who became quite indignant when he saw Glenn with his one sided moustache, his swollen lip and a sword cut over his left eye and Smith and myself with such unmistakable evidence of the beatings which we had received. I did not suppose him to be capable of such feeling as he exhibited. He characterized our guards as a "set of cowardly scoundrels" and gave expression to some very uncomplimentary opinions of Italians in general. He said that he would see that anybody from the ship who wanted to go into the interior hereafter was provided with a passport so that the Italians would not have the lack of a passport as an excuse for abusing "his men." We learned from him that the proprietor of the New York Hotel at Sarzana had notified the Consul of our arrest before our arrival at Spezia and that our position was known on the ship.

Thus our experience as Italian revolutionists ended. Twenty four hours in Italian prisons. Taken from town to town in irons. The examination of the American buttons on our clothes, followed by a significant shaking of heads. The hardship, the physical abuse and our inability to communicate with those outside who might look after our interests, made a profound impression on me. On recalling some incidents I would laugh and the next moment I would be boiling with indignation at the thought of our usage.

November 4
Spezia

Every one of the ship's company is interested in the details of our adventure. Our plight became known on the board yesterday through the Commodore who had been promptly informed by the Consul and it had been the talk of the ship all day. Everyone greets us with a smile or a significant look as we go about the ship today and those more familiar with us joke hard.

November 5
Spezia

Commodore Thatcher received today from the Prefect of Police a letter purporting to give the cause of our arrest. Several grounds are taken, but the principal is that we were without passports. It was stated that if we were abused they had a right to abuse us because we resisted arrest—that we were not abused—that we were so far from our ship that the presumption seemed justifiable that we had deserted and thereof we were arrested. There was no evidence that we were Americans. The American buttons on our clothes were regarded as a deliberate attempt at deception. Finally that our conduct showed us to be revolutionists and rebels to the Italian Government and that we were properly treated as such. There were also other lies which only an Italian official or a Chinaman would think or offering as an excuse for misconduct.

Commodore Thatcher who is very much incensed over our treatment replied to the effect that the communication was a clumsy fabrication of inconsistent lies and was unacceptable as an apology for the mal-treatment of American Naval Officers by the Italian Police or as an explanation of what actually occurred.

All boats are put out to bring provisions aboard from the Store House tomorrow. Our bread and beef and Paymaster's stores will be largely increased.

November 6
Spezia

This is the pleasantest day which we have had for a long time. Stores are coming aboard.

Reports reach us of a desperate battle in Kentucky. Bragg led the Confederates. Buell, McCook and Rosecrans were engaged on our side, also Lytle. Rosecrans did himself honor and won his double stars. McCook was killed and many other officers of distinction. Though not considered as a Federal victory at the time nevertheless the retreat of the Confederates followed.[29]

November 7
Spezia
Another pleasant day. I am receiving stores for my Department. The top-gallant masts are sent down. All the whiskey on the ship is sent ashore to the Store House.

The *Canandagua* is reported at Gibraltar. I presume that she will come here soon. I hear nothing more about the *Colorado* being in European waters.

The Governor and his wife and other ladies were on board in company with the Consul.

November 8
Spezia
Weather is quite cool. Preparing to leave here for winter quarters. Several of the men who have been on shore on duty return intoxicated. Kulver [?-name illegible] a German, was court-martialed and lost two months pay and was sentenced to 30 days solitary confinement and four days a week on bread and water.

November 9
Spezia
Sunday comes again, but I am sick and unable to enjoy the fine air and sunshine. Yesterday I ate some apples and they deranged my stomach. I am on the sick-list again as I was a fortnight ago. I attend muster but have to take to a hammock in the sick-bay.

One can accustom himself to the sick bay of a man-of-war. Here to find some seclusion although all sorts of sounds proceeding from the activity of 300 men reach him. If a man could not accustom himself to adverse conditions in life he would indeed be a miserable creature. The sick-bay of a man-of-war is a place to smother thoughts of a quiet home and tender bedside care bestowed by kind relatives, nor is one likely to find himself in a place where it is harder to dismiss such thoughts, in the turmoil of oaths, disputes, calls for this and that and a regular commotion at meal time.

November 10
Spezia
I am back on duty, but so weak that I can scarcely walk. I have not been so sick for a long time, if ever. I can eat nothing, but drink a little tea. I think I am wrong in attributing my condition to eating apples. I have a cold. I have not been well since the cold, rainy, windy disagreeable autumn weather set in and the immediate cause of my present condition is doubtless the sleeping on a wet mattress. While I was on shore in prison the rain penetrated the hammock nettings and soaked my mattress.

November 11
Spezia
I am still miserable, but on duty. I eat a little food. Newspapers give accounts of the destruction of fifteen American vessels by the Rebel cruiser *Alabama*, commanded by Captain Semmes, formerly of the *Sumter*.[30] The crews are put in irons, kept in the waist of the ship where the water can come on them and otherwise treated with cruelty. Nearly 200 have been put ashore at the Azores after their vessels had been plundered and burned. They are burned at night to attract others to the same fate.

November 12

Spezia

I am still an invalid and at noon had to go to the sick-bay and found a berth on a mattress on the deck. I have symptoms of a violent cold through my system. This is evidently the secret of the whole trouble. I have become very thin. I usually weigh 165 lbs. Without showing any signs of fat, but now I am below 145.

It is bad enough to be sick and confined to proper quarters, but it is perhaps worse to be on the "list" and allowed no rest or quiet because not considered sick enough not to be called from time to time to attend to various duties, but I do not feel disposed to complain in these times when so many of my fellow citizens are suffering on the battle fields and in crowded hospitals from wounds of hard fought battles. It is said that we are waiting for some of the Italian ships to leave Genoa to make place for us to go into winter quarters there.

November 13

It is like a cool November day in New England. I am somewhat better. Mails continue to come, but no letter for me yet. If they are all dead or gone to war I should like to know it, if not, I should like to know why I am discarded.

November 14

I feel much better today. Have an appetite. Will soon be well. The crew are laughing about the First Lieutenant. He let them have their bags today thinking that it was Saturday.

Crowded together on a ship with little to break the monotony of routine; men get tired of each other.

Open quarrels occur now and then among the men and the officers have numerous little difficulties among themselves. On this ship however the Marine Guard is entitled to the prize for squabbling. The Orderly Sergeant has his little clique and the non-commissioned officers who do not enjoy his confidence head another. The Orderly has been "to the mast" and has made so many general charges against his men that he does not obtain much of an audience now. He is in a trap through his own mismanagement and it would be brought out if he caused an investigation.

November 16

Sabbath comes again with its respite from regular duties. The day is fine and the sun warm, although snow is to be seen on the distant mountain tops. One of our anchors is up and we are waiting for a favorable wind to sail.

Several visitors came aboard and the gangway had to be shipped for them. In doing so one of our men fell overboard and the accident so affected one of the ladies that she screamed and fainted.

I find all of my woolen clothes eaten by moths. They are a great nuisance here.

November 17

We are finally off for Genoa.

All hands are exercised at target practice for two hours. 120 rounds of ammunition were used, being the amount allowed for two months for this purpose by the Navy Department. The target practice showed good scores.

November 18
Genoa

We entered the harbor of Genoa this morning and soon after moored inside the mole in the place reserved for us alongside several Italian men-of-war.

The appearance of the city is beautiful. The trees look as green as when we left here in June, and better since the summer dust has been washed off the foliage by the recent rains. Several American merchant ships are here.

It is reported that Mobile has been taken; also that Great Britain and France have recognized the Confederacy.[31] These reports lack confirmation. Such reports begin to circulate on the ship whenever we arrive in a port. There is no mail for me here. Five and a half months have elapsed since I have heard from my home or friends.

November 19
Genoa

Water froze last night and it is like a cold New England November day.

This is a busy day for me. We are dismantling the ship. Chains, anchors, sails, etc., are being sent ashore. Running gear, blocks, etc., are coming down from aloft with a rush and I have to look after the tallying or tagging. The royals and top-gallant yards are down and we will soon look like a ship in "ordinary."

The minstrels whose music we enjoyed so much when we were here before were aboard today. It was good to hear them again. Garibaldi's Hymn, which caused our arrest at Sarzana was the first piece which they played and sung. They are not allowed to play it ashore, but took advantage of our flag and the Italian officers who happened to be aboard seemed to like to hear it as much as we.

November 20
Genoa

A northerly gale and a piercing cold that reminds me of North America. The men are dressed in overcoats with "comforters" around their necks—and still they look cold.

We have visitors, many military and naval officers and cadets.

Top-gallant masts are sent down.

November 22
Genoa

The Marquis of Devonshire and daughter visited the ship. He is a man well advanced in years with grey hair, quite tall and a good specimen of an English gentleman. The Marquise is a true type of an English lady, tall and robust. Both were plainly dressed. The daughter is a really beautiful young woman and was dressed in keeping with her age.

The Marquis has a splendid yacht here with a small steam tender. The former is a ship rigged craft of a beautiful model. The crew are dressed in a blue uniform with red caps. On his yacht the Marquis wears a blue uniform with bright buttons. It is said that he employs a thousand men and has an income of 300,000 pounds a year. Tonight he gives a ball to our Commodore.

November 23
Genoa

This morning commences with a sad and fatal accident which calls to mind the death of poor Dyer on the 30th of June last. As top-gallant masts were being sent up this morning, William W. Clark of Portsmouth, N.H. was instantly killed. The mast-rope parted from an additional pull after the mast had reached its place. The exercise was by signs. No talking was allowed and therefore the words, "stop swaying" could not be passed down by the topmen. The consequence was that the mast-rope being affected by "dry rot," parted, letting the mast with all the rigging attached, down until it was stopped by the main top-sail yard. The rigging crushed poor Clark on the cap where he stood. His skull was fractured and his back, neck, leg and arm broken. The blood came down on the deck like rain. It was some time before his body could be extracted from the position into which it was jammed by the spar and rigging. He was lowered from the top in a cot but no signs of life were discoverable. The mast was left as it fell for the day.

It was fortunate that the topsail was bent. Had it not been the mast would not have stopped at the top-sail yard, but would have come down to the deck, and have killed and injured many in its fall.

Had the men been allowed to speak the accident would doubtless have been averted as the men seemed aware that the mast-rope was parting under the extra and unnecessary strain. It would have held the mast in position without parting. Still there was no reason to expect that the rope would part. It was large enough and was new and looked all right when rove for the purpose.

Clark was an agreeable companion among his shipmates and an active and efficient seaman and was beloved by all. He was twenty one years old.

His shipmates were deeply affected by his death and naturally kept referring to the necessity of keeping silence during such exercises. I hope this may be our last fatal accident.

November 24
Genoa

Preparations are being made to bury the dead. A coffin costs on shore $40. Stock enough to make one costs $15. Therefore one is being made by the Carpenter. Dying is expensive in this city. A subscription is being made by the crew to defray the expenses and as a purse for the family, $150 has been raised.

I sent a letter to my brother Edward, addressing it to Kittery. I also wrote to Mr. John Clark of Portsmouth whom I know and who is the father of the seaman killed yesterday.

The Commodore's servant Jose Fernandes, a native of Madeira is very sick and will probably die within two days. A few days ago he was a robust and apparently healthy man, but today he looks like death. His case is peculiar and is not understood by the surgeons.

November 25
Genoa

This morning the yards were manned and a salute fired in honor of the Italian Prince, a son of Victor Emanuel, who arrived in a large steam frigate. It rained incessantly during his debarkation. Officers in uniform waited in boats around his ship for nearly two hours before the Prince and his Royal companions stepped into the Barge to be rowed ashore. The Barge was a highly decorated affair with a gilded eagle covering the bow. The Italian warships were dressed with flags and salutes were fired from them as well as from a battery on shore.

Just before ten o'clock the Marquis of Devonshire came on board with a portion of his crew to serve as an escort in accompanying the body of young Clark to the services at the church ashore and to the grave. Our Commodore, Commander and master with about thirty of Clark's messmates and others of the crew started with the Marquis for the shore with Clark's body. It rained throughout the services, but the Marquis was well prepared for the weather, being dressed in a rubber suit with cow-hide boots. The Services at the Church were conducted by an old Scotch clergyman and were very impressive.

Clark was buried beside a former shipmate, who as Mate of a Portsmouth ship on which they had sailed together, was killed by one of the crew while we were here last May. These Portsmouth boys lie buried in a beautiful spot shaded by trees in the western part of the City of Genoa.

November 26
Genoa

Jose Fernandes breathed his last this morning. So soon has death come again into our ship. A few weeks ago he was the picture of health. Today he lies beneath the American Jack which covered Clark's body yesterday. Truly life is of uncertain tenure at the best.

November 27
Genoa

This is Thanksgiving in Massachusetts and observed as such by our mess. We had a turkey dinner.

I had five teeth filled by the dentist on board. He is a good mechanic although not well supplied with tools.

November 28
Genoa

A delightful day, calm and balmy. A Swedish steam warship came into port. The American ship *Mary* of Bath, Maine, was towed out and sailed. I came near being killed by the falling of a grating from the spar deck through the hatchways over the Store room. I was standing directly beneath, weighing myself on a "balancer" when the grating came down. It hit me on the muscle of my arm near the shoulder. Had I not instinctively moved as I felt it approaching it would have struck me on the head. It was fortunate that it did not break my arm. One is constantly exposed to accidents on a busy crowded ship.

December 3
Genoa

The men who have been going in liberty and coming back in good condition. Some are going every day.

Our minstrels are coming aboard at meal times. We all enjoy them. I made a contract with Sebastian White for caulking the ship, on behalf of the Carpenter. I am acting as attorney for the ship.

The wages of the contractor, who is a ship surveyor, are 13 francs; of a first class workman 6½ francs; of a second class workman 3¼ francs. Oakum is 32 francs and pitch 20 francs per 110 lbs.

A mail came today, but there is no letter for me.

December 5
Genoa

The men who are going on liberty are behaving very well. Thus far there has been no trouble. Yesterday one man, Riley, who had just returned from liberty and appeared at muster went off immediately afterward with the liberty party unnoticed. His absence was however subsequently discovered and when he returned today he was put in the brig.

The caulkers are making their confounded clatter all over the decks and the smell of hot pitch makes its way into every part of the ship.

December 7
Genoa

At eleven o'clock I visited the *Sylphide*, the yacht of the Marquis of Devonshire, in company with Hunter, our Acting Boatswain and a friend of his. We met the Captain and the Steward who invited us to dine with them Tuesday. From there we spent about two hours walking through the Eastern part of the city. We saw scores of women washing at the public fountains, places formed by stones laid in cement thus making numerous separate compartments. The buildings in this part of the city look ancient and, for the most part, are seven stories high. A building is occupied by many families, usually of moderate means and some apparently poor and destitute. Evidence of vice is conspicuous everywhere.

After dining we visited the more pretentious part of the city. We then hired a carriage and drove through the city to the West. Seeing the American flag at the gaff of a ship we stopped and went aboard. It was the *Eliza Schofield* of Brunswick, Maine. We had a pleasant interview with the Captain who had his wife and two children with him.

From there we drove to "Smith's Hotel" where we met some Englishmen and spent several hours with them, we all taking supper together, and at eight o'clock we went to the opera which lasted until eleven o'clock. The opera was good, but I must confess that I am not educated up to an appreciation of some of the exhibitions of vocal or musical skill. I am inclined to prefer music of a steadier sort.

At seven bells we were back on the ship and soon swinging in our hammocks.

December 8
Genoa

This morning rewards were offered for several men who were not on board when their liberty was up. Five were brought off by the Police, for which escort they had to pay $10 apiece, it being deducted from their pay. Some eluded the Police and came off to the ship "in their own boat." On the whole I think that the crew have conducted themselves remarkably well. There have been no quarrels and a comparatively few cases of drunkenness—such common occurrences among men-of-war's crews.

December 9
Genoa

Paint yards today. News comes of the promotion of Lieutenant R. R. Wallace to be Lieut. Commander. Now we have two Lieut. Commanders on the ship. Presumably one of them will soon be sent elsewhere.

In the evening Hunter and I went on the yacht of the Marquis of Devonshire to dinner. Besides us the Captain of the yacht, the mate and the Steward were at the table. After dinner we were shown over the yacht by Mr. Leonard, the Steward. In the cabins, saloons and drawing rooms are to be found everything conducive to comfort which a wealthy man would provide for himself in a cottage ashore.

The pleasantest feature of our visit was to observe the respect and esteem with which the

Marquis and his family were regarded by everybody on the yacht. Everyone to whom we spoke had some word of praise for them. "Lady" Alice is adored by the crew, her mother is a mother to them all and the young Lords are "most agreeable companions."

The Marquis is without a doubt one of the finest men to be found. He is charitable, sociable and possesses a large share of <u>common sense</u>.

December 10
Genoa

Liberty has now been extended to all the men and their conduct does them much credit.

This evening I received a letter from home. No letter ever came to me with a more hearty welcome. Eight months has elapsed since I had received any note or tidings from my kindred or friend in the wide world. The letter is from a woman whose family I know well. It is kindly and cheerful and refers to my brothers and relatives so that I feel that they must be well, but gives me no information about them. Presumably she thinks that I have been hearing from them.

December 14
Genoa

Hunter and I again visited the city. We had our photographs taken. We met several men from Maine who are here in ships. It is pleasant to run across persons from my own State among the vast throng who fill the streets of this city and speak a tongue which I cannot understand.

December 15
Genoa

We hear that General Fremont is in command of the Federal Army. This shows a vacillating policy in the conduct of our affairs not at all indicative of strength or confidence on our part. The control of affairs seems to be in the hands of politicians entirely. It is enough to make one sick.[32]

December 16
Genoa

The papers state that the *San Jacinto* chased the Confederate cruiser *Alabama* into Fort de France, Martinique, but that the *Alabama* eluded her pursuer, as always.

Everything is moving quietly on the ship now. There are few occasions for punishments and the men appear quite contented.

For several weeks I have been occupying my leisure in reading Macauley's *History of England*. It possesses all the attractions of a romance. It deals with the most stirring of human events and whether we read it for historical instruction or to be entertained it never fails to hold one's attention and interest.

I have decided to learn Italian and have engaged a highly recommended "maestro" to come aboard twice a week and give me instruction. Between lessons I will study and utilize my opportunities to practice here on the ship and ashore.

The Commodore received today instructions from the Navy department to clear the ship of all spirituous liquor. Under the order which abolished the spirit ration no officer is permitted to keep liquor except the Surgeon, but I presume that the Department thought the officers might expect a special invitation to discontinue the use of a private stock. So they did. Every officer who chose has had on hand as much liquor since the order went into effect September 1, as before. The officers have really been violating Navy regulations as much as the sailor who steals on board with a bottle, gets caught and is sentenced by a Court martial to loss of two month's pay and extra police duty. I spent the evening on the English yacht *Sylphide*. By special invitation I accompanied several of our officers. The spar deck was covered and decorated by flags so as to provide a spacious and attractive saloon in which a long table was set. Here our party dined with the Marquis of Devonshire at the head of the table. We had a regular English dinner, plum-pudding and all, and an abundance of good wine.

After dinner some of the crew dressed in favorite costumes danced and sung. No one appeared to enjoy the evening more than the Marquis. He seemed to delight in making others happy. I came back on board of our ship at eight bells.

December 21
Genoa
Sabbath comes again. I went ashore and took a long walk through the Northern gate and along outside of the wall. The day was delightful. The streets were thronged with people of every class. In almost every public square were acrobats who took up collections from the spectators after giving their exhibitions. The wall and other defenses for the rear of the city are really extensive and well worth seeing. They recalled the days when Genoa and Venice held the mastery of the seas.

December 23
Genoa
News reached us today of the capture of Fredericksburg by the Federal forces.[33]

It is also reported that the Confederacy has proposed to suspend hostilities and to come again into the Union under the old Constitution. They propose to pay their share of the expense of the war, unite with our armies, go into Mexico, drive out the French, make Mexico a State of the Union in which slavery shall exist and go on to the same old tune as of yore. This news seems rather too much of a pill to swallow.

December 25
Genoa
Christmas comes as a most delightful day. The sky is cloudless and the landscape ends in a clearly defined horizon. The weather recently has been clear and beautiful and the sun warm, to me an agreeable surprise as it was cold and rainy when we arrived and I supposed such weather was the regular winter climate. Our mess was provided with a good turkey and all the accessories for a real Christmas dinner, after enjoying which I went ashore.

In company with my fellow townsmen, Mr. Philbrick, the Carpenter of our ship, and a Mr. Nevins of Philadelphia, I visited the public grounds, or "Agua Sola" and various beautiful churches. At one there was a representation, "the birth of Christ." The shepherds and their flocks and the other animals were shown as most lifelike figures on the plains of Judea. The church was also elaborately decorated with flowers.

In another church there was the most exquisite decorative iron grill work that I ever saw. Here too were most magnificent marble columns about the rotunda and chapels. Some of these columns were inlaid, others were screw shaped. The paintings on the ceiling were superb and covered every part not gilded.

There was less evidence of public festivity than I expected to see, but most places of business were closed and on the whole the day seemed to be more appropriately observed than the Sabbath.

Yesterday as two cavalry officers were exercising on the public parade ground their horses took fright and ran off an abutment and fell onto a street forty feet below. Both horses and one officer were killed and horribly mutilated. One of the officers was caught in the branches of a tree and escaped with a few scratches.

December 26
Genoa
The rigging is being tarred down and the ratlines squared. To one unaccustomed to a ship at such times everything would seem to be in confusion. One of the men has been fighting this morning with a petty officer. The man was put in the brig and will be court-martialed. Another man was confined and put in double irons last night for a similar offense. These were among several men who have been intoxicated on the ship the past few days. Where the liquor has come from is a great mystery. The ingenuity which sailors will sometimes display in obtaining liquor is beyond belief.

December 29
Genoa
The ship *Portsmouth* of Portsmouth, N.H. came in port last night and I went aboard today to get the news. I learned with regret of the death from fever of Manning P. Waldron[34] who was in the 27th Maine regiment. He was one of my pupils and an able young man. He is but one of the many young men who have gone from Kittery and never will return. Dr. Mark F. Wentworth,[35] Lieut-Colonel of the same regiment has lost his eldest daughter who has died at home while he has been at the front. Mr. Langdon, our former Boatswain who left the ship in August is reported at home unemployed.

No definite news of my brothers, except that both are thought to be at sea and Edward somewhere with the Navy.

It is reported today that General Burnside has been driven back across the Rappahannock with heavy losses on both sides; also that general McClellan is again called to the command.[36]

December 31
Genoa
Today closes the year. It has been a sad and eventful one for our country and has brought hardship and sorrow to our people. Few if any of those I know are as happy as they were a year ago. May this cruel war soon cease its destruction of our national prosperity and domestic tranquility.

During the past year I have seen many new and interesting places and things and have learned much about the world and about men, but I have had much to oppress and discourage me. In other times and under other conditions how much more I would have enjoyed these new experiences which were pleasant.

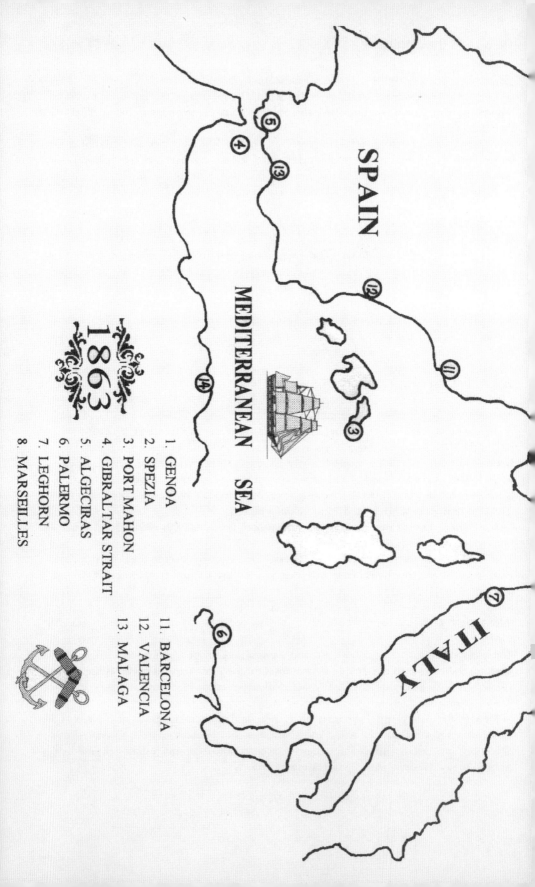

Chapter Three
January 1863 to June 1863

January 1, 1863
Genoa

At home "I wish you a happy New Year" used to be a common salutation when friends met. Today one naturally thinks first of the state of our country. I certainly wish that this may be a happier year for it than the last. Here on the ship I hear the wish, as a personal salutation, expressed on by a few of my most intimate acquaintances. Among the crew this New Year salutation is seldom heard and when so the recipient of the good wish and the giver look at each other as though they felt that their present condition boded anything but happiness for the future.

Today is the day for new resolutions regarding one's conduct in life. If any one on the ship is making such resolutions today he is keeping the matter to himself, so far as I have heard. Yet today it would seem that such resolutions might appropriately be made, notwithstanding our tendency in spite of ourselves to fall back in old ways and old habits and succumb again to our special temptations. Twelve years ago today I resolved to lead a life untarnished by the customary sinfulness of men, but I have fallen so far short of my ideals that sometimes I am doubtful whether I have been any better than the vast majority of men in fulfilling my obligations and my duties to God and man. I come to realize more and more as time goes on of the little inherent goodness in the hearts of mankind.

January 2
Genoa

The ship is in great confusion. Everything is removed from the gun deck which is being painted. All hands will have to crowd into the berth deck to sleep tonight for the paint to dry.[1]

Painting is also going on elsewhere about the ship. It is amusing to see how it is being done. Sailors who know as much about painting as about milking a cow are running about with pots and brushes from the Store Room to the spar deck.

The official report from General Burnside which we did get today gives our killed and wounded as 2,200 and the Confederates 1,800. Our defeat is evidently a great disaster.[2] I spent the evening very agreeably on board the yacht of the Marquis of Devonshire.

January 4
Genoa

I went on shore at noon and spent most of the afternoon with the German Consul. He is a man of intelligence and well acquainted in the United States. I met him quite accidentally. Some conversation followed his request of me in English for a light for his cigar. It related to the operation of some dredges which we were watching. They belonged to a German Company in which it appeared that he was financially interested. He discovered that I knew something about dredging machinery and then that I was a lawyer, that I had procured two patents for clients and that I had done some local work at home for New York attorneys for a Swedish patentee in connection with an infringement suit. The consequence was that we spent part of the afternoon together and I accepted an invitation to dine with him at five o'clock, the weather being unpleasant and unfit for me to carry out my other plans for the evening.

My new friend's name is Wilhelm H. Leupold. He lives at bachelor quarters with a considerable number of other men of various nationalities. Including guests about thirty of us sat down to dinner together. They were talking in Italian, German, Dutch, French, Spanish and English, all at the same time, and everybody except me seemed to understand what everybody else was saying. My host admitted that he understood seven languages. It was a company of fine appearing intelligent men.

I liked the way dinner was served. Wine, of which we had two kinds, was the only drink during the dinner and it was removed with the dessert. Then came coffee and cigars, only. We arose from the table at seven o'clock.

Mr. Leupold told me that he expected me to avail myself of his quarters and accept his hospitality during my stay here.

January 7
Genoa

A strong southeast gale made it advisable to send down our top-gallant masts. The harbor is exposed to wind from this direction and the gale today and the heavy sea which drove into the harbor put shipping in jeopardy. The rain makes the ship very damp and dirty between decks.

It is now reported that Burnsides lost 8,000 men at Fredericksburg.

Glenn has been sick and off duty almost ever since our experience at Sarzana. He had a bowel trouble somewhat like mine but does not recover. G. P. Vamisk who has been acting Master-at-Arms has not returned from recent liberty—and in my opinion will not.[3] I think that he had previously made arrangements to leave the country. He is a very peculiar person in some respects. I can imagine no reason for his desertion, save that he did not wish to do duty as Ship's Corporal or as Master-at-Arms. Should justice ever overtake him in spite of his aliases, he would, according to his own admissions fare badly. It is sad that one born of a respectable family of means and possessing talent, a splendid physique and an attractive personality should thus disguise himself and his origin. Many such cases are to be found in the Service.

January 11
Genoa

In the afternoon I visited the city alone and spent some time with the German Consul, Mr. Leupold, after which we walked around the "Aqua Sola." I then met my friends from the English yacht. We were together about two hours and I then returned to the ship. Hunter who went ashore before I did failed to keep his appointment with me and stayed ashore all night. From his appearance when he returned I think that he showed some sense in not returning. I wish that he could be more discreet. He now has the chance of his life. He is doing well as Acting Boatswain. I have been helping him and I will soon have him so that he will be able to pass any educational tests and work out any practical problems that will ever be given him to qualify for a warrant as a regular Boatswain in the Navy, and if he once gets his appointment and warrant as a Boatswain his weaknesses are not so much worse than those of some other Boatswains and so highly thought of by his superior officers in other respects.

Two other men have not returned from liberty and evidently have deserted. One of them, Gilchrist, is our mess cook.

January 13
Genoa

Last night an unfortunate affair occurred among the men ashore. Charles Moore, Gunner's Mate, cut Sullivan, a marine, with a knife and also injured him by beating him. The cut, at first reported to be fatal, did not prove to be dangerous. Intoxication, as usual, was the cause of this trouble.

I am sorry to see that this vice is confined mostly to the American and English sailors. I seldom see a native of this country intoxicated. Moore who is charged with this offense, is, when sober a very agreeable companion, but, as with many, spirits make a fiend of him. This is the second injury of a serious character which has been inflicted on men of this ship by their shipmates while intoxicated.

January 14
Genoa

Moore who committed the assault on Sullivan has been apprehended and is now in the brig in irons. The affair has been made the subject of proceedings by the civil authorities ashore. Mr. Kenion, the proprietor of the Queens Arms Hotel where the assault occurred has been adjudged by the court to "be the keeper of a disorderly house" and fined 200 francs.

January 16
Genoa

A stormy rainy dreary day, but I was cheered by a letter from my brother Edward, mailed at New York. He has received none of my letters. It is strange.

January 18
Genoa

I went on shore alone and later met Hunter by appointment at my favorite up-town cafe where we had luncheon, after which we walked out to see the newly erected statue of Christopher Columbus. It is the first work of the sort in a public square, the construction of which has been recently undertaken. The Railway Station which forms one side of the square is the best looking modern building in the city and architecturally is far better than any other in the vicinity. The statue is a real work of art and does justice to the memory of the illustrious navigator. It is of marble, resting on a marble pedestal. On the sides are represented various scenes in the career of Columbus. He is shown laying his plans before the Spanish court, holding a scroll in his left hand and the index finger of his left resting on a globe. We see him landing in the West Indies. His reception by the Spanish court on his return is pictured with the natives whom he has brought back with him. He is also shown being brought back in irons from a later voyage. On the corners of the monument are life-like figures representing the arts and sciences especially called into use by the discoverer of the new world. On the top stands Columbus, his arm resting on an anchor and holding a scroll in the hand, while his right hand is extended in an attitude of protection over an Indian woman who sits at his feet.

The whole is a fitting tribute of respect to the memory of one whose achievements entitle him to the place which he holds in the hearts, not only of his countrymen, but of the people of the new world.

January 20
Genoa

Recent private advices would indicate that our losses at Fredericksburg were no less than 30,000.

Several letters have been received from Kittery by the crew. All my friends there are apparently well.

Received a cask of olive oil for lamps on the ship. Sperm oil is not used here for lights.

Little is being done these days except to improve the appearance of the ship. It is surprising to see how busy three hundred men can be kept looking after a ship. No snow is seen in Genoa except on the mountain tops in the distance, but within the past week an unusual amount has fallen in this part of Europe. Railroad communication is interrupted and the Marquis of Devonshire who started for France yesterday had to return. Several disastrous avalanches have occurred in Switzerland. In one instance a church was destroyed and about forty persons killed.

It is reported that the ironclad war steamer *Monitor* has been lost off Hatteras with all on board. If true it is a sad disaster for our Navy.[4]

January 22
Genoa

The papers say that the proclamation of President Lincoln in respect to freeing the slaves in Rebel states does not suit all the people in the border states. Some from these states who hold high military positions have tendered their resignations. [5]

The papers also say that great complaint is being made because some of our soldiers have received no pay for six months.

January 25
Genoa

I went ashore at noon and found my friend Mr. Leupold, the German Consul at my favorite cafe. After a pleasant walk I accepted his invitation to dine with him at his quarters. Mr. Cox, my messmate was to meet Mr. Leupold at 7 o'clock. He had promised to help Cox pick out a costume for the Carnival tonight. Cox failed to keep his appointment and Leupold was noticeably provoked. He said that it was the second time within a few weeks that Americans whom he had kindly offered to help at personal inconvenience to himself had failed to keep their appointments with him. I felt sorry for I had introduced Cox to him.

Carnival is now being celebrated here and masquerade balls are among its features. I wanted to see one of these affairs and without telling any of my shipmates I hunted up a costumer and paid him ten francs to rig me out for the ball tonight. My dress consisted of a frock and pants, one half of the latter being white and the other red. Around the bottom of the pants, which were loose, Turkish style, was deep white lace. My blouse also had a lace collar. A sash and a pointed hat completed my disguise.

At eleven o'clock I entered the spacious hall over the opera room, where an opera was being conducted. The entire building was thrown open to the masqueraders when the opera finished at twelve.

The first person whom I saw when I entered the ballroom was our Carpenter, my fellow townsman, Mr. Philbrick. I addressed him in Italian, but with no attempt to disguise my voice. He was unable to recognize me until I told him who I was, nor did anybody else recognize me during the evening although I saw several whom I knew. The place was brilliantly illuminated. The floor of the dancing hall was mosaic. At the sides were numerous ante-rooms. Two bands gave us splendid music. There was plenty of good natured fun but no roughness or vulgarity or unseemly familiarity; nor did anybody show any signs of intoxication or of jealousy or rivalry, yet all classes of people were represented at the ball. Courtesy and civility prevailed and no disposition was to be observed to take advantage of his or her disguise in any improper way. I certainly admire the success of the Genoese in managing an affair of this sort without a single objectionable or disagreeable incident.

Our officers were there and for all that they or I know they may have danced with our sailors disguised in feminine attire. Several whom I recognized talked with me, but none recognized me. There were many laughable incidents which I will always remember.

It was half past five in the morning when the dancing ceased and as I had to go to the hotel and change my costume before returning on board it was an all night affair for me, but I have a pleasant memory of an Italian masquerade ball.

January 27
Genoa
Nemo an English ship broker and our Philadelphia friend Nevins, both of whom have shown us around Genoa have left here very unceremoniously. It has been learned that they have sailed from Havre for New York. Both were in financial difficulties. The former left his wife behind him as well as his creditors. He maintained a rather pretentious establishment and had a very pleasant wife with whom he seemed to be happy.

It is said that he left to avoid chapter-parties in which he had involved himself by hiring two ships which showed him a disastrous loss.

A report is received of our occupation of Galveston Texas. It is said that one of our war ships, the *Harriet Lane* grounded and was captured by the Confederates by boarding. Subsequently Admiral Harwood who was on the vessel lost his life when she was blown up. Reports would indicate that considering the number of ships which we had available for this undertaking it was a blundering sort of an affair.

It does seem that our acts in the prosecution of both naval and military operations are often very stupid. I read that Jeff Davis has recently made a speech in which he says that the North is not capable of governing itself; that the population of the North is composed of Dutchmen and bog-trotting Irishmen and that their lack of capacity for self government is the cause of the Rebellion. He would be glad to live under the old Constitution were it not for these facts.

I am inclined to believe that we are now less capable of self government than we were some years ago, but it is another case of the pot calling the kettle black for the South has been the worse source of elements which are opposed to good government.

January 29
Genoa

It is reported that Vicksburg has been taken after five days of hard fighting. Our loss in killed and wounded is reported at 10,000.[6]

Another battle has been reported at Murfreesboro, Tennessee, where General Rosecrans completely routed the Confederates after severe fighting, the Federal forces being 45,000 and the Confederate 60,000.[7]

There are such inconsistencies in the reports as they reach us that I doubt if a decisive victory has been gained, as claimed. Our fights seem to result in great slaughter without definite results.

The ironclad *Monitor* which was lost off Hatteras sprang a leak. Four officers and twelve men were lost in a boat belonging to the *Rhode Island* in attempting to rescue some members of the *Monitor*'s crew who were on the turret.

January 30
Genoa

Conti, the painter of Naples arrived today with portraits for officers of the ship, including mine.

Mr. Philbrick, the Carpenter received a letter from home stating that Ed. Dixon had been promoted from a Captain to Lieut. Colonel of the 27th Maine Regiment. Lieut. Colonel Wentworth has also been promoted.

The letter also mentions a singular coincidence. The same day that Wm. W. Clark, the seaman was killed on our ship his father received severe injuries in a fall at the Navy Yard at Kittery.

2,000 men are now employed on the yard.

January 31
Genoa

Last night an order was given prohibiting the further issuance of raw pork to the messes. As a result the whole amount of pork put in the "harness cask"[8] yesterday to be served out to the messes, about 150 lbs, was thrown overboard by members of the crew last night. Thereupon the Executive Officer gave notice that all "scouse kettles" would be destroyed at sunset tonight if the names of the men who threw the pork overboard were not disclosed by that time. Meanwhile the marine on duty near the "harness cask" has been put in the brig in double irons for failure to prevent the men from taking the pork.

The men have got in the habit of retaining a portion of their fat pork uncooked to eat with their bread and this practice has resulted in a smaller accumulation of "slush" in the Cook's coppers. The entire amount of slush accumulated during the cruise which was sold a few days ago was only four barrels. This means a small sum for the "slush fund,"[9] which is devoted to the benefit of the ship's crew in such ways as the Executive officer may deem best. Our Executive officer is believed by the men to be disappointed at the proceeds of the sale of "slush" as being insufficient to carry out his plans for expenditures for the crew and therefore wants to stop the practice of eating pork raw in order to get a larger "slush fund."

A bad situation has therefore developed which probably could have been avoided if the Executive officer had made his plans known to the crew and given them an opportunity to present any grievances on their part to himself or to the Captain, as they really had reason to expect. The unwarrantable acts which have been committed do not however have the approval or sympathy of the majority of the crew.

At six o'clock tonight all cooks were mustered with the "scouse kettles" and marched to the head where the kettles were broken up and dropped into the harbor.[10]

I hear from some of our officers that we are to leave here for Port Mahon the last of February. If so our winter here will be shorter than expected. I confess that we have been here long enough for me to welcome a change.

I have a severe cold, the first this winter.

February 1
Genoa

During the night some person or persons cut six gun breechings, removed and threw away ten bolts belonging to the guns and cut the fore-top-gallant mast rope in two places—in one it was completely severed, in the other the cut was slight. The breechings are rendered useless.[11]

These acts are base, villainous and in the highest degree aggravating and malicious. I deprecate such traitorous proceedings and hope that the offenders will be brought to punishment.

At general muster this morning Commodore Thatcher gave the ship's company a very cool and sensible talk regarding the affair of last night. He expressed his regret that he should have to be the instrument for inflicting punishment on members of his crew, whether by depravation of liberty, or of monthly money, or in any other way, but that the Navy Department and the whole country hold him responsible for finding a way to stop such depredations as had been occurring on his ship in time of war.

In the afternoon I went ashore, and as it was raining I spent most of the time at my favorite cafe, the Basseria. After dining here I went to Smith's Hotel where I met other friends including Captain Tarlton of the ship *Portsmouth*, who is a high class gentleman in every way. Among others whom I know on his ship are Card, the mate and Cate the Carpenter, who are both from Kittery. Most of my friends left me to attend the Masquerade ball at the Carlo Felice. I did not feel inclined to go and instead went to see some of my friends in the bachelor quarters where the German Consul lives and returned on board at nine thirty.

Boy Saunders is in the brig in irons as the result of making some remark indicating that he knew who were concerned in malicious acts committed last night.

February 2
Genoa

This morning we were surprised by evidence of the commission of more malicious acts. The panel work inside the bulwarks was cut all along from the gang-way to the fore chains.

The topsail sheets were also cut.

Samuel Tibbets is confined, accused of the former act and James W. Judge is in the brig accused of the latter. The evidence against them is circumstantial and not very strong, but more may come out.

This matter calls for summary measures and I hope convincing proof of the guilty persons may be quickly found.

Kenney, the marine who was on guard near the harness cask is being tried by court-martial.

February 4
Genoa

This morning I was sent for as a witness in the "pork case." But one question was asked me. It led me to infer that some testimony had been elicited indicating that the pork had been thrown overboard in a bag. One of the jacket bags is missing.

In the afternoon I went ashore with Hunter and in the evening visited my friends on the ship *Portsmouth*.

February 5
Genoa

The Italian papers state that an armistice for five years is being considered by the North and the South. The French papers which have the same report declare this to be equivalent to a permanent separation.

A diver in a diving suit has been down along side the ship hunting for the pork which was thrown overboard. It was not found. A few breech pins, a marlin spike and a scraper were brought up.

February 6
Genoa

The crew are being exercised with the sails and then the decks holy-stoned.

Hunter has received a regular appointment as Acting Boatswain from the Navy department. He at once took possession of the Boatswain's room on the ship and asked me to come ashore with him and assist him in procuring his uniform. We returned at sunset.

Business in Genoa is said to be very bad at present, but one would not think so from the crowds and activity in the streets.

February 8
Genoa

In the afternoon I went ashore with Hunter. After spending some time with him and Smith, the Doctor's Steward, at the Cafe Basseria. We all go to the Brignole Palace.

This is a substantial building on the principal street of the city and contains, in the upper story, the largest collection of paintings in any private building in Genoa. Two Brignoles, father and son, were famous Doges of Genoa.

On entering an attendant presents the visitor a card, describing in Italian and in French the subject of every picture in the collection. The rooms are square, very high and the ceilings frescoed. The floors are of marble, of different colors, so arranged as to present artistic designs. In the first room are portraits of the two Brignoles who were Doges.

I cannot now enumerate the pictures which I saw, but I recall the following which impressed me especially. The carrying-off of the Sabine women by the Romans, the division of the flocks and herds of Abraham and Lot, a portrait of William, Prince of Orange. Among other masters whose works are to be seen here are Reubens and Van Dyke.

On leaving the palace we went to Smith's Hotel where I met Captain Swanton and Captain Tarlton and others of my friends, most of whom were to attend the Masquerade Ball. I dined with Hunter, then went with him to see him dressed for the Ball and returned to Smith's Hotel and left there at eleven o'clock with Smith, the Doctor's Steward, and came off to the ship. The streets were filled with people in masquerade costumes.

February 9
Genoa

News comes of success of the efforts of Admiral Porter and his gunboat fleet in opening up the Mississippi River.[12]

No bum-boats are allowed to come to the ship now, and the men are unable to make purchases to supplement the regular ration which is not exactly a luxurious fare.

February 11
Genoa

The Court-Martial sentenced Kenney, the marine on duty near the "harness cask" when the pork was thrown away, to forfeit three months pay, to have two hours extra police duty in twenty four for three months and thirty days solitary confinement on bread and water part of each week. This seems rather tough, but I do not know what sort of a case was made out against him.

February 12
Genoa

When on shore last evening with Hunter I met a Mr. Davenport and a Captain Johnson, the latter being a "Secesh" who lately left New Orleans. He has run the blockade several times and seen action in the rebel Cause. He deemed it better for him to leave and avoid plans for his future which Ben Butler had made because of Johnson's alleged burning of a ship. We went to the Cafe Basseria as usual.

February 13
Genoa

George H. Smith and Munroe Nelson have been placed in the brig in double irons. They are suspected of being the men who committed the depredations on the battery and the mast-rope. It is not generally known what is the basis of their arrest, but from what I have learned I believe proof of their guilt will be forthcoming. Two men, Brown and Jay who, I suspect, are implicated in the affair went ashore this afternoon.

February 14
Genoa

It is reported that boatswain's mate Brown who went ashore last night has deserted. I doubt if he has really deserted. He owes money to everybody on the ship from whom he has been able to borrow, including myself.

February 16
Genoa

A reward has been offered for boatswain's mate Brown. S. Tibbetts is in irons.

The Court-Martial is still in session and many witnesses among the crew are being examined. The principal one to have been Joseph Ridgley. I hear that strong evidence against the accused is being brought out.

I received a letter from my brother Edward.

This evening Nolan, the painter, who is with me in the Store Room picked up a piece of paper. On it was written a note presumably by one of the men in the brig and intended for Joseph James asking James to accuse Joseph Ridgley of being one of the guilty parties. I reported the finding to Mr. Low and delivered the note to him. James was immediately placed in irons.

February 19
Genoa

Reports reach us of the sinking of the *Hatteras* off Charleston by a Rebel boat and the burning of several other U.S. ships.

I finished a letter to Kate B———.[13] It is quite long and, I think, dry, and probably there are some mistakes in spelling or English in it. But I will send it since it has taken so much time for me to write it. She is as particular about such matters as my mother was. Probably that is why my mother said that Kate would make a good wife for me.

An American ship hailing from Richmond, Me. Came in today. Maine is well represented by its ships here.

I went ashore in the evening for a walk and met Mr. Davenport. I returned on board with Messrs. Philbrick and Ryder.

February 22
Genoa

Washington's Birthday. —Flags are hoisted at the fore, main and mizzen, but no guns are fired.

The Commodore's Secretary read Washington's "farewell address" on the gun deck.

George H. Smith, Munroe Nelson and Samuel Tibbetts were found guilty of disabling the battery and sentenced to the brig for thirty days, loss of three months pay and extra police duty. While in the brig they are to have a full ration one day a week, the others on bread and water.

While leaving the harbor the Italian steam sloop-of-war, *San Giovanni* ran afoul of the ship *Holly Head* of Bath, Me. Both ships were damaged somewhat. The *San Giovanni* returned. She was bound for the United States via England.

The latest reports indicate that a conscription law is likely to pass Congress as our forces will be reduced by 500,000 men this spring because of the expiration of enlistments for two years and nine months. Such a law will of course be unpopular and trouble will arise in connection with its enforcement.

February 25
Genoa

Joseph Ridgley, the chief witness against the men recently convicted of crippling the Battery has been missing for two days. I think he has left the ship after the manner of Brown.

It is reported that General B.F. Butler has been appointed as Secretary of War. I did not suppose that he would be considered a proper man for such an important position.

Was ashore in the evening with Smith, Cox, Grainger and Ryder, the last three we found at a new place to me, "The Twelve Apostles."

February 26
Genoa

Went ashore in the evening for a walk and met Messrs. Johnson, of the ship *Carioca*, Coleman of the *Lallah Rock*, Davenport of the *Holly Head* and Boatswain Hunter. Davenport goes to sea tomorrow. We go around the city and have a fine time. It was twelve o'clock when I returned on board. The others spent the night ashore. It was a beautiful night, the last which I will spend with some of them here, or perhaps anywhere, so changing are the conditions of a seafaring life. We make friends in a place and in a short time they are gone, perhaps forever, the others who succeed them we lose in the same way.

One year ago today I first came on this ship to live when she went into commission. I well remember the cold inhospitable decks covered with ice and frost, on which the three hundred men of different natures and nations then first assembled to form for a period of three years a family of no ordinary magnitude.

How different they look upon each other today. How much better they understand each other now.

Some have left us in effort to find a place more congenial to their tastes. Some have been sent home because of physical infirmities. Some we have lost through death and at first have felt inclined to look on as intruders, the strangers who have come to take their places.

Ours is a singular family. There are those among us with whom one never feels acquainted and would hardly be missed were they to desert. There are those whom we feel to be of our family and whom we would greatly miss even though we might not speak to them for the entire cruise.

The officers too belong to this family, and we come to learn their weaknesses as well as those of anybody else. We come to look upon their exhibitions of petulance or arrogance as when such traits manifest themselves in members of a family. The crew of a ship learns to appraise an officer very closely to his true value. So do they also their shipmates who nurture the opinion that those in command are constantly plotting their discomfiture. When not so employed such men will be regretting acts in their past lives, deploring the causes which brought them on the ship and wishing that they were somewhere else. A man-of-war is certainly a great place to study human character in all its forms.

February 28
Genoa

With this day ends winter. It has been the mildest winter that I ever knew and soon now we will be off for our summer cruise and new scenes. It has been a pleasant winter and the months have flown rapidly by, nevertheless if we winter in this sea again I hope that it will be in some other place as I am satisfied with my sojourn in Genoa.

It is said that some of the men who have deserted the ship since we came here are in Marseilles. I doubt if any effort will be made to arrest them.

It is reported also that Lieut. Commander Low is to be relieved by some other officer who is to come from the United States.

One never knows where such stories come from or how to treat them.

March 1, 1863
Genoa
A springlike day.

In the afternoon I went ashore with Cox and Smith. They went to ride. I preferred to walk around alone and went to the Aqua Sola where I listened to the band and watched the gaudy equipages in which the fashionables like to display themselves.

March 3
Genoa
All the standing rigging is being overhauled and the berth deck is being caulked. With the clatter of two dozen caulking mallets over my head and several persons asking me at the same time for various articles for fitting stays my Store Room seems like a very busy place.

It is reported that the USS *Brooklyn* has been destroyed by the Confederates. I do not credit it.[14]

March 4
Genoa
Busy getting the ship ready to leave.

I did not mention that on the 1st inst. A "Secesh," known as Judge Brice, formerly of New Orleans, who came here with his family this winter appeared in a Confederate uniform at Smith's Hotel. It is said that he holds, or held, a Colonel's commission in the Confederate Army and was obliged to leave for New Orleans under the regime of General Butler, who said that Brice deserved hanging.

On the occasion of his appearance in his uniform, Brice was with Ex-Consul Paterson and Johnson my "Secesh" friend of the ship *Carioca*. The uniform looked as if it were made of blankets thrown away by some Union troopers at New Orleans.

The *Alabama* has escaped from Jamaica and destroyed two more merchant vessels. It is strange that with all our Navy we cannot rid the sea of this piratical craft.

Secretary Seward's reply to the French Minister with reference to the offer of foreign mediation has been received in France with considerable dissatisfaction, but I think that they will be content with venting their spleen on the wind, and on paper.

March 7
Genoa
The Conscription Bill has passed the Senate. According to the French and Italian papers a rupture of the Western States which has been threatening will be hastened by the enactment of this law.

It seems that the reports of trouble with France are not wholly without foundation. The French papers speak of issuing letters-of-marque, but this may be premature.

March 8
Genoa
At two p.m. I went ashore with Smith. We spent a couple of hours at the "Concordia" reading the papers and then I went to the American Consul's to make arrangements for procuring a bill of exchange on London. I am sending home 1,000 francs. Exchange is quoted $1.76 today.

After dining we went to the Pagnini Theater and saw the play *Jiudetta*, or *Judith*. The prima donna, Ristoriu, is probably the first actress in Europe today. Luigi Rezzana took the principal male part. It is a tragedy.

The theater is a substantial building. The interior is highly decorated—too much so, but there are many good paintings illustrative of music and the other arts. The ventilation was very defective and the air became so bad that I was obliged to go outside for a while to recover from vertigo. After the theater I met Paymaster Pangborn with whom I returned to the ship after refreshments at the Concordia.

March 10
Genoa

The event of the day is the marriage of the Prince of Wales to the Princess of Denmark.

Among other vessels which came into the harbor before the easterly gale was an American ship.

I am interested in reading the *Last Days of Pompeii* by Lord Bulwar-Litton.

March 11
Genoa

Gold is quoted @ 1.72. English exchange @ 1.88.

I went on shore in the evening with Hunter and "Secesh" Johnson. After playing billiards until eleven o'clock I returned to the ship with Lieut. Miller.[15] One year ago today I sailed from my old home in the United States. Just before the lines were cast off at the Navy Yard some of my friends, companions of my youth who chanced to be near clasped my hand and bade me good-bye. It was a sad moment, leaving old associations, those with the living and the dead; and my homestead even though robbed of former attractions by the loss of my father and mother. I did not even know where I was going, the ship was sailing under sealed orders, but I knew that scenes and experience were ahead that were going to be hard to endure. Worst of all, the future looked dark and precarious because I had given up my profession in which I was getting a good start, entrusted my property and affairs to the custody of others, and cast my fortune with a national government whose prospects of enduring did not, and do not seem very encouraging.

A year has passed on a man-of-war—a little world afloat with its hum and bustle of three hundred men. It is much larger, very different and more interesting than the other, diminutive floating worlds in which I have previously lived. Its manners and customs as well as its purposes differ from those of a merchant ship. I have known on merchant ships men who in a contest of rough, profane or vulgar language could doubtless hold their own with any man on this ship, but being surrounded here by mere seafaring men one hears more of such language. I have become more accustomed to such profanity and harsh or vulgar epithets, but I am sure that they have not become any less repugnant to me. Nor have I become so habituated to the rough and arbitrary usages as to exhibit them in my manner off the ship. I am sure that this is true, although I am aware that in my dealings with the crew I speak to them often in a manner uncustomary on shore. It becomes very necessary for me to do so in the position which I occupy on the ship in order to be understood and prevent being imposed upon. To talk easy with sailors here would be equivalent to a license to them to question whether one is in concert and means what he says.

March 13
Genoa

The American Minister at Turin and the Consul at Genoa, Mr. Wheeler visited the ship and were received with the customary salute.[16]

A British ship belonging to Georgetown, P.E.I. arrived today with the loss of the fore and main top-gallant masts and with the main-mast sprung. She looks as though she had had a tough time.

I am still reading the *Last Days of Pompeii* which is very interesting. One learns from it Egyptian as well as Greek and Roman customs and history.

I received a letter from my old shipmate on the brig *Cochico*, Richard Graham. He is on the U.S. Sloop *Portsmouth* in the Mississippi near New Orleans.

March 18
Genoa

It is reported that the Southern Confederacy has been recognized by France, but I think that this will not be done for some time yet, if at all.

"Secesh" Johnson visited the ship and I went on shore with him and Hunter for a short while.

I am still working hard on my Italian under the instruction of my "maestro" and am making fair progress.

While on shore with Smith in the evening Mr. Pangborn, the Paymaster invited us to come with him to the circus at the Andrea Doria theater where he had a box engaged. We spent the entire evening there, returning on board at eleven thirty.

It is reported that the English are building twenty vessels of war for the Confederates, two of which are to be ready in ten days.[17] They are being built under the pretext that they are for the Chinese Emperor.

March 21
Genoa

A tooth has been troubling me for several days. Our marine barber and dentist, Edsall, extracted it. He did the job well, if I can judge. It was a wisdom tooth.

Went ashore and met Mr. Leupold, the German Consul who has just returned from Germany and spent the afternoon with him going over papers which he brought back with him, relating to the affairs of his company in the United States. Took dinner with him, after which I went to Smith's Hotel.

March 22
Genoa

At one o'clock I went ashore to have a walk. I was not feeling well and had a headache. I went alone to the Aqua Sola and had spent a couple of hours there listening to the music when I met Messrs Bowles and Ross, of New York ships and went with them to the Basseria. They left me to go to the circus and I made my way to Smith's Hotel where I met "Secesh" Johnson and some of my shipmates. Returned to the ship at seven bells.

March 23
Genoa

The American papers which reach us state that the new British built Confederate ironclads are first to be employed in destroying the Federal warships in the Mediterranean.

In the evening I went on shore with Hunter and Johnson, who had been visiting the ship. I purchased a lot of lace and collars as presents for my friends at home. Although I am a poor judge in such matters I think that I purchased my articles quite cheap. I also bought some more views of Genoa and the vicinity to complete my collection.

March 24
Genoa

At two p.m. we dropped down the harbor and anchored outside the inner mole, ready for sea.

The Commodore is entertaining a party from shore at dinner.

"Secesh" Johnson sailed today. The *Carioca* is bound for New Orleans. I sent a letter by him for Kate B——.

March 25
Genoa

Sailing—At an early hour this morning all hands were called to unmoor ship. The anchor was soon up and we were drifting out of the harbor. It is almost calm, but a light air tells us that we may expect a fair wind. The day is delightful, the first which has really given us promise of returning spring. Soon a light breeze from off the land springs up and we sail along the high and rugged coast whose mountain tops are white with snow, enjoying the beauties of both sea and land. It seems quite novel to be again at sea after a confinement of four months among the shipping of Genoa.

Our Commodore seems to be uneasy. Contrary to his custom he is remaining on deck and is scanning the horizon with his glasses as though to discover if the ironclads reported to be out to capture us are in the offing awaiting our approach. These reports have persisted and the officers say that the Commodore has serious apprehension of an encounter.[18]

All hands are exercised at general quarters, guns are shotted, as is customary when going to sea and everything is put in readiness for spending the night at sea as the wind has died out.

The evening is most delightful, there is scarcely a ripple on the sea and how brightly the stars shine out of the azure sky.

March 26
Spezia

A beautiful day with light winds and calms. We are near the coast and the mountains covered with snow make pretty pictures in contrast with the mild spring-like atmosphere below.

At ten p.m. we come at anchor in the bay at Spezia, after using the boats to tow us in.

March 29
Spezia

This morning the proclamation of President Lincoln for the emancipation of the Negroes in the disloyal States and Counties was read together with some orders relating to the interests of seamen.

Mr. Low on being asked refused me permission to go ashore on account of my not reporting the Store Room closed, as heretofore. A misapprehension on my part, or an implied assent on his to dispense with such reporting was the reason, rather than disobedience, neglect or thoughtlessness. I am sure that hereafter no occasion for such a reproof will be found against me. I will use the "squeeze mark."

A fine day all right on board, but quiet. I feel a little blue, but that will be of benefit.

March 30
Spezia

The hold and store rooms of the ship are being cleared for restowing, while provisions and stores are coming on board rapidly. A large amount of cordage is being received in my Store room, mostly manila for braces, etc. I am completely filled up. Enough provisions and stores have been taken aboard for six months.

March 31
Spezia

This morning the men have the privilege of washing their blankets on the decks after they have been covered with all sorts of dirt from receiving stores. Humanity as well as decency would seem to dictate that a time be chosen for scrubbing blankets when the deck is free from dirt, as it usually is, but it seems to happen that the worst time is likely to be chosen for anything intended to promote the comfort or health of the men.

April 1
Spezia

This morning numerous men have come to me on all sorts of fool's errands, and have gone from me to the officers of the deck. Some have gone from one officer to another with a piece of paper endorsed "pass him along." Among so many men the practice of "April fooling" can be carried on successfully for quite a while.

April 2
Spezia

A boat drill. All boats are armed and manned and their crews land on the opposite side of the bay.

Stores are still coming aboard.

The papers contain accounts of an old coal barge fitted up with boards and pork barrels for smoke stacks to imitate an ironclad which was set adrift in the fleet at Vicksburg. It is said that the *Queen of the West* ran away from it and that the *Indianola* was abandoned and blown up by her crew when they saw the supposed ironclad coming in their direction.[19]

April 4
Spezia

A letter from home from I.D. Phillips Esq. Tells of the death of Robert P. Mitchell and of the illness of Captain Wm. L. Tobey, who is not expected to recover. Mitchell was drowned while sailing from Gloucester in a fishing vessel. Mr. Tobey was my first Lieutenant in the military company, an able man and a valuable seaman. Major R.F. Goodwin, landlord of the City Hotel in Portsmouth, died March 7. Every mail brings news of the death of some friend or acquaintance.

In the last State elections New York showed a Democratic gain of 100,000 and New Hampshire, of 2,000. Serious disturbances are expected in connection with the enforcement of the conscription law in Pennsylvania and some other States. I hope that the prospect of trouble will not give rise to any weakness in enforcing it.

April 5
Spezia

A fine Sabbath day. Some of the officers go on shore. I do not ask as I was refused a week ago and I do not wish to give Mr. Low the satisfaction of refusing me again today. Regardless of the matter of justification, one might suppose that an Executive would realize that his reproof had served the practical purpose of preventing a repetition of my failure to preface a request to go ashore with the statement that the Store Room was closed, but our Executive is not built on that plan. In accordance with his habit he has probably made a memorandum on his cuff of the incident.

April 6
At sea

We got under way last night at twelve o'clock and now we are some distance from land running before a light breeze in a summer sea—even though it is April.

We suppose that we are bound for Port Mahon, but apparently nobody knows yet where we are going except the Commodore. Our present course, SW by W ½ W is consistent with that destination—also with several others.

April 7
At sea

Light winds and little progress. During the forenoon we had target practice. The shooting was very good. The first shots tore all the cloth from the target. Some of the shells burst too soon—as soon as they leave the gun. This must be owing to some miscalculation or deliberate intention to render the shells ineffective on the part of those who filled them. Such occurrences have been frequent since the war commenced.[20]

Whenever the smoke of a steam vessel is seen it is watched closely to discover if it be one of the Confederate ironclads supposed to be after us. Some excitement was caused when a steam ship, hull down, was observed to change her course and come in our direction. She soon, however, turned and steered away. Our crew do not take our supposed danger seriously. I think that they would welcome a fight in which we stood any chance of winning.

April 8
At sea

When I came on deck this morning we were under a heavy press of canvas. The royals were furled. The wind was ahead and we were smashing into a heavy head sea which had made up very rapidly. A large part of the ship's company felt seasick. I did also. A deranged stomach was probably the cause. Poor Cox, my messmate, was again, as usual, on his "beam ends." I have not been troubled with this disagreeable affection since I have been on this ship.

April 10
At sea

A rough head sea continues and we are making slow progress. I am not well. I feel stupid and dull. I take some medicine, but it does no good. I do not like to patronize the Dispensary. One is usually better off without than with their drugs.

At "quarters" all bags were searched to find a pair of pants which were stolen from a boy who drew them yesterday. The pants were found, but not in the possession of the thief.

Thieves are seldom caught on a man-of-war. They manage to avoid being found with "stolen goods in their possession."

General Quarters at night—and a grand stampede.

April 11
At sea

We have a fine breeze, but cannot head within two points of our course. Our bottom must be very foul. When we first came out we would have made ten knots with this breeze. Now we are making only seven.

I feel better than I did yesterday, but am still very dull and sluggish.

At noon we were 80 miles from Port Mahon which is evidently our destination.

At sunset we took in top-gallant sails and single reefed the topsails, so as to check progress.

General Quarters again tonight.

April 12 & 13

All sail set, with a good breeze. Inspection and the usual routine of the Sabbath, including Divine service, etc. Soon after dinner the wind hauls to the Northwest. It is showery. Large schools of porpoises are playing around the ship. A small island is made on the weather bow, presumably one of the Balearic group.

At sunset we come within twelve miles of Minorca, but too late to enter the harbor, if that be possible at any time with the wind blowing out. They claim that it is not.

We keep off until daylight when we stand in and signal for a pilot. We fired a gun for a pilot during the night but none came off, the reason presumably being that he could not bring the ship in until the wind changed.

No pilot appearing we stand off shore. Light sails are furled, the courses hauled up, the ship layed to with the main top-sail aback and all Divisions are exercised at target practice, which does not cease until seven bells in the afternoon.

The practice was praised by everybody who watched it. Many old timers said that it was the best which they ever witnessed. Every target put out was quickly shot away after being thoroughly perforated. Bottles suspended from the fore top-mast studding-sail boom were rapidly smashed. Michael O'Rourke was the "best shot." He broke four bottles with five shots. The men all fired six rounds apiece.

After target practice we ran in near shore and then stood off and hove to for the night.

The shore is rocky and looks like the Spanish coast, and one also sees here on the promontories the little stone watch towers to prevent smuggling. The grass seen growing among the rocks looks different from the Italian grass. It looks more like the American.

April 14
Port Mahon

This morning the wind came fair and we entered the harbor and anchored at the quarantine ground.

On both sides of the harbor are ruins of ancient fortifications. The Government appears to be repairing those defenses which were laid low by Lord Nelson. Low stone buildings, barracks for soldiers, are to be seen behind the fallen masonry.

The land looks stony and barren near the town. The buildings to be seen from the ship are white and neat in appearance. There are however so many old stone walls and low stone buildings to be seen as to remind one of Pompeii.

On two islands in the harbor are hospital buildings.

April 15
Port Mahon

Still in quarantine. All communication with the shore has been via the island provided for smoking diseased people, etc. The quarantine officials will not even receive a written communication from the Commodore except with tongs. We are treated as though we were purveyors of the worst conceivable contagion. All provisions come from the little island at prices not favorable to modest purses. Enough fresh beef for one dinner for our mess cost us $5.00. There is evidently some inducement to keep us in quarantine.

The town opposite to where we are lying is called Georgetown. It is noted for its asses. From the ship it looks like a deserted fortress.

Since my earliest recollection I have heard of the lazy propensity of Mahon soldiers, but until today I never saw a concrete example of it. I saw several rowing a boat. They cared nothing for the progress which they were making, but dipped their oars lightly in the water to avoid the exertion which might result from dipping deeper.

The English papers of the 11th contain accounts of the burning of the USS *Mississippi* by our people after she ran aground in the river.[21] The attempt of our fleet to pass Fort Hudson was not successful.

A riot took place recently in New York and Negro dock laborers were driven off the docks.

New Jersey has enacted a law making it punishable by imprisonment for a Negro coming into the State to remain more than ten hours.

A steam vessel fitting out in England has been detained by the Government on evidence that she was intended for the Confederates.

The rebels have been making gains in Kentucky.[22]

I can see no advantage which has been gained by the Federals since the winter began. American affairs look as bad as ever. The prospect of war with England adds to the gloom which veils the future.

April 17
Mahon

This morning we left Quarantine and sailed up to the town, saluting the Spanish flag on the way. The passage is quite narrow and a sailing vessel needs a fair wind to come up. The town is built on a high bank on the left hand side of the harbor, many of the buildings being flush with the sides of the escarpment. We moored at the Navy Yard where we are to remove stores from the ship and clean the hold.

A Spanish frigate is here, but the Navy Yard appears more like a church yard than a Navy Yard. There is no activity here. There are a few low stone buildings, one of which we will use as a depository for our stores. A small steamer is on the railway and an American built ship, now a Spanish Naval store ship, is here. The Yard is surrounded by a high stone wall with towers or guard houses at frequent intervals extending beyond the line of the wall and commanding the approach to it. The water is deep enough for the largest ship to lie alongside the quay.

We formerly had a Naval Depot at Port Mahon, but moved to Spezia on account of serious trouble between the local population and the American officers. One Master in our Navy was killed here.

April 18
Mahon

We commenced to put stores ashore this morning. The weather is pleasant and the sun warm, but it is damp with very heavy dews at night.

Scores of women, old and young, come aboard the ship at meal time. The young ones are, I presume of the class which has given Mahon its chief reputation. Georgetown is famous for its asses and Mahon for its prostitutes.

Every mess has its regular collection of women at meal times who come to get what they can to eat. The decks are thronged with them and nearly every one has a little child with her to feed.

This place depended greatly on the patronage of American Naval ships when the Store House was here. They tell me today that the jealousy of the French Consul was the real cause of the trouble and the removal of the Store House to Spezia. Now few American ships come here.

Many of the inhabitants speak English and are well acquainted with the officers of our Service. One old woman who came aboard today was a servant in Lord Nelson's employ. She is still active and joked with some of our sailors whom she knew.

If one may believe the stories told some of our best American families have relatives in the Port Mahon population and it is asserted that the population would soon have become quite American had not our Naval Depot been changed.

April 19
Mahon

The anniversary of the battle of Lexington, but the gods have been unfavorable to me today. I have had my two upper front incisor teeth broken off and the sleeve of my coat torn as the result of a jackass ride to Georgetown. The careless beast fell while going on a downgrade and tumbled me over his head. My poor unfortunate teeth had to contend with an adamant roadway and yielded, but they put up a good defense for they were strong sound teeth. I chanced to be near the residence of an old patron of our ship and he took me in and cleaned my face with water. It was quite bloody.

This ride was taken against my desire to please my friends Hunter and Cox, and like that taken from Spezia to Sarzana for the pleasure of two messmates also resulted disastrously. In both instances I had a strong and unaccountable aversion to starting on the excursion. In the future, under similar feelings I will not yield to the claims of my companions and see if the following of my own inclinations will lead me to part with my teeth, but they were the price which I paid for a half an hour's ride on one ass.

On inspecting the town today with Cox we found the streets and houses very clean and quiet. Everything suggests the health and comfort of the people. The buildings are lower than in Italy but are better ventilated and seem healthier.

We met Hunter in company with a Mr. Jones at a hotel kept by a former shipmate of Hunter's.

One of the first things which we did after leaving the hotel was to inspect closely one of the numerous windmills. They are usually made of stone, are round and about forty-five feet high. At the top is a wooden turret through which runs a heavy axle to which the arms holding the sails are attached. The turret is made to revolve by a purchase so as to trim the sails to the wind. The power obtained from the sails spread on the arms radiating from the axle is very great by reason of the leverage exerted by the long arms, and in an ordinary breeze the axle turns quite rapidly.

We climbed to the top of one of the hills and found the solitary keeper sitting in his narrow attic and regulating his machine as the wind required. To the sails are attached various clewlines and brails to enable the keeper to reduce the sail area. At three thirty we attended vespers at the church which, it is said, contains the largest organ in the world.[23] It surpasses any that I ever listened to. Its tones are magnificent. Its range is very great. Upon it can be imitated the booming of cannon, the ringing of bells, the singing of birds, etc. I hope to hear its entire repertoire before I leave here.

From the Church we walked through the city and took the asses for the short ride of which enough has been said and enough will be felt to make me remember it to the end of my life.

After the ride I dined at the hotel with my friends and soon after went to my room for the night.

About 30,000 of Minorca's population of —— live in Mahon. The products of the Island, I judge, are not more than sufficient for home consumption. About 5,000 soldiers are stationed here. I met several men who have been in the United States Service. They all think very highly of Americans and regret that they do not come here as formerly. Mount Diablo, about twenty miles in the interior, is a popular resort.

April 20
Mahon
I came aboard with Mr. Hunter at two bells this morning. All of my friends expressed sincere sympathy at my misfortune. I must confess that I felt rather blue, but at the time of the accident I felt the sense of misfortune the most. I am quite reconciled today and feel that it is not good to lament too long such an affair.

All of the stores have been taken out and nothing now remains in the hold except the ballast and the tanks. They are now working on the latter, most of which will have to come out. The Commodore has promised the crew liberty when the hold is cleaned out and restored.

I am reading Tom Paine's *Age of Reason* for the first time. He was a bold writer, but my opinion of him and his arguments must be withheld until I have finished the book.

April 24
Mahon
We have had some very handsome bouquets of fragrant flowers presented to our mess by the little boys who have been coming at meal time for bread. At sunset I took a walk about the Navy Yard. Grass grows everywhere and the buildings are nearly empty. There is a railway where small ships are hauled out and repaired. How unlike the Navy Yards of our country at this time; but it would be far happier for all if no occasion existed to disturb the blossoming of flowers in our Navy Yards this spring.

April 25
Mahon
From the English papers arriving here it would appear that the war forces are inactive at present. The Confederates are represented as being in a destitute and almost starving condition, but are making no overtures for peace.

One year and two months ago today I came on this ship with the rest of the ship's company. Nearly half the time to be devoted to the cruise is probably past. A year ago I was in Cadiz. How soon the year has passed.

During the last year I have seen many places under different governments, where in many respects habits and customs vary, but how similar is man in every condition in life with respect to his wants and fears! Some elements of his nature ever stand prominent and what we learn of man in a limited circle of observation, if carefully studied, will be true, in a great degree, of all.

The English papers report that opposition to the arrest of deserters is encountered in Ohio, Illinois and Indiana and Federal forces have been required to suppress disturbances. The sale of firearms has been prohibited by the local authorities in these States and the Federal forces are confiscating them.

We are evidently called on to contend with a serious situation in our own part of the country and perhaps may be facing developments more difficult to contend with than any which have thus far manifested themselves.

April 26
Mahon

The quiet, rest giving Sabbath comes with springtime loveliness. Everything in Nature is superbly delightful—and how quiet! On the berth deck at every mess there is a bouquet of flowers which the patron of the mess has brought from shore. It looks quite gay.

In the afternoon I went ashore alone and to the Hotel. I found after talking with "Frank," the proprietor that I have met him before, in the United States. I then took an omnibus for Georgetown in which were some soldiers and with them an officer who invited me to go to the barracks. I accepted the invitation and found them spacious and well ventilated, but not so comfortable in many respects as our soldiers' barracks at home. The blankets are of very coarse material. The muskets are clumsy and not so well finished as ours. The uniforms of the soldiers are blue and of very good material.

I called on Señor Rafael as I had promised to do. He is the man who took me to his house at the time of my accident and I greatly appreciate the kindness of himself and his family.

From his long intercourse with Americans in years past the old gentleman is able to speak English well. The Señora does not remember English so well. He showed me his gardens and fruit trees and entertained me an hour in his house. His niece, a young woman whose husband is in New York, made me a beautiful bouquet to take back to the ship. I came back at sunset, visited the public square, listened to the band, saw the fashionables of Mahon promenade and returned to the ship at dark.

No donkey ride for me today. My shipmates whom I saw all invited me to join them in a ride, but I am resolved to ride no more donkeys in Mahon except in case of necessity. Cox was thrown from his beast some ten feet and cut his hand and bruised his knee, but was not so unfortunate as I. Mr. Hunter's animal fell many times, but did the rider no serious injury.

Various kinds of fancy work, representing flowers and other objects and usually enclosed in glass cases are made here with a high degree of skill which sometimes seems to surpass Nature. How durable they are I do not know. I suspect that the cement used may yield in our climate although durable here.

April 27
Mahon

Last night Frederick Raynes, a native of Oahu in the Pacific Ocean died after being but a month in the sick bay.

The poor fellow never recovered from the effects of a cold which he contracted when he first came on board the ship and which finally developed into consumption. Thus the poor Kanaka, away from his native isle, pined and died in a climate unsuitable to his constitution.

I am informed that a brother of his died in the Chelsea Hospital just before we left home. Kanakas are short lived in our climate. Raynes was a very industrious and peaceable fellow, never in trouble, always willing and ready to obey any command. He remained on duty longer than was advisable, but who would not avoid the sick bay as long as possible. With its crowding and bad air it is a place only fit to die in. This makes the fifth man that we have lost since we left home.

All provisions and stores are back on board and tomorrow the men will have liberty. One watch will go at a time.

Just before sunset all hands were called to bury the dead. The coffin covered with the American flag was placed in a boat and taken to the burying place on Hospital Island. Our Commodore and the American Consul accompanied the three boats detailed for the service. Very little feeling is produced among the men of the ship by a natural death like this one.

April 28
Mahon

This morning the entire port watch went on liberty, being the largest number of men away from the ship at one time since we left home. The absence of 150 men changes the character of the ship. Quiet prevails and she seems more like a merchant ship than a man-of-war. One can move around without coming in contact with somebody else. It has been a pleasant day for liberty and I hope that the men will enjoy it.

Two hours after he left the ship one Negro, Amos, was brought alongside in a state of unconsciousness from the effects of liquor, probably drugged.

In the afternoon the ship left the Yard and moored in the stream.

Joseph Cresus who lives here and who served as a seaman in the Frigate *Constitution* some years ago and was stricken with blindness has been given a donation of $150 by our ship's company. He is a native of this place and he has some old shipmates among our men.

His blindness is ascribed to sleeping on deck in the moonlight. His eyes are very much distorted, one is completely shut. Otherwise he is in good physical condition. He speaks English well although long out of the Service.

I learn that the American Consul here[24] has advices from the United States that war with England is imminent, but I see nothing in English papers to justify such a conclusion.

April 29
Mahon

The port watch remains on shore while the starboard watch is busy oiling ship outside and tarring down the rigging.

This afternoon the American Consul, accompanied by a few of his friends came on board and was married in the Commodore's cabin in the presence of the officers of the ship. The Commodore's Secretary performed the ceremony. The affair was brief and very unostentatious. After it was over some of the officers accompanied the Consul's party ashore.

At half past twelve at night three marines who had stolen a boat from a Spanish steamer to come off to our ship upset their boat while attempting to come aboard and caused considerable excitement for a few minutes. We had to lower a boat to rescue them and one of them came very near drowning.

April 30
Mahon

This morning the men who have been on liberty began to return. Most of them are clean and sober, but there are some exceptions and those are enough to disgust anybody.

Mahoney, ship's corporal, and two others are confined in jail ashore for some breach of the peace. The worst feature is to see among the drunken ones the young "Boys" of the ship who must have ruin before them if they begin thus early. The associations of a man-of-war tend to be corrupting. It is a poor place to trust the young without guardianship.

May 1
Mahon

The New Englanders are "Maying" today—may they have a happy time. A year ago I was in Gibraltar harbor—the day as fine as this.

The Spanish papers say that we have been repulsed at Charleston; that the USS *Vanderbilt* has captured the *Alabama* and the *Wachusett*, the *Florida*. If these two alleged captures be true they will be worth more than all the victories which I have heard of during the past winter.[25]

May 2
Mahon

The men are now coming aboard in much disorder—some late and many with bruised faces. Seamen Hyde and Thompson are confined in prison ashore for a breach of the peace.

The donkeys have had a hard time. During liberty sailors on donkeys could be seen everywhere. Their performances furnish entertainment to delighted crowds of natives. Today the berth deck on the port side is covered with men asleep sobering off. Some of them are lying up against each other like hogs. What ideas of having a good time some sailors have!

May 3
Mahon

At muster about forty bruised faces could be counted as the men passed around the capstan.[26] Many feel blue on more than one account—money lost or squandered, digestion deranged, head confused and premonitions of other disorders.

Last evening the United States Consul was advised that the British Government had instructed Lord Lyons, their minister at Washington, to demand the unconditional surrender of the steamer *Peterhof*, lately captured by a Federal Cruiser, and in case of refusal to demand his passport. If this be true it would seem that if a war be desired by our government a sufficient pretext is available.[27]

The Spanish officials refuse to surrender Hyde and Thompson, the two seamen arrested while on liberty and they are to be discharged from the ship. It is unreasonable to detain these men for such a trivial offense. Hyde was not at fault at all, but was trying to prevent

Thompson from assaulting a policeman. Assault and battery should not be an excuse for keeping them and it would not be in other times, but the United States does not command her former respect in Europe these days. How are the mighty fallen!

May 4
Leaving Mahon

We dropped down the harbor this morning and anchored at Quarantine. Why we did not put to sea I do not know. The Mahon parasites follow us down for their "loaves and fishes." They will miss the ship when we are gone.

A collection amounting to $150, was made up for Hyde to pay for counsel for him and to aid in his support while he is in prison. Twice that amount could have been raised for him just as readily.

Thompson is a British subject and, I hear, asks no favor from our government. No doubt he is much at fault, but according to our men, Hyde tried to prevent Thompson from doing any harm to the police officer who attempted to arrest him. Hyde assisted in taking Thompson to prison and when there was himself held.

May 5

This morning the ship's company sent Hyde a lot of books to read while awaiting the slow process of Spanish justice. Hyde is a noble hearted seaman, a true American and is in every way deserving of the sympathy of his fellow countrymen. I most sincerely regret to see him left behind.

The morning is occupied in supplying the messes with provisions and luxuries for an extended cruise. As I am caterer for ours some domestic responsibility devolves upon me. I have bought two vases of "shell flowers" which cost me $7. They may be a poor investment, but they are the only curiosity of any value which I have purchased thus far.

About six bells the pilot came on board and we were soon passing out of the harbor with a fair wind. Mr. Robinson, the US Consul, accompanied us outside the harbor.

May 6
At sea

Morning found us still within sight of the island of Minorca. General Quarters last night. At the roll of the drum out of their hammocks come the watch below; then begins the general scramble for the spar deck and the hammock nettings with the hammocks. Men returning below after stowing their hammocks crowd in the hatchways with men still coming up with their hammocks and with marines with their muskets striving to make their way to the spar deck. If in this hatchway jam a man does not have his hands trod on or his head bruised by a musket butt he may consider himself lucky. The tumult which 300 men aroused suddenly from their sleep will make in getting to their stations in the dark can hardly be imagined—it has to be experienced.

The afternoon is a perfect calm. For miles around the sea looks like liquid glass. The sun shines hot. The horizon looks smoky as in the topics.

In the twilight some of the Negroes dance in the starboard gangway for the entertainment of everybody. This is the first time the ship's company, officers and men, have interested themselves for so long in anything since the cruise began. Something extraordinary must be about to happen. It has been rumored that we are homeward bound, but I do not feel so sure that we are not going to have a hurricane within two days.

May 7
At sea

A fair wind, a smooth sea and a pleasant sail. We lost sight of the Island of Majorca at noon.

I am reminded of the inconsistency of orders which one receives. After being reprimanded because of following the practice sanctioned by our Executive of arranging to have the Store room opened by one of my men in case of need in my absence or by myself after the regular hours and being specifically instructed not to open it outside of prescribed hours, except by his express orders, I am now instructed by our Executive, Mr. Low that the Store Room is opened whenever necessary for the benefit of the ship. The new instructions have been issued because Mr. Philbrick, the Carpenter, after sending a man to me for an article went to Mr. Low and complained of the delay and trouble occasioned by my not being willing to open the Store room without orders from the Executive. I suppose these new instructions will have to be followed until some caprice leads our Executive to say that he never issued them.

Well, we are off again for some other port. The dull town of Mahon with its white-washed buildings, its rough streets and its serenading jack-asses will no longer offend our senses. Goodbye to its brawling women, its lazy soldiers and its brazen harlots. It will be a long time before some of our men cease to regret our sojourn at Mahon. I suppose no worse place could be found in which to let men loose to try to find diversion, from a sailor's monotonous duties.

May 8
At sea

A good breeze in the morning, but dying out in the afternoon. At night we are about fifteen miles from Cape Gata and about two hundred from the Rock. At eight bells John T. Nichols, a Negro, formerly Ward room cook, died. He had been on the "list" for more than a month. His disease was an affection of the liver which produced dropsy. An examination of the body was made. The liver had reached an enormous size and other organs showed a complication of diseases. I witnessed the autopsy.

Nichols was a very quiet man, of a rather melancholy mind. From time to time he came to me for advice when acting as waiter in the Ward room, saying that he could not succeed in avoiding the cruel censure and punishment which were often meted out to him. This was more common before "tricing up" was abolished.

We expressed much anxiety about his wife and child whose pictures he received in answer to a letter which I wrote for him. He showed their pictures to me. He used to tell me that he lay awake nights trying to think how he might act or what he might do to avoid the punishments inflicted upon him and others and so hard for him to bear because there was something wrong with his heart. A few days ago he sent some money to me for safekeeping. I have turned it over to the Paymaster.

Well, the poor fellow has passed through and beyond his troubles and no one sheds a tear of grief at his departure. His companions in the sick bay are rather glad of the room which his absence makes—cold hearted strangers in the most trying hour of life.

May 9
At sea

This morning after quarters all hands were called to bury the dead. After the usual reading of the service the body was slid from the lee gangway into the sea there to remain, while his shipmates whom he has left behind resumed their duties about the ship to await their turn with careless indifference.

We have had light variable winds all day and have made little progress. No land is in sight.

May 10
At sea

Off Cape Gata with light head winds. We have been in company with numerous ships and brigs for several days and out sail all that we meet, but we make only six knots when we should make eight if our bottom was not foul.

Everyone is anxious to hear from the United States. It is quite evident that our present purpose is to get outside the Strait, to avoid being trapped in the Mediterranean by the British ships if Great Britain declares war on us.

Mr. Philbrick, the Carpenter, is put below and suspended from duty. I do not learn the reason.

May 12
At sea

This has been a slow tedious passage and has made us envy the steam vessels which have been passing us. It has made me very discontented with my present lazy irresponsible life on this ship, but doubtless if I were frying in the West Indies or on the blockade looking at sand dunes I would wish that I were back drifting in the Mediterranean.

Just before sunset the haze, which has hidden the land all day, lifted and gave us a full view of the Rock, the Strait and of the coast both on the Spanish and African side.

May 13
Gibraltar Strait

It was calm all night. This morning a good breeze sprang up, but directly ahead. The tide also sat strongly against us and we have been beating against wind and tide all day. At one time we were in close to Couta on the African side. We have been in company with several other ships likewise trying to make headway through the Strait. They say that ships have been known to be held here for several weeks by head winds. In the afternoon however the wind favored us and we weathered the point of the Rock and came into the Bay and anchored of Algeciras at 5 p.m.

The U.S. Navy Store Ship is here. The USS *Tuscarora* has been to Philadelphia and has returned to Madeira, from which place she is daily expected here. Captain Pickering late of the USS *Kearsarge* has resigned his commission in the Federal Service, and I am informed that he is now employed in the Confederate Service.[28]

The Consul informs us that Vicksburg and Port Hudson have been taken and the Mississippi is now free for our gunboats.[29]

The questions raised by our seizure of the steamer *Peterhof* have all been amicably settled and there is no longer any apprehension of war with Great Britain on that account.

As this war scare is past we will doubtless start back immediately for the genial clime of Italy, probably touching first at Palermo.

May 16
Algeciras

We are still awaiting a favorable wind to sail. Some of the officers visited the Rock and returned in a jovial condition. American officers are not exempt to the weaknesses of the enlisted men.

George H. Smith who was found guilty of disabling the battery at Genoa was sent on shore. He received his money and his discharge from the Navy for making infamous proposals to the boy Coleman of this ship. Whether the accusation be true or not I cannot tell. He was not tried by Court Martial and was therefore not regularly found guilty. Whatever may be said of our crew the dominant American sentiment on an American ship makes short shrift of a man who betrays any unnatural proclivities and his stay on an American man-of-war is brief. It is generally believed that Coleman's charge was untrue and malicious. Coleman's testimony had helped to convict Smith of cutting the gun breechings and the boy was afraid of Smith and disliked him on that account. The officers also disliked Smith and wanted to get rid of him and welcomed Coleman's charge as a pretext to do so. Smith himself will be more comfortable off the ship, even though it may be unjust to discharge a man with this stigma against him without an opportunity to answer the accusation. However he has no good reason to complain of his treatment as a punishment for disabling the ship's battery, an offense of which he was regularly proven guilty. If he had received justice he should have been hung. He doubtless would have received a long term in prison, had it not been desired to avoid directing the attention of the Navy Department to the responsibility of our Executive for precipitating the mutiny.

A man named Andrew Turpay ran away from the ship's boat at Gibraltar while on duty. He had due him $160. He must have had some very urgent reason for deserting.

May 17
At sea

Last night after the men had retired, all hands were called to "unmoor ship." The remainder of the night was spent in getting anchors "set." The wind was so light that the ship nearly drifted ashore on the Rock of Gibraltar.

It was, "all hands out boats." Then came boat towing maneuvers to keep the ship from striking the shore. They would have been unsuccessful had not a favorable wind sprung up and taken us clear.

Amid the confusion there were some complications of an unusual character. Two officers were sent below because they were too much intoxicated to perform duties assigned to them. Disputes among other officers nearly led to blows. At seven o'clock this morning, however, the ship was sailing along quietly about fifteen miles from the Rock as though nothing had happened.[30]

There was no muster or inspection during the day, and for the first time the men had the privilege of reposing on the port side of the berth deck during their watch below in consideration of their loss of sleep last night.

May 18
At sea

We have been going at the rate of ten knots with a fair wind all day. Nothing could add to the pleasure of such a sail on such a day and in such a sea except the fact that one's ship was homeward bound.

I have been feeling rather blue lately, without apparent cause unless it be a physical one. Today's sail makes me feel better.

May 19
At sea
The wind is stronger than yesterday. The ship is making from eleven to twelve knots. It is a glorious breeze—how she flies along, making the water foam for many yards around her bow. During the last twenty four hours we have sailed 260 miles. On the berth deck there is a general scraping and the deck looks like the floor of a plaster mill. Every part of the ship is covered with white-wash dust. It is a regular work shop for the cooks and the "black-listers."[31]

May 21
At sea
A good breeze—royals not set—but a head wind.

The Divisions are being drilled with single-sticks and muskets on deck while below white-washing is the order of the day.

When not employed in dull routine of this sort occupation is found for the 300 men in keeping themselves clean and the ship in order. Their chief diversion would appear to a superficial observer to be to find fault with the way things are done, to growl about the injustice of the government in starving them or giving them poor "grub," to discuss various regulations or practices which have been in effect or in vogue in the Navy since it has existed, to describe the shortcomings of the port which the ship has last left and to extoll the attractions of that to which the ship is bound.

Intimacy of contact in our little floating world brings to our ears discussions which would not reach them in ordinary life ashore and focuses our attention on men whom we would not be likely to know ashore except through the police news column of the newspapers. After all, the ship's company of a man-of-war is a sort of cross-section of the male population of an ordinary good sized town. As in such a town we have the good, bad and indifferent. Like such a town we have our fugitives from justice, outcasts from home, the vicious and depraved. They are reinforced by those who are ever finding grievances in conditions for which they themselves are directly responsible, —all eager to listen to the political demagogue on shore or the "sea lawyer" on a ship. It is these elements which fill the columns of the newspapers as I find that they are filling the pages of my diary They must not be allowed to dominate either afloat or ashore. We may differ in our opinions regarding methods for their control, but they must be controlled or they would destroy a ship as they would wreck the peace and security of society ashore.

May 24
Palermo
This morning we made land, the Island of Sicily. A haze prevented us from seeing it sooner. The breeze under which we had been making ten knots increased and we beat up the bay under reefed topsails and came to anchor off Palermo at 12 m. The high wind causes clouds of yellow dust to rise above the city, but the mountain slopes and foliage look green. From the ship the city has the same attractive appearance as a year ago.

Our mail is received and for me it is a large one. Letters, some of them written more than a year ago, and directed to the care of the Naval Lyceum, Brooklyn, reach me.

Although these letters are old they are interesting and give me news not referred to in subsequent letters from the same persons. I am impressed with the numerous deaths of friends and other changes which have taken place in my comparatively brief absence of little more than a year.

Mr. R. R. Wallace, Lieutenant, has been promoted to Lieutenant Commander. Midshipman Blake is ordered home for examination. He expects to leave here in the steamer via Marseilles tomorrow.[32]

May 26
Palermo

I wrote letters to eight persons, including my brothers and my former shipmates Richard Graham and R. H. Seaward, who are both now on the US Sloop *Portsmouth*.

I said goodbye to Mr. Blake who sailed this afternoon on the steamer for Marseilles. Mr. Wallace is at present off-duty and we are now two officers short.

The steamer *Anglo Saxon* has been lost off Cape Race, N.F. with three hundred out of four hundred passengers aboard. This is the twentieth ocean steamer that has been lost and the sixth by the Montreal Company.

We get reports of a victory by General Hooker at Fredericksburg and that he has sent 5,000 prisoners to Washington; also that the conscription law is being enforced.[33]

May 27
Palermo

Mr. L. Monti, the Consul visited the ship. He is a man of literary distinction and was once professor of Italian at Harvard College. His wife is a great favorite with the Commodore and the officers. She is American, very talkative and quite aggressive for a woman. I think that she is the more important member of the co-partnership.

May 28
Palermo

Today for the first time this season all hands are dressed in white frocks and hats.[34]

The Russian, Turkish and British Consuls visited the ship together at noon. Later we had the General commanding all the military forces in Sicily. His staff accompanied him. The General is a mild mannered man of middle age, with a sandy complexion. His staff are fine looking men.

These distinguished visitors today called for the expenditure of considerable powder in salutes. The Chinese are more economical than we in this matter. It is said that the Emperor gets one gun; all inferior officials two.

May 29
Palermo

This morning when I awoke the air on the berth deck seemed so hot and oppressive that I could scarcely breathe. On going up to the spar deck I found the same difficulty. The wind was high, but the air felt as though coming from a furnace. At noon a squall came from the southeast like a tornado. The ship dragged her anchor and another was let go, but failed to stop her and had the wind not abated suddenly we would have gone on the rocks.

After the squall the air again became oppressive. We learn that the peculiar heat and the sulphurous smell in the atmosphere is due to the fact that the wind is coming from Mount Aetna.

Reports today state that General Hooker has been defeated and compelled to re-cross the Rappahannock with a loss of 10,000 men.[35] This is quite different from our first accounts. This is depressing. What a disaster with which to open the summer campaign! It is disheartening to think of the repeated failures of our arms, the terrible slaughter and how little we have accomplished in so long a time.

This evening the Governor and the Prefect of Police with their wives visited the ship and were received with appropriate salute.

May 30
Palermo

The first thing this morning the ship was unmoored and her position changed. After breakfast holystones and sand were in order. For the first time this season windsails were put down the hatchways. They make it much more comfortable below decks and especially in the Store Room.

The reports which reach us today put a more favorable aspect on General Hooker's operations. Our Gunner, Mr. Grainger had a brother wounded. "Stonewall" Jackson is reported to have lost an arm. Captain Demmick of the regular army is killed. I presume that this is Major Demmick of Portsmouth, an artillery officer.

May 31
Palermo

A beautiful morning much like summer in its richness, but New England also has its charms at this season as well as Sicily.

After dinner I went on shore with Boatswain Hunter. He wanted to see the catacombs and I agreed to go with him although I had been there twice before. We hired a barouche. We had the usual encounter with troublesome guides whom we did not need or want. We managed to get away without any, but one ran through a cross street, headed us off and mounted the seat with the driver. We told the driver to make the fellow get off, but the driver was evidently afraid to do so. I then told the driver to stop, get out, climbed up and grabbed the fellow by the collar and yanked him off into the street. I took him somewhat by surprise, but he was as quick as a cat and we both landed on our feet in the street together. He reached for his knife and I sailed into him. I was lucky. Before Hunter could reach us he was unconscious and I had his knife. I managed to hit him three times in the jaw, just where I wanted to. We re-entered the carriage and told the driver to go ahead, but he did not do so and people began to come running toward the fellow lying in the street. I climbed up alongside of the driver and said, "commi a, o ti faccio lo stresso," (move on, or I do the same to thee). He drove ahead, and as I looked back I was much relieved to see the fellow slowly stand up on his feet again, as I had landed rather heavily on the point of his chin with my left, and I have had all the experience with Italian prisons that I want.

We arrived at the catacombs without further incident, descended the stone steps and passed through the alcoves of the dead. The monk who went with us told us that in the course of the years 8,000,000 corpses had been deposited there.

My attention was attracted to the skull and forearms, including a gloved hand of some Ottoman dignitary, but of whom I could not make out. The Turkish insignia of royalty surrounded the niche and a marble tablet bore the chiseled head and the customary inscription to designate a royal personage. I never heard that a Turkish Sultan or any other Turkish personage of royal blood ever left his body in Sicily. I must try to think of somebody who might tell me about this man. The Catacombs usually contain about 4,000 bodies. Many are there who died in 1862.

I felt something break under my foot and I looked down and found it to be a human tooth which had fallen from its owner onto the floor.

Each body has its separate niche in the wall or is in a case. The women are in separate apartments. All virgins have crowns on their heads. They are usually dressed in colored drapery or in customary wearing apparel.

From the Catacombs we went to the "King's Garden." It was beautiful today. The fragrance of the flowers and of the fruit blossoms helped to make it most attractive. From the Garden we drove to the "Marino" and through the principal streets and stopped for refreshments at my old friend's place near the "Four Nations." After visiting the Cathedral we took a carriage and joined the procession of gay equipages on the Promenade.

We returned and took supper at my old friend's. He was very cordial and evidently glad to see me again after my absence of ten months. We invited him to visit us on the ship and he promised to do so.

Even while we were eating those pestiferous guides came to bother us, among them one who had been following us most of the afternoon. While we were walking along the street we at one time being followed by six carriage drivers soliciting us to hire them.

After supper we returned to the ship, having contemplated during the afternoon mortality and the frailty of human life in the Catacombs and its more brilliant aspects in the public drives and pleasure resorts.

Now that the day is over my mind turns to my encounter with the guide. At times I have been accused of being too ready with my fists, but I was none too quick with them today. As Hunter says, I suppose that this fellow and his Sicilians will "lay for me" when I go ashore. However, if one wants to worry he can always find something to worry about. It is no new experience for me to have to deal with men with murderous intent, and somehow I feel that my guardian angel who has always protected me on former occasions will not desert me here in Sicily.

June 1
Palermo

Agreeable to his promise my hotel friend from the city visited the ship today with several companions. I showed him the things of interest in our little floating world.

Anson Dunbar, an old man, who has been punished more than any other man in this ship lost a sum of money a few nights ago. He reported it to the Executive Officer who said that he was glad of it and gave Dunbar eight hours in one of the brig cells, or "catacombs," as the sailors call them. This seems rather hard for not reporting who the thief was as well as the fact of the theft.

Dunbar was ship's cooper at first but was disrated to seaman and then to ordinary seaman. He has been stretched on gratings with his hands and feet bound—crucified, as it is termed—lashed up in his hammock by the Captain's galley and heated so hot that the perspiration ran through mattress and hammock on to the deck. In short every means allowed has been taken to torture him, because he is so infirm that he cannot move around as quickly as a young man, or is a great malingerer—as they say he is. I have heard it stated that "this is an old game of his," to be invalided home. That he never completes a cruise; that "he is an imposition on the government."

I know not whether such charges be true or not, but they are no excuse for thus treating a man whose age would indicate that he might possess all the infirmities of which he complains. He should not be kept from the sick-bay when not well, nor pushed down and run over on deck, as has been done, no doubt through prejudice. I cannot understand how "an officer and a gentleman" can permit such treatment of a fellow being.

I understand that the old man is to be sent home soon and I am heartily glad of it for the sake of my own feelings as well as his. It is no credit, to say the least, to those who might prevent such cruelty to an old man who has been in the Navy for twenty years and has obviously outlived his usefulness, whether it be a case of can't work or won't work.

June 3
Palermo
Showers last night and the air is cool and bracing today. We have had many visitors on the ship.

I have found a biography of Commodore Preble[36] which I am reading with much interest. Poor old Dunbar is walking in the starboard gangway with a musket because he could not keep step in the division drill this morning. The old man holds on the hammock netting to keep up. It certainly is hard usage if he be actually so feeble.

June 4
Palermo
Reports which reach us regarding the doings of General Hooker about Fredericksburg are very contradictory. One cannot tell just what happened. The latest is that he has started a movement toward Richmond, keeping communications with Washington open and that General Lee has retreated to the defense of Richmond. The killed and wounded of both sides were left on the fields of the recent battles and the latter who crawled into adjoining woods to avoid the contending armies were burned when the woods caught fire.[37]

Nelson, the Painter, who is with me in the Store Room has just received news of the death of his brother who was killed March 12.

The *New York Herald* states that the USS *Macedonian* is to relieve our ship, but does not say where we are going.

When I took my monthly reports to our Executive, Mr. Low, he started a lecture on the need of being circumspect in our attitude toward the people with whom we come in contact ashore, reminding me that we were representatives of the United States and that it was our duty, especially at the present time, to do all we could to avoid friction with foreign officials. I assented and told him that I had always tried to conduct myself with this idea in mind, and then I found out what he was driving at. He said, "you pummeled a guide severely in the streets recently." Knowing that his knowledge of the affair could only be gossip which had reached him somehow from Hunter's mess, I said, "But did you understand, Mr. Low, that I was defending myself from a man who was trying to kill me?" He replied, "I understand that your habitual attitude toward those who solicit our patronage ashore is such as to invite trouble," an assertion which he fabricated because he saw the position into which he was getting in reprimanding me without attempting to learn the facts. I must admit however that I have not always been exactly polite to the scoundrels who have annoyed or attempted to cheat me, and probably, after all, it may be well that Mr. Low has pointed out to me the advisability of caution in attempting to reform Italian customs.

In looking over some old papers I find an account of Lady Hamilton who occupied with Lord Nelson a house which we can see just opposite to where our ship is lying. This intimacy lead Lord Nelson's wife to obtain a divorce from him. Lord Nelson met Lady Hamilton at Naples where she was an intimate of the Queen of Naples and in various ways had aroused the jealousy of the ladies of the Court. Her gay life closed with death in poverty in France.

June 5
Palermo

Weather delightful. I received several letters from home. They reflect discouragement from our conduct in military operations, and it would seem that people are prepared for the worst.

We reeve new braces today. This gives me more free space in the Store Room as I get rid of several coils of manila cordage obtained in Spezia this spring.

June 6
Palermo

This is the regular day for cleaning ship.

This morning the Commodore showed a company of English ladies around the ship. Nothing of interest, but much to disinterest me in a man-of-war. What a monotonous, purposeless life! Beside a lovely country caged in a damp hulk afloat. However my so-called cruise in this ship is probably about half over.

June 7
Palermo

This is a holiday here. In the afternoon I went ashore with Mr. Hunter and Glenn. We took a carriage and had a fine ride around the city, which in the evening was brilliantly illuminated. The gardens and public buildings looked splendid—the best display I ever saw.

During the afternoon there was a military review at the Marine. As a whole the troops do not exhibit the spirit to make such a parade effective, although some companies were exceptions.

The infantry is too thickly clad. They have heavy overcoats, not adapted to this climate at this season. Their evolutions were sluggish and they showed fatigue. The gens d'armes have showy uniform and made a fine appearance.

At six o'clock the national salute is fired from our ship which has been flying the Italian flag at the fore all day. Numerous visitors were received on board.

June 8
Palermo

At mess this morning Smith and Glenn had a little dispute which resulted in the latter striking the former twice in the head. This rather disturbed the quiet of the mess for the time being. Smith is inclined to be captious while Glenn is pugilistic, and this morning weather conditions were not favorable for the suppression of either propensity. Family jars are unpleasant for all affected.

Some officials from shore dine on board, among them our Consul and Lady who are great favorites on this ship as elsewhere.

We put three men on an American bark to be taken to the Naval Hospital at New York. I send letters home by the vessel.

June 9
Palermo

Although a report was made to the Executive officer of the affair at our mess yesterday morning between Glenn and Smith no investigation has been made to the satisfaction of Smith. I was the only one called up in reference to it and there the matter has apparently ended. It seems hard for Mr. Low to entertain a charge against the Master-at-Arms.

This has been a very quiet day. A mail arrived from Genoa. General Hooker appears to be doing nothing. A telegraphic report says that General Grant has lost 5,000 men at Vicksburg and that General Lee is marching on Washington. This is bad news if true, but who can believe what reports give us now-a-days.

Dunbar, the most abused man of the crew, went on the bark as an invalid with the others yesterday. I am glad that he is free from the ship.

At night a band was brought on board and the decks illuminated and a company from shore entertained at a dance.

There was more relaxation of discipline on board the old *Constellation* than I have seen since I have been on the ship. The men remained on deck or watched the performance in which they eventually began to take part. The "messenger boys" made quite free in the Ward Room and port Steerage, doubtless requesting wine for the spar deck more than ordered by the officers. Some of the men put on the overcoats, belts and caps of the musicians and sat with them on the spar deck. One sailor thus pretended to play a belaying pin as a flute; another appropriated the instrument of a musician who had stepped aside to trade his portion of wine with a sailor for tobacco. Other sailors were also ready customers for the Musicians' wine. Becoming bolder some of the men intercepted the caterer's waiters at the head of the steps at the gun deck and obtained bottles of beverages in transit, the waiters apparently not realizing that the wine was not going to those for whom it was intended. Later some of the men took advantage of the only occupant of the port Steerage when his back was turned and carried off a large demi-john, thus robbing the place of its entire supply. The Master-at-Arms, the man most needed on such an occasion, was not in condition to take his duties seriously and the young urchins of the ship infested every place where anything was "being kept for the occasion."

Except for taking part in the dancing the men had quite as much of a time as the officers. The company consisted of military officers and other Sicilian officials and their ladies.

June 10
Palermo

It is very quiet about the ship today. Neither officers nor men care much about doing any unnecessary work.

The Commodore is surveying the harbor inside the breakwater, with view, I think of determining the practicability of mooring the ship there to pass next winter. The space there possibly available for our ship is quite small.

The Commodore and other officers are evidently much more agreeably entertained here than at any other place which we have visited. The Consul's wife is a social leader here and a great favorite with everybody. I <u>think</u> that she is <u>capable</u> of being Consul, but I do not say that she <u>is</u>.

The weather is very warm. The heat below decks is almost unendurable.

June 11
Palermo

Fifteen months ago today we sailed from Portsmouth. The time spent on this ship is far too long for my benefit, yet it does not seem long so swiftly do the days go by.

Last night the crew were employed until a late hour setting up the head stays and making other preparations to sail, but this morning there is no sign of starting.

Two more men ran away last night, Bennett and Jackson. The former left the ship here a year ago, but was caught. If caught again he will not get off so easy.

June 12
Palermo

The men worked half the night on Thursday to make ready to sail, but there are no other signs of our departure.

The *New York Herald* of May 20 gives an account of the capture of Jackson, Mississippi a small town on the river.[38] The Army of the Potomac is quiet. General Hooker is to retain his command. Government credit seems to be good. No fears of foreign intervention are entertained at present. The French have not made the progress in Mexico that has been claimed. General F—— [illegible] is unpopular and much disorder prevails in the Army.

June 13
At sea

After receiving some communication from shore the commodore gave orders to hoist the boats and get up anchor and now we are clear of the harbor and are fairly out on the blue sea. An agreeable change.

June 14
At sea

The land is still in sight. Mount Stromboli is to starboard. We are sailing by the wind under reefed topsails with a good breeze.

It is rumored that we are going nowhere but are just out from Palermo for a short cruise, one reason for which is to lead the men who deserted to believe that the ship has left and thus make it easier for the police to capture them. The Commodore is undoubtedly very anxious that they be caught.

A Sabbath at sea is quieter than in port. There are no visitors and no going ashore. Here the watch below is reading or sleeping and that on deck similarly employed except when working the ship. I enjoy the quiet of the ship very much.

One might think that life on a ship like this would furnish an opportunity for study and mental improvement, but somehow the environment is not conducive to such beneficial employment. Too many disagreeable distractions are constantly occurring to disturb tranquility of mind and divert attention from instructive pursuits.

June 15
At sea

This morning finds us close under a small island. Targets are put out under its protecting lee and we engage in target practice for two hours and then we stand along by the wind again.

One of our Italian musicians tells me that this island is called "Bentrilli," as near as I can make out. Much of the land is cultivated and lies well exposed to the sun. In the southeast part there is a town of considerable size, and what appears from this distance to be a harbor.

I should like to visit the place to see if the inhabitants are so devoid of conscience as those of Palermo. As caterer of my mess I have not only learned that the latter never hesitate to lie or cheat, but what is worse, that the contemptible rascals take no offense if accused of so doing; neither do they appear at all disturbed if caught in the act.

The evening is calm and delightful.

June 16
Palermo

This morning we entered the bay of Palermo and are promptly boarded by the Consul. Accompanying him were gens d'armes bringing back our two deserters. The departure of our ship brought them out of their hiding place and resulted in their capture as we supposed that it would. They were dressed Sicilian peasant fashion, with dark felt hats, black pants and light colored print shirts. After taking these men on board we stood out to sea again and headed for the coast of Italy. Some say that we are going to Leghorn, others say to Spezia, but the Commodore does not reveal his secrets to anyone.

June 20
At sea

This morning after drifting about in warm weather and calm seas for three days a strong breeze brings us in sight of the Island of Corsica, and during the afternoon we also have Elba and Monte Christo in sight. The day is delightful. I spend much time in the fore-top to obtain a better look at the places of Napoleon's birth and banishment. At night we are very close to Elba. Napoleon came forth from this region like a meteor to shine for a while and back here to disappear.

June 21

This morning finds us off Leghorn, hove to and waiting for a favorable wind to go in.

"Ike" Simmons, the Negro cook's-mate was given five days in the brig in double irons for singing last night in the same place where he was being confined for another offense. According to "Ike," Nichols, the Negro, and Raynes, the Kanaka, who died recently on the ship appeared before him and danced in the brig outside of his cell and he sang to them. The ship's corporal told me as something which was puzzling him that this morning he found in the brig five buckets stacked up in a peculiar way and which had stood up in spite of the motion of the ship. Simmons was in a cell and could not have stacked them and the corporal had the only key to the door of the brig which was locked.

I am informed the mysterious occurrences or manifestations have annoyed and tested the nerves of men who have been confined in the brig before. Some of these incidents have been mentioned only to the Master-at-Arms. Twice on stormy nights last fall Campbell, the captain of the forecastle, whom we lost in the Atlantic was supposed to have been seen standing near the lee cat-head.

Whatever may be the explanation of these phenomena the sentence which Simmons has received will tend to discourage the men from giving undue publicity to their supernatural observations.

In the afternoon we sailed close under a small island with a large building in the center—presumably a summer resort. There are also on the island a collection of fishermen's cottages and many boats on the beach.

Two other square rigged vessels are with us awaiting a chance to enter port.

June 22
Leghorn

This morning we picked up a pilot and soon a favorable breeze enabled us to enter the snug artificial harbor of Leghorn. The extensive break-water which extends in a semi-circle outside the old mole is nearly completed and must have cost a great sum even though convict labor was employed upon it. It is about a mile long. There is an entrance to the harbor—end to the city—around either end, and through these passages there is a constant procession of arriving and departing vessels.

I think that there is more American trade here than with any other Mediterranean port. It is in fact an American city so far as appearances go and is unlike any other city in Italy which we have visited.

I relinquished the caterership of my mess today.[39] Glenn took it. It is impossible for one to please long. Five months have sufficed for me. It is quite a relief to be free from the duty. I have lost interest in trying to cater to the capricious appetites of a part of my mess. When a man cannot suit himself it is difficult for another to suit him.

June 24
Leghorn

Captain Page of the Rebel Service is said to be here waiting for a vessel to come here from England for her armament.[40]

We have had numerous visitors since our arrival. Two Americans who were on board today gave encouraging accounts of the progress of our military operations. One is from Ohio and the other from Indiana. The personal pronoun <u>we</u> was used frequently in telling us what the Federal troops had done, when in fact the "we's" to whom we were listening were in this very place to avoid fighting for the Union "so dear."

The ship *Evening Star* of Portland came in today, light, in tow, of a steamer.

Saint John's day is being celebrated today. Flags are flown everywhere, there is a large military parade and the theaters are crowded.

After supper I went ashore to purchase some clothing. Linen as well as cotton and woolen is cheap here. I ordered a suit of black which the tailor agrees to make for 84 francs or 15 Tuscan dollars. I bought some fancy patterns for pants and some linen handkerchiefs. I presume that we are paying for all these things much more than a native would have to pay.

June 25
Leghorn

The sailors have been daubing over the outside of the ship with black paint. They apply it with rags and brushes in a not very dextrous way and as a consequence get a large share of the paint on themselves.

In the evening I went on shore to make some purchases and to try on my suit. Mr. Hunter accompanied me. I met with Messrs. Wing and Elmes, chief mates respectively of the ship *Evening Star* of Portland and of the bark *Sumpter* of Boston. Elmes belongs at Augusta, Me. As I lived there two winters we had a pleasant time talking over old affairs with which we were both conversant.

The theater at Florence was burned last night while illuminated for a ball to celebrate St. John's day. Very few people had assembled there when the fire started, otherwise the loss of life would have been heavy. Doubtless the burning of the theater will be charged to the priests, who were opposed to the masquerade costumes adopted for the occasion.

June 26
Leghorn
Painting ship and tarring rigging and squaring ratlines. It is almost too warm to live in the Store Room where I have been kept quite busy. No windsail is put down because of the tar which is being used on the rigging.

Messrs. Wing and Elmes visited the ship.

June 27
Leghorn
In the evening I went ashore with Mr. Hunter to try on our new suits and to get a breath of air. We met Messrs. Grainger (the Gunner), Jones, and Glenn and we hired a carriage and all had a pleasant ride.

The officers are purchasing all kinds of wearing apparel here. I bought a bolt of linen for forty francs.

June 28
Leghorn
I went ashore in the afternoon with Mr. Hunter. We visited the *Evening Star* and the *Sumpter* and Messrs. Wing, Elmes and Drew joined us in a ride on the Merino and to the baths. The Merino extends for a few miles along the shore to the East. A more beautiful drive cannot be found anywhere. Hedges, gardens and groves border the way.

The facilities for sea bathing are good. Messrs. Hunter and Wing took the baths. There are numerous attractive restaurants, both open air and covered. We all had supper at the Café Americano and after a promenade we went to the "Casa" where Hunter and I had spent the evening before with Messrs. Grainger, Glenn and Jones. Mr. Philbrick and Mr. Rider came in just before we left. On my way to the ship I became separated from the others through my efforts to induce some of our petty officers to return to the ship as they appeared to be starting on a rampage. I succeeded in persuading them to return. While talking to them Mr. Grainger came up. From what we were told we concluded to try to find Glenn and three others, but we were unsuccessful and returned to the ship without them.

June 29
Leghorn
The men whom Mr. Grainger and I tried to find last night failed to return to the ship as thought. This morning Evans and old Buchanan, the quartermaster, came off, but McIntyre, the boatswain's mate, and Glenn still remained, delaying the departure of the ship which was to sail this morning. The police were notified and the customary rewards offered for the missing men.

Crowds of visitors throng the ship. It is St. Peter's day, a holiday. All shops and places of business are closed.

I went on shore at four o'clock with Mr. Hunter and went to the tailor shop to see if my suit might be ready, but the shop was closed. The tailor will therefore have to send it to Spezia, unless he can bring it aboard before we sail.

I mailed a letter to Kate C. B——, took a short walk with Messrs. Hunter and Philbrick and left them to say goodbye to some acquaintances after which I went to several places in an unsuccessful search for Glenn and then returned to the ship. Sometime later Messrs. Hunter and Philbrick arrived on board with news of Glenn and of a melee at the landing which they were neither able to prevent nor stop.

It appears that Glenn arrived at the landing shortly before they did, hired a boatman to bring him off to the ship and had seated himself in the boat which had proceeded some distance from the landing when either the police at the landing or the other boatmen waked up to the fact that he was the man for whom a reward had been offered and there was a mad scramble to "capture" him so as to bring him back to the ship and obtain the reward. Glenn resisted those in the other boats who tried to lay hold of him and in the struggle Glenn's boat was capsized. When they attempted to seize him in the water Glenn would grab the gunwale of the boat and throw his weight on it and capsize the boat. After swamping two or more boats in this way they began beating Glenn over the head and shoulders with their oars and managed to subdue him sufficiently to bring him to the landing. As soon as he got on his feet he broke away from those who were trying to hold him, slipped on his brass knuckles and soon had boatmen and policemen sprawling all around the landing. Finally they tired him out, threw him down and the police put the irons on him and carried him off to the Police Station, but not until Glenn had knocked the teeth down one man's throat and otherwise injured him and had done somewhat less serious damage to several others.

McIntyre came off on his own hook soon after dark, not only escaping the vigilance of the Police, but also managing to sneak on board unseen. He was most fortunate. He said that he had been back eighteen miles in the country lying under a grape vine "cooling off."

A band consisting of nine men was shipped today. Now we will have our own music in addition to other entertainments for our happy family on the *Constellation*.

Mr. Grainger and Dr. Clark were sent on shore to see Glenn who is represented to be badly cut and bruised about the head. After midnight Glenn arrives, showing only a few cuts and bruises about the head and face. His left eye is black and there is a cut of some size on his forehead. He complains of soreness about his shoulders and on the top of his head. He has been put in double irons under the charge of a sentry.

It was hard work to obtain his release from the Police. The man who lost his teeth was finally induced to accept a cash indemnity for his injuries. If Glenn had been taken to Court he probably would have received a severe sentence. I have heard only one side of the affair, but I suspect that Glenn might have avoided such trouble by different conduct.

June 30

This morning we got under way and left Leghorn by the western passage. Before leaving the market-man came to collect his bill against our mess. Glenn our caterer was oblivious to demands of all kinds, and besides was not in funds, having reached the ship with half a franc. A big Italian came to my hammock for Glenn's boat hire for the trip to the ship which ended so quickly and so disastrously, and at the same time the "bumboat" man,—*qui facit per alium facit per se*, and besides my reluctance to reassume the responsibility of caterer of the mess tended to be overcome by hearing, "an Italian wants some money and you owe it to him." There are cases when it is better not to try to argue—and this was one.

A favorable breeze sent us along on our way to Spezia at a fine rate. We reached Spezia at six o'clock and entered the harbor with our new band playing *Hail Columbia* and some Italian airs. It has been a very warm day, but a shower has cooled the air somewhat and the evening is lovely. Spezia never looked more beautiful and the fragrance of flowers and shrubbery is wafted to the ship on the evening breeze.

Chapter Four
July 1863 to December 1863

July 1
Spezia

I received a package of newspapers mailed just a year ago and which my brother Edward has mentioned in his letters. They are rather too old now to be of much interest.

Glenn has been freed from his confinement.

Had "General Quarters" this forenoon.

It is reported that General Lee is in Pennsylvania with 140,000 men.[1] France has made a proposition to Great Britain with respect to the recognition of the Confederacy. With what success I cannot judge at present. The French have taken —— [illegible] and are marching on Mexico City.

This place is more attractive than any other at this season, especially when viewed from the water, but Leghorn is my favorite city with respect to everything that concerns good living and comfort, although it is not free from beggars. The suburbs are also more attractive than those of the other Italian cities which I have seen. I like the streets and squares and the public and private buildings of Leghorn, but as elsewhere there are to be seen dingy habitations and squalid children giving the appearance of a surplus population. They make soldiers out of them and except for this employment they would be hard pushed for bread.

Tuscany can well boast of an ancient and honorable line of Dukes and other personages of distinction. Their influence is still felt.

July 2
Spezia

A warm day. My Store Room is almost intolerable but I am busy there on reports.

The woman tooth extractor was on board today and I let her take out the remains of my two front upper incisor teeth which were broken in Mahon. She is an admirable operator.

During target practice here a gun burst on the frigate *Garibaldi* and killed 7 men.

Three men, John Gray, Henry Carter and Alex. McLeod, the drillmaster, were tried by Court Martial today. The two first were charged with leaving the boat when on duty; the last with insubordination. Gray and Carter were returned to the ship by the police after rewards had been offered for them. Carter was absent two days.

McLeod desired me to act as his counsel before the Court, but I refused because of the nature of the offense with which he was charged. The Executive Officer makes the charge himself and any plea which could be made on behalf of the accused would inevitably bring up the propriety of methods of discipline employed by an Executive officer, a subject which it would be highly improper for any one holding a subordinate position on the ship to attempt to discuss as a counsel in a Court Martial.

July 3
Spezia

I am very busy making up reports. It is too warm to work in the Store Room during the day and therefore I work during the night.

It appears that the men who were accused of desertion from the boat had liberty from the officer in charge and would therefore appear to be guilty only of overstaying their liberty.

The band is practicing so as to give us some National music tomorrow. The men propose to give the band a dinner tomorrow and are taking up a collection for the purpose, even though these men have been eager without a good dinner than the Italian bandsmen have.

Flags are arranged to dress the ship and the Master-at-Arms has obtained some green boughs for the berth deck.

It is reported that General Lee is in Philadelphia and proposes to dine on Boston Common on the Fourth of July.[2]

July 4
Spezia

Again the anniversary of our Independence has come around. The ship is dressed with flags and the berth deck is trimmed with the branches of trees. Arches, bowers, etc. set it off very nicely.

The various messes arranged through a caterer for cooked dinners served on board at $10 a mess. There was however a great deal of complaint that they did not get enough and that the Italian "as usual" did not perform his contract.

I went ashore late in the afternoon and with Messrs. Hunter and Philbrick and witnessed, amid great excitement, a boat race between our fourth and fifth cutters. The fourth cutter won.

After supper I went off for a walk alone. It was not cool but it was pleasant and I enjoyed it. There are times when I liked to get away from company and do what I please without having to consider the desires and tastes of companions. With such brief opportunities for sightseeing one cannot afford to sacrifice too much time in concessions to others.

My walk in the moonlight reminded me of scenes pictured by artists, and also that a year ago today I was visiting the Museum at Naples, alone, as I was today. After my walk and finding that it was not too late I decided to call on Signore Maroni, a prominent local attorney whom I had met at the Consulate and who had invited me to his home.

I found that he occupied a rather pretentious house in the outskirts of the city. His family consisted of himself and the Signora, a daughter and three sons. All of the sons were away. The eldest, associated with his father in the practice of law, was in Mantua on business. The second was a Captain in the Army and the youngest was somewhere at school. The daughter, unmarried, was at home and was entertaining as guests two young women friends from Turin. Signore Maroni was the only one who spoke English. I have not made sufficient progress in my Italian to enable me to go much beyond conventional conversational phrases without tending to distress my hearers, but all the young ladies spoke French fluently and Signore Maroni spoke it as well as I did and I think that they as well as I had an enjoyable evening. I invited them all to take a moonlight ride in a boat down the Bay, and we started to do so, but a shower came up and we returned to the house to escape the rain.

As the boatman was taking me out to the ship my thoughts went from the events of this day to memories of other Fourths of July and where they had been passed—them off years when there was no war. It occurred to me that tonight men whom I know are perhaps lying wounded and neglected on some Southern battle field looking up at the same full moon which has contributed so much to make this evening enjoyable for me. In the Service for which I am best fitted chance has thus far kept me from sharing the dangers and suffering of some of my boyhood companions, but before this war is over I may see as much fighting as any of them. Within a week we may go down at our guns like the men in the *Cumberland* in a hopeless contest with a modern ship.[3]

I was awakened from this reverie by an "All's well," which came to my ears across the moon-lit sparkling waters of the peaceful bay. It came from the sentry pacing the deck of our ship. It was the voice of the United States Government in this part of the world. It was reassuring. I trust that it was prophetic and that I may live to reach my native land again and recall in times of peace pleasant memories of this Italian Fourth.

July 5
Spezia

The Sabbath comes to the ship as a respite from the duties and pleasures of the week, but on shore they are celebrating another holiday, Saint Somebody's day.

Towards evening I went on shore. With Messrs. Hunter and Philbrick I called on Mr. Kenyoun and his family, after which visit I left my companions to their own devices, took a walk alone and returned early to the ship, meeting and returning with Lieut. Backus, Master's Mate Wilson and the Commodore's Secretary Hinckley.

During my walk I met several of our crew and I was glad to see that they all were sober and quiet.

July 6
Spezia

The men on liberty all came off on time and sober.

I am receiving some stores in my department.

The Confederate raid into Pennsylvania is of less importance than at first represented. George H. Fletcher, ordinary seaman, has been examined and made a Master's Mate in the Service. He is a young man to whom much credit is due for reforming his habits since being on this ship. He is now a concrete example of temperance and propriety.

Some time ago personal letters to officers of the ship stated that Commodore Thatcher had been detached from our ship and Captain Stellwagen ordered to relieve him. Later advices however indicated that both orders had been countermanded. This morning word was sent me to take to Commodore at his hotel in Spezia certain reports on which I have been busy lately; that he was going to Genoa by the afternoon train and wished to see me before he left.

When I entered his room at the hotel he greeted me very cordially. He seemed almost jovial in contrast to his customary dignified demeanor. I almost expected him to call me by my first name as he used to do, but he addressed me as Mr. Safford, as he has seemed very particular to do since I have been on his ship.

We went over the reports and I made the memoranda from them which he desired. Then after an apologetic preface he asked me for legal advice regarding his personal affairs as he usually does when I see him.

At the conclusion of these business matters he inquired for my family and spoke of his friendship with my father. Then there unexpectedly followed an interview with him which I am going to try to preserve <u>verbatim</u> as nearly as I can. Turning abruptly from his reference to my father he said, "Mr. Safford I am going to leave you. I want you to know that I appreciate all that you have done for me in so many ways. I am sorry to part with you and others who have been loyal to me on this ship, but you will appreciate my feelings when I tell you that I have been ordered to the *Colorado* on our coast and that I hope now to have a chance in active service in my profession to save my name from oblivion."

I told the Commodore that I wished to assure him of my sincere wishes for an opportunity to bring to himself deserved recognition not only from the Navy Department, but on the part of the whole country.

I have never been able to condone his selfishness in appropriating me to look after his personal interests by having me appointed as Yeoman of the ship which he knew that he was going to command, nearly four months before she went into commission and I thought this to be a good occasion to show him how I felt about the matter and possibly interest him in making amends for his action.

I told him that I wished that it might be possible for me also to look forward to doing something more creditable in the present national emergency than filling the position of store keeper on a medieval ship; that my record as mate of ships, my proficiency as a navigator, my experience in the militia and a demonstrated capacity to lead and control men, to say nothing of my legal training ought to make me more useful to the country at the present time than filling my almost unendurable position; I did not regard it as unreasonable to expect that he might be interested in seeing that I was utilized by the Navy to better advantage.

He looked at me hard and then said, "Your feelings are perfectly natural. I must confess that I never thought of you as a mariner, but only as a young lawyer who was willing to do a patriotic duty in what must necessarily be an uncongenial position. From what you now say I infer that you were looking for a temporary commission in the Navy. If you still entertain such a hope you may as well dismiss it from your mind."

I replied that I had no idea of giving up a legal career and staying in the Navy, but that I saw no reason for not aspiring for a temporary commission when I knew that commissions had been given to others without my qualifications.

He then said, "If you had military ambitions you should have entered the Army which had to build up an entire organization and in which you might have obtained a commission for the asking."

I replied that it had not been my thought to use the country's military necessity for my personal advantage. My life's training and experience made me no more useful to the Army than anybody who had not had such a training, but that my training and experience did make me valuable to the Navy if intelligently utilized; that I was not so sure about getting a military commission for the asking. I had reason to believe that had not my political activities been of a character to make me a *persona non grata* with the new administration I probably would, at least, have been scheduled for a naval commission when I was "selected" by him as yeoman for the *Constellation*.

Thereupon the Commodore said, "I am going to tell you something to think over when you feel inclined to dwell upon your disappointments and also give you some fatherly advice which I trust that you will regard as such. Your life is ahead of you. Mine is behind me. I have been in the Navy forty years. I have always done my duty and have tried to be an efficient officer. This ship is my first command.[4] I was nearly 57 years old when I got it. At the outbreak of the war I saw other officers detailed to active war service where they had a chance to distinguish themselves, while I was sent to a foreign station with this 'medieval ship' as you call it, with no prospect of ever being heard of except through some encounter which would either make me pitiable or ridiculous. Now through the efforts of friends this chance has come to me of which I have just told you. It comes to me as an old man 58 years old with mental as well as physical habits fixed and adaptability to new situations and ability to meet new problems not what they once were."

"Now as to yourself. As nearly as I can see you are in a *cul de sac* from which you cannot hope to extricate yourself. For reasons which you ought to appreciate the promotion of a man to a commissioned position on a ship on which he has been serving as yeoman is unthinkable. It would be unwise even though he possessed the combined genius of Lord Nelson and Napoleon Bonaparte. This is no reflection on you or your position. A man who has the qualities which command respect will obtain respect in any position—on a man-of-war as anywhere else, but practical considerations require that we accept an established institution as it is—not as we think it ought to be."

"The only practicable possibility of gratifying your desires would be to find some place for you in connection with naval operations back home in the South. You are right in saying that men less qualified than you have received commissions. Even the fact of your familiarity with the Navy since boyhood tends to make you better qualified, but in spite of your experience in the merchant service and your familiarity with the Navy I believe that you overestimate your usefulness to the Navy."

"The Navy was badly depleted by the resignations of Rebels and it has been obliged to take in men like yourself and place them in positions of respectability, but as Naval officers they have been disappointments to a great extent. They have lacked proper training and have been undependable in emergencies. They have failed to meet situations which trained Naval officers of less natural ability would have met satisfactorily as a matter of course. Much more is demanded of a Naval officer than mere ability to handle and navigate a ship and control men. This is not a matter of abstract knowledge either. A man's usefulness anywhere is largely determined by his adjustment to his environment. A merchant ship-master or mate feels like an intruder and a misfit when put in a Naval officer's mess. It is hard enough for officers who have trained together in the Navy to preserve reasonably amicable relations when thrown together in each other's way on a ship week after week and month after month. I question whether in spite of your familiarity with Naval usages you would find life in the Ward Room or Steerage of a ship any more congenial than your position as yeoman, and the chances of your doing anything more satisfactory to yourself would be infinitesimal. It is too bad that we cannot have more men qualified by training to act as Naval officers in an emergency, but such training must begin when they are young and must lead to a consciousness that they belong to the Navy—that they fit into it as cogs in a machine."

"Be content to do your duty where you are. This war is more nearly over than superficial observers believe—thanks to my Navy and your Navy. Our Navy was crippled by the Rebels before the war started. What was left of it has resisted the efforts of our politicians to demoralize it and now has the South blockaded and split by possession of the Mississippi and held as in a vice, waiting for the Army to punish the Rebels until they cry enough. Thousands of men will be sacrificed to military incompetency before hostilities cease, but Secession is a danger of the past. I doubt if it could succeed now even with foreign aid, but this is our greatest danger, and the Navy shares with the State Department the task of preventing international complications. Our ship is on this Station, like the ships of other nations on foreign stations, as an adjunct to the diplomatic machinery of the government whose flag we fly. Through our Navy Department and through our consuls I have been kept in touch with our State Department. That is one reason why I feel able to speak as confidently as I have regarding the present status of Secession."

After delivering himself thus, as nearly as I can recall his words, he stopped abruptly as though he had intended to say something more, but decided not to. After a brief pause he arose, extended his hand, saying, "I assure you of my good wishes," and indicated by his customary Commodore Thatcher manner that I was to consider the interview ended.

July 7
Spezia

The olive oil is coming aboard and is being put in the tanks. This replaces whale oil for our lamps and other lights. Paint oil is also being drawn off and put into tanks. This makes a dirty mess in the Store Room.

The Consul-General came aboard and was received with the customary salute.

News reports dated June 21 state that Harpers Ferry has been taken by the Rebels[5] and that they are marching on northward ninety thousand strong opposed only by the militia.

July 9
Spezia

Everybody was cross this morning because turned out at four o'clock. The reason was unknown. No work except the regular washing of the decks was done until after eight o'clock. The men attribute this order as a desire for some purpose to make them uncomfortable. If so it certainly succeeds. It is so hot below decks that they get little sleep until towards morning when it cools off a little. The air on the berth deck is also very offensive with so many men sleeping there in hot weather.

July 10
Spezia

The raid into Pennsylvania is not of much advantage to the Rebels. General Hooker will probably cut them off. The surrender of Vicksburg seems to be only a question of terms now. No fear of Johnston is apparent. The Federal rear and flanks are too well protected. The Rebel ironclads have been destroyed by our boats. It took only six or seven shots to do the business. General Stewart with a cavalry force has also been defeated.[6]

July 11
Spezia

This is a lovely day and not as warm as usual because there is a good breeze. The Commodore is absent and there is no inspection.

In the afternoon Mr. Hunter and I took a sail and landed at "Boy Jack's" where we returned for supper after a walk about the Bay as far as The Store House. After supper we met Mr. Philbrick and we all went to Spezia where we met Mr. Tatem and spent the evening with him, returning to the ship at five bells.

July 13
Spezia

The Italian papers say that General Hooker is concentrating his forces around Washington; that General Lee has his headquarters at Frederick City, Pa,[7] 10,000 strong.

Commodore Thatcher returned this morning bringing with him Captain Stellwagen who also has his own son with him. The Commodore is making arrangements to leave immediately for the United States. It seems quite probable that our ship will remain on this Station three years from what our new Captain is reported as saying.

July 14
Spezia

The new Captain has not made his official appearance yet. It is rumored that Commodore Thatcher will accompany us to Marseilles, but I think this improbable.

Our band is being exercised more than is agreeable. I think that they make music more than half the day.

The men are having liberty in small numbers.

July 15
Spezia

This morning Captain Stellwagen came on board in citizen's dress. His son was with him.

Lieut.-Commanders W.W. Low and R.R. Wallace are to be relieved and return home. So it seems that a thorough change is to be made in the government of this ship. Whether or not it will prove of advantage, it will be hailed with delight by all hands.

After supper I went ashore, landing at the lower village, and walked to Spezia and returned on board at eleven o'clock.

July 16
Spezia

Captain Stellwagen and his son came on board this morning. After dinner the Governor visited the ship and was received with an appropriate salute. The Rebels are reported to be within thirty miles of Philadelphia.

The Revenue Cutter *Caleb Cushing* was taken by the Rebels in Portland harbor. They boarded her from a fishing schooner, the *Archer*, which they had captured in the Bay of Fundy. They got out of the harbor with the Cutter, but were pursued and captured by two armed steamers, the *Forrest City* and the *Chesapeake*. The Rebels put up a fight. Before surrendering they set fire to the Cutter and she blew up. She was well armed and quite a formidable craft. Her Captain was killed in the fighting.

July 17
Spezia

It is reported that General Meade has had a fight of three days with General Lee and that the latter has been repulsed.

July 18
Spezia

This forenoon Captain Stellwagen called all hands to muster and read his order from Secretary Welles to assume command of this ship. After doing so he said that Commodore Thatcher gave the crew a good name; that he hoped that no crime or misdemeanor would occur on the ship, and that for the present, at least, all existing regulations and orders for the government of the ship would remain in force. Thereupon he assumed command of the ship.

I know nothing about Captain Stellwagen except his hydrographic work. He appears to be a frank, business-like, straight-forward kind of a man. His son who is to be his clerk is about twenty two years old.

Three men who overstayed their liberty were brought on board by the police.

July 19
Spezia

This morning Captain Stellwagen inspected the ship. He made a very thorough examination of every part of it, not excepting the "Brig," or prison which is seldom without occupants. When about to enter the one which contains the "sweat boxes" better known as the "catacombs," Mr. Low said, "This is used only in cold weather." How far from the truth! The truth is that the hottest nights are selected to put men into them for punishment, because in cool weather confinement in them is not considered punishment. If he had been disposed to tell the whole truth he would have added, "We sometimes hang a leaky bucket of lime water over the head of a prisoner and allow the 'white wash' to drain down slowly onto him so as to spoil his clothes and annoy him. We think that it also tends to improve discipline to laugh at him as though it were a good joke when he is brought up on deck after his confinement."

In the afternoon I went on shore with Sergeant Robbins. We walked around to old Porto Venire. The day was very warm. We sat down on the cliff by the old church at the headland and watched the sea breaking against the rocks. This place always calls up memories of Julius Caesar the ruins of whose works we still see about us here. At sunset we returned to town and had a supper of eggs and fish for which we were charged double the worth. We paid and walked away feeling that Americans can afford to pay more than anybody else "because they are rich."

Provisions are coming aboard and the men are breaking out the hold to take account of those on hand.

Captain Stellwagen is making a careful examination into every department of the ship. He has ordered that all work shall cease at seven bells except in emergencies, declaring that work after supper is a nuisance on a ship. He inquired regarding the practice of working at night.

According to a telegram received by Mr. Low from Lieut. Abbot who is in Genoa, he will be here at ten o'clock tomorrow to relieve Mr. Low.

It is reported as quite certain that our Naval steamships *Niagra*, *Susquehanna* and *Shammocken* are coming here.

July 21
Spezia

Lieut. Abbot came on board this morning. Mr. Low is packing up. Wood, stores, and provisions are being received on board.

Vicksburg is reported to have surrendered unconditionally. General Lee is reported to have been severely whipped. Like all similar reports they lack confirmation.[8]

This afternoon Commodore Thatcher took his leave without any ceremony and Mr. Low in the same manner soon followed him.

The petty officers went to the mast to see the Commodore before he left in relation to replacing the "scouse kettles" which were destroyed last winter. He replied that he did not know that they not been replaced and that he would see Captain Stellwagen and have it done. Apparently however he said nothing to Captain Stellwagen about the matter before leaving the ship. The men could not believe that the Commodore did not know that the kettles had not been replaced and they regard conduct in the whole matter as unmanly.

Perhaps no cheers were asked for the Commodore as he left because it was feared that the response would have been so feeble as to be really disrespectful. I doubt if there would have been much of a response to such a request. It is most unusual for a commanding officer of a ship to leave without being given rousing cheers by his men. The bearing of the Commodore as he left was that of a man who realized that he did not have the confidence and respect of his crew and felt that he might not have done his duty in looking out for their welfare. None of the remarks which I heard our men make regarding the Commodore and our late Executive indicated a high estimate of their character or ability as Naval Officers, but invariably a contemptuous feeling toward them. It must be very unpleasant for men to leave a ship as these two did with the consciousness that they had been failures in the positions of responsibility which they occupied, for the attitude of the crew toward them as they left really meant nothing less.

Mr. Abbot is a man of different bearing from Mr. Low. Mr. Abbot is deliberate and quiet yet authoritative in his manner and shows the heritage of a gentleman.[9] A capable man has succeeded to Mr. Low's position, if I can judge from appearances. Everybody feels more comfortable as he leaves the ship and no one, so far as I know, will regret the change.

As Mr. Low went over the side—it was during the dinner hour—some men who chanced to be in the starboard gangway made groans and other disrespectful sounds. While this was indicative of the general feeling toward him the demonstration was disapproved by many of the crew as being in bad taste. They contended that absolute silence in watching his departure would have been a more effective rebuke.[10]

When the crew of the gig took the Commodore ashore they naturally expected the five or ten dollars which it is customary for a commanding officer to give his gig's crew when he leaves a ship as a sort of recognition of the many hours of loss of sleep and physical discomfort in all sorts of weather which they have suffered at boat landings ashore awaiting convenience, but "nary a red" did they get. Instead the Commodore said that he would not bid them "goodbye" for he expected to see them again in three months, apparently intending to have them to infer that he would join them again on this station. Perhaps he regarded this as a practical application of diplomacy.

July 22
Spezia

It is astonishing to observe how great a change has taken place in our ship's company, fore and aft. Everyone seems to breathe freely. Everything goes on more quietly, and with a will. All are glad that the two chief officers have left the ship and that men of <u>more</u> <u>apparent</u> <u>worth</u> have succeeded them.

A man was sent to the mast today for growling at work. Mr. Abbot said to him, "Go and do your work like a man. If you give me any further trouble I may have to report you to the Captain to determine what shall be done with you." This had a better effect on the man and on the crew than 12 hours confinement in the "catacombs."

This is the first time that a man on this ship has been informed that his conduct would be referred to the Captain for consideration. No matter of discipline ever went further than the Executive for adjudication who hurried the unfortunate off to summary punishment, often without permitting the accused to make any statement. It remains to be seen how the new regime is going to work with our crew, but I am glad to see the ship governed by men of a different character.

News is received by telegraph that the steamer *Southerner*, lately built in England, has arrived in the Mediterranean.[11]

In the evening I went on shore and spent a few hours with Messrs. Hunter and Philbrick at the residence of Colonel William L. Long. He has a fine residence, beautifully furnished and containing numerous paintings. He is an old bachelor, a jovial companion and an old resident of Italy. He has long been Navy Store Keeper here.

July 23
Spezia

The papers contain the report of the defeat of General Lee with the loss of 30,000 men.

After dinner preparations are made to go to sea. The boats are hoisted and before supper everything was made ready to sail before supper, not being left as formerly to be done by night work.

July 24
Spezia

This morning the mail arrived for which we were waiting last night. The defeat of General Lee is confirmed. 116 pieces of artillery were captured and over 20,000 prisoners taken. General Longstreet was killed. The Rebel retreat is cut off and the whole army likely to be captured. Jeff Davis was with Lee's army, but had left. The fighting was most desperate and whole regiments were sacrificed.[12]

About noon we left Spezia on our way to Marseilles. Never before since the ship went into commission have the men worked with such snap as when we got under way. Topsails were hoisted with a <u>will</u> in record time. In sixteen minutes the anchor was weighed and the ship moving under sail. Mr. Wallace looked on in a sort of sneering amazement. It was evident that he realized that the crew were showing what they could do as a rebuke to him and his late departed but unlamented colleague. Officers have to command the regard and respect of their men to get the best service out of them.

As we passed out of the bay we saw a large steam ship of war under sail apparently intending to enter, but soon she took in her courses and stood on the wind as though waiting for us. This indicated that she was the *Southerner* as we had suspected and was waiting to give us battle. We went to quarters and stood toward her. Soon we saw that she showed the Italian flag, but we kept on and worked to the windward of her thinking that the Italian flag might be a ruse. Not until we approached very close did we feel sure that she was Italian and not a Rebel craft. Our men were very eager for a fight. I do not know what we could have done with a steam ship like this one, but before she had finished us they would have known that they had been in a fight.

Our musicians who for the first time are experiencing the motions of a ship are laid out in all places unfit for service and their harps "hung on the willows" where they seem likely to remain until the sea becomes smoother.

July 25
At sea
This morning we are not far from Genoa with a fine breeze and banging into a heavy head sea. Our studding-sails are set. The air is refreshing after the heat at Spezia.

A French brig wishes to speak us and we heave to. The Captain wants to know our position. The coast is in sight. Later in the day the wind dies out. The ship is cleaned as usual in every part and we have a very quiet day. The bench of the Carpenter and the forge of the gunner are taken out of sight and the ship does not have so much the appearance of a workshop.

A spirit of peace and contentment prevails on the ship.

July 26
At sea
A beautiful Sabbath morning. General Muster and Divine Service on the spar deck. The custom today of reading prayers is an improvement on our old custom—those who are present do not feel that it is for an exclusive class.

In the afternoon top-sails are reefed. Our flying jib is blown to pieces by the parting of the rope on the after leech. Before sunset the wind is gone and the rough sea tosses our ship around without steerage way. We are in the Gulf of Lyons.

July 27
At sea
This morning we are in sight of Toulon, with a light wind and at noon about fifty miles from Marseilles.

July 28
Marseilles
This morning we are within sight of the old lighthouse of Marseilles and the pilot is aboard, but there is little prospect of entering the harbor until this afternoon when the sea breeze sets in. It comes about noon and we start up to the harbor in company with numerous other square-rigged vessels. We outsail and pass all of them.

The entrance to the harbor is spacious and well provided with lighthouses, one of which is located on an artificial island about ten miles out in the bay. The land about the harbor is of a dull white color suggesting a limestone formation. The coast is prominent and well defined, but not so high as the Italian coast.

We receive reports to the effect that Port Hudson and Morris Island in Charleston Harbor are captured; also that a riot has occurred in New York. Colonel O'Brien was hung to a lamp post by the mob. Negroes were driven out of the city and many of them killed. The Governor informed the President that he could not enforce the conscription act.[13]

A similar distrubance occurred in Boston in connection with the enforcement of the conscription act, but it was suppressed.

General Lee has made his escape into Virginia.

The Mexicans are to vote for their form of government the 29th. General James has embarked for New York.

July 29
Marseilles

This morning the U.S. Consul and his lady visited the ship.[14] I had a long talk with him in the Store Room after learning that he knows some of my friends in New York.

We saluted him as well as the French flag. This consumes the last of our saluting powder. Until we get a new supply we will have to use our best quality powder for this purpose.

July 31
Marseilles

The Captain and the First Lieutenant return from the city with a party of ladies who are entertained at luncheon after which there is a dance on the spar deck.

I obtained permission to go ashore and was accompanied by Mr. Grainger, the Gunner and the two Master's Mates. We all took rooms at the Hotel Restaurant de Marseilles. The son-in-law of the proprietor and his wife have both lived in the United States and speak English.

When walking near the Consulate we met the Consul accompanied by a Mr. ——(?) of Ohio who "is traveling for his health" and to whom Mr. Grainger was introduced by the Consul as Mr. Jackson of South Carolina and I as Mr. Vallandingham of New York. We all sat down in a nearby café where we were joined by two of the Consul's friends. Taking a hint from the Consul Mr. Grainger and I started a political argument which became so hot that the Consul had to separate us and thereupon the supposed Mr. Jackson challenged me to a duel which I promptly accepted and asked the Ohioan to act as my second and refused to consider his excuses for not wishing to do so. After we had succeeded in making the Ohioan feel very uncomfortable the Consul and his friends managed to establish a sort of armistice between the supposed "Mr. Jackson" and myself. A few minutes later when Mr. Grainger and I arose and said good bye to the party and started off amicably together the Ohioan realized that his feelings had been stirred by "horse play," and joined heartily in the general laugh. As a result he accepted our invitation to join us in seeing the sights of the city. Among them was the Zoological Garden which is most artistically laid out and contains specimens of many species of animals.

The Ohioan was good company and when he left us in the evening he said that he had not had so much fun since he left home.

August 1
Marseilles

This morning after breakfast we left the hotel to return to the ship, but tarried on the way at the bath houses near the mouth of the harbor opposite the Chateau d'If, where was confined the *Man With the Iron Mask* and also made famous by M. Dumas' *Comte de Monte-Christo*. After having a good swim we reached the ship at 12 M.

The rest of the day passes quietly and pleasantly on the ship as it usually does after a trip on shore. One seems in a new place on returning to the ship after an absence of a day or two. The ship looks so clean and attractive.

August 2
Marseilles

After dinner I went on shore with Messrs. Grainger, Philbrick, Miller, and Cox. We called at our favorite hotel and had refreshments and then went to the Amphitheater or Hippodrome to witness the contest between several wrestlers. One match was for a purse of $60.

The manner of wrestling was new to me and I think peculiar to the country. Many men were present to see the sport—if such it may be called. To me much of it was dull and uninteresting. The liveliest contest was between the champion of Marseilles and a traveling wrestler. It was decided in a short time in favor of the Marseillais who finally tossed his opponent in the air and slammed him down on his back. After the exhibition was over we met and congratulated the champion. He and his friends were very proud that the championship remained in Marseilles.

I hear of a sad accident to one of the boats of Captain Swanton's ship, the *Holyhead*, which lay in Genoa with us last winter. The ship was loading in the Black Sea with railroad ties for Marseilles. The boat which was returning to the ship was in some way capsized and Mr. Baker, the Second Officer, and a contractor and five seamen were drowned. A boy saved himself by swimming to the ship.

August 4

We leave Marseilles. The wind is light and the sea smooth. The atmosphere is very damp. I am sick and apparently have a high fever. I can scarcely attend to the making out of my monthly reports.

August 5
At sea

I had a queer time last night. I was living a French life all over France. I suspect that I was delirious. I feel somewhat better today, but unfit for work. I seem to have a violent cold.

The ship is damp throughout. Dew falls day and night. This is the most humid climate that I have ever seen. The sails gather moisture during the day.

August 6
At sea

We are bound for Barcelona. I am still sick, do nothing and eat little, but feel somewhat better and think that I will be well again in a few days.

August 7

I feel somewhat better and eat something, but my head troubles me badly. The coast is in sight and a pretty country with some large towns are to be seen. The large buildings and the tall chimneys in the vicinity of Barcelona would indicate a busy manufacturing district.

Unlike Mr. Low, our present Executive when on deck watching the crew does not write down the names of men on the wristbands of his shirt so as to remember them for the blacklist. If men sit on the boom-cover he does not punish them for it. "What harm does it do?" he asked, when a Master's Mate handed him a list of such offenders.

August 8
Barcelona

After muster I went on shore with Augusto Bartolini, the leader of our band. He claims to speak Catalan which is the popular brand of Spanish here as well as at Mahon. We rambled about the city and took in the plazas, public buildings, gardens and cafés.

Barcelona is a very handsome city and compares favorably with Marseilles if it does not excel the latter in its general claims to beauty. There is not so much life and gaiety here; there is the air of dignity and reserve characteristic of Spanish cities and which tells you that this is not France. The streets are clean, well paved and wide. The restaurants or cafés are attractive and well managed and among them is one said to be the largest in Europe. The shops appear to be stocked with all sorts of goods. One is impressed with the wide variety of fans exhibited for sale. A Spanish lady and her fan are inseparable and to judge from the shop windows she might be expected to have a special style for every occasion.

There are numerous artistic public fountains about the city.

We visited an old church, the Santa Maria del Mar, which contains some remarkable specimens of stained glass art.

The "Rambla" is an important street. It extends for more than a mile straight through the city. It is very wide with a mall in the middle and is shaded by large trees.

We dined in a fashionable restaurant at a reasonable price.

August 11
Barcelona
We are watering ship and making ready to leave.

I am troubled with dyspepsia which is a new experience for me. It is probably the result of my recent sickness.

An American captain has been killed in Valencia by a Spanish Customs-House officer on board his own vessel. We are to go there.

General Prim visited the ship today and has invited our Captain to attend the theater this evening to see a play which is to be a special social event of the season. General Prim commanded the Spanish forces in Mexico, acting in conjunction with the French and the English.

August 12
Barcelona
It is reported that Jeff Davis has asked for peace. I do not believe it. It would be good news for all if peace could be effected on a firm basis. At 5 p.m. we get under way for Valencia. We have the U.S. Consul on board.[15]

August 13
At sea
We are floating around in a calm. It has been excessively hot in port and is now just as hot at sea.

A Ward Room steward, John Castle deserted at Barcelona. He is indebted to the Paymaster and others are complaining of being out on his account.

During the evening the band on the poop and the viol on the forecastle furnish entertainment for everybody. The men waltz and dance and enjoy themselves. It is only comfortable on deck. It is stifling below.

August 14
At sea

This morning early we passed a life-buoy and some say that what appeared to be the body of a man was seen just before floating past us. The body was not picked up as I should have supposed, but was allowed to float by although practically alongside.

Calm and light head wind. We make no progress all day. How awfully dull is a calm at sea! How hot too. Gracious Heavens, one can scarcely live!

At night the berth deck is like a baker's oven. I remain on deck half the night, half dreaming, half thinking, with my face upturned gazing at the sky.

August 15
At sea

This morning the men are talking of the peculiar maneuvers which a steamship performed around us during the night. Some expected her to attack us. When daylight came she was not to be seen. It might have been a Rebel ship looking for a load of coal—or a coal vessel looking for a pirate ship. Yesterday we showed the French flag to a Spanish brig.

This afternoon we stand in close to land. I notice a high rocky promontory on which a town is built. It seems to be connected with the mainland by a long narrow isthmus. The wind is ahead and light all day. We gain very little on our course.

August 17
Valencia

We had a good breeze last night and it continues this morning and we anchor off Valencia, just outside the breakwater.

The water is not deep enough to allow us to enter the harbor. Only 16 feet can be carried over the bar.

An American ship, the *Inspector*, lies at anchor outside and five others inside the harbor.

The day is as warm as usual. I am scarcely able to do my duty. I feel very weak and can eat nothing.

The wind blows a gale and we pitch and roll heavily at anchor as though at sea. I feel a little better this morning. I took no medicine last night. The Doctor's men were on shore or not to be found. Neither they nor the doctors ever seem to be available if needed. What humbugs doctors are. It seems strange that more has not been learned about health and the human body in the three or four thousand years which men have had an opportunity to study these matters. The doctors today do not seem to know any more, if as much, as was known at the time of Moses and what he knew was probably common knowledge among the ancient Egyptians. It seems as though our present day doctors lose faith in their own teachings and reconcile themselves to being plain frauds, claiming special exemption from that personal accountability to which men in any other trade, profession or business are customarily held.

So far as the sailors are concerned the medical department of a ship is something which they would be just as well off without. The expense of anything which would be of benefit to a man, no matter how small the expense, is to the doctors always a sufficient reason for not doing it. Our doctors have not even the gumption to commute the ration of a man in the sick bay to purchase something proper for him to eat. They tell a sick man what he shall eat and shall not eat, but they make no effort to see that he may get what they prescribe. They tell him that he must not eat salt pork, but he must eat it or starve.

Both Captain James Cook and Lord Collingwood have demonstrated what can be done to benefit the health of sailors on ships. As nearly as I can learn their methods were their own deductions, most surely not the prescriptions of the medical profession.

This evening Tom Mahoney, Ship's Corporal had an altercation with Joseph James growing out of a "work up job" and Mahoney received a cut across the left cheek. Quite a feeling exists among the berth deck cooks who are generally admitted to be an abused class, James is confined in irons. There the matter stands.

August 19
Valencia

This is an anniversary that I never forget. Seven years ago today a kind mother stooped with me over the bedside to catch the last words of my dying father. It is now nearly three years since her mother's care for her children also ceased—unless the spirits of the dead are still mindful of the welfare of the living whom they have loved. It would be a comfort to me today if I knew that this was so. I am barely able to attend to any duty. I have spent most of the time reclining on the deck with a couple of life buoys beneath me. What a luxury would be a bed and a quiet chamber at home away from the harassing turmoil of this ship! But here I am and it would only make me feel worse to entertain such thoughts. Instead I try to imagine that I never had a better place to rest, certainly thousands today who are also sick and miserable are not nearly so comfortable as I. Why should I complain?

There is little news. The latest accounts say that the attack on Charleston was unsuccessful. The fighting at Fort Wagner was most desperate.[16]

The establishment of a French Empire in Mexico seems to be stirring up considerable feeling in the United States. No one can foretell to what consequences the French policy will lead.

August 20
Valencia

Last night I never felt sicker in my life and I went to the Doctor. The visit tended to confirm my belief that the less one has to do with Doctors the better he will be off in the long run. The old fraud asked me if I had been eating pork. I replied that I had eaten very little recently. Then he prescribed for me a medicine for worms! It is evident to me that I have contracted some sort of a remittent fever, probably something peculiar to this part of the world and it does not seem unreasonable to expect a man supposed to have a medical education to recognize what it is even though he may not be able to do anything for it.[17] As a ship captain my father was a stern disciplinarian, but he took an interest in sailors who were sick and tried to do something for them, although what he did might perhaps not always have been for the best. Treating the sick was not his business, yet I cannot help contrasting his attitude toward a sailor in need of medical care with the indifference and humbug of those whose professed business is to take care of the sick.

I retired early and perspired freely and felt better this morning and this afternoon much better.

We receive numerous visitors to the ship today, among them the captains and mates of several American ships in port. Some of the captains have their wives with them. Mr. Perry our Minister at Madrid also came on board in connection with the murder on the American ship here.[18]

It seems that he met a lieutenant of our ship and our Lieutenant of Marines on shore and told them who he was and asked that a message be taken to our Captain to meet the U.S. Minister at a designated place on shore. Our officers declined to forward the message until the Minister should establish his identity to their satisfaction and subjected him to some cross questioning which did not indicate either good breeding or common sense on their part. They finally accepted an old soiled visiting card as proof of his identity. The Minister related his experience to the Captain in amusement rather than in the way of complaint, but I am told that the Captain is considerably provoked at what he regards as an "exhibition of asininity" on the part of Naval Officers.

August 21
Valencia

I feel much better today. I have lost considerable weight and look sick but think that I will now soon improve so as to be able to go on shore with pleasure.

The local American Consul[19] dined aboard with some of his friends. He was saluted with some Spanish powder that made no report. Only two guns charged with American powder made any noise. The Spanish powder is damaged, it is claimed. They would sell dirt for powder. The Paymaster bought this powder. The Gunner who usually attends to this matter did not even have a chance to test the so-called powder.

A sailor belonging to an American ship came to see our Captain in relation to the payment of the wages of himself and his shipmates who were inveigled on board, "worked up" the whole passage and then turned on shore without pay. It does not appear why the Consul and our Minister should not have straightened out this matter without obliging the men to appeal to the Captain of a Naval ship.

The practice of maltreating seamen seems to be on the increase. There are other examples of it here. The Captain of the ship *Inspector* has been up to something of the sort. When he saw our ship come in a guilty conscience caused him to run away leaving his wife and his interests in the ship of which he is part owner, to the mate.

Another American Captain is under arrest on his own ship.

The man who was shot by the Spanish here was a <u>mate</u> not a captain. He belonged to the ship *Chas. D. Martin* of Boston. He went on board another ship to help to quell a disturbance that arose in connection with the mooring of the ship. An anchor to moor the ship was being taken out to the designated place by a scow in charge of Spaniards and by accident was lost overboard. The Spaniards on the scow regarded it as a great joke and some Spanish soldiers stationed on the ship by Customs House authority joined in the laugh. The Captain of the ship and a visiting Captain forcibly resented the amusement of the Spaniards and before the melee between the Spaniards and the Americans was over the mate of the *Marvin* had been shot and killed.

August 22
Valencia

Last evening a squabble occurred on the forecastle in which Mr. Miller, the Master's Mate, became involved. He tried to stop a fight between two men and others who had been drinking joined in and one of them, Rutland, got Mr. Miller by the throat. Following the affair a considerable number of men were around the mast and when ordered to disperse by Mr. Wallace hooted at him. This occurrence shows a spirit which cannot be tolerated and I am confident that our Captain will find the proper corrective. Rutland is now in the Brig in irons.

August 23
Valencia

This is a delightful day and very comfortable.

Evans returned on board on his own hook, although a reward had been offered for him. He was dressed in a corporal of Marines' uniform and presented a very soldier-like appearance. He exchanged clothes with a shipmate. Ludicrous incidents often happen in connection with sailors' liberty parties.

On my way to shore this noon I visited the ship *Chas. D. Martin* to see if I knew anybody on board.

At Grao, the port of Valencia, there is an extensive and popular bathing beach patronized by the people of Valencia. Grao is also the landing place from shipping. In consequence one cannot look about there without being overwhelmed by carriage drivers soliciting his patronage, for one must hire a carriage to go to Valencia.

One finds a peculiar sort of vehicle here. It has two wheels which turn in a plane about ten degrees off the vertical, the top of the wheel being about that much out beyond the part on the ground. It is drawn by one horse. The driver sits on one of the thills. The body of the vehicle rests on the axle without springs. It is covered, usually with an enameled cloth. Inside there is straw on the floor and two seats run fore and aft along the sides. They accommodate eight passengers. One enters and leaves by the rear, stepping on a bow bent down from the frame work supporting the body.

The distance to Valencia is about three miles. The road is level and straight, but one of these vehicles will give the passenger over this road a jolting and shaking that will tend to make him lose his dinner if he has lately dined.

All along the route large shade trees overhang the road, and the neat white stone dwellings with their thatched roofs contrast pleasingly with the green fields and foliage about them. The country gives evidence of great fertility.

After crossing a large stone bridge over the Guardalaviar the vehicle is examined by a Customs officer and then passes on to the gate through which one enters this ancient walled city.

From the tower of the large Cathedral I obtained a splendid view of the city and adjoining country for a distance of fifteen miles. It was an attractive panorama of fertile fields, green foliage and luxuriant crops, studded with neat white buildings. The Cathedral is the largest on the floor that I have ever seen. It contains many paintings and other features of interest.

The most extensive modern building in the city is the amphitheater where the bull fights take place. In one such exhibition about two weeks ago between twenty and thirty old worn out horses met their end with considerable suffering, I am told. The structure is of brick, but similar in general character to the Colosseum of ancient Rome with window like open spaces at regular intervals along the walls. It is capable of seating 15,000 people.

After seeing some of the other interesting sights of this city I returned to Grao to take the sunset boat to the ship. I found a strong wind blowing directly from the sea into the port. There was a party of officers on shore and there were twenty six of us in all which the boat had to convey to the ship or swamp. It was dark when we started. Like the others I got drenched with salt water, but we finally reached the ship without any more serious mishap. In this we were really fortunate for in his desire to frighten Mr. Wallace whom he disliked, Jack Ripley, the captain of the main top, acting as coxswain of the boat, jeopardized the lives of all of us repeatedly by his slowness in luffing when squalls struck us. So far as anybody could detect however Ripley's efforts to disturb our Lieutenant Commander were a complete failure. He did not appear even to be interested and made no attempt to interfere with Ripley's management, or rather mismanagement, of the boat which kept men constantly bailing. Mr. Wallace certainly gave his men a remarkable demonstration of self control.

August 24
At sea

This morning we started out with a light breeze, but by afternoon we were under reefed topsails running on our course to Malaga at the rate of eleven knots. It seems good to be out again on the open sea with a strong breeze. I must admit that I like the sea, especially after I have been ashore a while dealing with dishonest people.

August 25
At sea

Beating all day against a head wind with the island of Iviza in sight. Towards evening the wind increased with the prospect of a gale. We reefed topsails and after the jib was blown away furled the mainsail.

August 26
At sea

Still beating against a strong head wind. We are not so fortunate now with respect to fair winds as when Commodore Thatcher sailed this ship, for the wind now is usually ahead while Commodore Thatcher generally had fair wind. The sailors say that he took all the fair winds with him. This evening Cape Palos is just abeam of us to the leeward.

August 27
At sea

Last night topsails were reefed, the wind being ahead and blowing fresh. This morning all sail is set. Several ships are in sight and three close by. Every one has studding sails set and is enjoying a fair wind but ourselves. We are still pegging away against a strong head wind. An old quartermaster told me that the wind came fair once last night, but the Captain and the First Lieutenant appeared on deck and the wind immediately changed to dead ahead again. He thinks that we will have no more fair winds while they are in the ship.

August 29
At sea

Last night we were under double reefed topsails, reefed foresail and furled mainsail with the wind blowing a gale. The gale still continues and the sea is rough. Our ship creaks and snaps like an old corn basket as we keep her close hauled in the heavy sea. Rough as it is the decks are holystoned as usual and everything goes on the same.

I finish the reading of Virgil's *Aeneid* in which I have been interested for some time.

August 30
At sea

This morning finds us in a smooth sea off Cape de Gata near the land. In the afternoon two boats from shore came alongside with fruit to sell. They wanted $5 for four watermelons and their prices were proportionately high for other fruit. They promised to bring us some potatoes in the morning.

August 31
At sea

Very little wind. We make only 25 miles all day, but are working against a three knots current. Several square rigged vessels are in sight at dark.

The evening is delightful. It is calm. How still a man-of-war is on such a night as this! Who would believe after observing the bustle and turmoil of the day that 300 men could be so quiet at night and with half of them "on watch." Part of the secret is that most of them on deck are also curled up asleep. It takes but little to arouse this nest of sleeping men. a bursting shell—the first beat of the drum calling to general quarters—would make this ship seem like a greatly magnified hornets' nest which a boy had struck with a stone. The ship would at once be filled with a mass of hurrying men, butting and bumping their heads in the dark, a jamming of gangways and hatchways by men going in opposite directions, dressing and arming themselves, as they go, each on his way to his proper station and no one disposed to allow consideration for the convenience of others or regard for the safety of their heads or limbs to delay his arrival where he is expected to report for duty.

September 1
At sea

This morning finds us not far from where we were at sunset last night. The wind is light and variable.

A Court Martial is in session trying Joseph W. James for assault with a knife on Thomas Mahoney, ship's corporal, and Joseph W. Low for drunkenness when on duty as coxswain.

It is announced that because of the hooting at Lieutenant Commander Wallace when he ordered men from the mast, the Captain has decided to bring every act of disorderly conduct before a Court Martial.

We are in need of provisions for our mess as are most of the other messes aft. I hope that we will soon reach some place where we can find something to eat. This has been a most tedious passage considering the distance to sail.

I feel very well these days—much better than for several weeks.

September 2
At sea

We have a fine breeze this morning and had to double reef topsails—but the wind is ahead as all good breezes are this passage. We are in company with several ships and barks and are outsailing them all.

About 4 p.m. we stand in close to land near Almonecan. It appears to be a town of considerable size. We can see what seem to be sugar mills and wine factories.

Three short years ago today my kind mother died. It was the Sabbath. I well remember how beautiful everything in nature appeared. Everything appeared cheerful but me.

September 3
Malaga

At ten a.m. we anchored outside the harbor of Malaga about a mile from shore.

We receive reports that since France has occupied Mexico and evinced a greater disposition to aid the South, Great Britain has become more disposed to support the North. The *Florida* is still going and has been committing depredations on our commerce in the English Channel. At last accounts she was coaling at Brest.[20]

Fruit in abundance is being offered for sale and much needed provisions are coming off to the ship.

September 4
Malaga

During the forenoon the Governor, with two military officers of distinction and the French and American Consuls, were received on board. Each received an appropriate salute.

The prices of fruit and provisions here are exorbitant and the fruit is inferior in quality to that which we found at Valencia.

All hands are busy painting the ship on the outside and repairing rigging.

September 5
Malaga

Last night I had a dream which has made a very profound impression on me, but lest I appear credulous in respect to such matters I will not mention its character, but I cannot forget it.

In the afternoon our Captain went on shore and soon afterward he sent a message to the First Lieutenant to the effect that our Charge d'Affaires at Madrid reports that France has recognized the Confederacy.

September 6
Malaga

The report that France has recognized the Confederacy is causing much talk on the ship and many speculations regarding the events to which it may lead and how it may affect future movements of our ship.

After dinner I went on shore with Mr. Fletcher, Master's Mate. We hired a carriage for a ride and the driver took us to the Campo Santo, the public cemetery. Apparently this is regarded as one of the attractions of the place as are the catacombs at Palermo.

The Campo Santo is enclosed by a heavy wall inside of which and directly in contact with it are built vaults to hold the bodies of the dead. The vaults look something like ovens. They are five tiers or stories high and have an arched top. The body is pushed through a small doorway which is then sealed up and covered with a piece of marble bearing the usual gravestone inscription. The vaults are entirely above the ground. In the center of the cemetery tombs of a different character and private burial lots with pretentious monuments.

The cemetery is laid out in an artistic manner with weeping willows and shade trees and flower beds, all of which are well cared for.

From here the driver took us to the "English Burying Ground" at the east of the city. I noticed the monument of a midshipman, Coddington, of the U.S. Navy. If one may judge from the inscriptions many foreign young men have come to Malaga in an unsuccessful search for health.

The city is unattractive. The streets are narrow and crooked. There are some very good buildings, of which the Cathedral and the Customs House are worthy of mention. The former is an extensive edifice which was commenced by Philip II after his marriage with Mary of England.

The women of Malaga have a reputation for beauty, but I cannot see that they are any better looking than the women of Barcelona or Valencia.

The trade of the place has been nearly destroyed by our war. It is said that formerly it was not unusual for twenty or thirty vessels to leave port in a single day for the United States, laden with fruit and wine. Now there is only one ship in port flying the American flag. There are however still several sailing between here and the United States under the British flag.

There are beggars at every corner and they fill the doorways of public buildings. Some are licensed by the government and others appear to be plying their vocation on their own account. Some have a piece of wood strapped to the back of the hand and forearm to hold the arm steady while they crawl over the sidewalk to intercept pedestrians. Naked children are often seen in the streets.

September 9
Malaga
It seems that France only recognized the Southern States as "belligerents." This is no worse than Great Britain did at the beginning of the war.

Two of our officers who went to the city of Grenada have returned. They say that the visit was very interesting and well worth the trouble.

September 10
Malaga
The Captain, the Surgeon and Mr. Wallace returned today from the Alhambra dusty and tired.

September 11
At sea
We sail early with a fair wind. At noon the Rock is in sight. At sunset we are within ten miles of it. It is about sixty miles from Malaga. At nine p.m. we anchor off Algeciras.

September 12
Algeciras
This evening a packet loaded with an assorted cargo for the officers came from Gibraltar. This is a good place to stock up with cigars etc. and I secured a supply.

September 13
Algeciras
Last night the wind increased to a strong gale. At eight bells we let go the port bower anchor and prepared to send down the top-gallant masts, but found it unnecessary to do so as the wind abated.

Our distance from the shore is so short that we have little room to drift. Three ships of war drifted from Gibraltar half way to us. The Italian frigate *Eurydice* lost one of her boats from the boom.

Thick clouds hung over the Rock. No boats can land at Algeciras on account of the surf.

Some of those trying to sleep on the berth deck last night received surprises unpleasant to them but amusing to others. The berth deck air ports were open as is customary in port. As it became rough and the ship began to tumble about Boatswain Hunter was awakened by a stream of water the full size of the air port which came in and struck him in the chest and face.[21] A wave dashing through the open air port in the Dispensary doused the Doctor's Steward who was sleeping there, soaked his desk and papers and made it necessary for Smith to give up sleep and start bailing out the room. A wave came through another port and over the "bag rack" and struck "Boy" Hurley and filled his hammock with water.

It is too rough for the boats to land ashore. The ship is pitching and rolling and everybody is trying to take advantage of the weather to sleep.

September 14
Algeciras

The gale still continues and quiet prevails on the ship. The general diversion today seems to be the drinking of ale. Unless we find work to do soon or go to sea a new supply will be needed. Dark clouds are rolling over the Rock bringing thunder and lightning and violent squalls.

My diversion is the reading of Bayard Taylor's *Travels in Central Africa*.

At seven bells p.m. the "messenger" is brought up. This is a sign of an unmooring of the ship.

September 15
Algeciras

I want to go ashore to buy some needed articles. A boat went to Gibraltar today, but it was so full of officers and stewards that I decided not to crowd in.

The men who were working in the spirit room managed to get intoxicated, as often happens somehow. Low, one of them, was court-martialed and disrated a few days ago for being in the same condition. How foolish these men act when they find a chance to obtain liquor.

September 16
Algeciras

I was again unable to go to the "Rock," but Mr. Philbrick and I went ashore at Algeciras.

The city is built on uneven ground. The buildings are low and neat and clean on the outside, as in all Spanish cities. The people sit in their houses or in the shade nearby. Most of the children are poorly clad. Some of them run naked in the streets and others wear nothing but a cotton shirt. The resources of the place appear to be meager. I am unable to see how they support themselves.

The market is well supplied with fish. The fruit which grows here is not very good. The grapes are inferior to those of Malaga.

The "Almada" is a cool and well shaded place for a walk and contains some attractive beds of flowers. Near it is a bull ring, recently built.

On the west side of the city crossing a ravine is an aqueduct which has the appearance of a bridge.

Near the bull ring is an old cemetery from which have been removed all the vaults, and the bones, as well. A new burying place has been prepared near the water in the eastern part of the city. It is square, enclosed by a high masonry wall and has a pretentious arched gateway entrance. The whole is whitewashed and looks like a fort from the distance.

In the front of the principal church of the place is a public square paved with large smooth stone and containing various monuments.

In the evening we are joined by Messrs. Grainger and Smith with whom we spend the night on shore.

September 17
Algeciras

We return on board at seven bells this morning at the same time as the Captain and the Paymaster and others who have been to Tangier.

Newspapers which reach us state that Fort Wagner has been taken but leaves us in doubt as to Charleston.[22]

Commodore Thatcher has taken command of the *Colorado* and Mr. Low of the steamer *Aurora*.[23] It is reported that the USS *Kearsarge* has captured, near the Azores, one of the steam vessels which the English have just built for the Confederates.[24]

September 18
Algeciras

We get under way with a wind so light that it is nearly sunset before we pass Europa Point.

"Now for Mahon," as everybody is repeating. The men are to have liberty there. They are saying that they would prefer to have it at some other place, but when the time comes it is safe to predict that few will fail to improve the opportunity to go ashore.

The evening is delightful and as the ship sails along on a smooth sea Mr. Hunter and I pace the deck and talk of the pleasure which we will feel in being homeward bound, for the next time when see the "Rock" fading from sight astern we hope that it will be in the opposite direction. Hunter remarked that if we were the same distance from New York that we are from Mahon how light-hearted and joyous all would be. I hope that not much more than six months from now we will all feel this pleasure of being homeward bound.

September 19
At sea

This trip begins with the calms and head winds which have been our fortune recently.

The papers which were brought on board before we left Algeciras give an account of the death of Commander G.W. Rodgers of the Steamer *Catskill*. He was first on the staff of Admiral Dahlgren and was killed with the Paymaster in the pilot house of his own vessel.[25] He was a brave and efficient officer and a close friend of our Gunner J.R. Grainger over whom he has exercised a fatherly care and interest. Mr. Grainger is feeling very sad and at his request I have framed for him two letters of condolence, one for Commander Rodgers' widow and the other to be sent to his brother C.R.P. Rodgers, U.S.N.

September 20
At sea

Wind ahead except during the afternoon when we were able to stand on our course. I spend the day quietly in reading. The Sabbath brings to one on a man-of-war at sea a grateful respite from the daily routine and a quiet hour to think of the pleasures and the misfortunes of the past, and to enjoy something in the way of pleasure and personal improvement which the present may offer.

One sees today on the ship many employing the Sabbath quiet to read while others who have been reading are now intently occupied in overhauling their "ditty bags" and fishing out old letters and their worldly treasures, trinkets, curios, foreign coins, articles of jewelry for which a sailor has no conceivable use, etc. Mr. Low who destroyed sailors trinkets whenever they came in his way received the nickname of "Ditty-Bag Jack."

September 21
At sea

This morning at sunrise fifty two vessels were in sight, sailing ships, steam ships, barks, and brigs. We overtake and pass two Italian ships which left Gibraltar a day ahead of us, as we do all the other ships. The wind freshens until we are making eleven knots. We overtake and pass an Austrian steamship which passed us in the morning. We hold our speed during the evening. How finely she sails along! I remain on deck until seven bells, almost to midnight, admiring the ship as she makes her way on her course.

September 22
At sea

Our good breeze continues and we are still making eleven knots. In the afternoon we begin to roll considerably as the sea is getting rough. The only two ships which we see today we overtake and pass.

September 23
At sea

We arrived off Mahon during the night, but a squall struck us requiring all hands to be called to shorten sail and reef topsails and this morning we are tumbling around becalmed in a rough sea a long distance from Mahon. Towards noon a light breeze springs up and we slowly make our way back towards Mahon. While I write it is difficult to sit or stand. Frequent lurches of the ship require the use of both hands and feet for one to keep his position. Every now and then a crash of crockery attracts attention, and strikes terror in the hearts of the stewards and cooks. We try to eat dinner and at the same time hold onto the dishes on the table.

We take a pilot on board, but the wind heads us and we have to wait outside the harbor.

The Consul comes aboard and brings us letters and papers.

September 24
Mahon

At 7 p.m. the wind finally becomes favorable and we stand in toward the harbor. The wind is sufficient for the three topsails and spanker until we enter the narrows when the courses are put on her and we sail in the beautiful moonlight close to the rock on the port—so close that we could almost touch the rock with an oar as the water is deep alongside.

As we pass the old fortifications at Georgetown groups of people who have gathered there to see us pass greet us with wild cheers.

On board everything is as still as a church that any orders may be distinctly heard. Every man is on deck and at his station ready for the quick execution of any command which may become necessary in the narrow passage.

At eight o'clock we are past the hospital and at anchor within a third of a mile of the Navy Yard, just opposite the factory. Astern of us is the residence of the "Golden Farmer," so named from being the wealthiest man in Mahon.

September 25
Mahon

All day I have been hearing the men greet each other with the salutation, "Georgetown and Port Mahon—all same." This expression, borrowed from the natives is common among American men-of-war's men.

Seaman Hyde, the man whom we left in prison here is still detained, but is allowed to walk out in the streets. He speaks in great praise of the Consul and his wife who frequently visit him.

The old women who used to frequent the ship at eight bells to get food from the messes at breakfast are with us again, but few young women are seen with them. It seems that the women here played such havoc with the health of a regiment of soldiers recently sent here that the Governor deemed drastic measures to be necessary. Accordingly all women reputed to be prostitutes were gathered up and sent off to some place to be given an opportunity to recuperate whether they need it or not.

A telegram from the mainland announces the capture of the city of Charleston and all the batteries. This is good news, but it has been so long expected that it is hardly news.

The men are painting the ship and the boats. I am reading Ramsey's *Universal History*.

September 26
Mahon

The reported capture of Charleston is contradicted today. The news which we are getting is not worthy of attention. Another report today states that several regiments of Rebel troops threw down their arms and cheered for the Union. I suspect that this is about on a par with yesterday's report of the capture of Charleston.[26]

The old women accompanied by little boys continue to appear on the ship at meal time with baskets for "grub." It is amusing to see the little urchins with beef-bones in their hands making their way through the crowd to deposit the bone in the basket kept by the old women. The little fellows can say "biscuit, food" and several other English words which the crooning matrons have doubtless taught them in anticipation of the arrival of our ship.

Efforts are being made by the Consul, our Captain and others to have Hyde discharged from prison so that he may rejoin our ship. He is sick and discouraged on account of his present situation, although much has been done to cheer him. He says that he would prefer to work for two years for nothing than remain here in prison a month after the ship leaves.

In anticipation of our visit to Mahon one of our marines produced the following poetical effusion which his shipmates have been trying to sing to various tunes:

"La Estrella de Mahon"

I have sailed o'er the sea of the East and the West,
I have bowed at the shrine of the brightest and best;
But Beauty's ideal to me was unknown,

> *Till I met Catalina, the star of Mahon.*
> *Oh! Fair are the daughters of Genoa, the proud,*
> *As the blue sky above me unstained by a cloud,*
> *But on that peerless beauty the sun never shown*
> *Who could match Catalina, the Pride of Mahon.*
>
> *The soft evening breeze that ripples the sea*
> *As the cheeks of the daughters of green Sicily,*
> *But no softer cheek ever pressed to my own*
> *Than thine, Catalina, bright Star of Mahon.*
>
> *There are white bosoms heaving on many a shore,*
> *But thine are the beauties a god might adore,*
> *For charms never dreamed of are girt by the zone,*
> *Thy slender waist clasping, bright Star of Mahon.*
>
> *I have worshiped gay beauties in cottage and hall,*
> *But in thine lies a charm that surpasses them all.*
> *For thou art my Queen and my heart is my throne,*
> *Catalina Querida, pretty Star of Mahon.*

After dinner I went on shore with Mr. Hunter. We took the omnibus to Georgetown and called on the pilot and then on Señor Raphael and his family. We then visited the officers in the military barracks whom we met during our first visit to this port. In the evening we returned to Mahon where we spent the night.

September 28
Mahon

I came on board at eight bells and started at work immediately on my monthly reports.

This is the anniversary of my birth. Two have now been spent on this ship. How soon they come, but I fear that not enough of wisdom or of good comes with them. One year ago I was on the coast of Syria; before another comes I hope to be at home.

September 29
Mahon

It is reported this morning that the new Confederate cruiser, *Southerner*, which was in Malta a few days ago is now off this place waiting for us.

September 30
Mahon

Seaman Hyde, in prison here, for whom a subscription was to be taken today, wrote, yesterday, a saucy letter to the Consul charging him with being the chief cause of Hyde's detention. The officers who were to head the subscription now feel that they cannot properly do so and the Captain has stated that he would not approve any order for the payment of any money to Hyde.

General Quarters this morning, otherwise the day is very dull. At noon there was a heavy shower with thunder, lightning and hail. It obliged the women who came aboard at dinner time to remain part of the afternoon. It was discovered that some of the women were recent arrivals from Majorca. It is presumed that they think that the local supply has been so curtailed recently as not to be equal to the demand, but in this they are mistaken as the Captain has changed his mind and our men will not be given liberty here.

The report that the Confederate cruiser, *Southerner*, is laying for us off shore has apparently been confirmed by a dispatch from our Charge d'Affaires at Madrid.

October 1
Mahon

A warm and beautiful day.

I receive a letter from a Spanish Lieutenant of Engineers accepting an apology addressed to him for what he termed an offense and which I most willingly conceded as such, being due to thoughtlessness which I regret exceedingly.

The Captain seems to be holding the ship here for Hyde, hoping to hear from Madrid that his release has been ordered.

More females arrive. The wife of the ship's cook whom he met and married while we were in Barcelona came today on the steamer from there "by special request," whatever that may mean.

The women here are a disgusting nuisance on the ship. They almost rob our tables. I presume that the Captain does not forbid them from coming aboard because it is an ancient custom of the place when a man-of-war of any nation is in port and he feels that we do not have to put up long with an annoyance that the people of the place have come to regard as a vested right. For my part I hope that we shall go from here soon and never return. I dislike the place so much that I do not want to go on shore. There is really nothing to see or to do.

October 2
Mahon

It is reported this morning that an American steam ship of war was signaled passing this port. As no such ship is known to be in these waters it is presumed that the ship signaled was the Confederate craft flying the Union flag.

General Burnsides has resigned. General Franklin is reported to be marching on Texas with 30,000 men.[27]

There are some signs of going to sea. I hope that it will be soon.

October 3
Mahon

The war ship flying the American flag is again reported off the harbor this morning.

The Captain is still on shore. It looks as though he might be awaiting some dispatch from Madrid regarding the movements of our ship.

Today the horrible rumor started in the ship that we will winter here.

October 4
Mahon

This afternoon I went on shore. I had to go on business. After calling on J. Hyde at the prison I went to the Consul's. While my visit was primarily official I enjoyed it very much. The Consul is affable and evidently a gentleman of integrity and with a high sense of honor.

His wife is handsome and the most charming and interesting woman that I have met since I have been in Europe. She shares the Consul's interest in Hyde.

We talked the Hyde affair over and the Consul explained to me the tedious Spanish procedure in contesting a case of this kind. Hyde was convicted, or perhaps more properly indicted—for his trial is not yet considered completed—under an old Roman law in which the smallest penalty is $50 and the largest $500 with long terms of imprisonment attached. Meticulous compliance with all prescribed legal forms is exacted. Every sheet of paper on which testimony is recorded must bear the government stamp and every document intended for the appellate or reviewing authority at Madrid must be otherwise duly authenticated. The expense and delay incident to a trial in this country can never be estimated beforehand.

The civil Governor and the principal citizens of the place have united with our officials in petitioning the Queen for a pardon or reprieve for Hyde. It is believed that he will eventually be released.

October 5
Mahon
The Captain returned on board today and immediately gave orders to prepare the ship for an engagement. The ship is stripped as far as practicable. Everything unnecessary about the decks is carried down and stowed in the hold. Extra preventer backstays with tackles are rigged. The gig is taken in on deck. The bulkhead of the forward cabin is made ready to take away. The guns are ordered to be double shotted and small arms to be loaded. The Gunner, Mr. Grainger, has been directed by the Captain to take charge of the 30 Pdr. Parrott gun on the forecastle in the operation of which he has shown remarkable results at target practice and I am ordered to take the Gunner's regular station, in charge of the forward magazine. Everything indicates that the Captain expects us to fight—to hunt for and engage an antagonist of superior force. It is to be conceded that the steamship for which we are looking has its motive power presumably below the water-line while ours is up in the air where it makes an ideal target, and that we could do little with a steam warship in a calm or a light wind, but that may not be the story. We have a thoroughly trained crew with respect to both sails and guns, and they can be depended on if it comes to boarding. Both our Captain and our Executive have the confidence of the men. Our men have been doing some really extraordinary work at target practice. We are now rid of the unreliable shells with which the ship was fitted out—the kind that exploded as they left the gun—and we now have a good supply of shells which Mr. Grainger and his men loaded at Spezia. We have also gotten rid of the stock of powder which our smart Paymaster bought at a bargain in Valencia. We have now an entire stock of good powder. I do not believe that the Armstrong guns which the English are said to have put aboard of our antagonist will outrange our Parrotts. Give us plenty of wind and a little good luck and we may be able to send this British–Confederate pirate with its British steam engines and its British Navy-trained crew where they ought to be. If our Captain be not too scrupulous about following this craft's practices with respect to the display of national colors we may be able to get close enough to it under the Greek or Austrian flag as to disable it so that it cannot get away from us by running to the windward. It surely would be great for us if our old sailing ship should be the first ship of the Navy to put a Confederate commerce destroyer out of business.

October 6
At sea

After waiting for wind finally at 3 p.m. we weigh anchor and sail slowly by the walls of old Fort St. Phillip and then around the parapet of the new fortifications and out to sea. All along the shore crowds watch us go out. There is no cheering as we were greeted when we came in. The natives are now silent and awestricken, doubtless reflecting their thoughts at the expectation of losing their source of income in our prospective encounter with the Confederate cruiser.

It seems good to be at sea once again, to smell the sea breeze and to feel the motion of the waves and the movements of the ship—and especially to leave behind a place which has so few attractions. I confess that I have always liked being at sea. I have not forgotten my boyish seasickness on my father's ship, nor can I ever forget my hard experience for a boy of 14 during my first voyage on my own hook, but I continued to follow the sea longer than I ought to have done, even though intermittently, and I am chagrined when I realize that I get out of the sea a kind of satisfaction that I cannot expect to get from the practice of law, if I be alive to return to it when this war is over.

October 7
At sea

We are bound for the African coast. I learn today that our Captain received information that a British vessel loaded with coal was lying in the harbor of Algiers waiting to coal the Confederate cruiser which we expected there soon. It is the Captain's plan to intercept her. Owing to the difficulty in obtaining coal as well as its cost Rebel ships do most of their cruising under sail. The *Florida* which we saw in Gibraltar was bark rigged. The one for which we are looking is said to have a full ship rig. While it would seem incredible that they would not keep some coal in reserve for emergencies it is not at all improbable that she will make her way to Algiers under sail and it is not impossible that we may come upon her on the way or surprise her on her approach at Algiers when her fires are out or banked with the steam down. Our men feel that there is a good prospect that we will give her a chance to try her battery.

Our start is not very propitious for a quick passage to Algiers. We have had a head wind all day and at night are opposite the western end of Majorca.

October 8
At sea

Last night all hands were called to reef topsails. A gale sprang up and continues today. We are now under three reefed topsails and it is very rough. It is a disagreeable day. The ship leaks in her upper works so that even the berth deck is wet.

When I took some monthly reports to Captain Stellwagen today he asked me if I were a relative of Captain Safford who used to send to the Navy Department magnetic and tide and current observations and other hydrographic data. I told the Captain that the man he named was my father. He then said that all he ever knew about my father was he was a "Down-easter" who was highly esteemed by New York shipowners and asked me questions about him. He then asked me how it had happened that I was not a ship master instead of a ship's yeoman and this brought out my life history also. Captain Stellwagen is very courteous in his manner, but very business like and does little talking himself to give an opportunity for conversation or to let one know what he is thinking about.

October 9
Algiers
After a rough night under three reefed topsails and an equally rough disagreeable day we entered the port of Algiers at 2 p.m. without having seen sign of our quarry on the way, nor is she in the harbor. The information which we obtain from our pilot is to the effect that she has not been in here.

I find the sight of the city of Algiers from the water much more imposing than I had imagined. Instead of low mean Oriental buildings with little evidence of modern influence I see a well built town situated on an eminence showing off to good advantage buildings which must have been designed with respect to size, character and even color so as to give the city a pleasing aspect from the distance. Architecturally and in general appearance it is decidedly French.

Several rows of arches cross the front of the town on which streets are built. A large mole and fortifications enclose the harbor.

The Captain has gone ashore to communicate with the Consul and has left orders to have the ship ready for sea on his return.

October 10
At sea
The Captain returned last night at ten o'clock from his visit to the Consul and we immediately got under way and put to sea. The information which our Captain obtained from the Consul leaves considerable to be desired in the form in which it reaches me. It is as follows. A British steamer was in here and supplied coal to a steamship which arrived, supposedly from Alexandria with 300 passengers. Besides coaling this ship took on cotton here for Tangier. It is thought, on what evidence it does not appear, that the cotton was used to conceal guns and other armament obtained from the coal steamer. The Consul admits that he is without definite information that this is so, since he could not demand the breaking of her cargo. The ship flew the British flag while in port. The Consul feels sure that this ship is now sailing as a Confederate privateer with her passengers as her crew and has left her cotton at Tangier, or elsewhere, and has now passed out beyond the Strait. She left here together with the coal steamer nearly two weeks ago. As she flew the British flag we could not have done anything with her had we caught her here, without stirring up more trouble than Captain Wilkes did with his *San Jacinto*.

We have been going ten and twelve knots all day with a fine breeze. Our course would indicate that we are returning to Mahon. The orders to the men and the vigilance which is being maintained make it evident that the captain is still expecting an encounter. Towards night the wind freshens and the light sails are taken in. The ship is sailing along at a great rate.

I have been feeling very sick all day and have spent little time in the Store Room, but how enlivening it is to sail along with a fair gale even though one be ill. Today's sail and C. Lever's *Romance of Life* have almost made me forget that I am sick.

October 11
At sea
It was quite rough last night. The ship leaks badly in her top work. The berth deck is very damp and uncomfortable—so much so that the Boatswain had to find drier quarters.

The ship has made great progress the last 24 hours, 14 knots at times. At 8 p.m. tonight we passed Mahon Light. We then changed our course and now appear to be on our way to Spezia. I hope so. Next to being "homeward bound" with the prospect of seeing again the somber rocky headlands and the pine clad hills of my native Maine I prefer to be returning to Italy. There as elsewhere in Europe one has to contend constantly with frauds, cheats and beggars, but Italy offers something else. Both Nature and the hand of man have contributed to make Italy attractive and beautiful. It is everywhere historically interesting. Its people are patriotic, active and industrious, and cheerful, even in poverty and misfortune.

October 12
At sea

An unpleasant day. Cold and rainy, but we have a fair wind and are making good headway in spite of a cross sea into which the ship plunges heavily at times. Below everything is damp.

I am used up with a cold. I never had such a severe headache in my life.

At 4 p.m. we are opposite the Island of Corsica.

October 13
Spezia

This morning at 8 o'clock we are at anchor in the harbor of Spezia opposite the Store House. It seems good to be back in my beloved Spezia again. Its present attractive beauty and its reminders of the glory of ancient Rome endear it to me.

A large mail is received on board. I have one letter from home. Among other news it states that my brother Edward has been released from the Service on account of "physical disability," the nature of which is not specified. He wrote me some time ago that a foot and an eye had been hurt in an accident, but I did not understand that there was any serious or permanent injury.

Mr. Abbot, our Executive, has been informed in a private letter from home that the steam frigate *Niagara* is to be sent on this station and he feels very certain that our ship will go home this autumn or early in the spring.

October 14
Spezia

The ship is the scene of great activity. Stores are coming aboard for the Carpenter's and the Boatswain's departments. I am also very busy breaking out and restowing the lower Store Room.

An American bark is in port. She brought iron for the railway here.

October 17
Spezia

The crew is still working on the ship. We will have to have the ship caulked before we do much cruising. We expect to go to Genoa for the purpose. I am quite dull these days and am losing interest in reading history. I am <u>really</u> sick.

October 20
Spezia

A busy day for everybody. I am attending to my duties, but am nearly used up. I showed the swelling in my leg to the Doctor last night and commenced poulticing it today. I do not want to lay up unless necessary.

October 23
Spezia

The Genoese tailor, Ancelini, is here from Genoa to collect his bills against the officers. The 27 francs which I owed him had increased to 67. He pretended to discover that I was right after referring to an old bill. What Jews![28] Even the 27 francs was twice as much as he ought to have charged me for the pants which he made for me.

The men are having liberty. About 30 went ashore for twenty four hours yesterday. Some returned drunk today, as usual; others have overstayed their liberty and rewards have been offered for them. What fools they make of themselves.

October 24
Spezia

More men go on liberty today. Several officers are absent. Some have gone to Florence; others to Genoa.

I find that my swelling will oblige me to "lay up" for a few days.

Our band serves to cheer the dull hours.

October 25
Spezia

The Sabbath again comes to the ship with its welcome quiet. By request of the Governor no men are allowed on liberty today. All my mess-mates are on shore. I do not feel able to walk, nor do I think that it would be prudent to attempt to do so. I am much interested in reading an illustrated edition of the *Life of Washington* by Lossing.

October 26
Spezia

This morning I go on the "sick list." I make arrangements to leave my business with my assistant. It is necessary to keep quiet and I have a cot on which I am to lie all the time. There are a half a dozen men here in the sick-bay who make a nuisance of themselves by talking all the time. I have my *Life of Washington* here with me to read and went once to the Store Room today to write up my log.

The men on shore yesterday had a good deal of trouble. Several were cut with knives; some were struck with full bottles. The Master-at-Arms was cut in the back of the neck.

October 27
Spezia

All the liberty men who were arrested have come on board. Joseph W. Low, a seaman, has his right ear bitten off so that its beauty is spoiled; his face is also badly bruised. It has been a rough time ashore.

One hears in the sick-bay all kinds of discussions, including ghost stories, etc. It must be very distressing to Anderson, our old quarter gunner, to listen to such stories as are told within his hearing. He has been a long time sick with a consumption and will probably not survive many days.

October 28
Spezia

Lieutenant Commander Rush R. Wallace is ordered home. He takes his leave today. A farewell dinner was given to him in the ward room at which the Consul and his wife were present. I presume that no one will <u>weep</u> at his departure for he was not a favorite with his mess-mates, nor with the ship's company generally. He frequently has failed to exhibit good judgement, but the feeling against him on the ship is largely due to the fact that he is a Rebel sympathizer and has taken no pains to conceal his satisfaction at reports of Rebel successes. He is not of the stuff of which Farragut is made.

We have not waited to go to Genoa for caulking and the clatter of their mallets about the bows and the talk and noise of the crew going about their work make the sick bay a poor place for a very sick man. Fortunately this racket does not annoy me and I feel very comfortable when lying quiet.

October 29
Spezia

A rainy day—dark and dull in the sick bay. I am chiefly interested by hearing the steward read to me the *Life of Washington*. It is becoming very tedious to have to lie so much on my back.

October 31
Spezia

A rainy, damp day, dull and cheerless.

I could write a volume about the incidents which are occurring here in the sick bay but it would not be a pleasant task even if I had the patience to attempt it. When Anderson, the poor quarter gunner, who is nearly dead groans in his sleep I hear the remark, "Somebody is on the side tackles." It was his duty as quarter gunner to keep men from lounging on the guns or yielding to the temptation to sit on the side tackles and poor Anderson was very solicitous of his guns.

November 3
Spezia

Today Anderson and Wilson who have consumptions are landed and put in the local hospital to await the arrival of the Navy supply ship on which they will be sent home if possible. The ship is expected daily. The farewell of Anderson and his shipmates is doubtless final, but it is characterized by the coolness usually to be observed in men of his class on such occasions.

November 4
Spezia

Anderson who died last night will be buried tomorrow near the Store House where repose the remains of several seamen who have died on our ships here. The day is pleasant, but the weather is growing colder. My confinement is becoming very irksome. How much we ought to appreciate health!

November 5
Spezia

Anderson was buried this morning. He had quite a respectable funeral. I am expecting to have my swelling cut every day. The prospect is not pleasant to contemplate.

November 6
Spezia

Today the doctor came with his instruments and after administering a dose of whiskey and a few drops of laudanum he commenced operations. I had suffered more in anticipation than in the actual cutting.[29]

November 7
Spezia

I lie on my back all day and all night. I am quite tired and talk nonsense and make all the fun possible. I feel rather stiff since the cutting.

November 8
Spezia

I have not been down in my Store Room for four days. Today I go down and make my reports and write my log. I am very well today.

November 12
Spezia

I am quite well, but am obliged to keep quiet. The Doctor says that I will be out of confinement in ten days or a fortnight. It is becoming quite cool and in some ways the sick bay is preferable to being on deck. Snow appeared today on the higher mountains around Spezia.

November 15
Spezia

The Doctor says that I will be taken off the sick list tomorrow. I am feeling very well, but how thin!

November 16 to 22, inclusive
Spezia

Activity too soon has necessitated my confinement to my cot for the past six days. Today I venture to visit the Store Room, make my reports and write my diary. I also go on deck and take a look around. A large fleet of Italian men-of-war is in the harbor.

During the past six days the usual scenes have been enacted in my place of confinement. Life in the sick bay of a man-of-war would furnish material for a harrowing melodrama. One hears blasphemous talk regarding death. There is no apparent sympathy for the afflictions of others. Their misfortunes are made the subject of jibes and jokes. One hears, "Are you dead yet?; it takes you a long time to die; Damn it, I wish you would hurry up, for I want your cot; Well, you are a candidate for the 'bone orchard'; The Devil will soon be picking your bones." These and other similar remarks will be liberally interspersed with profanity.

There is however no such lack of humanity among this class of men as one unacquainted with them might infer from their talk. Any intention of being cruel to a suffering fellow being is most exceptional. A good deal of such talk springs from a stupid idea that it will be taken as a joke and tend to make their hearers minimize their misfortunes. It arises too from an effort of those who make such talk to screw up their own courage. A great deal of the profanity is bravado, incited by apprehension. Back of it is a vague fear that a future existence is going to be unfavorably affected by a persistent disregard of the voice of conscience in this.

November 23
Spezia

The officers of our ship have been such assiduous patrons of the ugly *prima donna* who performs at the small theater in Spezia that they have incurred the enmity of the Italian officials. In showering bouquets and purses of money on the stage our officers have made the contributions of the Italians look cheap. A few nights ago a hundred francs were tossed on the stage and two hundred more held in reserve to meet any possible Italian competition. In retaliation our ship's band has not been allowed to play at the theater. What fools Americans manage to make of themselves abroad!

November 25
Spezia

I feel much better today. I think that tomorrow will find me on duty again.

Tomorrow has been set by the President of the United States for a general Thanksgiving and preparations are being made for a Thanksgiving party and dinner on board.

Since finishing the *Life of Washington* I have been reading Bayard Taylor's *Travels in Greece and Russia*.

November 26
Spezia

This morning the Doctor informed me that I could go on duty. Thus commences a more agreeable life outside the hospital. The day is fine, the sun warm and I enjoy a visit to the upper deck for the second time within the past month.

Preparations are being made for the dance on the quarter deck. The inside of the awning is covered with flags and chandeliers are hung. The gun deck and the berth deck are also decorated with flags to very good effect.

At dusk the guests, gentlemen and ladies from shore began to arrive. Then our band which was stationed on the poop started up the music. The supper in the Ward Room was a lively and enjoyable affair, to judge from the popping of champagne stopples and the loud toasts in Italian which reached my ears in the Steerage.

The affair did not lead to such boisterous sideshows as that at Palermo, because effective precautions were taken this time to prevent uninvited participation on the part of the ship's company. As it was old May, the Quartermaster and Orderly Sergeant Robbins who were invited into the Ward Room with the band to have something to eat in recognition of their special services in connection with the affair, had to be removed for engaging so hotly in a political discussion as to be inconsistent with good social usage. May was delivered to the sentry for safe keeping and Robbins was put in his hammock.

It was half past one in the morning before the last guest had departed and leave takings were indicative of some bad heads and deranged stomachs both on ship board and on shore in the morning.

November 27
Spezia

Clear bracing weather. I take long breaths of the atmosphere of which I have been so long deprived. I have not lost so much weight as I thought. I find that I am able to attend to my duties and am improving every day.

Just two years ago today I entered the Service by engaging to go as yeoman of this ship.

It is beginning to look as much like winter as it does in this part of Italy. We will soon be going to Naples where we will probably lay up for the season.

November 28
Spezia

Cold and windy. Overcoats and the crawling of the sailors under the lee of guns and into corners indicate that winter is here. After my long confinement it seems good to be able to come up on deck and get breaths of pure air whenever my duties permit.

I have been bestowing more of my leisure time lately on *The Count of Monte Christo* than I am accustomed to give to a novel. It is quite fascinating.

November 29
Spezia

In the afternoon I went on shore for the first time since the ship has been in Spezia. I accompanied Messrs. Hunter and Fletcher. At a café where we went we met Lieutenant Bacchus who introduced us to Judge Dwyer and Dr. Davidson. The Judge and the Doctor have charge of affairs of the United States government here.[30]

The Judge is evidently a Western man as he likes whiskey and has a large fund of interesting anecdotes. The Doctor does not object to anything *drinkable*. He has the appearance of a newspaper man rather than that of a diplomat. The Judge has one eye which he holds steady, but the other is likely at any time to start up dives and gyrations which have the effect of suggesting an uncanny perspicacity on the part of the Judge. This unstable eye is very disconcerting to any one who may be trying to make an impression on the Judge in the way of conversation.

After leaving them I went to the hospital to visit Wilson who was put on shore a short time ago with Anderson. He complains of having little to eat and being very lonesome. The "Sisters of Charity" were singing in various parts of the building during my stay. Wilson says that they are anxious to convert him to "Christianity."

The place looks clean, but it is gloomy and cold. The rooms are high and well ventilated, but to one who cannot understand the language of those whom he meets life must be very dull and dreary.

Mr. Kay, the Paymaster's clerk, is to give a birthday party at Lucas' Hotel this evening. A few select friends only are invited.

November 30
Spezia

Preparations are being made for sailing. One anchor is hove up. Sails are being bent and the running gear "rove off." In every part of the ship there is the kind of activity to be seen on a man-of-war prior to leaving port and which the uninitiated might mistake for confusion. The change will be agreeable to me as we will find more life and less cold in Naples than here.

My long walk yesterday did me no harm. I am improving every day by exercising in the open air.

December 1
Spezia and the sea

At noon the anchor is weighed and our good ship falls off before the light breeze which blows out of the beautiful bay of Spezia. There is enough wind to make sailing a pleasure. The view as one enters or leaves this place is always delightful and today the blue hills and the snow capped mountains behind them give us a picture which no artist could duplicate.

The air is cool. As we sail out on the blue water I feel that I am again free. I know how an imprisoned bird must feel when he escapes from a cage and flies high up in the air away from the earth and the sense of confinement. Poets may talk about the "cruel wave," but there is always something grand and soul inspiring when we sail out and meet the heaving sea with a bark under us which we feel that we can make the mistress of the storm.

This evening as I sit below reading *Monte Christo* and hear the constant tread of the watch on deck and the sound of the water rushing by the ship's side as we glide along in the darkness I know that I am again at sea, even though it be smooth.

I finish *Monte Christo* just as we near the very island where Dumas placed the fabulous palace and treasure, —where Haydie and Valentin were made so happy in the presence of Morrell and the Count.

Edmond Dantes in his farewell letter to his friends on the little rock said, "There is neither happiness nor misery in the world; there is only the comparison of one state with another, nothing more. He who has felt the deepest grief is best able to experience supreme happiness. We must have felt what it is to die that we may appreciate the enjoyments of life." Wait and hope is the lesson taught in this narrative of remarkable coincidences.

December 2
At sea

After a good breeze all night this morning found becalmed with Corsica to starboard, Elba and Pianosa to port and Monte Christo ahead. During the forenoon we practiced target shooting.

Soon after meridian the wind came ahead with the appearance of a storm. Over the high land of Corsica it was seen to be snowing and shortly after we had rain. It was cold and disagreeable on deck.

Our cook is drunk again today. He has been fighting on the spar deck and is now confined in the brig in irons. The dinner which he had under way was left in the pot until a late hour when cook N. 2 had it served to us in a rather raw state. This is not an unusual culinary incident in life on a man-of-war.

The ship has made little progress today.

December 3
At sea

Last night was one of the most disagreeable which we have experienced during the cruise. A downpour of rain, thunder and lightning, mix intense darkness and heavy shifting winds all contributed to make our position among the islands a matter of unpleasant uncertainty. Once we kept away to run back and get clear of Corsica, but we had not proceeded far when the wind suddenly shifted and came out of the North in terrific gusts. Away we went before it like a frightened bird and this morning we were still going followed by all the wind which we needed with reefed topsails. Owing to our recent speed on our course our net gain in the twelve hours previous to eight o'clock this morning was 108 miles.

An occasion like last night is a real test of the ability of an officer in charge of the deck of a ship. If he meets the situation and unexpectedly changing conditions so as to get from his men that unhesitating response to his orders which is indicative of their confidence in him, then he knows that he has passed the test successfully—and what is there that can approach the sense of satisfaction which comes to one in command of a ship when he sees his crew give such mute testimony of their confidence in an emergency?

We have passed several craft today. Some have been running as we; others have been hove to under short sail.

December 4
Naples
At daylight the island of Ischia, or <u>Epomeo</u>, is in sight. The wind is light. It looks like rain. We have all sail set. At eight bells the sun breaks through the clouds bright and warm and Gaeta appears in view. We sail along close by the frowning city of the rock where the late king was besieged so long, and then we come opposite the Castle of St. Ermo. Here the ship is hove to and the Italian flag is saluted. Thirteen guns are also fired for the Italian Admiral in port. Two Italian officers come on board to assist in putting the ship inside the mole where she is to lie. After much noise and confusion we at last reach the designated spot. At 1 p.m. the operation of mooring commences. No dinner is served and when night comes the mooring is still unfinished.

December 5
Naples
This morning the work of mooring is recommenced and continues half the day. The remainder is occupied in sending down top-hamper and cleaning up the ship.

It is a cold and rainy day. The ship is in much disorder throughout. We have a very good place to lie although the dark and gloomy wall of the old buildings which shut us in do not furnish an attractive view.

As I sit at the mess table and look through the air port I can see the Castello di Sant' Ermo and the Chièsa di San Martino. The latter is a most interesting edifice. It occupies the site of a former country house which was converted into a sacred building in 1525 through the efforts of Charles, Duke of Calabria, son of Robert of Anjou. The church and monastery were endorsed by Queen Jane the First.

The Navy Yard is just ahead of us and the large mole astern. Several ships of war lie near us.

It has not been the practice to allow foreign war ships to lie here. The granting of this privilege to us indicates a relaxation in local ordinances. As a special privilege also we are allowed to keep our powder on board.

No shore boats are permitted by the authorities to approach the ship and all persons passing to or from the ship must go through the Navy Yard gates. By reason of such restrictions we will probably have few visitors.

December 6
Naples
All decks are holy-stoned—an unusual performance for the Sabbath but there was not time yesterday. All hands were turned out at 4 a.m. to breakfast and to this duty. Many of the officers have gone to Pompeii. I remain on board all day.

December 7
Naples

The sails are loosed to a fine breeze for drying them and then they are unbent and with the running gear which is unrove are put below. The men are busy. Some are painting; others tarring chains. All the bright work on the gun deck is being cleaned.

It is believed that we will remain here about thirteen months. This will give me a good opportunity to resume my study of Italian and to see everything of interest about here. According to reports Naples is not very agreeable to the present king. He is charged with impoverishing the people by high taxes and in favoring people from other places in government work. Even the government paper and tape is procured in Turin. Another row may be expected here soon. If Garibaldi would lead the time would not be far distant when Naples would set up a republic. A local artist tells me that the expected insurrection will aim at such a form of government.

December 8
Naples

Preparations are being made to receive the Prince, or Admiral of the Italian Fleet. Every part of the ship has been cleaned and put in the most perfect order.

The Prince has failed to appear. The Consul accompanied by some American ladies came near night and received his appropriate salute.

Everything is stowed away for the winter. The ship is clear in every part except the hold which is crammed full.

Some of the officers visited Vesuvius yesterday, descended two hundred feet into the crater and took luncheon, including eggs which they cooked there. They say that the trip to the summit of the mountain is very tiresome and that one requires the assistance of a guide to do some pulling up in places.

The Assistant Secretary of the Treasury of the United States accompanied by several ladies came on board in the evening.[31]

December 9
Naples

I have found that the man, the ship's painter, who has been stationed in the Store Room as my assistant, has forfeited the confidence which I placed in him by committing petty larceny, stealing some small articles of clothing and putting them in his own bag where I found them. This is the acknowledgment which I get for my kindness for allowing him to take when I was sick some articles of my clothing which he needed to wear and did not have.

We are still awaiting the visit of the Italian Prince, and are standing in readiness to receive him and his company.

The Italian frigate *Garibaldi* and a school ship in tow went to sea this afternoon. They are bound for Spezia. The *Garibaldi* is a fine frigate of 54 guns. My assistant will not remain longer in his position.

December 10
Naples

This has been a summer day. The bay of Naples looks as we would always like to see it—a place of extreme beauty. The surface of the water is undisturbed by a ripple and steamers and feluccas are headed in every direction. The atmosphere is clear over the hills and Vesuvius appears at its best. The Prince has not come and the marine guard have again been kept waiting in their dress uniforms.

M. Conti, the artist, has brought on board a number of portraits which he has painted. Mr. Grainger, the Gunner, has one of his brother in a uniform full length. It is good.

December 11
Naples

The weather is still pleasant and warm. A winter here is much preferable to one in Genoa.

M. Conti still continues to bring on board portraits and other paintings for the men, ordered when we were last here. I have heard of none which have been rejected or sent back for alterations. I should judge that a hundred of our crew had given him orders for pictures. I went ashore at sunset. Naples is, as ever, full of life and bustle. The same assortment of persistent annoying guides salute you at every turn. Carriages fill the streets and its palaces and squares have not changed.

I visited Byrn's English Hotel and there met a man who is a native of Philadelphia and at present attached to a Spanish steam warship as an engineer. He was very companionable and showed himself to be a Union man by his conversation.

In the evening I attended a circus at the King's Garden. The performances were very common. It is the same company which I saw at Palermo and once a year is often enough to see it.

This is the first time that I have spent an evening on shore for three months.

December 12
Naples

The pleasant weather tempted me to go on shore again today. Smith and I visited the Bourse and some other public places after which we took a carriage and with "Louis," the guide we went to Virgil's tomb. A winding and twisting flight of stone steps brought us to the high land above the grotto overlooking the city and the bay of Naples. On a plain marble slab in a quiet nook is the following inscription, said to be an epitaph dictated by Virgil himself:

P. *Virgilio Maroni. Mantva me genvit; Calabri rapvere; tenet noc Parthenope. Cecini paseva, rura, Duces. 1840 Consacré au prince des poets latins.★*

Beneath is the following, *Par F.G. Eichoff bibliothécaire de S.M. la reine des Francais.*

★*Mantua bore me: the Calabrians took me away; Naples (parthenope)has me now. I have sung of pastures, of fields, of chieftains.*

From this place we drove on the new Posilipo road which commences at the Point of Morgellina and extends to Cape Coreglio opposite the little island of Nisida. Near the beginning of the roads, on the right, stands a newly repaired cottage said to have been the habitation of Sannazaro. It is on a high hill and may be reached through the grounds of a private house in front. On the left stands the ruins of an ancient edifice called "Palazzo di donna di ogni ánno" first erected by the Princess of Stigliano. Repairs which were undertaken by a prince of Thora in 1711 were, for some unknown reason, discontinued.

There are many splendid country residences along the road and attractive gardens the entire way. This drive affords one of the finest views of the city. We then went to the Campo Santo which is to the eastward of the city. On our way we pass the Royal Poor House or Recluserio founded by Charles III. It is now 1,630 feet long. A portico of three arches give it an impressive appearance. Nearly 6,000 persons of both sexes are employed here. It has an annual income of 240,000 ducats, besides public and private donations.

Close by at a place called "Ponti Ropi" are vestiges of an ancient aqueduct. It was built, it is said, by Claudius Nero to bring water from Serino, a place about thirty five miles from Naples, to the country houses of the Romans at Posilipo, Pozzuoli and Baja. The new cemetery or Campo Santo covers the whole hill of Poggie Reale and is one of the most remarkable in Europe, both on account of its size and its situation. Here one sees a statue of religion by Angiclini, a Gothic edifice or hospice for the waiting friars and a great number of costly and well kept Oratories and Chapels. The grounds are adorned with shrubbery. We found flowers still in bloom. My chief reason for visiting this place was to see the manner of burying the poor people regarding which I had read some not agreeable accounts.

The places set apart for this purpose are square courts paved with lava. There are 365 distinct subterranean vaults. Above each is a square removable slab of lava, each numbered and provided with a ring-bolt for the purpose of lifting it.

Each day a slab is removed and toward night, the times when I was there, the bodies of the dead are thrown into the vault. But one was put in today. It struck the solid bottom on its back. It was the body of a man. Another body brought here today for disposition is being kept in the "dead house" for a "post mortem" examination as the person died suddenly.

I had read that the bodies were stripped of clothing and thrown in naked, but such is evidently not the case now as the body which I saw had on the clothing in which the person died.

The manner of throwing the bodies into a deep vault so that their bones must be broken when they strike the stone bottom is an unnecessary procedure which offends our sensibilities.

We returned to the city by another way and entered at the gate of S. Gennaro. The streets in this part of the city are not so clean, nor are the buildings so fine as in the western part of the city, but there are many important public structures here of ancient appearance.

After taking supper and ordering some clothing and at an "English" establishment we returned on board.

December 13
Naples

An Irishman preached to the ship's company for an hour and a half in a very energetic style. This is the first *ex tempore* preaching I have heard since I have been on the ship.

A report reaches us that General Burnside has been captured.

December 15
Naples

This morning a native of Portsmouth N.H. was on board. His name is Lock. He left Portsmouth in 1827. News of the fight between Herman and King for the championship has reached us. Herman was beaten in thirty five minutes.[32]

December 17
Naples

All the talk to be heard is still concerning the prize fight. According to all accounts it resulted in a square and complete defeat for Herman. Thus has ended the greatest pugilistic contest ever known.

Groups of men may be seen all over the ship discussing the affair. Some say that they had rather have lost huge sums of money than to have Herman whipped.

We have rain and sunshine, but less rain than in Genoa. The sun is as warm as in May there.

I went on shore and visited Byrne's Hotel and returned on board with Mr. Mallett.

December 20
Naples

A missionary came on board and preached for half an hour. He is the same man who preached a week ago.

After dinner I went on shore with Mr. Hunter and we visited M. Conti, the artist. It gave me an opportunity to see how an artist lives in Naples. We ascended a rough dark stairway in an old building in Str. S. Maria, rang a bell by pulling a hemp string and were admitted into M. Conti's studio.

The walls were covered with pictures and the usual implements of an artist were scattered about the room, on tables and in chairs. A narrow window looking out on a dark narrow street furnished all the light of the studio.

Arousing himself from his Sunday nap the artist came forward to meet us. In response to our greetings he replied that he did not feel well and his melancholy expression was intensified by the general gloom of the place.

How many lives have thus been passed since shadows first began to fall in the Strada Santa Maria? This part of Naples is very ancient and is kept in a very dirty state. The grey old walls bespeak their antiquity. In this vicinity are the palace of former kings of Naples, now used as prisons and barracks for soldiers.

On leaving M. Conti we went into a café and were charged four centimes for lemonade because we were Americans. It would have cost a native one and a half, but what is the use of contending with these imposters over trifles?

Hunter, Smith and I spent the evening at the Fondo Theater.

December 21
Naples

It is like summer. Many walk the deck without coats.

General Grant's success over Bragg is confirmed. Other news also begins to make the cause of the Southern Confederacy look dark.[33]

While on shore today I purchased many photographs of Naples and the vicinity. Captain Stellwagen and Paymaster Panghorn have gone to Rome.

December 24
Naples

This morning I appeared before a Court Martial as counsel for James McNamara, musician in the Marine Corps who is charged with theft. Michael Gaul is also charged as an accomplice. McNamara is tried alone. The second specification under the charge is a breaking and entering of the Marine store room in the cock-pit for the purpose of robbery. To this I demurred. The demurrer was not sustained and the prisoner was put on trial as the charges were.

The prosecution commenced to examine witnesses by asking questions of any kind and in any manner which pleasure suggested. Leading questions and irrelevant testimony were sanctioned. If I objected I was required to be silent, or if the objection was listened to, I was overruled by the Court. They cross examined their own witnesses in an unwise manner which really saved me the trouble of doing so.

The evidence was all hear-say and much of it came from a man, who when he was put on the stand, confessed that he knew nothing about the matters in question. Those who gave him as their authority presented a very detailed account of the affair. It was evident that somebody was lying. The chief evidence was in support of the confession made by Gaul who was charged with the same crime.

Of course I felt that my position was unpleasant and peculiar. I was only nominally a counsel—nothing more—and I was about to retire when at the request of the prisoner I consented to remain and take the minutes of the proceeding.

The Court adjourned until tomorrow. In the evening I went on shore and took a walk. The day has been very pleasant, but my employment has not been so. I do not feel happy in a Court Martial.

December 25
Naples

Christmas comes again. During the night a constant discharge of guns and fire crackers was kept up. Sky rockets and fireworks illuminated the whole city.

Today the chief streets and avenues of Naples are filled with all classes of its population. Conspicuous among them are cavalry officers with swords clattering as they walk along. Confectioner's shops are crowded with people buying cakes and sweetmeats. Old women selling candles blend their voices with those of fishmongers selling snails and products of the sea.

At ten o'clock this morning the Court reconvened and the orderly came for me. The Court informed me that it would proceed no further with the charge and specifications against the prisoner, but would adjourn from day to day until Captain Stellwagen returns from Rome. The demurrer which I made had caused the Court to determine to proceed no further with the trial until the Captain could be consulted.

I had no sooner left the cabin than I was called back and Lieutenant Commander Abbot told me that his attention had been brought to a remark which I had been reported to have made reflecting on the dignity of the Court, to wit; that I had "bluffed the Court." I indignantly branded this charge as false as well as being a coarse and ungentlemanly expression which I would not think of using in connection with proceeding in my tribunal. I added that as a matter of fact and of policy I had made to no one my reference to proceedings in this trial and would not do so while it was in progress. I demanded as a right that an investigation be made as to the origin of this allegation.

Mr. Abbot said that he would investigate the matter tomorrow, but from the way he spoke I declined to act further as counsel for the prisoner and informed Mr. Abbot that I would never again appear as counsel for any person on trial while I remained attached to the ship.

I am well convinced who the person was who reported or intimated that I made this remark. He is anxious to convict McNamara and would like to keep me away from the trial and would not hesitate to lie to do so. I know of no man who possesses so little that an officer of his rank should possess.

After dinner I went on shore with Glenn. We took a carriage and drove out on the Puzzuoli road, stopping at an oyster-house where we partook of several dozens of the bivalves. We then drove back through the city to the Capo di Monte palace erected by Charles III. Its situation renders it one of the most delightful of the Royal buildings. From the mountain on which it stands we had a fine view of the city, the bay and the surrounding country. About the palace is a park or Royal "chase," the "Bosco di Capo di Monte." It has an area of about three square miles and is surrounded by a wall. Nearby are the seats of the Duke del Gallo, Marquis Ruffe and Princess Avella.

Opposite the palace is the Royal Astronomical Observatory founded in 1819 by Ferdinand I. On the way into the city one sees many grottoes, arbors, stone stepped passages etc. which add to the attractiveness of the drive.

Our coachman who wore part of his uniform as a Garibaldean soldier kept us interested in him because of his manifestations of devotion to his King, but especially to Garibaldi. All along the drive he was recognized as a well known personage, and judging from the manner in which he was saluted it would seem that he was considered to be an important genius, but in what way other than in abetting revolutions we were unable to learn.

He gave us a dramatic description of the reception of Garibaldi in Naples and made comparisons between the police of different governments that revealed a wider experience than with local affairs. The English and Americans he referred to as advancing, going forward, while France and Italy, or Victor Emanuel, he described by placing the five fingers of each hand beside each other in parallel lines.

By removing his cap and looking at the zenith he emphasized his faith that God will bring about a higher destiny for Italy—that her domains will be enlarged and Rome again be her capital.

We dismissed our interesting John at dark and after having refreshments I left my companion, Glenn, and joined Castell, the Spaniard, with whom I went to the circus. The place was crowded when we arrived, but we secured good positions to see the performances. The acting was superior and changed the opinion which I had previously formed of the company. The performances of an Englishman and his children were really remarkable in all respects. One was only two years old, the youngest performer that I ever saw. Under the guidance of his father he carried through his acts like a veteran although not quite firm on his legs. He was a wonder.

A trained horse was made to dance and stand on a box 18 inches square.

On our way to the Navy Landing we hunted for some time to find a place where we might get a decent supper. We were unsuccessful, but we got into some places which for noise and confusion beat anything that I ever heard of or imagined. They were gambling places and men of every social class and grade, including soldiers and officers in uniform, were scrambled together in turbulent crowds engaged in all sorts of exciting games.

December 26
Naples

I hear nothing of the investigation which Lieutenant Commander Abbot promised me that he would make in relation to my alleged remark derogatory to the honor and dignity of the Court Martial.

I have concluded that the idea of accusing me of making this remark was suggested by some member of the court and agreed to by the others for its effect on me. Instead of believing that I said that I had "bluffed the Court" the Court tried to "bluff" me and succeeded.

I think that the proper action to take regarding my demurrer puzzled them and they thought that they might divert attention from the fact that they were paying any attention to my demurrer as a defense by putting me personally on the defensive. Their action in staying proceedings was, I think, the result of advice which they sought off the ship—probably from the Consul.

Their action in the affair is practically an admission of their own weakness and is going to be so recognized on the ship, for there are others talking if I am not.

December 27
Naples

After supper I went on shore and met Mr. Wilson and Smith at the Arsenal gate by appointment. We had a short walk and then went to the San Carlo Opera House to see *William Tell* for which we had previously procured tickets. The building which is one of the best in Europe was well filled. The singing was good, but the ballet was not attractive. The principal tenor has sung all over Europe and in the United States. He is worth $20,000 and after an absence from the stage for nine years is now filling an engagement for three months at $2,000 a month.

The theater is connected with the Royal Palace and is 288 by 144 feet. On the front appear the names of celebrated Italian composers. The stage is 105 feet long and 53 feet deep. There are six tiers of boxes containing 30 boxes each. Each box will comfortably seat twelve persons.

December 28
Naples

Painting the true gun deck today and the usual changes and confusion attends it.

I feel that my attendance at the opera last night will satisfy me for the winter unless something extraordinary is presented here. I must admit that I do not have a great passion for opera. I like to hear sung what should be <u>sung</u> and <u>talked</u>, what should be talked—to me the combination is not as effective as either alone.

December 31
Naples

The painting of the ship is being delayed on account of the rain.

General Longstreet is reported to have been defeated and captured with his artillery and 3,000 men. Various other reports are also at hand regarding the progress of the war, but I have practically given up the habit of reading foreign papers since I have learned that no dependence can be placed on anything which one reads in them. I see one report today that is probably true. It is that John C. Breckenridge has died of his wounds.[34]

With this day closes the year. It has passed quickly. I trust that before another shall have passed I shall be relieved from my "imprisonment."

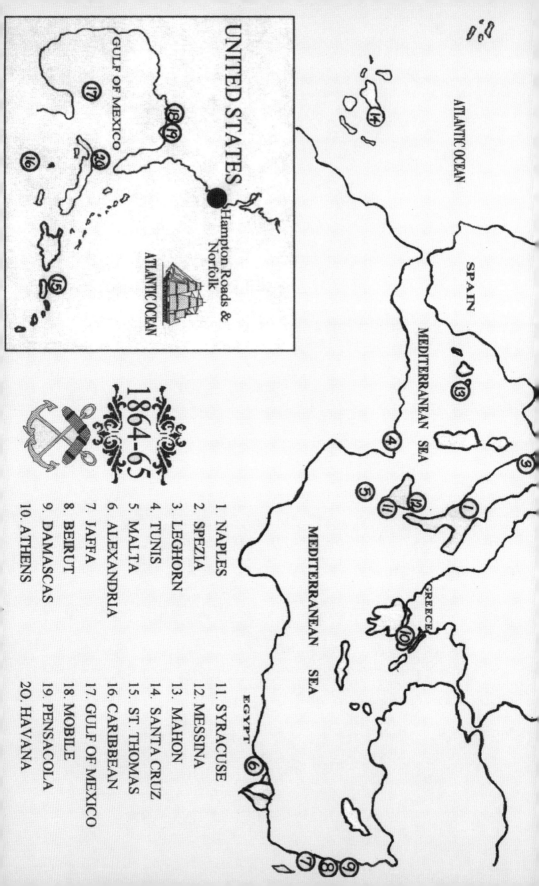

UNITED STATES

GULF OF MEXICO

Hampton Roads &
Norfolk

ATLANTIC OCEAN

1864-65

ATLANTIC OCEAN

SPAIN

MEDITERRANEAN SEA

MEDITERRANEAN SEA

GREECE

EGYPT

1. NAPLES
2. SPEZIA
3. LEGHORN
4. TUNIS
5. MALTA
6. ALEXANDRIA
7. JAFFA
8. BEIRUT
9. DAMASCAS
10. ATHENS

11. SYRACUSE
12. MESSINA
13. MAHON
14. SANTA CRUZ
15. ST. THOMAS
16. CARIBBEAN
17. GULF OF MEXICO
18. MOBILE
19. PENSACOLA
20. HAVANA

Chapter Five
January 1864 to June 1864

January 1, 1864
Naples

This morning the wind blows strong from the South. A Prussian bark bound into port mis-stayed and drove on shore just outside the outer mole and in less than an hour she sank. Several steamers were near enough to have gone to her relief and taken her off. One started to do so after delaying to land some passengers, but by that time it was too late.

She was a new bark, loaded with railroad iron, and was waiting for the pilot to come aboard. She had been inside the harbor once and was standing in again when the accident occurred. The Captain and crew escaped without saving any of their personal effects. A boat from our ship went to their assistance, but could be of no use. Several boats also went from the Italian men-of-war in port.

A cool and disagreeable day. I write a letter to Miss Kate B——.

January 2
Naples

This morning, for the first time this winter, snow appears on Vesuvius.

At evening I went on shore with Smith and Fletcher and attended a Neapolitan Theater—one of the truest kind. The play was local in its conception and domestic in character. It was well done and very amusing. There was a full house.

January 3
Naples

This morning the snow extends down the sides of Vesuvius and in the afternoon snow fell on the ship. Divine service is held on board at one o'clock, being conducted by the same man as last Sunday.

A man from the Prussian bark came on our ship for marline spikes, axes, etc. to use in stripping her, after the loan of such implements had been refused the Prussian Captain by the Italian Admiral. This would seem to be the limit of meanness on the part of the Italians as the bark was chartered by the Italian Government. The Captain of this bark has been most unfortunate lately. A few days before the loss of his vessel his nine year old son was lost overboard and drowned.

January 4
Naples

The cold wind that blows down from the snow clad slopes of Vesuvius is giving us a sample of a Neapolitan winter.

Today brings the sad news of the death of my old schoolmate and neighbor, Howard Cutts, Attorney at Law and Clerk of the U.S. Navy Yard at Kittery. Two from that family have thus passed since I left home. Howard Cutts was a young man of exceptional promise, just making his start. It is hard for the young wife and child whom he has left.

January 5
Naples

Cold and windy. Jackson, our mess cook has left the ship. He went on liberty two days ago and presumably has deserted together with Reuben Hart. This is Jackson's second attempt to desert and will probably be successful. Our mess has lost two cooks in this way.

January 7
Naples

Everybody is engaged in doing nothing. Some of the sailors are occupying their time in growling because the Paymaster is still away on his visit to Rome and they can get no "monthly money;" others are swapping conjectures as to the future movements of our ship.

January 8
Naples

A delightful day. In the afternoon I went on shore with Messrs. Hunter and Wilson. We visited the eastern part of the city and kept on through the gate St. Gennaro to the English Cemetery. Here lies buried poor Dyer, who was killed on our ship by falling from aloft while we were lying in the Bay of Naples, June 30, 1862. A good marble slab bearing an appropriate inscription has been placed at the grave by his shipmates.

I noticed the graves of many Englishmen, officers and men of the Navy and English residents of the city on whom death has laid its hand during their sojourn in this "sunny land." I observed one pretentious tomb erected to the memory of a Captain in Her Majesty's Navy who died on duty here a few years ago.

Near here is a district, consisting chiefly of one street of old buildings, known as "Castle Rag (?)," where the late King attempted to segregate the prostitutes and keep them under strict regulation for the protection of the soldiery. Whether this idea has been given up by the present government I do not know. It is said that while soldiers and sailors in uniform who go in this district may expect a cordial welcome, persons in civilian dress are subjected to considerable annoyance, having their hats snatched off or even set upon and robbed.

On returning into the city we visited M. Conti, the artist, after wandering through long narrow dirty streets in the middle of which runs a stream of water that makes the entire street damp and disagreeable. We found the artist working in his cold cheerless studio which the light of the receding sun had almost forsaken. Among his paintings I noticed portraits of Com. Bell,[1] Levy and Lavalette of our Navy.

I purchased some views and a stereoscope. We then visited the French Café where we spent a couple of hours in company with Italian officers. We left them to go to the Theater of San Carolina where I again witnessed the humorous national play which I saw a week ago. At eleven o'clock we returned on board.

January 9
Naples

A no more delightful day could be desired. I went on shore with Cox and we proceeded directly to the Royal Academy of Study where are deposited the relics of Pompeii and Herculaneum. I cannot attempt to enumerate all that we saw, nor will I mention those things which I saw on my previous visits and have already mentioned in my Journal, but will note the following which especially claimed my attention on this occasion. In the gallery of marble statues is the so-called Farnese Hercules, which according to the inscription was executed by Glico, an Athenian; another, the Farnese Flora, also of Greek workmanship and celebrated for its delicate representation of drapery. Both of these statues were found in the baths of Caracalla at Rome. In this gallery I considered these also to be especially notable. The famous Venus Calypso and a Venus group, found at Capua; a statue of Aristides found in the theater at Herculaneum; busts of Augustus Caesar, Tiberius, M. Aurelius, Seneca, Cicero, Bacchus, Isis and Minerva. There is a hall containing Egyptian antiquities where I noticed a peculiar representation of Diana of Ephesus with two slaves, each with a knee on the ground in the act of arising with burdens on their backs. They are of a beautiful marble and their features are finely chiseled.

In another hall are Etruscan objects, bronze and marble statues, bas reliefs etc., almost all of which formed a part of the famous Borgia collection which was purchased by Ferdinand I.

The Papyrus Hall contains an immense number of ancient writings executed on Egyptian papyrus which were found at Herculaneum and Stabio. The rolls look like bark and are hard and stiff, but a process has been discovered whereby they may be unrolled and many of them deciphered.

My attention was distracted by a collection of some 30,000 coins and medals, bracelets, rings, earrings, etc. Then there was as interesting collection of ancient paints and other substances used in the arts in antiquity and specimens of grain, figs, bread, prunes, peas and other articles of food suggesting the manner in which people lived in Pompeii.

In one room I was impressed by two designs in crayons, one by Michelangelo and the other by Raphael. There is a library containing 32,000 volumes, many of them very ancient, and also 4,000 manuscripts.

After spending more than five hours at the Academy we dined, purchased some views, visited a lava and coral manufactory and then went to the French Café with Mr. Philbrick where we spent the time until seven o'clock when we went to the ship.

January 11
Naples

Last evening Captain Stellwagen and the Paymaster returned from Rome where they have been for the past three weeks. The Paymaster's return is welcomed by many of the men who are short of money.

Mr. Henry R. Philbrick received today his warrant as Carpenter in the U.S. Navy. It bears the date of January 9, 1861.

I am informed by an officer of the ship that my demurrer or motion to dismiss the charges preferred against McNamara and Gaul, made by me as their counsel, was referred by Lieut. Comdr. Abbot, as I suspected, to the U.S. Consul here and he said that it should be sustained on the grounds taken. This accounts for the action of the court on the second day. My informant also told me that he was asked by the Consul, "Who that lawyer on board the ship <u>was</u>," and that on being told something about me sent through my informant an invitation to me to call on the Consul some evening at his house. This is a most unusual concession to a petty officer in the Navy. I will however do him, or myself, the honor of calling on his Excellency when I have an opportunity.

January 12
Naples

I hear that we will go to sea about the 25th and proceed to Leghorn; that if the Captain does not receive orders to return to American waters in the spring we will cruise in the eastern Mediterranean the coming seasons.

Reports reach us today of apprehension of a mutiny among the two-years men of the Mississippi fleet, whose term of enlistment has expired and who have not been discharged by the Government.

January 14
Naples

Mr. Philbrick informs me that a letter to him from home tells of the death from wounds received in battle of two more of our young fellow townsmen, Charles Peckham and Augustus Butland.

The Court-Martial sentenced James McNamara to 30 days confinement in double irons, loss of three months pay and extra police duty for a like period. The Captain however refused to approve the sentence, because, in his opinion, the evidence was insufficient to justify conviction, thus virtually rebuking the officers composing the Court for their action.

The Court is now in session trying Gaul.

January 15
Naples

Gaul's sentence was announced this morning at general muster. It was contrary to expectations. He is to lose three months pay, be confined 30 days in the brig in double irons on bread and water and perform three months extra police duty after his release.

Some of my mess mates and others formed a party to accompany an American from Philadelphia in an ascent of Vesuvius. I was planning to go, but a bowel disturbance made it inadvisable to do so.

They returned in the evening with indications of having been roughly used, but all well satisfied with the trip which was a perfect storm of fun from beginning to end.

Jones returned with no seat to his trousers or drawers, but fortunately with the tail of his coat still remaining to cover the badly scratched portion of his body which was exposed. Some had their hands torn and all had their faces more or less scratched. Jones lost his hat and in attempting to recover it slipped and slid down a declivity for five hundred feet bringing an avalanche of small stones and earth in his wake.

January 16
Naples

The thermometer is 38 this morning. Ice formed on deck last night. We had snow squalls yesterday and the slopes of Vesuvius are again white. It is also sending out a large volume of smoke or vapor.

In the afternoon I went on shore and spent a short time with some Italian officers who spoke English and then took a long walk.

On my return I happened to see Glenn meet Messrs. Kay and Cox, the Paymaster's Clerk and Steward who were passing along just as Glenn came out of the café du Commerce. He was intoxicated and insulted and struck both of them. He was in company with Italian officers and citizens at the time.

Glenn is most unfortunate in his conduct on shore and his company is not to be sought by any gentleman. I most earnestly hope for his own good he may be stopped from going on shore any more.

January 18
Naples

Cold and disagreeable. I receive 210 gallons of olive oil for the lamps. This will last five months at the present rate of consumption.

The Captain has decided not to put to sea until about the 12th of next month. I hope that he will wait until March. I learn that there is snow in Genoa and that the weather is very cold there.

Prince Umberto gives a ball tonight at the Palace and some of our officers will attend.

January 19
Naples

Cold and cloudy. Lieut. Comdr. Abbot is indisposed today from the effects of last night's ball. Prince Napoleon and Princess Clotilde were present.

At noon a Swedish man-of-war arrived and was properly saluted.

A mail arrives from the United States but brings nothing for me.

Preparations are being made for the ball on board Thursday night.

January 21
Naples

This is the day for the great ball. Awnings, flags, green shrubs from shore and chandeliers have really converted the ship into a very attractive ballroom. I contributed my part by painting some small American flags for the chandeliers and making some suggestions as to the arrangement of larger flags and then after supper went on shore to sleep as past experience had proved that I would get little sleep if I remained on board. The invited guests were already beginning to arrive at half past three in the afternoon as fast as the boats could bring them.

After spending the early evening with some of my shipmates who had also come ashore for the night I went to my lodgings about nine o'clock to turn in, but failed to secure the sleep which I was planning on as I got in conversation with my landlord and discussed local politics with him in Italian until midnight.

January 22
Naples

I returned on board at eight o'clock this morning. I found the caterer's waiters removing bottles, jars, empty ice cream containers and the debris of last night's entertainment.

Over 300 guests appeared—more than were invited. This does not include members of the ship's crew who took advantage of some unintended opportunities to participate in the festivities. It seems that when the caterer's men were heating various pots of liquor in the galley some of our crew saw their chance and made off with the liquor and drank it concealed between the guns before it could be recovered. Preparations for making the punch or "hot toddy" were resumed with a new supply of liquor and a sentry stationed at the galley.

At one time the Master-at-Arms was engaged in a lively fist fight with his two corporals and had considerable difficulty in subduing them to his satisfaction and putting them in double irons in the "brig." In the meantime a general row started between the Orderly Sergeant and some of his marines and all the prisoners in the "brig" became involved. New developments in the row occurred so fast that the Master-at-Arms in his drunken condition became puzzled as to what he ought to and gave up trying to do anything. The affair quieted down through the physical exhaustion of the participants.

During the night two men, Judge and Bennett, left the ship and have probably deserted. Bennett has attempted to desert twice before but has been caught. Four other men who were on liberty have not returned and very likely do not intend to.

The day is warm and springlike and gives a glow of cheer all around.

Mahoney the corporal is "broken" and a new one is made, an Irishman of course, O'Roque. "Jimmy Legs" (*i.e.* Glenn, the Master-at-Arms) appears today somewhat chopped and bruised about the face and forehead where the prisoners used their "irons" on him. Officers have gone ashore to convey an apology to the Prince who was not invited to the ball and has flattered them with the hint that he feels slighted. Moreover he is reported as saying that he would have come if he had been invited. I cannot imagine what the envoys from our ship can concoct in the way of an apology. Such an incident makes one feel ashamed of official representatives of our government. Our ship has been given its berth here this winter by a special act of official courtesy which disregarded all precedents. Our officers were recognized as representatives of the United States government by invitations to attend the Prince's ball and it would have been a very easy matter to have ascertained if an invitation to our ball would have been acceptable to the Prince. Every time our officers arrange a social affair they manage to make some *faux pas*. If, as Commodore Thatcher maintained, Naval Officers are "adjuncts of our diplomatic service" they ought to receive better training in their duties. They ought not to expect to be excused as "sailors" whenever they disregard social usages which children reared in good homes instinctively observe.

There is another ball ashore tonight which our officers will attend.

January 23
Naples

News by telegraph announces the capture of Charleston and the sinking of the Confederate *Florida* by the steam sloop *Kearsarge* off Brest after an engagement of seven minutes.[2] The former report may be true, but the latter I do not believe.

The weather is warm and I think that the worst of the winter is over. It has been the coldest in Europe since 1830.

George W. Phelps is discharged and took passage today by steamer to England and thence home. He is an invalid, but defrays his own expenses home.

The men who remained on liberty have all returned except Judge and Bennett. It is said that they have been arrested.

In the evening I go on shore and walk through a cheap market district. Every variety of produce from peanuts up is to be seen exposed for sale in stalls which line both sides of the street. The street is damp and covered with a thin layer of mud and slime and is jammed with a motley crowd of the lower classes working their way through in both directions. There are old hags of women and dirty boys and girls all bare headed and chattering. With their shrill notes are blended the sonorous voices of the male fishmongers as they pick the fish out of baskets and hold them up to view.

After a walk of about four miles I return to the square Nuevo and spend an hour at the "Dutchman's" where I have a bottle of lager beer and converse with the Captain of the Prussian bark which was lost on the mole recently. He speaks English fluently and seems to be a man of unusual intelligence for his profession. There is a wholesome frankness about these people which is refreshing. If they are frugal and industrious they are also usually honest and hospitable. I am not unmindful of the pleasing qualities of the better type of Neapolitans, but they are different. They lack stability. They may, as an act of spontaneous kindness, do you a favor which you cannot fail to appreciate, but they will not forget it either and they may afterwards embarrass you by making it the basis that some unreasonable request may dictate.

January 24
Naples

A warm and delightful day. After dinner I go on shore with Hunter and Smith. We visited Signore Conti, the artist, and looked over his new pictures and then proceeded to the Church of San Martino.

Asses are provided at the foot of the hill for persons who desire them, but we prefer to walk for the exercise. Although the ascent is long it is quite gradual.

We enter through the principal door of the edifice and go to a balcony on the west where a splendid view of the city can be enjoyed.

San Martino is a church and monastery combined. It was converted from a royal residence into its present use by Robert of Anjou in 1325 and endowed by him and his queen. Two centuries later it was remodeled according to a plan of Chevalier Farisega. Its interior decorations may include variegated marbles, gilt work, precious stones and stuccoes. The marble statues are the most highly polished of any which I have ever seen and are beautifully executed.

On the upper part of the Church is a painting by Chevalier Massime representing Jesus Christ and the Virgin Mary. On the sides are two others depicting Moses and Elias, by Spagneletto. On the ceiling of the nave are the *chef díoeuvres* of Spagneletto[3]—the Prophets, comprising eight separate paintings. The sublimity of the design, the variety of character, the naturalness of the facial expressions, and the beauty of the coloring render these paintings superior examples of the painter's art.

The grand altar is of wood, designed by Solimena. The small altars are ornamented with mosaics and inlaid with amethysts and other precious stones. A painting, *The Baptism of John*, by Charles Maratta is his only work to be seen in Naples. The Chapel of St. Anselm contains two good paintings by Vaccari.

In the Chapel of St. Genaro is to be seen a very fine *basso rilievo* by Vaccari and that of St. Bruno by Massimo is looked upon as one of his best works. *The Savior in the House of Pilate* is the work of three artists, Vivinni, Massimo and Fansaga. It is a valuable. Another picture in the Sacristy represents St. Peter denying his Lord. It is by Michel Angiolo Caravaggio. Adjoining this room is another where all the paintings are by Jordaens except one representing Jesus Christ dead which is one of the finest works of Spagneletto. In niches in one chapel are bones of several patron Saints which have been brought from Rome. They are bound with lace and decorated with rosettes.

One room is covered with inlaid mosaic-like work in Brazilian woods depicting Old Testament history. This work was done by a German, Fra Benaventura and must have occupied him for a long time.

The view from San Martino is grand—the most imposing that I ever beheld. On one hand are the beautiful hills of Posilipo, on the other Capo di Monte and below the Campagna Felice: in front is the Bay of Naples; back inland are the mountains, Tifata, and beyond the majestic Apennines. It is a view to be seen and appreciated.

As I look down the waters of the Bay appear like a beautiful blue sheet, which here and there takes on a deeper hue as the surface is ruffled by a flitting breeze. The ships and steamers look like toys. A boat just outside the mole is a mere speck on the blue. In comparison with the Bay the city and the surrounding towns seem small in extent, although I see the habitations of more than a million human beings.

The region which I look down upon has been the scene of centuries of human endeavor and a part of its charm comes from its historical past. Everywhere something stands out as mute evidence of efforts of man to meet his needs or to gratify his ambitions or his passions. Contests for the possession of power have repeatedly laid waste what has been slowly built up in periods of peace. Thus one's thoughts are lead back to that remote age when the delightful valley of the Campagna Felice showed no marks of civilization, when there was nothing to suggest a Parthenope or its future castles, squares and devotion to the arts, and the natural beauty of the region alone appealed to the adventurous bands of Greeks who landed here.

We gave our guides a few francs and took our departure from the beautiful edifice much pleased with the visit and with the courteous manners and genial good nature of these monks. Although ever in the presence of relics of the dead and reminders of human mortality they preserve a joyous countenance which makes them attractive to the visitor. I must acknowledge my great respect for the members of this religious order and my utmost regard for their observances. On parting with them one said to me, "Trust in God, depend upon faith," and something more which my knowledge of Italian did not enable me to catch.

The gate of the Castle of St. Ernois is close by the entrance to the monastery and I resolved to make a second attempt to enter this formidable old edifice. We were refused permission because we had no papers from the proper authority, as are demanded of Italians, but just then the Commandant happened to be coming out and he gave us permission to enter because we were Americans.

This stronghold was first begun by the Normans as a tower. The entrance to the central square is kept closed and guarded. The passage to it is winding and paved with irregular stones. We entered and ascended the parapet and walked around the entire fortification which is in the form of a hexagon. A counter scarp cut in the rock and a ditch or moat surround the castle. Underneath and to almost the entire extent of the structure is a large cistern.

The view from the castle is superb. The castle is considerably higher than the monastery. It was beginning to become dark and clouds were gathering with signs of rain when we began our descent into the city. On arriving there we went to the Café du Commerce and then to the Fondo Theater, returning on board at eleven thirty.

January 25
Naples

This morning a party of our officers went to Capri to see the Blue Grotto. Carter and McIntyre, the Boatswain's mate, who went on liberty yesterday have not returned and it is believed that they have deserted. It is supposed that they took the steamer for Genoa which left last evening.

A Dutch man-of-war arrived and was properly saluted.

January 26
Naples

I wrote a letter to my brother in relation to business of Peterson of this ship who wishes to entrust his bank-book to some person who will remain in the locality of the deposit. Carter's wife has it and Peterson fears that Carter, having deserted will remain in England and send for his wife to come there to reside.

I learn today for the first time that Carter's letter received the day before he left mentioned the sickness of my brother Edward and stated that he was recovering. His sickness of which I thus learn probably accounts for my failure to hear from him. I am anxious now, fearing that something serious may be occurring at home.

Isaac Simmons, a Negro, was found missing when all hands went to quarters. Upon inquiry it was learned that he was taken off the ship by a shore boat about one p.m. and landed at the Navy Yard. This is pretty good, that a man can leave the ship in open daylight.

January 27
Naples

I receive a letter from my brother John. It tells of the death of Mrs. B.S. Grace who died very suddenly. Edward has been suffering from a troublesome if not serious inflammation of one or both eyes as the result of his accident, but is now recovering. He has been unable to write.

Most of the crew have been employed today breaking out and restoring the hold. The weather continues delightful.

January 28
Naples

Isaac Simmons, the Negro, who ran away was returned on board this morning by the police. The Swedish man-of-war sailed today. The Italian papers report the arrival of the USS *Sagamore* at Spezia.

January 30
Naples

This morning I went to Conti's and sat three hours for my portrait in his cold gloomy studio. I found it more tedious than one would suppose. When I left he had a fair picture of me. He says that one more sitting should suffice. When I came from the studio a strong cold wind from the east was blowing and people whom I met on the street wrapped in their warmest clothes and shivering.

An Ensign, Brown by name, has reported by telegraph from Spezia to Captain Stellwagen. He has been ordered to join our ship.

Most of our officers will attend a ball on shore tonight.

A caricature of the recent ball on our ship is to be seen in the shop windows in Naples. In it the Pope is at one end of a telegraph line and Napoleon at the other. An American and an Italian are represented as trying to swallow a big fish, one having the head and the other the tail in his mouth. The Pope is informing the Emperor that the Italians and the Americans are becoming very friendly and intimates the Emperor had better watch them.

January 31
Naples

When on shore today and walking in the eastern part of the city with Hunter and Jones I noticed many hunch-backs and other deformed people and many persons with loathsome and disgusting skin diseases. It is unbelievable that human beings can live in the miserable holes which serve as dwellings for whole families in this part of the city. Dark prison like vaults into which no light can enter except by the door are the abodes of hundreds of people who have hardly clothing enough to keep them from freezing during cold days and who depend upon begging to supply them with bread to eat.

In a square I saw the same troupe of street acrobats who performed in the streets of Genoa last winter. One of them executed some extraordinary feats on a pole some forty feet high and held by another person.

February 1
Naples

Mr. William Brown, Acting Ensign, reported for duty today.[4] His orders were dated October 7 and directed him to proceed on the first sailing ship bound for Gibraltar. He did so and the consequence is that he has been nearly four months in reaching our ship. He is not needed on the ship and why he was sent nobody knows. He is a native of Buenos Aires and has been a lieutenant in the Naval service of that Province.

February 3
Naples

The Spanish steam war ship which left here a few weeks ago is reported to have been destroyed at sea presumably by a magazine explosion. A French mail steamer passed through wreckage, including buckets, etc. which had the Spanish ship's name on them. All hands were lost, and with them my friend the Philadelphia-born Spaniard who was the Chief Engineer. Poor Castell; he was a good fellow. He took supper with Hunter and me and spent the evening before he sailed with us. I receive several letters from home giving the news which is mostly deaths and marriages.

The Prince was expected to visit the ship today but he failed to appear. The Italian officer in charge of the water-boat supplying our ship has been disrated and put in prison for attempting to smuggle liquor on board.

February 4
Naples

The "bum-boat" man who has been supplying the ship's company with fruit, vegetables, etc. has been prohibited from coming to the ship again because he has been enticing men to run away and then selling them out to the police for a share in the reward.

We are to have another ball on board February 22. The Captain is much interested and this means that the ship will not leave here until March.

February 5
Naples

At ten o'clock I went to Conti's to sit for my portrait. The studio was damp and dark and within its cheerless walls I spent not a very agreeable three hours, just sitting. The continual noise on the street does not help to make a stay in the studio any more endurable. Above all else one hears the loud penetrating cries of the vendors of fruit and small wares. One fellow who omitted shrieks at regular intervals sounded like a mad man. If the artist does not spoil my picture I think it will be very good. It was raining when I left the studio. Today the streets of Naples are as dirty as a pig's pen. Mud covers the pavement in every street. What a dirty place!

Mud and poverty when mixed seem to intensify both. An old lady of genteel appearance, her head covered with a handkerchief, came into a café where I had taken shelter from the rain and offered for sale matches which she had in a little basket. It seems hard that an old lady of her age bearing unmistakable evidence of refinement should have to go out and peddle matches in the mud and rain of today, but Poverty is a hard master.

She was followed by an urchin who came in and took out from under his wet coat a monkey and proceeded to give an exhibition of the monkey's accomplishments, which were very creditable, both to the monkey and its trainer. He was followed by a succession of musicians—all looking for the needful money.

February 6
Naples

The day begins with the regular holy-stoning of all decks. The olive oil sold to us here for the lamps is not good and the Captain has ordered it all removed from the ship. This has been done today and better is to be supplied. "Cheat if possible," seems to be the motto of every one with whom we trade.

February 7
Naples

At muster the Captain read the law relating to desertion and made some remarks to the crew respecting their conduct which he did not regard as being to their credit.

The Prince opened the carnival today, but as I do not care to see it enough to get wet with rain and tread around in the mud of Naples I remain on board.

Despite the rain and mud the procession, headed by the Prince, passed through the principal streets. A ship containing sailors and various other elaborate floats were included in the pageant. Those in the carriages and the spectators on the streets pelted each other with confetti, bags of confectionary flour, muddy bouquets and even with hard oranges and other fruit. Missiles for the occasion were supplied by dealers along the route. The Prince's supply of ammunition included a large quantity of dough balls. Everybody was privileged to "soak" anybody else. Nobody was considered exempt. Bouquets were not barred if they had been used and fallen in the street and become saturated with mud. Most of the people provide themselves with clothes suitable for the occasion, and wear wire masks over their faces, but no one can claim consideration for fine clothes. A good target must not get offended. The only defense is to outdo others in an offensive of pelting. Once on the street there is no escape. You must pass along. The police prevent people from going back or turning off into side streets. Our officers did not realize what they were getting into and returned on the ship with swollen noses and bruised faces and with their clothes smeared with flour and mud.

February 9
Naples

After the rain stopped today I went on shore. The three days of festivities in wet weather had just finished. I view the scene from a distance which is enough for me. The principal street is white with flour out of which the rain has made a sort of doughish mud that is very hard to get off one's clothes.

February 11
Naples

It seems that the bad weather has just commenced. It has rained every day for a week. Today a gale is blowing outside and several steamships and other craft have put in for a harbor. Our ship's company are huddled together on the gun deck. It is dark and gloomy below decks.

The gale increased and two of our stern fasts were parted and the chain on the port quarter pulled up the stone post to which it was attached. If we had lost all of our stern fasts the others would surely have parted and we would have been blown out of the harbor. This is the first gale that has disturbed us since we have lain here.

The Dutch man-of-war parted her stern fasts and swung against an Italian war ship doing considerable damage to the latter. The gale soon abated and all became quiet again save the cracking of things over where these two ships were locked together.

February 12
Naples

Beautiful weather has apparently established itself again. I went ashore in the evening and listened to the band at the Royal Palace and bought photographs of the Royal personages of Europe.

It is reported that the king of Denmark has abdicated the throne. Fighting is the order of the day in that part of the world and soon other powers are likely to become involved.[5]

February 13
Naples

I visited Mr. Conti's and purchased two pictures, one a Madonna and the other, *The Flight into Egypt*, for which I pay $25 and $12 respectively. Just before sunset I started from the Villa Realle and walked through the Grotto of Posilipo and for about a mile beyond. The Grotto is lighted by gas. On my way I met numerous parties returning from pleasure trips and groups of peasants strolling along. Their songs and the rolling of the carriage wheels echoed through the subterranean passage. It is about twenty feet wide and twenty five feet high paved with stone and well lighted, day or night. Although alone I enjoyed this walk very much. I witnessed a most beautiful sunset through the western entrance just as I was coming in at the opposite end.

On my return through the city I met the Prussian Captain and went with him to the "Dutchman's" where we sat down with friends and rested a while and then we took a stroll about the city.

If I should try to record all which I see that is interesting on my almost daily walks ashore in Naples I would soon have a large volume written.

February 15
Naples

My forenoon is occupied in delivering cordage needed for various purposes in making the ship ready for sea. I also receive our new lamp oil and some other supplies. In the afternoon I went on shore with Mr. Hunter. We walked and rode until tired of both, but not of enjoying the fine scenery and delightful sunshine of this glorious day. I bought a photograph album. We met Cox and others at the Café du Commerce and returned on board with them at sunset.

February 16
Naples

This morning Prince Umberto sailed in a steam sloop for Castellamare. We made preparations to man our yards and salute him, but just before he left he sent a request to us to omit such recognition. We saw him as he passed. He was dressed in citizen's clothes.

At sunset the Prince returned from his inspection of the Navy Yard at Castellamare. The Admiral's ship fired a Royal salute and all the ships in the Arsenal dock manned their yards and gave him three cheers. The Prince removed his hat in acknowledgment of each salute as he passed to the shore in his barge.

February 17
Naples

We commenced this morning to reeve off all the running gear—braces, sheets, clewlines, buntlines, reef tackles, etc., etc. This makes considerable business for me as old cordage is being replaced and I have to figure out the lengths of new needed.

Conti, the artist, brought on board all the pictures that he has finished and was notified that he must close and present his accounts with the crew within two days.

February 18
Naples

I went on shore alone and visited the artist, Rica, of whom I bought some photographs and then took a walk toward Capo di Monte. On my return I stopped at the glove manufacturer's, Bossi's, and bought some gloves and then proceeded to the Café du Commerce where I met Messrs. Miller, Allen, Cox, etc. and with whom I spent about an hour. Most of the party remained on shore to attend the circus, but I returned on board at four bells.

February 19
Naples

The ship is "dressed" for the Dutch who have a holiday of some kind.[6] I noticed that all hands had a drill around the deck with small arms. They wear long hats of an ugly shape and so large that I do not see how they find sufficient space in the ship to stow away the supply for all hands.

Mr. Conti receives from the Paymaster payment in full for the men's paintings. The Italian papers state that Charleston is taken and that an attack is about to be made on Mobile.[7]

Governor Madison of Illinois is in the city. A British Navy Captain and the Chief Engineer of the Italian Navy visited the ship today.

February 20
Naples
After dinner I went on shore and visited Sgr. Conti, the artist, and then rode with Cox to the west and where we bought some tortoise shell sleeve buttons, shirt studs, etc. A great demand for this sort of work has developed lately. Combs are finished with great beauty. I bought one because it seems to be the proper thing to do, but who the lady will be to receive it is a matter of great uncertainty.

I met Messrs. Kay, Rider and Philbrick at the Café du Commerce. We went to the Café Nand for supper. It was excellent. We then returned to the Café du Commerce where we played billiards until eleven o'clock.

As the wind was blowing with great fury we had difficulty in finding a boat that would attempt to take us to the ship and then more difficulty in getting on board as the ship was rolling and pitching heavily.

The ship *Ella* of Bath, Maine, arrived this morning, loaded.

February 21
Naples
In the afternoon I went on shore with Mr. Fletcher. We walked out toward the Capo di Monte, dined with several officers of the ship at Nand's and in the evening I went to the theater San Carlo where a new opera is being presented. Its composer is a Frenchman, Gound, by name. It is based on Goethe's masterpiece,—*Faust*. The presentation was the most magnificent that I ever saw. The singing was exquisite. The ballet surpasses anything that has hitherto appeared here this season. The prima donna who took the part of Margarete has the finest voice that I ever heard and she is a beautiful woman.

His Satanic Majesty and his deputies were shown with appropriate royal splendor. The conception of Paradise was that of a rural scene of striking beauty and adorned with sparkling fountains. The opera well illustrates the subtle weakening influence on the unwary of the artifices of those inured to evil deeds even though cloaked in the garb of attractive respectability. It also has a religious appeal in the Divine forgiveness of one who has been wronged and in the hopeless condemnation of those who use their special gifts for evil purposes.

February 22
Naples
The warmest day of the season, and delightful. A letter from home states that my brother Edward is recovering, but does not yet use his eyes to write.

This being Washington's Birthday our ship is dressed in flags as well as the other ships in port.

At noon we fired the national salute by permission of the Italian Admiral and his ship did Washington the same honor.

The ship *Ella* with stores for the Italian Government hauled alongside in the tier.

In the afternoon I went on shore with Mr. Fletcher to examine some paintings. By appointment we met at the Café Europa with Mr. Farrell who went with us. We visited the studios of the artists, Scardini and Baridillani.

I purchased a Madonna, Raphael's Holy Family, and a Mary Magdalene and ordered a view of Paestrum and a copy of Zingarella to be painted and delivered at Spezia within thirty days.

I called at the Consulate for mail and to say good by to the Consul and had a long talk with him before leaving.

When I went for the photographs which I ordered three days ago I found that none of them had been finished. This is according to the Italian idea of doing business. They will not do more than the customary amount of work in a day under any circumstances. I called for my tortoise shell studs ordered Saturday, bought some more combs, dined at Nand's, took a short walk and returned to the ship at eight p.m.

February 23
Naples

There is unusual activity in the police department of the ship. It is occasioned by the putting in irons of the crew of the ship *Ella* by request of the Consul. It is alleged that they refused to do their duty. Some of our officers and marines were sent on board with "Jimmy Legs" to do the "ironing."[8] The men have unquestionably been abused by the officers of the ship if one may judge from what has taken place with our sight from our ship. I saw the first officer kick a man in the face while attending to his duty. No reason whatever for the act apparent to a spectator. The fault is doubtless with the officers, perhaps due to a consciousness of their own incompetency, to which my father was accustomed to attribute acts of cruelty on ships.

In the evening I went on shore with Mr. Hunter and attended a "Dutch Ball" with the Prussian Captain, Lund. He has become a regular companion of ours and a very agreeable one, with whom I shall be sorry to part when our ship leaves here.

February 24
Naples

My portrait and the other paintings have been delivered on board. The four additional paintings which I ordered yesterday are to be sent to me at Spezia when completed.

The Master-at-Arms who went on shore last night and probably was not in condition to reach the ship unassisted appeared today on board the *Ella* with the cook, in whose company he was, and proceeded to introduce his old practice and "triced up" the men whom he put in irons yesterday. He attracted attention from our ship by striking a man on the head with a belaying-pin, inflicting a serious wound. The men were "triced up" between decks and were some distance apart but the tricing line lines were led up through the hatchways and were observed and recognized from our ship. An officer was immediately sent on board the *Ella* to order the men let down and to bring the officious Master-at-Arms to his own ship as he was entirely without official authority on the *Ella*.

What inhuman creatures live in human guise! A being who will get into a condition of fiendish irresponsibility is unfit to be entrusted with any authority in the government of men.

February 25
Bay of Naples

All hands were called at one bell this morning to "unmoor ship." At eight bells we were free from our fasts and entering the Bay. The city rapidly receded from our sight and we were once again afloat on the open sea. The Castle of San Ermo and a few other prominent objects make us the final adieu of our winter abode. The wind just permits us to head out of the Bay by Ischia. It is smoky but we have a very good breeze and a smooth sea.

The evening of the 23rd which I spent in the city is probably my last visit to Naples. I feel that I will never see it again,—that I must say farewell forever to this favorite spot where the streets are filled with men of every nation, attracted thither by the charm of its climate, its history, its devotion to art and its human activities. Yes, I feel that Naples with its princes and splendid equipages, its palaces and churches; its famous paintings, its busy artists, all have passed out of my life except as a memory. Probably never again will the hoarse voices of the vendors of fish and poultry greet my ears. It is not likely that my eyes will ever again see the wrinkled visages of the old women who sell roasted chestnuts at the corners of its streets, nor that I will ever again test my fluency in Italian in bargaining with its competing coachmen and guides.

Mr. Fogg, our Minister to Switzerland and Mr. Farrell are on board.[9] They are going to Spezia with us.

February 26
At sea

Two years ago today I commenced to live on this ship. It was a cheerless inhospitable abode at that time. Ice and frost were to be seen on every deck when the new ship's company had been assembled to witness to hoisting of the stars and stripes. Not all of those who took part in that ceremony are here today. Very many are absent. Some have died; more are still living, but in other parts of the world. Today the weather is thick and rainy. The wind is fair but so light that we are making little progress.

I have been below all day busy making requisitions for needed stores to be taken at Spezia. I have also been looking over some old letters and I find that my friend Miss Kate B——'s last letter is dated March 15, 1863. This is very infrequent correspondence but I have sent two since receiving the last and therefore it is not my fault.

Near sunset the weather cleared and we can see land and some islands and an isolated rock which looks like a ship in the distance. It has been as quiet as though we were in port and when below I forget at times that we were at sea.

February 27
At sea

A light head wind and a smooth sea.

In the early afternoon we were near the mouth of the Tiber and could plainly see the dome of St. Peter's church and the cross at the top. Everyone is using glasses to observe as much as possible of this famous structure. It is said that the dome of this church can be seen thirty miles at sea. We are not half that distance away.

February 28
At sea

Rainy with a light fair wind. At noon we have the island of Monte Christo abeam and are making nine knots with the lower studding-sails set. At four p.m. the islands of Elba and Corsica are in sight. The rain has ceased and the sun is out.

February 29
At sea–Spezia

Last night about midnight the wind came ahead. Topsails were reefed and soon a strong wind struck us. At six bells we made land near Spezia and after crowding on sail we were able to head up for port. At noon we were about six miles from the lighthouse with the wind dying out.

The mountains all along the coast are covered with snow. Up towards Genoa the snow comes down close to the base. The wind feels very different from that of Naples—it is decidedly chilly. At Naples it was as warm as summer. We must expect at least a month of cold rainy weather here.

As we near the light house the clouds break away and the sky becomes clear. At two p.m. we anchor in the beautiful bay of Spezia. The sun shines brightly and the wind has died down almost to a calm. I like this retired little place with all its rain, for when summer comes a lovelier spot cannot be found.

Several Italian men-of-war lie here. We salute the admiral with seventeen guns. Mr. Fogg also receives the same salute when he leaves the ship. The admiral's ship also responds to his salute.

A large amount of mail comes on board and is followed by trades people from shore whose familiar faces are beaming with hope as they solicit the patronage of the ship's company. The Lieutenant of Marines was, as usual, on deck dressed for the shore as soon as land was distinctly made out. Until then he had not been seen on deck during the passage. He is always ready to step on <u>terra firma</u> and is of quite as much service to the ship there as anywhere else.

I am informed by some of the officers who have received letters from reliable sources that we will receive orders to proceed to the United States next month. "At any rate that we shall go home this spring."

Lieut. Comdr. R.R. Wallace is in command of the *Shenandoah*.[10] I hope that he will do his duty. It is reported that the Confederates have of late been successful in Tennessee. We are also informed that the Government is to do its best this spring to put down the rebellion; also that the South will do likewise to sustain it.

Visitors to the ship state that there has been very little pleasant weather here for a long time. Six inches of snow fell in the last storm when we had rain at Naples.

March 1
Spezia

The sails are loosed for drying. They are to be unbent and put below together with the running gear. We will probably be here a month or longer. Admiral Albini of the Italian Navy visited the ship at noon with his Aide.

A long time is occupied in completing the mooring of the ship and in putting in the swivels in order that the chains may nor foul or the anchor "trip." It recalled occasions when, although handling somewhat lighter chains, I have done the same with fifteen men in one third of the time and with less than one tenth of the noise. It seems to me that it takes too long to do these things when there are so many men available, but every one has his own way of doing things, and in a man-of-war the easiest way is not always adopted. The day ends with the coming down of sails, blocks, etc.,—and a late supper.

March 4
Spezia

I am very busy receiving stores in the Boatswain's, Carpenter's and Sailmaker's departments.

Anselmi, the Genoese tailor, arrived to collect bills and receive orders for new clothing. The rats on this ship eat everything left in their way. Two nights ago they took my last pocket handkerchief.

Speculation regarding the future movements of the ship constitutes the chief subject of daily conversation on a man-of-war and this subject is now tending to monopolize conversation entirely both fore and aft on this ship. In spite of the confidence with which some assert that we shall go home this spring, others maintain that we shall take a cruise to the East.

March 5
Spezia

Last night all the officers were ordered on board at sunset. Some said that this order was issued because of trouble which had taken place between one or two officers and Italians. Others said that there were to be general quarters. About 9 p.m. as I was sitting in the Paymaster's issuing room the springing of the rattle and the sounding of the gong suddenly struck my ears. The Paymaster's Steward, with whom I had been talking, and I ran to our stations.

There was the usual scene when quarters are sounded at night. The men had turned in. Most of them were asleep. The surprise was practically complete. As my hammock had not been unlashed I had a better opportunity than had ever come to me before to look on and see the fun. A man would start up the ladder with two turns around his hammock and the lashing dragging behind him. The man following would step on it. This would check the headway of the first man and in trying to gather up the trailing lashing and take another turn or two around his hammock a collision would occur between him and a man running down the ladder on his return from the hammock nettings where he had left his hammock to his station with the 5th Division. Meanwhile the shouts from the Master-at-Arms and his corporals to "hurry up" tended to increase the confusion and make collisions more violent. By this time marines carrying their muskets and at the same time trying to buckle on their various accouterments began to appear on the hatchway ladders in transit to the spar deck and the sailor who got in their way was likely to feel a punch from the muzzle or butt of a musket in whatever part of his anatomy that the marine could reach the most quickly. This scene lasted about seven minutes when the bustle subsided with the arrival of the men at their stations.

I received today for the Carpenter's department, for burning purposes 202 gallons of olive oil. It arrived at a very inopportune time, just after the Store Room had been cleaned for inspection.

I received a letter from Miss Kate C. B——, who is now living in Boston—the first letter from her for nearly a year. It is certainly welcome. I am very glad to hear from her. I expected a letter before, but I cannot blame her for not writing as one that I sent her was not received.

I have a sore throat and feel mean. I hope that I am not going to be sick.

March 6
Spezia

Clouds and sunshine alternately throughout the day. I do not go on shore for the reason that I have no money. Most of the officers are affected with the same complaint. The Paymaster has gone to Leghorn to procure money. I wrote a letter to Miss Kate C.B—— in reply to hers of February 14.

Like many others I have a sore throat and a bad cold owing to the extreme dampness of the decks this cold spring weather. Too much water is put on them and it is bound to be unhealthy between decks at this season on this account. The Doctor does not take notice of such matters nor interest himself in the health of the men, nor has he ever shown any disposition to do so. Conditions affecting the health of the men on the ship are left to the Master-at-Arms who neither knows nor cares about such matters.

March 9
Spezia

Mr. Pangborn, the Paymaster, returned from Leghorn. He was unable to obtain any money there and therefore we shall be obliged to go moneyless until next month at which time he will be able to "draw."

I have a bad bronchitis and many others are similarly affected because of the cold damp conditions below decks. It is very different weather here from that which we left at Naples. There is great rivalry among our boats' crews with respect to the sailing qualities of their respective boats, and they race whenever occasion offers. Today just as dinner was piped the first cutter which had been sailing with some other boats belonging to the ship was reported capsized. She was about five miles distant from the ship. The launch and the third cutter had been in company with her, but were then not very near, and being to the leeward, the nearer probably could not reach the capsized cutter within an hour.

There was intense anxiety on board the ship as it seemed impossible for the boat's crew to be saved. The fourth and fifth cutters were manned and pulled off in the direction of the first cutter which could be seen from the ship with a glass when on top of a wave. Fortunately the accident was observed by the crew of a shore boat which happened to be not far away and all of our men were rescued by this boat and had been landed when our two cutters from the ship arrived on the spot. The crew of the first cutter consisted of eight men and five boys. Seven of the crew could not swim. It was very rough and it was difficult to cling to the bottom of the boat. Boatswain's Mate Burns, who had charge of the cutter, and Rose, the two best swimmers were of the opinion that they as well as the rest of the crew would have drowned had it not been for the quick work of the shore boat. We on the ship were certainly glad when we saw them all safely back on board.

We were told that the fore sheet of the cutter got foul just as she went in stays and before the sheet could be cleared she went over, the wind catching the fore-sail on the other tack with the sheet to the windward. The real cause of the accident was carelessness, and when imminent there was failure to avert it by the proper quick action.

March 10
Spezia

The weather continues cold and dull with an occasional heavy shower. The men who saved our boat's crew yesterday came on board this morning and received from them a substantial present in money.

Owing to old custom regulations and commercial practices which still obtain among the various regions and provinces of Italy certain articles which may be purchased in Naples for a franc are worth here four times as much. This seems all the more strange because such articles are of Italian manufacture.

The sailors have a protégé whom they have dressed in a complete ship's uniform. He is a little fellow who gave up his business of boot-blacking to attend to the ship, doing errands for the men. He comes and goes regularly in the boats, but always manages to be on board at meal times for his food. He is a bright and interesting little boy.

March 11
Spezia

One year ago at this time we had not left our winter quarters at Genoa, but the weather was more summer like than now. Two years ago today we sailed from Portsmouth. It was a pleasant day but the feelings of many on the ship were not of the same order. That evening it was apparently gay on board. Singing and instrumental music enlivened the occasion, but it was a forced gaiety.

How quickly these two years have passed away! Indeed they seem to have been scarcely one, yet the changes wrought in our country are greater than any which have taken place during an equal period since the foundation of the government.

March 12
Spezia

Some letters and papers were received by the officers and crew today. The surgeon is informed by a letter from Dr. Hinckly our former Captain's clerk that the frigate *Colorado* is to be fitted out for this station to relieve our ship, but that it will be five or six months before this will take place. The report is quite plausible.

Life on board goes on about the same as ever, the general topic of conversation being the future destination of the ship. I am employing my spare time in writing a sort of biographical account of different events in my experience to add to my record of the cruise. I feel greatly the need of more exercise and better air, but the effort to leave anything which interests me has kept me confronting this undertaking without accomplishing much.

The boats are out sailing again this afternoon, but since the recent accident it has been quite apparent that boat racing is not quite as popular a diversion with the men as it formerly was.

March 13
Spezia

This is the most delightful day which we have had this season. In the afternoon I went on shore and took a walk on the road leading to Genoa. On my return I stopped at Lucas' Hotel where I spent a short time with some of our officers whom I met there and returned on board at sunset.

I mailed a letter to Miss Kate C. B——whose address now is East Boston, Mass.

March 14
Spezia

This is the anniversary of the birth of Victor Emanuel, King of Italy. All the ships of war in the harbor are dressed with flags and three salutes from each are being fired during the day, our ship also taking part in this observance of respect to the King. Five ships firing twenty one guns at the same time makes quite a salvo. At sunset a boat race came off among the boats of the Italian fleet. Thus ended the day celebrated as the birthday of the now king of Italy.

We sent up our long top-gallant masts today.

March 15
Spezia

All hands are employed in "rattening" rigging and tarring them down. By the middle of the afternoon the men also had the sides of the ship scraped ready to receive a new coat of paint. The black paint is to be applied to the entire sides of the ship, thereby covering the white streak which has hitherto shown along the gun ports during the whole cruise.

Towards evening Cox and I went on shore. We walked to the Store House and visited Anderson's grave at which has been erected a fine marble slab marked with an appropriate inscription and device. We called at "Boy Jack's" and then took a stroll on the road toward Spezia. After passing two hours very pleasantly in this way we returned to the ship.

I always enjoy a walk at twilight where I can view the beautiful scenery of Spezia Bay. Its enjoyment is enhanced by an agreeable companion and conversation reminiscent of scenes of our distant homes and of such incidents and experiences as we have been enjoying together during the past two years. The pleasure would doubtless seem small to those accustomed to the diversions of a different sort of life from ours, nevertheless these walks will always live in my memory.

March 16
Spezia

In the afternoon I went on shore alone and made my way up to the mountain gorge where a railroad to Genoa is being constructed. The water is diverted from a narrow stream by means of steam pipes to facilitate the boring of tunnels through enormous ledges. For tunneling they have a newly invented machine on trial and a desire to see it in operation induced me to make my visit to this place.

After my inspection of the railroad construction work I took a look around the mountain. I was astonished to discover how high up and how extensively these mountains are cultivated. Where one would not expect to find a pathway people are constantly being met on much traveled zig-zag paths so constructed with stones laid crosswise as to enable one to descend without sliding. The olive trees grow everywhere on the mountains and shut out of view the houses of the peasants which are located at considerable distances from each other. These dwellings are built of stone and some of them appear very small to accommodate a family.

I saw about twenty young girls and old women who were employed in carrying in baskets on their heads, earth and stones from the bed of the river up to where the ties for the new railway are being laid. It is astonishing to see how great burdens these women will balance on their heads and take up the steep mountain pathways without any support from their hands.

On my return to the town I took a warm bath at the "Maltese Bros." On my way to the boat to go on board the ship I met Mr. Wilson and accepted his invitation to spend the evening with him on shore. We attended a serenade at "Peter's" where I got into a long political discussion with Mr. Mallett, our Master.[11]

I returned to the ship with Mr. Philbrick, leaving in a rather oblivious state those who remained for the night. Our officers have great entertainment there.

March 18
Spezia

Our Captain is quite ill on shore. It is stated that he has been affected with an aberration of his mind, but the cause I do not learn. I suspect however that he has merely been delirious from some acute disease.

I receive letters from home and learn that my brother Edward has been very sick, but is recovering. I am grieved to read of the deaths of many persons in my town. It has been very sickly there the past year. Among those who have died is Mr. Joseph Mitchell, a brother Odd Fellow and a near neighbor. I left him in perfect health.

I have such a cold in my head that I can scarcely think. My warm bath was productive of ill instead of good. I will try a cold one the next time.

March 19
Spezia

This is a great "giurno di festa" with the people here. Old and young from the country around are in town. Young men from the rural districts and their favorite lassies throng the streets. They are chiefly engaged in eating filberts which they have on long strings. Nearly everybody on the streets has a string of these nuts. The well dressed, those in gay attire and the ragged, all mingle together and seem to feel equally happy. I learn that this peculiar form of celebration is in honor to a Saint of the town, who, I believe, is Saint Joseph. Circuses and shows of all kinds were in full blast from five a.m. until midnight. During all this time one could see the rather amusing sight of groups of peasants, men and women, eating nuts from a string as they passed along the streets.

March 20
Spezia

After dinner I went on shore with Messrs. Grainger and Kay. We landed at the Store House and walked to Spezia. It was a most delightful day. The sun shone brightly from an azure sky. Only a few golden clouds hung on the northern horizon. We spent nearly three hours on the walk, resting occasionally on the way. On reaching Spezia we spent an hour at "Peter's" and returned to the ship at sunset.

March 21
Spezia

An Italian sloop-of-war, the *Etna* arrived this morning. Liberty men came off full of American whiskey, many of them "tight." Our Captain is reported to have a relapse of his disease.

Quiet and pleasant. I spend the day in the same manner as usual, including a little exercise and reading.

March 22
Spezia

I asked permission to go to Leghorn for the purpose of obtaining some clothing which was made for me in June last. I was authorized to see the Captain. I called on the Captain who is at Colonel Long's and obtained permission to be absent three days. I returned immediately on board in the sunset boat.

March 23
Spezia

My assistant returned from liberty this morning in very good condition, but as preparations were being made for manning and equipping all boats I remained on board during the forenoon and was kept quite busy.

At one p.m. I went on shore and was soon en route to Sarzana with an Italian peasant. His was the only conveyance which I could find at that hour of the day and although my journey time started without pomp or magnificence it was to me a novel experience and not devoid of pleasure. Our team was not fast and the owner and an old lady on the seat with me fell into an agreeable slumber after we had passed out of town into the rural districts. Although somewhat annoyed by the swaying of the old lady to and fro with an inclination to remain resting against me I said nothing until I saw that we were approaching a railroad crossing on the way. Then I gave the old woman a lift into position with my left arm and aroused the driver by calling out, "Guarde! Avanti!" They both showed signs of life during the remainder of the journey. From time to time they offered me snuff apparently in polite effort to get me to break my silence which they probably attributed to surliness.

The distance from Spezia to Sarzana is about twelve miles. I remembered it as a route over which I passed about fourteen months ago with two messmates as a prisoner in irons escorted by two gens-de-armes. Familiar scenes along the road revived my memory of that trip. I never supposed then that I would be traveling the route again. About eight miles from Spezia two suspicious looking men with canes asked permission to ride with us. Our driver consented although our poor old horse could scarcely drag us three along. The additional load required more frequent use of the whip. Two additions to our party were bad enough, but I was made more anxious when a third man, who appeared to be one of their party in advance, joined us a little further on the road near a small shanty. I had no weapons of any kind, but I kept a sharp watch on the movements of these passengers and resolved that they would not get my 500 francs without realizing that they had been in a fight. From the appearance and peculiar reinforcement of these men I suspect that they were brigands. Had it been night the situation would have been more unpleasant, but if I had been traveling at night I would have been armed.

I arrived at Sarzana too late for the last train to Pisa and accordingly called on my old host the proprietor of the New York Hotel. I spent the remaining hours of the afternoon in examining the ancient town of Sarzana whose walls shut out warlike foes centuries ago.

Outside of the wall, to the eastward, an old castle stands on a high eminence overlooking the town. I found it well worthy of my visit.

A new railroad which will connect Sarzana with Genoa is under construction, but as the country is unfavorable for railroad building it will be several years before the new line can be completed.

Just before reaching Sarzana there is a large stone bridge crossing the river Magran which must be a stream of considerable size at certain seasons although I found its bed bare in places.

March 24
Sarzana, Pisa, Leghorn

The landlord called me at 3 a.m. to take the four o'clock train for Pisa, where I arrived at six-twenty. The air of the morning was cool and damp. A heavy dew covered everything in the valley of the Arno. As I was quite chilly I walked about outside the walls of the city to warm up while awaiting the departure of the train for Leghorn, not attempting to revisit the sights of the city which I had seen in June 1862. The morning sun had come out brightly when I left for Leghorn at half past seven and I enjoyed the ride of a half an hour very much.

I found my friend Mr. Romiti, Sr. in good health but his son confined to his room by sickness. The forenoon was spent in making purchases of various sorts for myself and my friends and I arranged with Mr. Romiti to have the goods shipped to Spezia. I also called on Mr. Romiti, Jr. whom I found suffering from fever and a cough, but now able to be out of bed some of the time. I hope that he will not be long so confined as he is an active and worthy young man—an old soldier of Garibaldi with a good record during the Revolution.

March 25
Leghorn
A delightful day and Good Friday. Everyone is visiting the churches, including the inmates of the Poor House whom I saw going in procession led by the proper church functionaries. Great preparations are being made for Easter.

In the afternoon Mr. Pangborn, our Paymaster, arrived to procure money for our ship.

March 26
Leghorn, Spezia
The day began with rain. I took the train at 9 a.m. for Pisa. I was disappointed in not being able to send my goods on a felucca which left for Spezia last evening. I had to leave them to be sent by Mr. Romiti at the first opportunity. The strictness of the Customs officers prevented me from taking with me even the smallest article which I purchased. Had I done so I would have been subjected to detention and trouble which I had to avoid to prevent possible failure to reach the ship before the expiration of my leave. My carpet bag was not particularly explored, but people with trunks were subjected to great inconvenience by the officers in charge at the city gates.

On arrival at Sarzana I found that I would have to hire a special conveyance to reach Spezia that day. Outrageous prices were at first demanded, but were finally lowered within the bounds of reason. I arrived at Spezia at three-thirty in such a rain as is only known in this region.

I find that our Gunner, Mr. Grainger, is very ill at Lucas' house in charge of the two surgeons of the ship.

I dined at Peter's and subsequently called on Colonel Long and on Mr. Rice, the Consul to deliver a message from Mr. Pangborn and to present the compliments of Signore A. Vincenso Calvi of Leghorn who was a recipient of the hospitality of Colonel Long and of Mr. Rice during the revolution.

Colonel Long is a gentleman of the old school, kind and hospitable and one of the jolliest men to be found. A visit to his house is always attended with pleasure and one never goes away without feeling lighter at heart and with an increased regard for the bachelor host.

I returned on board in the sunset boat well pleased with my journey and also glad to be back again on my ship, especially so after the rain and inconveniences of the last two hours of travel. Why is it that a man finds on a ship a kind of contentment that come to him nowhere else?

March 27
Spezia

Some of the officers have received assurances from the Navy Department at Washington that our ship will be kept on this station as long as the war may last, if she will hold together that long. This predicts in a rather indefinite way the duration of our stay in this part of the world.

The Pope of Rome is said to be dead and that his death has not been made public.[12] I do not place any reliance on the report. This is Easter Sunday and is being observed accordingly ashore.

March 28
Spezia

Mr. Grainger was not expected to live last night, but he is some-better today.

News comes of the taking of Mobile, but the report lacks confirmation.[13]

March 31
Spezia

Today hope is entertained of Mr. Grainger's recovery. I am somewhat disturbed by the fact that my goods which were to be sent here from Leghorn by packet boat have not arrived.

Hyde, the man who was imprisoned at Mahan has been released and now is in Genoa. He sent a letter to one of his shipmates stating that he is destitute of funds and clothing and cannot find employment. He had a row with the Consul at Mahan and struck him in his office. The Consul at Genoa and the Captain of this ship have doubtless been informed of the fact and will do nothing for Hyde. The Captain will not have him on board again.

I have lost all interest in Hyde after this affair. The Consul at Mahan and his wife did for Hyde all that could be expected of them had they been his brother and sister. Hyde wrote a letter to the Philadelphia War-Press, so he says, and the editor forwarded it to the Navy Department at Washington and as a result the State Department reprimanded Mr. Robinson, the Consul, for not reporting the case. In the mean time the editor published Hyde's letter. Hyde claims that this made the Consul hostile to Hyde. I believe that this story about the letter and the reprimand is a lie. Mr. Robinson certainly gets no thanks or gratitude for all his solicitude for Hyde. I wonder if Hyde is mentally deranged?

April 1
Spezia

The usual number are made "April fools" this morning, including Orderly Sergeant Robbins, who was told by a private in the Marine store room in the cock-pit that the officer of the deck wished to see him.

Up comes Robbins in slippers, stepping from grating to grating,—for the decks were being washed—and presents himself before the officer of the deck with all the dignity of a General Bluecher in spite of his slippers, saying, "Do you wish to see me, Sir?" "No," was the reply, "it is the 1st of April, Sergeant." The old man went away indignant and gave poor Kenney, the marine who fooled him, a terrible lecture, saying among other things, " . . . do you know that you are liable to court-martial for such disrespect to your superior?"

In the afternoon I went ashore to visit Mr. Grainger and to see if I could be of any help to him. I found him still improving and I think that he will recover if no other relapse occurs. He has the best of care and the Doctor stops with him all the time.

General Sherman is reported to have returned to Vicksburg and Admiral Farragut to have drawn off from Mobile.

April 3
Spezia

In the afternoon I went on shore with Cox. We walked to the Lazeretto and returned to Spezia and dined at Lucas'. I find that Mr. Grainger is improving. I think that he will soon be able to leave his bed.

In the evening Cox and I are joined by Messrs. Hunter, Drew and Ryder. We look around to see how the Italians spend their time. I got considerable amusement in watching my companions in a Café where they join in dances with the plebeian Italians to the music of the viol and harp.

April 5
Spezia

The Captain is more ill today. We shall not sail from here so long as he and Mr. Grainger remain ill. We will therefore be here at least a fortnight longer.

As a result of what Mr. Abbot directs me to do and of requests for help from the gunner's mate I seem to have inherited the duties of gunner of the ship during Mr. Grainger's illness. I do not object. It gives me something new to think about, including some matters to which I have never before given any attention. Lieut. Backus has loaned me a treatise on ballistics which I find both new and interesting.

Charles Lever and other company visited the ship today. Mr. Lever received a salute.

Mr. Conti, the artist of Naples came on board, but as a consequence of meeting some of our officers on shore previously and drinking too freely of whiskey with them he was unable to carry out his purpose of taking orders for pictures. I felt very sorry for the man who probably has not been drunk before for ten years, if ever.

Some of the sailors who went on shore to clean the boats returned on board drunk and a grand "hub-bub" ensued until a half a dozen were put in the brig.

April 8
Spezia

Our probable departure for home continues to be the chief subject of conversation on the ship. The report of the taking of 10,000 men from the Army for the Naval service makes some confident that we will be relieved this summer.[14]

Mr. Romiti of Leghorn arrived on board to inform me that my goods are shipped. He feared that the ship might be gone and is kind enough to take this trouble for me.

I went on shore in the afternoon to entertain Mr. Romiti. We visited Colonel Long where we also found Mr. Pangborn. I spent the evening with Mr. Grainger and remained with him all night to watch and relieve his regular attendant.

April 10
Spezia

In the afternoon I went to Lerici with the gig. I found the felucca that had my goods on board, but was unable to obtain them because I had no permit from the officer of customs at Spezia.

This ancient town contains an interesting old tower and is otherwise noteworthy because of its narrow streets and the many old people whom one sees in them. I am told that it furnishes a thousand men for seafaring pursuits. Nearby are the lead works of Potuosala. The ore also furnishes a large percentage of silver. The industry is now in the hands of an English company and it is said to be very profitable. Not far away is the residence of Shelly, who with his fellow poet, Byron, spent a portion of their lives on the border of this delightful bay. Shelly was drowned in its waters and his body washed up on its shore. Shipbuilding is carried on at Lerici and a coastwise trade with feluccas enlivens the port.

After a rough sail we reach Spezia just before sunset. The band from the Admiral's ship was playing in front of the theater and the streets of the little city were crowded with the usual Sabbath crowd of out of town people who come in to visit the cafés. I took supper with Fletcher and Smith after which we visited with Grainger and returned on board at eleven p.m.

April 11
Spezia
Today we are twenty five months from the United States. I went on shore at one p.m. and called on Mr. Rice the Consul and on Colonel Long. I returned at sunset with all who were on shore and who had been ordered to return at that time. This was an indication that general quarters would be called during the night.

At one a.m. the sound of the rattle was heard and the usual scenes ensued. A half an hour later we returned to our hammocks to be quiet for the remainder of the night.

April 12
Spezia
I received my goods from Leghorn, all right, through the Customs. After supper I went on shore and had a very pleasant walk with Cox to the Lazeretto. We returned to Fizzana, to "Boy Jack's," and came on board at dark. I shall always remember these quiet rambles at evening among the unusual scenery of this romantic place. The broad bay at sunset is an object to delight every beholder.

April 14
Spezia
What a lazy life! As I look on deck I see 300 men employed in doing nothing and expecting still easier times. I fear that they will never be found. There is a gull which sits continually on our anchor buoy with its head tilted slightly looking up at the ship. The men say that it is "Cocky" Anderson our quarter gunner who died here last November. Anderson was slightly cross-eyed and had the habit of holding his head in a similar manner.

Mr. Jones and Glenn had a fight on shore with some Scotchman this evening—all pretty drunk.

April 15
Spezia
A few nights since a small pet hedgehog which is kept on the berth deck got into the Ward Room during the night and attracted attention by the noise which it made on the carpet. The Asst. Surgeon and the Lieut. of Marines, thinking it to be a rat drew their swords and commenced an onslaught which stopped when the Doctor recognized the animal, he having seen it before. Its life was saved but one of its legs was broken. If all the rats in the

ship could have their legs broken it would be most fortunate for nothing can be kept from their destructive raids.

A scarcity of news increases the dull monotony, made worse for the men since for some reason liberty has been stopped.

April 16
Spezia

It seems very dull. In the afternoon Mr. Hunter and I went on shore at "Boy Jack's." Mr. Hunter paid forty francs damage claimed for the breaking of glass and crockery during the fracas of Jones and Glenn a few nights ago.

I walked to Spezia and called on Mr. Grainger who is now sitting up in his room and will soon be able to come to the ship.

April 17
Spezia

I went on shore alone in the afternoon and spent two hours wandering through the olive groves near the Store House and then walked to Spezia. The leaves are just coming out on the fig trees and the grass is fast shooting up. Last year on this date vegetation was much farther ahead. I enjoy these quiet walks and quite as much alone as in company, for Nature now offers enough to claim one's undivided attention.

April 18
Spezia

Our officers were attracted on shore by a ball at Colonel Long's. Some came back "high flavored." Some did not come at all.

Most of the men who had liberty yesterday remained on shore because a lieutenant ordered them out of the ship's boat after they had been kind enough to pay some fellows who had followed the lieutenant to the landing in effort to get him to pay them four francs which he owed them. What unlooked-for scenes appear among both officers and men when whiskey is the agent.

Our eccentric old orderly sergeant is again in trouble. He has again discovered a plot against his life. He has secured the admission from some of the marine guard that one corporal Connelly was to have $50 to poison him. Others were to kill him in his hammock with billets of wood. He has officially revealed his discovery and formally charged his "mutinous scoundrels" with the aforesaid vile purpose. The conspiracy is set forth in several lengthy documents which also attest his untiring energy in unearthing the villainous machinations of his subordinates.

Oh! That Charles Lever might write up the hair-breadth escapes which this "Irish-American" has experienced and the infernal combinations with which he has had to contend since swearing allegiance to his adopted country; and above all that Lever might appropriately set forth our sergeant's valuable services to the American flag and the super-human ability with which Nature has endowed him for ferreting out mutinous conspiracies and hellish plots for the overthrow and subversion of authority on shipboard and elsewhere. Charles O'Malley, the Irish Dragoon would be nowhere in comparison with our Orderly Sergeant in such matters.

I note in papers from home the death of Mrs. Parmelia, the wife of Capt. Daniel Frisbie. Indeed those whom I left in health and happiness have fallen often.

April 19
Spezia

The most common salutation that now greets one on the ship is: "I am tired of being here—how dull it is—I wish that the ship would be ordered home, or somewhere." But little relief is found from the monotony by going ashore except that there is more room to promenade and the return to the ship furnishes something now to think about.

The men bask in the sun from "morn till eve." Some do nothing but eat and sleep; others act the part of tailors. The old Orderly is still continuing his investigations in the cock-pit and has several additional sheets of foolscap well filled with important disclosures of vile acts which have been perpetrated on the ship from the commencement of the cruise to the present date. I doubt, however, if at the present time there should be an actual attempt to set the ship afire that the officers would exhibit much interest in the discovery of the guilty person. Everyone seems to feel that he has fulfilled his obligation to his government so far as this cruise is concerned and should now be expected only to await orders to return home and receive the benedictions of his countrymen for his faithful services.

April 20
Spezia

The summer is rapidly advancing as I come to realize during my ramble on shore today.

I find that a discreditable opinion of the officers of this ship in comparison with those of our Naval ships which have previously been in this port is being created among the people of Spezia because some of our officers are appearing on the streets and in public places with women whom they have invited here from Genoa and who are of a kind that these officers would not want to be seen with in public in their own country. When one is in a foreign country there is a relaxation of certain restraints which one always feels at home among his own people, especially so because his superficial observations tend to lead him to misjudge the real sentiment of the foreign people with respect to some matters. The adage that "a man is judged by the company he keeps" holds as true in Italy as it does in the United States.

The fifer who is the Orderly Sergeant's chief source of information regarding the identity of those who have committed the various "depredations" on board this ship has told, among other things, who the culprit was who took the money from the pocket of my pants in July 1862. The person so accused by the fifer, McNamara, of the theft came to me this morning and gave me my first information regarding the charge by accusing McNamara himself of stealing my money, evidently supposing that I had already been informed of McNamara's accusation.

A more perfidious set of human beings than these marines would be hard to find. The acts of the informers which they themselves admit would be sufficient, if proved, to send them to the yardarm in a noose. According to the story of McNamara the crime of disabling the ship's battery was committed by men other than those who were convicted.

April 21
Spezia

Last night the officer of the deck was somewhat disconcerted by hearing the Captain's answer to the challenge of the sentry being given, the word "Constellation." The officer of the deck thought that the Captain who has been sick and staying on shore had come off at night to surprise us. There was a grand scramble for side lanterns by the quartermasters and other hasty preparations to receive the Captain properly when there appeared the Captain's Negro servant Francis.[15]

Last night also, Crosby, who was one of Walker's filibusters[16] came to the starboard gangway with the Ward Room officers "hail" and was met on the ladder by Mr. Mallet, who replied, "That's right Crosby, I like to see you come off in style."

In the afternoon I went on shore and called on Mr. Grainger with whom I met some English engineers belonging to the Italian ships of war. I then took a walk on the road to Genoa and back through the town, returning to the ship at sunset.

April 22
Spezia

The hills in the distance are white with snow. The air is cool but the day is pleasant.

I learn that the *Re d'Italia* made the passage from Gibraltar to Naples in seventy four hours. No citizens of Naples are allowed to go on board except by written permission of the Admiral. The engineers who came out in her have £ 40 a month—$200! Doubtless the expenses incident to the delivery of this ship in the hands of the Italian authorities will wake up the financiers of the government.

Two other ships have arrived here and two princes are expected to come tomorrow. I hear that there is to be a grand Naval review in the Bay in a few days. The crews of the Italian ships drill every day, landing from boats and taking howitzers ashore.

It was a beautiful sight this morning, when the sun was partly obscured by clouds, to see the bright green of the mountain slopes where the sun's rays fell. Nature is just dressing in her gayest attire and we now see her in her greatest beauty before the dust of summer falls upon the delicate hues of the foliage.

Few places possess the features which here combine to make such a delightful landscape as that furnished by the amphitheater of hills which surround the beautiful Bay of Spezia, the little villages scattered about the hills and in the ravines and the castles and church spires, reminding us of the history of the past and of human aspirations for the present and future.

April 24
Spezia

Letters say that the steamer *Ticonderoga* has sailed from Philadelphia with orders to join the Mediterranean fleet. Any news thus indicating that this ship is to be relieved is of interest to us all. I hear that we will remain here for three weeks longer and then if no orders are received that we will proceed to Mahon.

After general muster I went on shore with Cox. We walked to the Lazeretto and there took passage in a boat to Porto Venire. After walking about and visiting the old church of San Lorenzo we sailed back. We dined at "Boy Jack's," visited the village to the westward and returned on board at 9 p.m. after having had a pleasant time and got some good exercise.

So many of our Italian bandsmen have left that the band is of no use now. Unless more men can be secured we will lose our musical entertainment.

April 25
Spezia

Preparations are made to receive the Prince, but he does not come. He has disappointed the people of this place once before since we have been here and may repeat the performance.

Kimball and Crosby, the two men who created the disturbance when on shore three days ago have been conveyed to the fort where by the Captain's orders they are to be kept until the ship sails. It serves them right. A U.S. Naval steamer is reported to have arrived at Gibraltar; also the Italian war ship *Re Galantuomo* which was supposed to have been lost.

April 27
Spezia

We shall soon be off. All hands are employed in taking stores on board. Mr. Grainger came on board for the first time since he was taken sick. He looks very well now. Mrs. Rice the wife of the Consul visited the ship in the afternoon. She is certainly a <u>handsome</u> woman.

One of the bandsmen returned this afternoon dressed in a suit of dandy's clothes. I learn that the others are ready to come back now that they have spent their money. I think that the Captain will make a mistake if he keeps them. Three men deserted today from a boat at the landing.

April 28
Spezia

The Italian fleet in port have received orders to proceed at once to Tunis where trouble has occurred between the foreign residents and the natives. The *Etna* and the *Garibaldi* the two Italian ships which arrived there from here a few days ago have been forbidden to pass out beyond the fortifications on penalty of being blown up. It is said that they went up too near the town.

The French and Italian Consuls have been killed and their houses burned. Several French and British war ships have already assembled at Tunis and others will soon join them. The *Duke of Genoa, Maria Adelade*, and the *Magenta* sailed for there this morning.

Thompson, one of the men who left the boat yesterday, was brought on board drunk today and put in irons.

April 30
Spezia

We shall go to Tunis next week. I am glad that we will soon be away on the move again and especially so at the prospect of being mixed up with something so interesting as the affair at Tunis promises to be. All boats were taken in this morning and provisions and water having been taken aboard nothing but wood remains to supply our needs. The forenoon was employed in unmooring ship.

A letter from home tells of the death of Edward Collins and others of my acquaintance. Many too are sick.

I took a trip on shore in the afternoon, but derived little benefit from it as I have a severe headache and feel sick. While on shore I saw Mr. Queto's beautiful child who is not expected to live. The poor little thing cast up its eyes as I approached it; the mother was bending over it in grief. How hard it is to see such little ones suffer!

I had chills after I returned to the ship. I am nearly used up. Dr. Messersmith prescribed the blue pill and I retired.

A Dutch man-of-war arrived last night. It is the same one which was with us at Naples. Four men have died on board her from exposure in their thin clothing.

May 1
Spezia

I felt pretty blue this morning, but the pills seem to have been what I needed. My headache has nearly gone and I think that I shall soon feel very well.

After muster I went on shore with Cox. We landed at Fizzana and walked to the Lazaretto. On our return we rested on the bank and took a nap. The beauty of the locality was enhanced by the songs of the birds and the distant sound of the bugle from the ship.

May 2
Spezia

Like yesterday this is a beautiful day. My walk on shore made me feel better.

We are receiving the running gear; everyone is looking for the blocks, sheets, braces, clewlines, buntlines, etc. which have been stowed away for two months. The sails are also bent and everything made ready for sea.

Castelli, the Ward Room steward is discharged at his own request. He is one of many who have served in this capacity and his going makes room for Lucas, the Makonite,[17] who keeps the headquarters for the officers on shore.

May 3
Spezia

Mr. Kay, the Paymaster's Clerk, received today the appointment as Acting Assistant Paymaster and orders to report at the Philadelphia Navy Yard. All social conditions and ranks of people come to look over our ship. I noticed an old lady yesterday who accompanied her husband around the ship with one of her shoes in her hand. Her stockingless bare foot did not make a very striking contrast to the other foot so far as color was concerned. A handkerchief covered her head and a skirt served the purpose of a gown. Many of such rustic people visit Spezia, especially on the Sabbath. The bare foot is as common as the clad one among these people who visit the ship. No restriction is placed on any person of this class who may wish to examine any part of the ship.

May 4
Spezia

Everything is ordered to be on the ship today as we are to sail tomorrow. A new cook has been employed by the Captain. I hope that this change will not result in curtailing our privileges at the galley where our mess does its cooking. This news is followed by other to the effect that the Captain has trouble with an eye and in consequence we will not go to sea this week.

A battle is reported to have taken place in Louisiana in which General Banks lost 2,000 men and that the black faces at Fort Pillow were massacred.

May 5
Spezia

The pilot who is to go up East with us came on board today. He is from Leghorn.

Two boys were shipped today. They represented themselves to be French, but they are

Genoese. They are bright young fellows, but do not speak English.

I went on shore with Cox. We walked to Spezia and returned to the ship at 10 p.m.

May 7
Spezia

I went on shore at one o'clock at the Store House where I spent two hours alone in the grove of olive and fig trees in the rear of the buildings. Messrs. Hunter and Brown coming along in a carriage espied me in my lonely retreat from the main highway and invited me to accompanying them. With some reluctance I parted with the sweet songsters of the grove and boarded the carriage of my shipmates.

We had a pleasant ride of about three hours driving to the Lazaretto and through Spezia and finishing with a few miles on the road to Sarzana. A double carriage with two horses costs three francs an hour. We took supper at "Peter's" where I made the acquaintance of several officers of the Dutch man-of-war. After supper we all went to the Y.O. where we spent most of the evening. We then returned to "Peter's" and listened to Cox's music on the accordion and conversed with the Hollanders. On arriving at the landing to return to the ship we found the wind so strong and the sea so rough that "John" the boatman would not take us to the ship. Accordingly all hands went back to spend the night on shore. Some selected the "Grand Hotel d'Odessa," others "Peter's." I went with Hunter to Y.O. Hunter is known there as "aqua Frésca."

May 9
Spezia

The gale still continues with rain and I defer going on shore. Some excitement was caused this morning by the capsizing of a felucca within view of the ship.

Notwithstanding the weather we, as a mark of respect to the Dutch man-of-war, dressed ship and fired a salute of twenty one guns in honor of the birth of some Dutch Prince or Princess.

This was to be our sailing day, but it is not being observed as such. Next Thursday is now set as the day to sail. The officers believe that we will not go home until autumn, but from the delay in sailing I suspect that the Captain is awaiting some important orders from the Department.

The Dutch ship has received orders for home and will leave immediately.

It is reported that the Bedouins have command of the fortifications in Tunis and that forty thousand more of these lawless fellows are coming down from the interior. The affairs of the Bey would appear rather dark if this be true. His attempt to increase taxation is likely to prove to have been a disastrous experiment for him.

May 11
Spezia

Chafing gear is put on and the battery is secured for sea. All bills are settled and we are again free. The day is pleasant and if I were home I would not be happier than I am here today, unless peace should lighten the cloud which now casts its shadow over our beloved country.

A dinner party was held on board to which Mr. and Mrs. Rice were present with the Captain and Colonel Long. The French Consul also visited the ship and on departing received the customary salute.

We shall be absent from here for several months and perhaps we may be saying farewell to Spezia forever if orders are received at Tunis to sail for the United States.

May 12
Spezia

The Captain came on board this morning. The gang-way ladder was then unshipped and other necessary preparations made to get under way. The wind was so light however that we could not sail and the gangway ladder was again put in position to accommodate an English family that visited the ship.

Last night Mr. Grainger and Mr. Mallet had an altercation during which the former struck the latter over the head with a glass bottle for calling him a s—of a b—. Both men have quick tempers, but as this is not the first time that Mr. Mallet has offended in a similar manner I do not consider Mr. Grainger so much to blame. Such rows are disgraceful and a discredit to anyone connected therewith. These men subsequently "made up" and the affair will probably not be reported to the Captain.

I am more and more convinced that in all such companies as have <u>spirit</u> for the host may be found the most unpleasant occurrences for which our natures are responsible. Deliver me from them.

May 13
Spezia

A head wind prevents our departure. In the afternoon the boats are again lowered and the officers go on shore. Even though Spezia be a dull place it seems to have some attractions for them.

I am reading the memoirs of Garibaldi in which I am much interested.

General Banks has gained a victory on the Red River.[18]

A mail is received. In a letter August is named by Mr. Tullock, Navy agent at Portsmouth, as the date of our recall, but he probably knows as little about it as anyone else. It is amusing to hear the arguments on the subject among the sailors.

May 14
Spezia

At two p.m. a good breeze blew out of the harbor. The anchor was hove short and the Captain sent for, but before he arrived the wind had died out and the sails were furled for the night.

It seems as though we would never get away. Tonight the wind blows strong into the harbor so that we would have made little progress had we gone out.

May 15
At sea

Last night at ten o'clock we got under way and left the bay with a gentle breeze. At eight bells this morning we were 40 miles from Spezia with no wind. In the afternoon a breeze springs up and we pass the island of Gorgona, off Leghorn. Several Italian brigs dip their colors to us.

It is indeed a pleasant change to be sailing again on the sea. The sun shines with a mellow light upon the sea and the distant islands and upon the numerous vessels of all sorts within our sight. Capraia and Elba may be seen. How many men who have left their names in history have passed where we are sailing and have looked upon the scene which now meets our gaze.

May 16
At sea

A good breeze all day. We sight the Island of Monte Christo. At 4 p.m. Corsica is still plainly in sight. At sunset Sardinia comes in view. We think that we can make out Maddalena and Caprera, the home of the Italian patriot. It is a pleasant sail and I feel quite happy. I am kept busy with my duties and have the wind-sail in the Store Room for the first time this season.

May 17
At sea

Although yesterday I felt so well during the forenoon, last evening I was taken suddenly sick with a fever and a violent cold which came on me. The cough which has been troubling me for a week has increased. My right lung is very sore and my symptoms indicate an increase in the affection.

The wind has been moderate all day, but fair. A good breeze will bring us in Tunis tomorrow. I spent most of the afternoon on deck in the sun. Cox is also sick. The mess is therefore minus half its numbers. I fast all day.

May 18
At sea

Sardinia passed out of sight this morning and all day the good ship has been going on her course under a light breeze. I have not eaten for two days. I feel very weak and my cough remains the same. I spent the afternoon on deck in the warm sun which makes me feel comfortable. The berth deck which is wet down every day had not become dry at 5 p.m. This is probably the explanation of the sickness which prevails on the ship.

Dr. Clark, the Assistant Surgeon, informed me that there was no cough medicine on the ship. He said that he "could not help it." Perhaps <u>he</u> cannot, but <u>some</u> <u>one</u> should. The Government pays the medical faculty of this ship $3,500 a year for looking after the health and well-being of the men, yet these doctors neglect or refuse to provide a kind of medicine which is almost constantly needed. If a sailor were guilty of a comparable failure to perform his duty he would quickly find himself in the brig. It might appear that the Navy Department provides positions as medical officers in the Navy in order to enable certain favored doctors to live as gentlemen of case rather than to care for sailors who are sick and give attention to the effect on their health of the sanitary conditions of quarters in which they must live. This, I think, is not the intention of the Department, but everybody has become so accustomed to seeing medical officers neglect their duty and do nothing that nobody now expects them to do anything. Perhaps after all I am fortunate that they have nothing on the ship which they thought of giving to me for my cough. Very likely they might have given me something which would do me more harm than good.

Near sunset land is reported in sight. There are several sails in sight. We are evidently nearing the African coast.

May 19
Tunis

At 9 a.m. we come to anchor in the fleet off Tunis. About us are three French line-of-battle ships, three Italian frigates and one steam sloop and one steam tender, three Turkish steam sloops and one Portuguese steam sloop. There are also several smaller armed vessels up the harbor, the nationality of which I cannot make out. An officer from the British ironclad, *Royal Oak*, is the first to pay us an official visit. This appears to be the only British Naval ship here.

He was followed by an officer from the flag ship of the French fleet. He came in a steam launch. These steam launches are a great improvement upon the old ones.

By this time the wind was blowing heavy and it had become quite rough. The atmosphere is like that of a hot mid-summer day at home.

Our next visitor was the American Vice-Consul,[19] who I am told either does not speak English or will not speak anything but French. With him came a Customs official of the port. Then came a boatload of Italian officers. Last but not least was an officer from one of the Turkish ships. He was a fine looking man. He had a well dressed crew and a splendid boat.

The visits were followed by salutes. Twenty one guns for the Bey of Tunis, seventeen for the Turkish Admiral and fifteen for the French and the same number for the Italians. I am told that the Turkish Admiral has seven wives with him on his ship—quite a luxurious <u>ménage</u> for a sailor.

May 20
Tunis

The air is filled with little flies. They cover the side of the ship, but a breeze springs up and soon drives them away.

Several of our officers who went on shore yesterday returned this morning and brought with them the Consul, the Vice-Consul, the Consul's daughter and two other ladies. The Consul is a Rhode Island man, whose manners I much admire. His name is Berry. His personal servant is a splendid physical specimen of a Turk. He carries an umbrella as well as a sword, in accordance with the custom of the country. He is an intelligent man and must be brave if appearances count.

The Consul's party spent the forenoon on board and the Captain and some of our officers accompanied them on their return on shore.

One of the French ships sailed today. A funeral was held on board another.

I feel a little better in some respects, but my cough is even worse than yesterday. I feel quite blue and become easily cross and annoyed in the performance of my duties.

May 21
Tunis

Very hot. After the usual routine of cleaning the ship the men stretch out at full length under the awning.

All the officers except two are absent from the ship. Two Turkish officers visited the ship, but there was no one to receive them. They went away without going below deck. My cough is worse than ever. I cannot take a moment's peace.

May 22
Tunis

Some of the officers who were going on shore asked me to join them. In a few minutes I was ready and on my way. I regarded myself as hardly fit to go, but as it was probably my last opportunity I decided to improve it.

We landed at Goletta which is the place where all goods are shipped and received for

Tunis. It is three miles from the ship. There are extensive fortifications here and several large public buildings. Goletta is in fact the gateway to Tunis by water.

On landing I noticed, entirely out of water, a large ship of war which probably had been built for forty years. How they intended to put her afloat I cannot imagine, still it seems incredible that men would construct a ship in such a place with conceiving of some plan whereby they thought that she might be floated.

A canal about one third of a mile long divides Goletta into two parts and connects with a large lagoon or lake, called, I believe, "Lake Carthage," on the opposite side of which is the city of Tunis. The cannon in the fortifications at Goletta are of brass and some of them are elaborately decorated with various designs in relief. Many Maltese live at Goletta and act as interpreters for the officers and men of the British and other ships which come in port.

Messrs. Hunter, Wilson, Fletcher, Glenn and I boarded a boat at the canal, bound across the lagoon for Tunis. The boat is a long open craft with two masts—a kind of felucca—rather narrow, with seats at the stern covered with bamboo mats for passengers. Along the sides of the boat, forward and extending to the space for passengers are places for the crew to walk when the boat is propelled by poles.

We have a light wind and start under sail. Our skipper is an Italian. Besides ourselves we have as passengers, one Turk, one Arab and three Italians. We have fewer passengers than the other boats because the skipper takes us for five francs—more than he would get for a whole boatload of natives at the customary price of a few sous a piece. In the canal we pass British, French, Italian and Portuguese boats belonging to the men-of-war in port, several of them with ladies on board.

The water in the lagoon is about four feet deep in the principal channel. The bottom is sandy and in some places is covered with a fine greenish weed. Spires of grass float on its surface and its general appearance is that of stagnant water. After a passage of two hours and a half we reached the city of Tunis.

Tunis is a beylik containing a population of 25,000,000. The city has a population of about 100,000. It is situated on rising ground commanding a fine view of the lake. On approaching its appearance is white as all the buildings are of stone. At the landing are scores of half naked Arabs who manifested some curiosity at our arrival, but were too indolent to show it long.

On leaving the landing my attention was attracted to a quarrel between two Arabs who had simultaneously seized the valise of a passenger arriving in a boat. They tugged at the valise alternately and then together. Then they would stop and give all their attention to talk—what a noise! A third Arab appeared and put in his claim. I left the owner standing by and witnessing the contention and putting in an occasional rejoinder and I do not know what the outcome was.

We made our headquarters at the Hotel France. This appears to be the only place agreeable to Christians. We met here our Captain, the Consul and other officers. We secured a carriage and a guide and our party started out to see all of interest in the city.

We first visited the Garden of the Bey which is about four miles outside of the city. The grounds are tastefully laid out and flowers are grown in great profusion. Here are the summer houses for the reception of guests of the Bey. They are furnished in good style. I noticed in them some fine specimens of carpeting. About are myrtle, orange, lemon, olive and other trees, all loaded with an abundance of fruit.

There is evidently a strong aversion to the French here. They made inquiry regarding our nationality at the gate. Our guide told us that they would not let Frenchmen come in. The blacks are slaves and are marked by several straight lines, scars, extending from the scalp over the side of the face. Each town has its special mark and consequently some of the slaves have many scars.

On our return we visited the encampment of the Bey's troops in front of his palace. There were several thousand soldiers. We passed inside the lines and conversed with some of the soldiers through our guide. They made inquiries regarding the ranks of the members of our party. The soldiers showed great curiosity about us and crowd around us in large numbers.

We crossed the street, passed through a gateway and entered the Bey's palace. Here we saw more troops awaiting the war-cry of the Bedouins. Their arms were of an ancient pattern. The muskets were "flint lock" and were rusty. The bayonets were of the old style. The soldiers were dressed in red pants with short black jackets. The universal head dress is a Turkish cap or fez bearing a brass device in front.

On entering the grand square of the palace the harem is directly in front, occupying the western wing of the building. The glass in the windows is stained blue, thus preventing the curious from seeing anything within. We were told that the Bey has seventy five wives, thus confined and guarded by his harmless and trusty eunuchs. We saw them sitting in the grand entrance shining in ebony blackness. We soon reached the limit set for our curiosity and we had to turn back after taking a good look beyond, where we were not permitted to go.

The floor of the palace was of white marble squares and very good, but the interior of the palace generally, so far as we were permitted to see it, did not measure up to the political importance of a Bey.

The country around has the appearance of great neglect, although it seems to be fertile. It is covered with grain. There is good grazing for the cattle and they are in good condition. There is a steady procession to the city of natives on horses laden with fruit and other productions of the country.

Finally our guide, a Maltese and a "sharper" told us that we had seen everything of interest outside the city. We entered the city on foot, leaving our coach because the city streets are too narrow for a carriage. The city is entirely surrounded by a wall on which brass guns are mounted. In few other respects does it differ from Smyrna or any other Turkish city. The bazaars are very good. Some of them are arched over the top with stone. Jews are to be seen here as in most corners of the world where money is to be made. Everywhere in the city evidence of indolence and of poverty abounds.

We all went to a bathhouse and took a Turkish bath. We entered, removed our shoes, and stepped up on a platform covered with bamboo. Here we undressed. A cloth wrapper was placed about our loins. We descended to the floor, put on a pair of wooden slippers and were conducted through a narrow passage way to the bath rooms. The whole place was very hot. Even the marble floor was too hot for the bare feet.

Soon the perspiration began to cover our bodies. Three of us immersed ourselves in the same vat of hot water after several attempts to stand the heat. Then we passed into an adjoining room where all of us stretched ourselves on our backs on marble platforms. Then the attendants whose duty it is to go through with the various manipulations of the trade began their work.

Meanwhile I hear shouts in Arabic from some who have passed through the first stage and suggesting that they were being "done up" by being scalded alive. I had seen or felt nothing to make me shout and I thought that perhaps that the noise was the result of some ecstatic condition produced by the bath and that our turn would come.

My attendant, a dark villainous looking son of Ham, kept up a brisk rubbing and soon my skin began to yield and come away in flakes. Suddenly he stopped, looked me in the face, and said inquiringly, "Francais." I replied, "Americano." He responded "Americano, bueno," nodded his head approvingly and resumed his rubbing.

The Tunisians dislike the French intensely. They distrust the French and suspect their political intentions. A few days ago two French officers who were on shore were stripped of all their clothing and personal effects.

My attendant then took me into a small room and after rubbing me from head to foot, using much soap, he turned a stream of water on my head. I suspect that this was what made the natives cry out, but it did not feel too hot for me after my douche in the "hot tank." This procedure being completed I passed into an adjoining room. Here bandage after bandage was thrown about my body as I sat in this room which was piled with all the linen required.

This was the final stage of the bath. We were conducted to the place where we undressed and reposed at full length on field cots. A Turkish drink, very palatable, was brought us. After that we had coffee and then cigars. The feeling in this stage is very agreeable. The perspiration continues to flow until the bandages are removed.

As it was late and the dinner hour was approaching we could not devote as much time to this stage of the bath as is customary and desirable, and perhaps necessary for health. I feared that I might take more cold in my shaky condition, but I escaped. The benefit to my cough was great. The bath relieved entirely my distress in breathing. We returned to the hotel where dinner was awaiting us and were joined by several of our officers who had arrived during our absence. We had a very nice dinner, served in French fashion, which I find is the best in these countries.

The landlord has five very comely daughters who all look and act alike. They did all the waiting on the tables and did it in a very agreeable and efficient manner. The mother was equally praiseworthy.

After a short walk in the evening our party retired. Some of our officers went to the opera which is under the control of Mr. Hall, an American, whom we met at Naples last winter. He is learning to sing Italian Opera and is appearing in small or out-of-the-way places. We may hear him sometime in America after he becomes accomplished. I am told that he is considered a fair singer and otherwise an artist of some merit.

Some of our officers on returning from the opera found their rooms occupied by others and their belongings a little mixed up. The landlady said that we all looked alike and that on so short an acquaintance she could not identify us so as to dispose of us as she otherwise would have done. However everybody quieted down after a while and silence reigned in the hostelry, save for the buzzing of the mosquitoes. Tunis appears to be an awful place for these insects. I was fortunate in coming through the night with demonstrable evidence of only four bites.

May 23
Tunis

At four a.m. our coachman true to his word gave us a call. We were to ride to Carthage and spend a short time there before returning to the ship. A boat was to be at Goletta waiting for us at 10 a.m.

A delay was proposed and adopted and we waited for breakfast at seven. In the meantime we took a walk about the city. As the bazaars were not yet open we could not see what they had to offer.

After breakfast we drove to the site of ancient Carthage, twelve miles distant. The road which leads around the border of the lake is poor. The ground is soft and unfit to travel in rainy weather.

Extensive grain fields were to be seen on the left all along the way and occasionally a camp of Bedouins with their flocks and herds. These Bedouins, barbarous and dirty, with a few rags drawn over their bodies present a picture of depravity and domestic wretchedness.

The ride brings us to the site of the once powerful city, or rather cities of Carthage. Rains and fragments of ruins are all around us. We enter an enclosure and visit the tomb of Saint Louis of France. Here is a chapel containing a fine statue of this sainted king. It is characterized by a most benevolent expression. He holds a book under the left arm. The statue bears two dates in gilt figures on a black background, 1270–1840.

To the right is an ancient Corinthian column very well preserved and standing on a mosaic foundation. Near is a statue of somebody, I do not know who. The head is missing, but the other parts are well executed. There are also two rude busts in dark marble, apparently only about half finished.

We next look at the ruins of a church which are made visible by an excavation directly in front of the tomb of Saint Louis. Two of its former chapels are discernible and the immense size of the blocks of stone which formed the side of the church indicate the extent of the destructive and burying forces to which the really magnificent buildings of the former Carthages have been subjected. Another Corinthian column and another statue of a man completes the list of all that I noticed of interest within the enclosure containing the tomb of Saint Louis.

We then drove to see the ancient cisterns, passing over a very bad road which threatened to overturn us every moment. So thoroughly has the surface of the ground been ploughed down through the centuries that fragments of ruins are distributed everywhere. The ground is covered with small stones. Occasionally in the side of a hill may be seen an arch of masonry.

The coach stops and the driver tells us that we are opposite the ancient cisterns. We start to travel on foot over the stones and through pathless fields of grain and tracts of poppies. Soon we see a ruin which proves to be the roof of a cistern. There are about a dozen of these structures, each about seventy five feet long, twenty broad and perhaps forty feet deep. The arches over them are firm and with few exceptions almost perfect. Presumably these cisterns were intended to provide a reserve water supply for the city.

Fragments of ancient buildings are also to be seen lying about in this locality. Even on the sea shore are to be seen marble columns dark with age. Most if not all of the ruins which we see are those of the Carthage rebuilt by the Romans, beginning under Julius Caesar about 122 B.C., and which was destroyed by the Arabs at the close of the seventh century A.D.

As one stumbles over fragments of ancient building material and walks on the hillside slopes where grain and the wild poppy flourish now his thoughts go back to a time when here stood the city which once contended with Rome for the supremacy of the world. Where now no human habitations are seen was once a city of 700,000 people who had extended their dominion over Sardinia, half of Sicily and all of Spain and sent elephants with their armies to trample Roman legions into the soil of Italian plains. This rival of ancient Rome began its career of commercial enterprise and of conquest 800 years before the Christian era. As one reads of the critical periods of its history he feels that Carthage might have conquered Rome and have imposed its civilization on Europe and the Western world had it not been for the interference in military operations by the envious politicians composing the supreme governing council of the state.

It may be that the visitor does not see vestiges of this older Carthage, but we know that the hill over which we have been rambling was the Byrsa, the site of the citadel, the acropolis of most ancient Carthage. Where we now find buried the royal leader of the eighth crusade whom the scheming Charles of Anjou had diverted to Northern Africa to perish with many others from the plague and we see a chapel dedicated to the teachings of a gentle Savior was once the temple of Beal-Ammon, the "Moloch," whom the Carthagenians sought to please by tossing into the arms of a huge bronze idol living children and watching them fall into the flames below.

One hundred and forty six years before the birth of this Savior, it was here on the Byrsa, in the temple of Eshmun or Aesculapius, the patron god of Carthage, that Hasdrubal and the faithful remnant of his followers after years of fighting made their final stand against the merciless Roman invaders whose motto was *Carthago delenda est Carthago* with which Cato had ended his speeches.

Carthage was destroyed. Aemilianus did what he was expected to do. The torch was applied to the citadel and to the rest of the city. The stone walls of its buildings cracked and crumbled in the heat of the flames.

It was here where we see the tomb of Saint Louis that Hasdrubal prostrated himself at his conqueror's feet and asked for mercy for his soldiers, his wife and two sons and the 900 deserters from the Roman army who had taken refuge with the Carthagenians in the temple of Eshmun. When the doors of the temple were thrown open Carthagenians and deserters alike were put to the sword or perished in the flames which followed. When the wife of Hasdrubal realized the hopelessness of her husband's entreaties in her behalf she appeared in her best apparel on the top of the temple, stabbed her two children and leaped with them into the flames.

The destruction of the city was complete. It was pillaged. Pliny calculated that four million four hundred thousand pounds of silver in weight was taken away by the Romans in addition to all the other plunder. More than fifty thousand women and children were shipped to Italy as slaves. The burning of the city is said to have continued for seventeen days. Remaining walls were thrown down, the ground ploughed over and human habitations within the area forbidden. Utica became the capital of Rome's African domain.

The time soon came when it was necessary for us to leave the reminders of the tragic fates of the rich and powerful cities that once flourished on this historical spot. A drive of a half an hour brought us to the port where we spent two hours waiting for the boat which we expected to find there awaiting our arrival. We finally reached the ship after a rough passage in which we all get thoroughly wet.

May 24
Tunis

This being the "birthday" of Queen Victoria of England all ships in port are dressed in flags and a national salute is fired at noon.

In the afternoon the French line-of-battle ship which left here a few days ago returned bringing with her *The City of Paris* and another line-of-battle ship, the iron-clad *La Gloire* and a steam tender. A little later a French store ship arrived loaded with coal. This makes quite a formidable French fleet here. I learn that the British fleet is also to be augmented very soon.

May 25
Tunis

Troops were being landed all night from the French ships, This afternoon the boats of the French ships are engaging in a boat drill.

The Captain came on board with the Consul, the Vice-Consul and several ladies. After dinner there was a short dance.

We have shipped two musicians who left a French ship. One of them has been a band master in the French and in the British service. He brought with him enough music to last for years. He had several bags of sheet music much of which he had composed himself. He ought to make a great addition to our band.

May 26
Tunis

The Captain is visiting the ships in port. Some of our officers went on shore at Carthage and returned with a great quantity of relics There were some marble slabs so heavy that they had to be hoisted on board from the boats. Everyone of the boats' crews now has several substantial souvenirs of one or the other of the ancient Carthages.

May 27
Tunis and the sea

This morning after breakfast the ship was got under way and with a fair wind the port of Tunis was seen far astern. We are bound to Malta. In going into the magazine today for powder to load the battery the Gunner found six inches of water.

It was soon discovered that there was a leakage in the port bread room which let the water into the sail room whence it found its way into the magazine, the sail room being over the magazine. After these rooms were emptied the water was found to have come through a leak in the ceiling on the side of the ship under the fore chains.

We leave the island of Tembra on our starboard and soon are up to the island of Pantellaria whose abrupt sides present an effective barrier to the pounding of the old Mediterranean.

My cough is improving and my appetite is returning. By the scales I have lost ten pounds.

May 28
Malta

At eight a.m. the island of Gozo is made ahead. We pass a British bark and a brig. The brig is going in the same direction as ourselves, but we quickly leave her astern. There is considerable sea and the wind is increasing, but we keep the royals on her and she flies like a thing of life. This is the kind of sailing I like and I remain on deck the entire forenoon.

Some settlements are to be seen on the island of Gozo, but the appearance of the land is sterile.

At eleven o'clock we are off the harbor at Malta and are hove to for a pilot. One soon reaches us and at one o'clock with a heavy breeze we pass into port under double reefed topsails. The entrance is narrow and the wind will just permit us to keep the ship (i.e. the sails) full enough to enter. A large number of small boats filled with Maltese follow us, also the tug boat *Bull Dog*. An American bark, the *Jasper*, lies here. She arrived a few days ago from New York.

May 29
Malta

Very warm. After dinner I went on shore. I was reminded of the description of this fortress given by Byron and others. It is a great place for stone steps. I kept thinking that St. Paul did not have to travel them when he was here. The guides are as annoying here as anywhere. Some of our party took a carriage for St. Antonio. Smith and I went to the Governor's Palace. It was also used for this purpose by the Knights of St. John, perhaps better known as the Knights of Malta.[20]

An attendant showed us the various apartments. We first entered the grand hall or ball room used by the knights. It is without a carpet or any furniture. The walls are white and are decorated effectively by rich gild work.

We next inspected the drawing room. The furniture is the same as three hundred year ago. As ancient as anything is a clock which will show not only the hour and minute, but the day of the week and of the month, and even the time of sunrise. The clock was not running, but we were informed that it can be made to do so merely by winding.

In this room are portraits of the two first Grand Masters or Commanders of the ancient order. There are the complete armors of four Grand Masters, French, German, Spanish and Portuguese. The costly tapestry in the room is in good condition.

We next visited the Council Chamber which is still used for this purpose. The walls are hung with the most elaborately wrought tapestry that I ever saw. It pictures Oriental scenery. It was made in Paris expressly for this room at a tremendous cost.

We next passed into the Armory of the Order. The passage leading to this room is beautifully decorated by mosaics in the floor and paintings above. Along the walls of the room are life-size figures dressed in the armors of the order, each figure holding a spear vertically to the front. Here in the Armory we see the Charter by which the island of Malta together with Tripoli was in A.D. 1530 granted to the Knights in perpetual sovereignty by Charles V. Here also is preserved in a glass covered case the sword of Dragut, the Bey of Tripoli, used by him at the siege of Malta by the Turks in 1565. Here likewise safeguarded we see the trumpet which sounded the retreat of the Knights from the Island of Rhodes and a bull of Pope Clement VII.

There are all kinds of swords and muskets used by the Knights. Some of the muskets are rifled. One is breech loading, about eight feet long and mounted on a pivoted arrangement. There are scores of coats–of–mail, rapiers, shields, etc., etc., a howitzer of brass and numerous models of guns and mortars. We are shown the armor of the "Spanish Giant" and his sword. The casque is very thick and weighs about twenty five pounds. A second sword lying by the statue is a sword and pistol combined. It would appear from what we saw here that the inventions "of these times," "modern inventions" are not all entirely new.

The Armory is about 250 feet long. It is one of the most interesting places that I ever visited. As we passed out we saw in a court like enclosure the state carriage of the Grand masters, the same in which Napoleon rode in 1798.

The Church of St. John is probably surpassed by none in Europe in the matter of elaborate decorative art. In the floor of the building are 400 sepulchral marble slabs marked with the epitaphs of the Spanish, French and Portuguese Knights and other dignitaries of the Island. On either side, to the front of the main altar are the thrones of state for the Bishop of Malta and for the representative of the British crown.

In the crypt under the Church are the tombs of LaValette, Philip de l'Isle Adam, Vignacount the Latin Secretary of deValette, and some others.

The Phoenicians are believed to have established themselves in Malta 1,500 years before Christ. There are remains of a still earlier race and culture on the island. The Carthagenians came to Malta in the 6th century B.C., succeeding the Greeks who had ruled it for more than a century. In the struggle between Rome and Carthage Malta passed into the hands of the former, the Maltese delivering up the Punis garrison to the Romans. Charles V, King of Spain and Emperor of Germany conveyed it to the Knights of St. John of Jerusalem, together with Gozo and Tripoli, in 1530.

The Knights had abandoned their headquarters in Jerusalem when it fell into the hands of the Turks in 1187. In 1291, Acre had been the stronghold of the Knights since 1191 was likewise taken by the Turks and the Knights settled in Rhodes. Here Mohammed attacked them in 1480, but was repelled. In 1522 Solyman moved against them with a force of 140,000 defeated them and they quitted Rhodes January 1, 1523, and came to Malta. They were besieged here by the Turks in 1565, but after a hard struggle the Turks were driven away.

May 30
Malta

In the afternoon I visited Brumola alone. There are three separate islets or harbors on this side and the Navy Yard is here. I spent my time inspecting the dry dock, rope walk and other Naval works and shops. As the British war ships are absent the place was unusually dull.

The ships have gone to Corfu to bring to Malta the troops which have been stationed at Corfu. The fortifications there have been blown up as Corfu and some other Ionian Islands are being evacuated by the British.

The sunlight is exceptionally strong and I find it difficult to keep my eyes open at all when exposed to it.

I crossed over to Valetta, met some of our officers with whom I spent a few hours and returned on board before 9 p.m.

The ship has been filled with visiting soldiers all day. The 100th regiment is stationed here. It was largely recruited in Canada and contains many men who have been residents of the United States and some who are citizens. The soldiers are finding former neighbors and some even relatives on our ship. The praise of our flag is in all their mouths and no doubt they would all be glad to go away with us. Some will probably try to do so.

May 31
Malta

We have a diving-bell under the ship's bottom to repair the copper which has been torn away or damaged in several places. The day is hot, as usual, and we have a large number of visitors on board. The ship is surrounded with boats from shore. I do not like the looks of the Maltese, nor their actions and I have learned from a brief experience with them that they are a great set of "Jews."

June 1
Malta and the sea

At eight o'clock we cast loose from the mooring and sail out of the fine harbor of Malta and say good-by to the reminders of the once famous Knights of St. John.

It appears that A. McLeod, the swordsman, has deserted. He went on shore yesterday on liberty and has not returned. His time in our service had expired and he said that he wished to be free, but if he has entered the British service he will be pledged to twelve years more of a service less desirable than ours. How foolish some men are. A little spirit probably has caused him to bind himself to an indefinite separation from his wife who is anxiously awaiting his return to America.

The pain in my eye has increased to a severe attack of neuralgia which confines me to my room and puts me on the sick list. Consequently I am unable to give a farewell glance to the frowning fortresses of Malta as we sail out on to the open sea. We meet shortly the mail ship from Marseilles and heave to. A mail is brought aboard with letters for some of the officers and crew. Contrary to my expectations I receive nothing. We are off now for Alexandria. I am nearly crazy with pain in or about my eye.

June 2
At sea

A fair wind and a smooth sea. The ship is sailing quietly while everyone appears cheerful, especially the Ward Room officers who are drinking English ale and laughing like jolly fellows.

My head is worse than ever. What a pain! I have an awful cold all through my system. The Carpenter on going into the port bread-room, forward, discovered a "stowaway" in the ship's uniform. He was brought out and taken to the mast. He is evidently a soldier, but says not. He will be delivered up to the British Consul at Alexandria. The Admiral of the port of Malta gave positive instructions that we should ship there nobody but American citizens.

I have a blister, etc., on my head, but the pain continues the same all day. At night it abates. I have obtained no help from the medical department. I did not expect to and am therefore neither astonished nor disappointed.

June 3
At sea

We are sailing along at the same rate.

I am confined to my berth all day suffering the most excruciating pain in my head and through the left eye. I cannot bear light, with which fortunately I am not troubled much, not being on deck at all.

June 4, 5, 6
At sea

Confined with the trouble in my head. Such pain I have never before endured. The ship has been quietly sailing along. Now and then studding-sails are hauled down and shifted from one side to the other. It is the most quiet sailing I ever knew—except for me.

June 7
Alexandria, Egypt

Last night land was made; also the light at this port. At eight a.m. we were at anchor in the harbor and the native pilot leaving the ship. We have made a good passage for this season of the year when the winds are very light.

On looking through a port I see that the harbor is filled with steam ships and all other kinds of crafts. Apparently from everywhere in the world.

The "stowaway" is in process of being delivered up to the British Consul, but I hear that he has said that he is going to make his escape from the officer who has him in charge.

We salute the Turkish flag and receive a return from the Turks.[21]

Soon merchants and small ware peddlers swarm on board. The decks present a great display of Oriental merchandise. Shawls, caps, pipes, tobacco, slippers, fancy work in beads and shells, etc., are exhibited in great quantities and sold for big prices.

June 8
Alexandria

I hear that a second "stowaway" left the ship this morning after having eluded the officers' search by remaining all the passage from Malta in the fore-top. An officer went there in the search for "stowaways," but somehow the "stowaway" escaped detection—with the help of some of our crew, of course.

I hear that the other "stowaways" whom we delivered to the officer from the British Consulate yesterday knocked the officer down and escaped and has not been recaptured.

The Viceroy is giving a grand ball at the Palace tonight in honor of the circumcision of a son. All the officers of our ship are invited to attend. The Palace is close to the shore and near the ship. The entire building is brilliantly illuminated.

My neuralgia, or whatever it is, is growing more easy, but I cannot go on deck nor read yet. The pain leaves me now at night and commences again at about eight o'clock in the morning. In addition to that I have a cold and cough which has destroyed my appetite and makes me very weak. My messmate, Cox, is as weak and feeble as I and there are many others on the ship as miserable as we are, or worse.

Perhaps the weather may be partly responsible because of the condition which it tends to produce below deck on the ship. The ship is damp in every part. The decks are dry. Here in the East a dampness which feels like "night air" comes down with the wind. Even the sails are damp. I will be glad when we are through with this cruise in the East. The ship however appears to be an unhealthy ship at all times. Before a man can recover fully from one kind of sickness he acquires another. I hear that a ship of this type has the reputation of being especially unhealthy for a ship's yeoman and that they are usually invalided home before the end of the cruise, because they spend so much time down in the foul air of the unventilated Store Room in the smell of paints, turpentine and other stores, and with a big lamp burning in order to be able to see to work.

June 9
Alexandria

This morning a Turkish Brigadier General visited the ship and expressed himself as being much pleased with her appearance.

My head is improving slowly, but I am not yet able to go on duty.

The officers who attended the ball returned this morning. They describe the affair as a magnificent demonstration of Eastern splendor and luxury. They say that it surpassed, by far, the Prince's ball at Naples last winter. The Palace was gorgeous. The supper included every dish and table decoration which the culinary art has devised. Although the host was a Muhammadan champagne flowed like a river.

There was a room set apart for gambling and into it Turkish merchants and Englishmen gathered with bags of gold which were carried by special personal attendants for this purpose. Gambling is a popular pastime here. Most of the people who attended the ball wore European dress. They were chiefly Englishmen, Frenchmen and Italians.

The fireworks which we saw from the ship were most elaborate.

June 10
Alexandria
The wind blows from the land this morning. It is quite a day. I spend some time on the gun deck to get the air and am feeling much better. We are living principally on vegetables here as it is not permitted to bring beef or eggs on board. Eighty thousand head of cattle have died here this spring and meat is considered unfit to eat. As it is meat costs fifty cents a pound. All other provisions are proportionally high.

June 11
Alexandria
McLeod who was supposed to have deserted at Malta came on board this morning, having followed our ship here on a French steamer. He acted wisely.

June 12
Alexandria
The wind is off the land. It is very hot and brings with it swarms of flies which are very annoying. They make it almost impossible to stay on deck.

Some of the ship's company went to the Bethel ship to attend divine worship.

Captain Weeks of Kittery who is in port here with his ship, the *Brazilian*, visited our ship and dined with the Ward Room officers.

My head is much better, but during the hours of the sun's greatest power I still suffer considerable pain.

June 13
Alexandria
I am making out my reports.

The Captain, Paymaster and Surgeon returned from Cairo where they have been for four days.

A British steamship arrived with the Captain deceased. We put our flag at half mast as do all the British ships in port.

My head is better. I am much improved in every way.

June 14
Alexandria
In the afternoon Grainger, Cox and I went on shore to see this ancient city which has been the scene of so many important historical events.

Passing numerous steamships, one of which is American built, we came to the landing. It is a dirty rude place thronged with laborers who are landing merchandise or taking it away; also dragomen and boys with asses who try to block the passage way so that you may be obliged to mount an ass in order to get clear. The scene reminded me of Bayard Taylor's description of this landing place. These donkey boys speak English very well and they used it in proclaiming to us the superb qualities of asses which bore such names as, "Yankee Doodle," "Jenny Lind," "Billy Wilson," "Stonewall Jackson," "General Siegel," etc.

We hired a carriage for the afternoon for $3 and an interpreter for an additional $1, and drove off to see the sights. We first went to Pompey's pillar. This peculiar monument of the past is crumbling at the base and unless soon repaired will fall. The pedestal on which it stands is cracked and giving way. Several acres around the pillar are occupied as a Turkish burial place. The ground is covered with little white stone tombs, built above the surface and only large enough to contain one body.

From here we went to the Catacombs of the ancient city. On the way we passed a Turkish funeral procession which offered some features new and strange to us.

There is little of interest in the Catacombs, except signs of great antiquity. They do not differ in their internal arrangements for the reception of bodies from the Catacombs at Naples.

We then came to the Nile, or the canal which leads into it—at any rate what we saw contains water of the Nile. Here were river boats loading and unloading goods of various kinds. All along the bank are baths where were lounging the most indolent and dirty people that I ever saw. There were many people who had lost the sight of one eye and beggars who were blind in both. Around what was once an eye but which now looks more like a boiled onion was usually to be seen a black fringe of flies.

We drove for two miles or more along the banks looking at the river boats which lie along the way waiting to be hired by Europeans or other travelers who want to go up the Nile. These boats have high sterns containing a spacious cabin and a place forward for the crew. They are also decked forward. They are rigged after the felucca style.

As we drove along I noticed the most beautiful flower gardens that I ever saw. Oleanders appeared in the greatest profusion.

On the outskirts of the city and on the borders of the Nile were low miserable huts occupied by the Arabs. Women, practically naked, were washing clothes in the dirty water of the Nile. Naked children were all about. Groups of people were sitting under some sort of a rude protection from the sun talking or eating or sleeping like pigs.

We came to the celebrated Needle of Cleopatra.[22] It is an obelisk of ordinary dimensions. It is covered on one side by what appeared to me to be Arabic characters. It stands in an enclosure with quantities of rubbish and waste building material about. There is at present nothing near it indicating that it occupied any important place in a city. There are no buildings or signs of former buildings in the vicinity. It stands in one of the roughest and least inviting places that I ever saw honored by a similar monument of antiquity.

We next came to the Palace of the Viceroy. The grounds are extensive and evidently require the employment of many servants and laborers. A large court-yard separates the Palace from the Harem, which is of itself an extensive building.

European Square is the most important and sightly place in the city. About it are hotels, banking houses, express offices, ship and other transportation agencies and English and french post offices. It is only here that one feels that he is in touch with civilization.

I noticed nothing about the bazaars that was different from what is to be seen in any other Eastern city.

We saw children making lace and cords. They had bad eyes, but the dexterity with which they handled their spools showed that they could almost do the work without the use of eyes.

On completing our sightseeing we went to wait for a boat from the ship, into a ship chandler's, which in some seaports serves as a rendezvous for mariners. Evidently because company was being entertained on the ship no sunset boat came for us, and we had to apply to the natives for transportation.

The first boatman had the impudence to ask us six shillings to take us to the ship. Our Italian pilot who had joined us gave the man a lecture and we went looking for another boat. One was offered to us for five francs and we thought that the matter was settled, but the boatman suddenly turned back and brought us to the first boatman of whom he was evidently afraid. After storming and haggling we finally had to pay the first man his six shillings and he insisted on being paid in advance. After considerable delay we eventually reached the ship, wishing that all the Egyptians were in their Nile with its dirty water three feet over their heads. I am glad to leave them and their dirty city behind us forever.

June 15
Alexandria
Today we are off for Jaffa.

At eight a.m. the steam yacht of the Viceroy was alongside ready to tow us out of the harbor, but owing to delay in obtaining a bill-of-health we do not leave until afternoon. The Turk who took the clothes of some officers on shore to wash them returned the clothes today in such a condition that everybody who saw them laughed—except the owners and the Turk. They had apparently been laid in some dirty water and then wrung. They still had the original dirt on them and more, smelled very bad and looked as though they had drifted all the way down the Nile from Cairo. The indignation of the owners made us laugh as much as the appearance of the clothes.

I feel quite well today and am glad to be again at sea and to be free from intercourse with such places as Alexandria.

June 16
At sea
I came off the sick list today after having been on just a fortnight. My head still pains me a little occasionally and my cough is not yet well.

We are having a pleasant sail and it is not uncomfortably hot.

The sailmaker is making canvas haversacks for the officers who are planning to go to Jerusalem.

June 18
At sea
At noon land is reported from aloft. We sail along the coast within sight of the cities of Giza and Askalan. The officers who are to go to Jerusalem are stirring about making their preparations. Permission to go is granted to several petty officers, to me among them. This swells the party to twenty six. I am informed that I must be ready to start tonight. A general excitement prevails among the "pilgrims." They are packing their haversacks and cleaning and putting in order swords and pistols. My equipment includes a Bible, two boxes of sardines and some ship's bread; also a flask of water for which I find room in the Carpenter's, Mr. Philbrick's sack.

By four p.m. however the wind dies out to complete calm and the tide setting us in toward the low sandy coast we anchor for the night. The start of the expedition is called off until tomorrow.

June 19
Jaffa
Early this morning the paymaster went on shore to make arrangements to take the party to Jerusalem. The names of the "pilgrims" were called soon after and we passed into the

boats and made our way to the shore. Jaffa is a poor place to land. The natives come to the beach to take you ashore on their backs and practically fight each other for the possession of a passenger.

I find that the American Consul here is a native of the country, but he speaks English well. He is a Doctor of Medicine. I am informed that he is a brother of our Consul at Jerusalem.[23]

An agreement is made with a German by the name of "Herman" to take the party of 26 to Jerusalem and back for £ 105 Sterling which means about $20 apiece. Hotel bills in Jerusalem are to be paid by the dragoman.

It is arranged to leave the city at 4 p.m. today. We return to the hotel. It is kept by the father of our dragoman. It appears to be the only hotel in the place and no one would suspect it of being a hotel from outward appearance. We order dinner for 2 p.m. and put in the intervening time in looking over this ancient city.

We visit the house of "one Simon, a turner, by the seaside" and find in it a Turk asleep. He wakes up quickly and asks for "baksheesh." I drink from the well and pass on.

In going into a narrow street nearby, Mr. Jones and myself came unexpectedly on a Turkish woman standing in the doorway of her house. She shrieked, placed her arm across her face which was bare and retreated.

On turning and going in another direction we came to a school, but nobody from a Christian country would have imagined what the children were brought together for. They were making a great noise when we appeared, but soon quieted down. Then the master who was sitting with his legs crossed on the stone floor, received from each pupil a tablet of tin upon which were written Arabic characters, apparently the letters of the alphabet. The master examined carefully what the pupil had written, rubbed out the characters and returned the tablet to the pupil. The pupils sat around the room in rows, facing each other. Soon the master started the commotion going again and meanwhile lighted his "chibouque" and began to smoke. The school was open to the street from which it was shut off only by a wooden gate. Opposite is the shop of a saddler.

The streets are very narrow and once I nearly had my clothes torn off by passing asses loaded with bushes for firewood.

The bazaars are about the same as in any Turkish city. Many of the houses are practically in ruins and are occupied more like the caves of wild people than civilized dwellings.

We passed through the gate to the market outside the town. Fruit and vegetables chiefly are sold here. About the market are coffee houses and booths of all kinds. The land around Jaffa is fertile and the scenery very fine. Palm trees, figs, plums, lemons and oranges grow in profusion and grapes are everywhere to be seen.

We get our first insight into the conduct of the local export trade by seeing beside a store house at the shore a man with very dirty feet treading raisins and other dried fruit into sacks. Some of our party declared that they never could eat raisins again. I noticed on the shore three large church bells. They were probably contributed by some Christian society for some church in Jerusalem, but as there is no means of transporting them inland here they remain.

We have a very poor dinner for which we pay 5 francs. Soon afterward we assemble at the Consulate for the start. Horses are brought up. Our names are called. Each one is given an animal. The cavalcade soon passes out the gate of the city and on the sandy road to Ramleh. The people along the route look at our troop armed with swords and pistols with some curiosity perhaps, but with their peculiar nonchalance. We may look something like the old Crusaders whose path we are following to the land of Judah and the city of Jerusalem. At any rate we are pilgrims.

A ride of five miles brings us on the valley of Asharon. The fertile plain which stretches away to the left is the Valley of Labana.

Herds of cattle are grazing on the green plains and fields of grain wave on every hand. The scene reminds me of the sacred poet's description of the beauty of this region. The "rose of Sharon" and the lily of the valley still blossom in Palestine, although further on toward the "Holy City" the land seems to be cursed with barrenness.

After a ride of four hours we arrive at Ramleh. If Jaffa is celebrated for its gardens and to be remembered as the place where Jonah fled when he shrank from delivering the message to Ninevah, the place where Peter restored Tabitha to life and where he beheld the vision which instructed him to offer salvation to the world, Ramleh is recalled as the home of Joseph and of Nicodemus and the place of the defense before the Danhedrin.

Along the way in many places hedges of cactus or prickly pear form an effective barrier on either side of the road and furnish a cool shade as well. Ramleh means sandy. The city is surrounded by gardens in which are trees loaded with delicious fruit and with olives. The palm tree flourishes here and they with the minarets of several Mosques make the place one of peculiar beauty.

Ramleh has a population of about 30,000. Here is one of the largest convents in Palestine. A conspicuous feature of the town is a square tower about 120 feet high. From it a fine view is to be had of the country as far as the sea and to the North, east and South. Ludd or ancient Lydda was pointed out to me. It is reported to be the birth place of St. George, the fabulous patron of England in Popish times. Lydda was a town of Benjamin. Here Peter preached the gospel to the "saints which dwelt at Lydda." It was there also that he said to Eneas who "had kept his bed for eight years," "Jesus Christ maketh thee whole."

While at Ramleh we stopped at the Convent where pilgrims are entertained. Here our horses were fed and coffee was served to our whole party. Some managed to get naps during our brief stay here.

Adjoining the Convent is the house of Nicodemus from the roof of which I had a moonlight view of the city. It was very quiet and the majestic palms stood like sentinels over the city in its solitude.

We "form company in two ranks" and pass through the gate of the city and out on the plain beyond. A ride of four hours brings us to a stopping place at the entrance of a mountain gorge. Our route lay along Habab, Latron, Bab-el-Wady, Huryet-el-Enab and Kutenich. The road is very good for traveling until the gorge is reached.

Up to this place nothing interrupted our progress save the delay in waiting for Surgeon Messersmith and Sailmaker Tatem to come up from the rear. They fell behind from their inability to ride, the former being advanced in age[24] and the latter very corpulent.

Here at the entrance to the gorge is a stone hut where we made coffee, had some refreshments like sardines and bread, and fed the animals. We found other parties stopping here for the same purpose. We also tried to get some sleep here, lying or sitting in what might appear to be a comfortable place. A heavy dew fell upon us. It was almost like rain and mingling with the dust with which we were covered made us look like real pilgrims.

The Surgeon and the Carpenter lay down on a bed in the hut for a short time, but soon came out, having discovered that they had acquired lice as well as fleas. I reposed on a somewhat elevated flat stone in the rear of the hut but was not sleepy enough to enjoy it long.

After a rest of about two hours we were again on the road, which is gradually changing in character. We are now entering a mountain pass that appears like the bed of a dry river. Rocks of all sizes obstruct our passage and the mountains rise almost perpendicularly on either side. We are obliged to go in single file and are ordered by the guide to keep in "close order." I never traveled such a road before and more than one of our party repeated, "Jordan is a hard road to travel."

At three o'clock we are saluted by some mountaineers who parley with our guide for a while. We halt. The baggage is brought up and we make ready for an attack. No hostile demonstration is made and after a time we move on without being able to determine how many men there were concealed behind the bushes and rocks on the sides of the mountains. I could distinctly hear men talking with each other within fifty yards of me, but could not see them. If they had intended to attack us they were probably overawed by the size of our party.

June 20
Jerusalem

Daylight finds us emerging from the gorge to climb hills and descend into valleys, over roads little better than that which we had left behind. They are full of stones and ledges. Over on our left the guide points out the Wadi "Albagosh," the place where Sampson slew the Philistines.

We came to the village which the guide called "Anata," but I think he must be wrong as according to my map "Anata" is east of Jerusalem. This place the guide tells us is the birthplace of Jeremiah.

From here on to Jerusalem there are no more towns or villages. Along the way are guard houses, each occupied by five men who are provided with horses and arms to assist travelers when attacked by robbers, but the guard houses are too far apart to be of much help in such an event.

By morning we all have become much fatigued and we are obliged to go very slowly to keep in sight of the Doctor and the Sailmaker on their donkeys.

At eight o'clock I see the Holy City and when within a short distance I drive in the shade of a building and wait for our rear to come up, They soon appear and we enter the Jaffa gate and are within the most interesting city ever built by men. Just outside the city and near the Jaffa gate is a Russian Convent, recently built. It covers considerable area. It is enclosed by a wall and presents a splendid appearance on approaching the city as we did.

Near the gate I observed several beggars and leprous women. They reminded me of the ancient Hebrew custom with regard to persons afflicted with leprosy as well as offering me examples of the disease itself. The faces of some were much disfigured and they could not speak aloud.

One of the first objects that met my eye on entering the city was a cask marked "Medford Rum." With the recollection of the road over which we had just passed so fresh in my mind and its painful reminders so keen, it was quite natural that I should inquire how they got a cask of rum here. Before reaching the hotel where we are to stay it is necessary to dismount. The pavement is so smooth and the street so sloping that the Gunner's horse fell and the Gunner with him, but fortunately escaped injury.

At 9 o'clock we are safely ensconced in the Mediterranean Hotel. After eating most of the party retire to their rooms. It is decided to do no more today, but to start at eight o'clock tomorrow morning.

The American Consul, Mr. Murad, invites us to the Consulate.[25] Captain Stellwagen and Messrs. Jones, Philbrick and I accept. The Consulate is up on Mount Zion where the stars and stripes float in the breeze above all other flags in the city.

The Consul is a native of this country, but a citizen of the United States. He was a Captain in a New York regiment at the beginning of the war, but was obliged to leave the service on account of ill-health. He has no family and complains of his exile from his associations and his friends in New York. Here are there are no places of amusement, no society, no diversions and no enterprises to interest him. He says that the people here will not lift a hand to do anything whatever if they can avoid doing so. He spends his time in reading and writing to his friends.

He offers us some "Jerusalem wine," the "pure juice of the grape." It is the color of Marsala, but has not the same taste. It is pleasant however, and very clear.

As the sun shines too hot to go about the city we conclude to return to the hotel and sleep and postpone until 5 o'clock the acceptance of the Consul's offer to show us about the city.

At the appointed time all our party are at the consulate where first we register our names. We then go to the Church of St. James, Armenian. Here is a tomb said to contain the head of St. James. Above the tomb is a splendid painting of Christ. It is in a beautifully wrought gold frame valued at $50,000. A fine portrait of St. James is preserved in the chapel. The church has a beautiful altar and contains several other excellent paintings. We are sprinkled with rose water by the priests as we pass out. Via Dolorosa, the street through which Christ carried his cross to Calvary is still extant with its ancient arch. We pass through it and enter the "Street of Mourning" through which Mary Magdalene walked, and wept as Christ passed by to be crucified. The street is arched, dark and otherwise in keeping with the name that it bears. We pass the ruins of St. John's Hospital and the Church of the Holy Sepulcher which we shall visit before we leave.

After purchasing some photographic views of the city we return to the hotel.

June 21
Jerusalem

We start for Bethlehem at 8 o'clock. We pass out through the Jaffa gate and take the road leading to the North. We pass the valley of Hinnom which is a continuation of that of Jehosaphat, separated only by a causeway. A short distance along our route we see the "Field of Blood" or "Potter's Field." We come to the "plains of Ephraim" which is the most beautiful slope to be seen on this side of the city. It terminates at Mount Elias. Here is the place where Elijah was "fed by the ravens." Now it is the site of a Greek Convent.

Just above and in the middle of the road is the well where the "Wise Men" saw the star which led them to the place where the newly born Christ lay. Near here we are shown the place where Benjamin's house stood. If however our guide be out of the way regarding the location where the ravens fed Elijah he may be wrong also with respect to the site of Benjamin's late residence.

Near the road, about half the way to Bethlehem stands Rachel's tomb. We dismount and enter the chapel where without doubt was laid the body of this woman whose name is familiar to us all. It is a small Turkish mosque that covers the place. In it lights are kept continually burning. I satisfy myself with a few pieces of the ancient tomb and ride on to the wells of David from which the three mighty men of his host drew water. From the well a ride of a few minutes brings us to the gate of Bethlehem. Bethlehem is built upon a hillslope. The houses are of stone, substantial castle-like buildings. Hills and valleys encompass the town. To the East one sees the hills of Ammon and Moab. Among these hills David was keeping his father's sheep when called to be anointed King of Israel. On these plains stretching out before us was heard the angelic chorus of "Peace on earth and good will to men."

How many minds have turned to this little town of Bethlehem! From it what inspirations and influences have gone forth to better men's condition and prepare him for a higher sphere. Yet in the present day inhabitants of the very place where Christ was born what miserable representatives do we see of the doctrines which he taught.

Bethlehem was the "City of David." Abijah, Obed, Jesse, Boaz and other scriptural characters were also natives of this place. It requires but little imagination to enable us to see Boaz and Ruth gleaning in the field before us. The feeling which comes over one who finds himself in the midst of the scene of recorded Biblical events is such that the whole experience seems unreal.

The great point of interest in Bethlehem is, of course, the "Church of the Nativity" together with the Latin Convent, supposed to be built over the spot where Christ was born. The Convent was built by Helena the mother of Constantine.

To the "Grotto of the Nativity" the descent is about twenty feet. The place is illuminated by costly lamps and adorned with expensive marbles. The precise spot where Christ was born is marked by a star, or "Glory." Numerous lamps are kept burning there.

A short distance away is the place where the horse and ass eat. Except for the star this place is accorded the same care and distinction as the spot where Christ was born. Lamps are likewise kept burning here.

At the place just referred to members of our party, including officers, lay various articles to bless them—even swords and watches go on. It would appear that our party are as superstitious as were the Crusaders of old.

Tapers are lighted and we descend into the vault beneath the Church. Here we are shown the tombs of St. Paul, Jerome and Josephus, and that of infants beheaded in Bethlehem by order of Herod. Here also is the study of St. Jerome where he translated a Bible from Hebrew into Latin about 400 A.D.

The present inhabitants have the reputation of being clannish and unruly. As we pass through the streets they surround us in large numbers importuning us to buy such articles as brooches of mother-of-pearl, beads of olive wood, sandalwood, etc. These were also exhibited at the Church in great quantities.

From Bethlehem we go to Bethany, on the side of the Mount of Olives. On our way through the Valley of Jehosaphat we come to the wall of Job. From it some Arabs give us water to drink. The well has several buckets fastened to long ropes by which the water is drawn up.

A short distance from here is the "Pool of Silcam" where the blind man washed and was made to see. There is a stone basin connected with the pool, arched over and reached by stone steps. I go into it, but the darkness prevents me from seeing the water. Some of our party obtained bottles of the water to take away.

We next come to the "Brook Hedron." Its bed runs between the Mount of Olives and the eastern wall of Jerusalem. For a part of its course it skirts some excavated tombs. The rocks on which this wall is built are at some points not less than 300 feet high, while the bottom of the valley there is about 150 feet wide.

On the right of our route are the tombs of Absolom, Zachariah and others. On the slope of the "Mount of Olives," opposite this point and near the city wall and close to the "Golden Gate," as well, are numerous Turkish tombs.

A circuitous road over ledges, worn by centuries of travel soon brings us to the village of Bethany. As we gaze on the road to Jericho over the dreary plain we think of the lesson taught by our Savior's story of the man beaten by robbers, the priest, the Levite and the "good Samaritan." The route to Jericho is no less dangerous now for travelers than it was when Christ chose it for this parable.

Bethany is said to mean "the House of Grief." It is about two miles southeast of Jerusalem. From it we have a fine view of the Dead Sea and of the river Jordan. It is now a village of about twenty families and though embosomed in olive groves has a forlorn and dreary appearance.

We are shown the house of Mary and Martha, the tomb of Lazarus and the remains of his house. We are lighted into his tomb. It is reached by 26 stone steps. This tomb is cut in the solid limestone rock. It calls for more credulity than I possess to believe that the body of Lazarus ever lay in this sepulcher.

Here in Bethany was the residence of Simon the Leper where the woman anointed the feet of our Savior, using for the purpose expensive material from an "alabaster box" and arousing the protest of Judas Iscariot against the proceeding as an unjustifiable extravagance.

It was from Bethany that Christ sent two of his deputies to bring the "colt of an ass" on which he rode on the occasion now celebrated as "Palm Sunday." It was here that He wept as Mary wept, and "all men saw that he loved" Lazarus. It was here that he "raised Lazarus," pronouncing the words, "Lazarus, come forth!"

It was from Bethany that Christ finally led out his disciples when he was about to return to "his God and our God." Nowhere in Palestine can a Christian feel that he is in a more sacred spot than at Bethany.

> *Upon that bleak and barren brow*
> *The very sun shines sadder now.*

Here the Savior found his nearest approach to a home.

Our route now takes us to the Mount of Olives. In some places we are obliged to dismount and lead the horses. We meet women on the way with babies slung to their backs in a kind of sack. The "innocents" were asleep with the scorching sun shining full in their faces while their eyes and mouths were rimmed with flies. I have noticed Turks sleeping in their bazaars with flies so numerous in their mouths as to make the interior of the mouth look black. This is a matter of custom. Children seldom brush flies from their eyes. I judge that these insects have much to do with producing the dreaded ophthalmia so common in this country.

There are both a mosque and a church on the Mount of Olives, and nearby is a village occupied by Arabs. The view of Jerusalem from this point is the best to be obtained. The city lies spread out like a photographic map before us. We can trace all the public buildings, streets and squares. Our view is from the tower within the enclosure of the convent—from the cupola of the "Church of the Ascension."

In the Mosque we are shown a mark in a stone, being, we are told, a footprint left there by Christ when he ascended to Heaven. There is, of course, no account of his ascension from this spot.

We see the mountains of Pisgah, Samaria, Mount Nebo, Frank Mountain; the Dead Sea, the River Jordan, the Valley of the Jordan, the road winding to Jericho and other Biblical places.

Taking leave of the Mount of Olives we descend by a nearby straight road to the Garden of Gethsemane. On the way we meet several Arab women carrying babies on their backs. They all ask us for "baksheesh." They are miserable degenerate looking beings.

We are soon in the retreat where Christ went for prayer that trying night when he was to be taken by his persecutors to be crucified, and when those who were to watch with him fell asleep. Near here he was identified by Judas to the servants of the high priest as the one for whom they were looking.

The northwestern corner of this garden enclosure is about 145 feet from Kedron. The western wall is about 160 feet in length and the northern about 150. Within the enclosure are four olive trees, doubtless of great antiquity, but which were probably not here at the time of Christ, as we were told. The Garden is now the property of a Franciscan monastery. Various shrubs are cultivated here and although we were not allowed to take a twig of the olive trees we were freely handed flowers and herbs. The gnarled trunks of the olive trees will doubtless be cherished a long time whatever their origin may have been.

Not far from here is the tomb of the Virgin which we pass without entering. We then cross to St. Stephen's Gate, outside of which is pointed out to us a flat ledge where, we are told, St. Stephen was stoned to death.

We are now on the road to Sychar which brings us to the "Tombs of the Kings." A pathway cut in the solid rock leads down to an open court about 40 yards square also excavated in the solid rock. At the end of the court is a portico decorated with exquisitely chiseled flowers and fruit. To the left of the portico is the entrance to an ante-room about twelve feet square. From here we enter another and much larger room and through this we pass to six or seven others, all cut out of solid rock and containing niches for the reception of the dead. The coverings of the niches had evidently once been richly carved, though now, but for the most part demolished. The doors of the chambers, of which none remains entire, were made of stone panels, the doors swinging on stone hinges moving in stone sockets. The decorations of the place are joyous rather than grave or melancholy. They are largely obliterated except on the portico. These tombs are well worthy to be the last resting place of royalty.

This visit completes our party's scheduled tour for the day and we reach the Jaffa Gate by passing the Damascus Gate, thus making the circuit of the city in the day's ramblings.

As we approach the Jaffa Gate an infantry company appears, coming from the valley where they had been for drill. We halted and permitted them to enter first, observing their military bearing and listening to their peculiar music.

I could not refrain from the thought that although the Crescent of the Turk now rules here supreme after centuries of fighting during which one flag after another has been planted on its blood stained walls and hundreds of thousands have lost\ their lives in deadly strife to possess this city made sacred by the life and teachings of Christ, there <u>will</u> come a day when those whose right it is to hold this hallowed place shall enter it in triumph ever to remain.

We arrive at our hotel glad to find here a respite from sightseeing and relief from the heat of the sun. A good dinner is served and eaten by everybody with relish and in a short time we feel much more energetic.

My room at the hotel is very cool and convenient. I look from my room on the "Pool of Hezekiah" which is alongside the hotel and furnishes it with water. The pool is about 250 feet long and 150 feet wide. The water is about 4 feet deep. The water is not used for cooking purposes, only for washing and bathing.

From the roof of the Hotel I have a splendid view of the city towards the east. The Mosque of Omar, <u>Kubbet es-Sahra</u>, "The Dome of the Rock," is directly in front. I can look down upon this sacred area, the scene of so many acts of religious devotion and of fanaticism and cruelty. I see the Church of the Holy Sepulcher and everything east of Mount Zion as I am on its eastern slope.

In line with the Mosque is the consecrated mountain to which our Savior so often rested to pray and to teach. It is so near that it seems like a mighty citadel within the city walls to protect the inhabitants

I enjoy the cool breeze of the evening on the Hotel roof, which like other roofs in Jerusalem is fitted with lounges on which to sit or lie and take comfort during an evening like this. I am also reluctant to give up my recent opportunity to gaze upon the interesting scenery which I must soon leave forever, perhaps before I have another chance to see the sun as it sets beyond the sacred landscape now before me.

As I look at objects nearer at hand I notice the house roofs of the city. They look like streets as they stretch away in the distance. They are flat and one might travel over them for blocks without descending to the street.

It is most difficult for me to bring myself to realize during this visit that I am really in Jerusalem; that I am actually looking at places to which I will often advert in the future and which have claimed and will always receive much attention from the students of Christian history, wherever they may be. Other travelers to this land have described the same feeling of unreality that I am now experiencing.

Later in the evening I take a walk with some of our party. We find that a walk in Jerusalem at night is not such as we might enjoy in our home towns. The gates of the city are closed at sunset—the shops likewise. No lights are to be seen in the streets, save the occasional paper lantern of some foot traveler. The streets are narrow—and dark—even in the daytime. Many of the streets are arched or covered with roofs. The pavements are uneven and smooth, so that one must walk cautiously.

Jerusalem at night! What solitude and cheerlessness! The solemn sound of a millstone "grinding," like the rattling of a railroad train in the distance, alone breaks the gloomy monotony of the hours of night until the cocks begin to crow.

We plod along until we come to a lighted building. Our guide tells us to walk in. It is a Jewish "Singing House," but it would seem that it might be as appropriately called a "smoking house." We go in.

We find about twenty five men seated around in various places, chiefly upon elevated platforms covered with mats. They are smoking and drinking coffee. Five or six are singing and playing on a violin and various other instruments which I cannot name without studying a description of ancient musical instruments. The singing is of the Arab sort—harsh and unpleasant. It is powerful, apparently relying for its effect on the strong vocalization of certain notes rather than on melodious tones.

We take coffee which is served as soon as one enters and then comes the "chibouque."[26] The singing is kept up without any intermission save to change the piece, and sometimes not even for this. I must compliment them on their rendering of the *Marseillaise Hymn*—and in French. It was creditably done. The strength of feeling which they put into it produced the desired effect.

We send for a servant of Lieutenant Commander Abbot to give them some samples of American music on the viol. Probably for the first times the strains of *Yankee Doodle, Dixie Land, The Star Spangled Banner* and other American tunes are heard in this place. They all listen attentively and our guide tells us that they pronounce our music good. Their violinist then follows with a solo to show what <u>he</u> can do alone. It seems to me that his performance is lacking in variety of tone as well as in melody.

At 9 o'clock we return to the Hotel. We are to begin our sightseeing at 5 a.m. tomorrow morning.

June 22
Jerusalem

The morning is as lovely as any that ever dawned in the "Holy City." Before breakfast we are on our way with the Consul to the Mosque of Omar. We travel again the "Via Dolorosa" and lest our interest flag we are shown the place where Christ fell under the weight of the cross and left the print of his arm in the solid rock of the building opposite, the stone now being worn and smoothly polished by the pilgrims who have rubbed their arms into the depression since it and its origin had been pointed out to them.

At the foot of this street we are shown the house of "Dives, the Rich Men" from whose table Lazarus was fed. It was in remarkable condition for a house so old and I noticed nothing peculiar about it except the blue stained window panes of its windows which suggested an extravagance of some modern "Dives."

A short distance from here we gaze at the place on the side walk where Lazarus received his donation of "crumbs." The place is to be identified by a curb stone somewhat different from those adjacent.

Opposite is the house in which Lazarus himself lived. If he were the owner and kept up this house in his time he could not have been a poor man, or perhaps his poverty was due to his inability to maintain such an establishment, or perhaps, as I suppose we ought to assume he was a "Tenant at will."

We now approach the place which we have far different reasons for regarding as sacred ground. We stand upon the steps beneath the ancient archway which admits us to the area of the Mosque of Omar, "The Dome of the Rock" a mat is spread down and we take off our shoes and either put on the slippers brought for the purpose or walk in our stocking feet over the broad pavements of this enclosure where once the Temple of Solomon stood. Many times since his day it has been the scene of carnage. Here the blood of men, women and children has flowed in the fury of wild fanatics. One such occasion was when Godfrey de Bouillon entered the captured city with his Crusaders on June 7, 1099. He found it a city of 70,000 inhabitants whom he massacred, a large part of them here in the Mosque of Omar where they had sought refuge. No mercy was shown to age or sex. It was said that the place where we now stand flowed knee deep with the blood which floated corpses away into the courts below.

We enter the Mosque. Permission had been obtained by the Consul and during the required twenty four hours' notice of our coming such persons and things as we are not permitted to see had been removed and mats spread upon the floor.

In the center, surrounded by iron railings is a rock. We are told that it is the rock on which Abraham offered Isaac as a sacrifice. A canopy is spread above to prevent any dust from falling on it. On the side we are shown the print of the hand of the Angel Gabriel.

We descend some stairs, go through an archway and come beneath the rock where is shown the print of the turban of Mohammed and also the aperture through which he passed to Heaven. Near here is the Tabernacle of Elias—*Sanctum Sanctorum.*

On the floor above we are shown the Throne of David, the shield of Al Hanen and furled above the Rock, the banner of Omar and close by the saddle of Mohammed. These articles of unquestionable antiquity are venerated as priceless by the Turks.

There is nothing about the interior of the Mosque to admire. It looks about the same as the interior of hundreds of churches. The roof is of cedar. The windows are of stained glass and of fine quality. We see no person about except the officials in charge who accompany us. Before leaving there is pointed out to us the place beneath the floor where Mohammed confined the Devils and sealed them up. On the opposite near the door is Solomon's gilded pitcher with its two blue colored doves on its sides. It is very pale and shows evidence of antiquity.

We pass through Solomon's Court, or the place where he dispensed justice. The judgement seat is entire as well as the columns which support the whole chapel. They are said to be the remains of the ancient temple as also are other columns and arches which we pass.

We then enter the Mosque of El Aksa, first built by Omar himself. Here we are shown the tomb of Aaron, the place where the boy Christ disputed with the Doctors and where the Virgin sat waiting. Here are the pulpit of Omar and two pillars placed close together. If one be able to squeeze between them good luck will attend him throughout life—he will not only have numerous wives, but still be rich. Needless to say all of our party managed to squeeze through. I went through with little effort.

In a passageway beneath the Mosque we are shown a portion of the foundation of the ancient Temple of Solomon. The stones are very large and impress one with the massive construction of the old Temple of which they almost certainly formed a part. Leaving here we are shown where the Dervishes were confined and the "Place of wailing of the Jews."

We now come to the "Golden Gate" or "Porta Aurea." It is walled up and has been for centuries. Some say that it is sealed up because the Muhammadans are awaiting the arrival of a king who will enter through it and rule the whole earth. Others say that it was walled up as a protection against the marauding hordes of the desert. It is called by the Muhammadans the "Gate of Mercy." It is claimed that not only Christ but Omar and Godfrey de Bouillon with his victorious Crusaders entered the city through this gate.

Near here we descend into a sort of chapel where we are shown the "cradle of Christ." It is of stone or marble, hollowed out to resemble to form of the human body. That it ever held the body of the infant Christ overtaxes my credulity.

Near here is an aperture in the wall through which we look out on the valley below. Projecting through the wall above is an old pillar upon which Mohammed is to sit when all return to judge the whole world. We were cautioned not to step outside as a Frenchman who did so about a year ago slipped and fell to the rocks two hundred feet below.

The tomb of Solomon is the next thing of importance to be shown to us. We are not permitted to enter, but look through a barred window. On it were fastened many small pieces of cloth. The people who have hung the cloths there believe that when they are taken away and washed any sickness or infirmity which the person may have will disappear. A short distance from here, near St. Stephen's Gate we see the "pool of Bethesda" which has been dry for two hundred years. It is about 360 feet long, 130 wide and 75 deep, exclusive of the rubbish which has been accumulating in it for ages. It is faced with cement and at one end are some arches which may have had some connection with the porches referred to by the Evangelist.

Entering the "Via Dolorosa" again we come to an arch which crosses a street called "Ecce Homo," where, according to tradition, Pilate united with the Jews in mocking Christ and said, "Behold the Man."

Then we see the place of the "sacred steps" which are in Rome now. They led to the tower of St. Antonio, I think, but I do not know the whole story connected with them. Christ is supposed to have passed over them after his arrest or at some stage of his trial. Just opposite on the right we enter the "Judgement Hall." Here we are told was where Christ was condemned. The room is not large and the roof has a modern appearance, but the floor looks ancient. There is an altar and the place appears to be a chapel. If we could throw aside our incredulity and believe that we were actually upon the very spot where Christ was condemned our feelings would be very different.

The next thing pointed out to us is a pillar in the street supposed to mark the spot where Christ was relieved of his burden by Simon the Cyrenian.

It is now nearly eight o'clock and we go to the Hotel for breakfast.

After breakfast and some rest we start for the "Church of the Holy Sepulcher." Everyone is carrying something to be blessed. Some have brought with them articles for that purpose. Others are buying Bibles with olive wood covers. I buy a Bible as a souvenir.

This church was built by Helena, the mother of Constantine and dedicated A.D. 335. Its unfolded doors which have admitted countless thousands since that date let us in.

It is supposed to be over the burial place of Christ. Even Islam concedes it the second place of importance in the city, the Mosque of Omar being first and second only to Mecca, and certainly Christians should hold it first.

We are shown the stone of "Unction" on which we are told that Christ was laid out after being taken from the cross; then the place where the Virgin sat, designated by a design of light and dark colored marble in the floor and a pulpit above; then the tomb of Adam. We see in succession a "representation" of the cross on which Christ was crucified; the place where the cross stood, as indicated by a "Glory," or golden star; the place where the cross was found by laborers, in a pile of stones and earth; the place where Helena, the mother of Constantine, sat watching the excavations. It is illuminated by a lamp which is kept continually burning.

To each of the following a chapel is dedicated, viz: the place where the soldiers cast lots for Christ's raiment; the place where he was "again scourged;" the place where he sat when he was crowned with thorns and in a little niche in the wall the crown itself covered with glass. In a recess where it can be seen only by introducing a lighted candle is the "stone of Flagellation." It is round and finished as for a pillar. It is less than a foot long in diameter. Its length I could not see.

In a choir of the Church is a fine reproduction of da Vinci's *Last Supper* in tapestry, wrought by Persian artists. The expressions are excellent.

We are shown the sword and spurs of Godfrey de Bouillon, leader of the Crusade of 1099 and King of Jerusalem. The tombs of several other distinguished crusaders are in the same place, but is not certain by whose bodies the tombs are occupied. The sword of Godfrey de Bouillon is two edged and tapers to a point. The edges are still quite sharp, but on the whole the sword is an ordinary affair for so distinguished a personage.

The place where Christ appeared to Mary Magdalene is designated by a peculiar star-like device of different colored pieces of marble in the floor near the entrance door of the Church.

We now come to the "Holy Sepulcher" itself, the most important—and impressive—

place in the Church, whether it be looked upon as the actual resting place of Christ's body or as a symbolic reproduction commemorating a momentous historical event. The significance of Christ's sepulcher to Christianity was what inspired the Crusaders from the time of Peter the Hermit to try to establish a Christian government in the Holy City and rescue this symbol of Christ's power over death from the infidel. It animated them in all their discouragements and disasters and in the face of every adversity.

We enter through a low doorway and see a marble sarcophagus. Upon this numerous articles are laid by members of our party to be "blessed." Two priests enter, sprinkle the articles with "holy water" and bless them.

Before the door of the Sepulcher there is pointed out to us the stone on which the angel sat. Lights are kept continually burning here. In the wall on either side is a hole though the "holy fire" is renewed during Lent.

On coming out the priest sprinkled us all with "holy water." Mass is to be said at eight o'clock tomorrow morning for our safe return to Jaffa.

We pay 50 francs to enter the Church of the Holy Sepulcher. At the Mosque of Omar we paid $42—$1.50 apiece. Formerly a single person had to pay $30 or $40 for permission to enter. It was not long ago that a Christian was not admitted at all.

The last place pointed out to us in the Church of the Holy Sepulcher is "the center of the world"—the navel. We take leave of the functionaries of this Church who remind us that it is illuminated by two hundred lamps, that every hour in the day priests are saying masses or repeating prayers and conducting services in all the languages of Southern Europe and that here the Spanish, Portuguese, Italians and French may find a place for worship and listen to some portion of a service, at least, in their own tongue.

Passing the "Iron Gate" we enter the house of Caiaphas, the High Priest. Here we are shown the place where Peter denied Christ, and then the cock crowed, etc. Here is an altar in front of which is the stone which was rolled away from the Sepulcher. Lights are kept burning in all the important places here. In the court is a well from which I drank some excellent water.

Near here we are shown the house where Christ met at the Passover and instituted the "last supper," the communion. The room is devoid of furniture, the table having been removed to Rome, we are told. We are shown where it stood. We may perhaps really be standing in the very room where Christ and his disciples stood.

From here we enter a place where we are shown the tomb of David. Two dirty Arab women and a young child go out of the room in order to give us possession, leaving behind a peculiar cradle and much dirt. Can this be the tomb of David? The top only is to be seen. It projects about four feet above the floor and is protected from dust by a cloth hung above it. We cannot enter the tomb itself. No Christian is permitted to do so. The Prince of Wales offered a large sum for permission, but it was refused.

As we finish gazing at the top of this tomb the curtain rings down on the scenes of which we have been reminded in this theater of momentous events. The time has come for us to return to our Hotel and prepare for our return to our ship. We are to dine at 3 o'clock and start for Jaffa at 5 p.m.

At the time set we are on our way and passing out of the city's gate. At the wayside near by leprous women ask us for alms. Some have badly disfigured faces and have almost lost their voices. They are most pitiably abject and forlorn, reminding one of the scriptural references to such people and the way in which they were customarily treated. We saw no beggars in the city and apparently old customs are being adhered to at least so far as leprous beggars are concerned.

The worst part of the way is to be traveled first and this is some advantage. I feel as comfortable in the saddle now as if I had been riding a month. We all proceed in regular order, Doctor Messersmith riding in his "box" between two mules.

At 1 a.m. the "mountain pass" is behind us. I dismount to take luncheon in the bright moonlight at the old "Coffee House," or I might say the "Bad Coffee House" for the water in which dirty cups are washed forms the principal part of the subsequent supply of "coffee."

Here we meet a large party "bound up." While eating on the shawl which my partner and I had spread out beneath us I had opportunity to observe a company of Turks at prayer, or performing acts of religious devotion. They rise to their feet, then fall on their knees and then on their faces. They go through with this performance repeatedly.

After a stay at the "Coffee House" of an hour and a half we are again on our way. It is a ride of four hours to Ramleh. Instead of giving you the distance in this country they give you the time required to perform the journey.

Before reaching Ramleh we were startled by the sound of two gun shots in the rear. I rode back in the direction whence they had been heard. Some of our party had "heard the balls pass near them." Orderly Sergeant Robbins said that they passed close to his head. I was unable to get any further information regarding the source of these shots, but enough in significant shaking of heads to satisfy me that the two almost simultaneous shots had come from the pistols of members of our party and that they had been fired to scare Sergeant Robbins. As the bullets were doubtless sent as close to his head as we deemed prudent it is quite probable that he heard them. It certainly afforded the party a good deal of amusement to hear him talk of an "ambush" and to see him cautiously scrutinize every hillock and ravine for the rest of the way.

Just as day was dawning in the east we reached the Convent at Ramleh, very weary and sleepy. The Paymaster and a guide had ridden ahead and had the table spread for us when we arrived, but no one cared to eat or drink. We all slept for some time—on chairs, on the floor, or anywhere. I found a place in the court on a pile of stalks, but the fleas within and the mosquitoes without reinforced by the rays of the rising sun soon compelled me to leave this couch. I never saw men more tired and sleepy than some in our party, but at 5 a.m. we are ready to take the coffee which the monks had prepared for us.

It came as somewhat of a surprise to me to see one of the "humble monks" give a smart kicking about the place to a servant for some infraction of discipline, and also to give a good pounding to two of our guide's servants for coming into the kitchen with lighted cigarettes. The recipients of such punishment made no resistance nor protest. The monk was a big fellow and I could not help laughing at the way that he landed his blows on the backs of our guide's servants.

June 23
Jaffa

At 9 a.m. I am at the Hotel in Jaffa with four others, an hour in advance of the rest of the party.

The last part of the journey was a wild ride for a sailor, who was never accustomed to horses and knows nothing about them. The vanguard with which I rode into Jaffa an hour ahead of the rest was composed of the real horsemen of the party, men who had been put in the saddle in childhood. When any need of keeping the party together for protection ceased as we approached Jaffa these expert riders naturally tended to draw away from the rest. I kept company with them simply because my stallion was interested in a mare ahead, probably the fastest of our animals.

I have been called a "natural rider." Today such aptitude was put to a severe test. I held the bridle in my left hand as nearly like a cavalryman as I could. The pieces of stone and marble which I had gathered as mementoes of the numerous places visited in and about Jerusalem, I had tied up in a large neckerchief. They made a bundle of considerable size. It was quite heavy. This bundle I held in my right hand. It served me as ballast to keep me in the saddle, but in order to preserve my balance as we galloped along the crooked trail I had to use it as "shifting ballast," such as is employed in yacht races, and at times my ballast was being held out at right angles to my body.

I had little occasion to try to steer my horse with my bridle and my knees as I had been shown. He followed the mare. Furthermore the winding trail had been so worn down by ages of travel that except where it had a rock formation it was a veritable crooked ditch, so deep that the top edges in places were level with my stirrups, or above.

When I dismounted I could barely stand and my right arm which held the bundle was almost paralyzed.

Before noon we are all back on board of our ship. In a few minutes the anchor is up and the ship is under way and the pilgrims are seeking needed rest and sleep.

June 24
At sea

The wind enables us to keep our course. We pass the city of Acre in the morning and in the afternoon the city of Tyre. The returned pilgrims are to be seen reposing in various places about the ship trying to make up lost sleep.

The ship is heaving about in a heavy swell entirely disproportionate to the wind. I have noticed this phenomenon in the Levant to a greater extent than in any other sea where I have ever been.

June 25
Off Sidon

We have been hove to most of the night and this morning come to anchor near the port of Sidon. We have missionaries here and a native Consular Agent. It appears that the former have complained that they have not been accorded rights which have been guaranteed them by our treaties with Turkey. Two natives come on board and by them the Captain sends word to Mr. Eddy, one of the missionaries.

This city now called Saide, is very ancient and according to tradition was the second to be built after the flood. In recent centuries Romans, Saracens and Turks have successively held it. In former times it had an excellent harbor, but now it has none for large ships. It has some trade along the seacoast and with Damascus and upper Syria.

It is said that glass was first manufactured here. Its artists were employed on Solomon's Temple, and its mariners sailed his ships. Paul touched here on his voyage to Rome and was "courteously entreated" by Julius. The rise of Alexandria appears to have contributed to the decline of Sidon.

At present it has a population of 15,000, subjects of the Sultan. We are to remain here twelve hours and then proceed to Beirut.

June 26
Beirut

At 9 p.m. we are in the harbor of Beirut at anchor. Two British and one French ship of war are here.

Beirut looks the same as when we were here two years ago. It is an attractive looking city from the water, but its charms disappear when one lands and enters it.

I receive a letter from my brother Edward informing me of his ill health and the partial loss of sight in one of his eyes. He is anxious to see me home and fears that if our ship does not return this year he will never see me again. He is not able to attend to his business and feels discouraged. I sent him from Alexandria a letter expressing the same sentiments as are contained in his. I am very sorry now that I sent it. I fear that it will give him great concern. I fear that he is much worse off than I thought that I was when I wrote my letter. I hope God will spare him until I return and that I will see him again.

By his letter I learn of the death of two friends. One was killed in a recent battle in which we lost 45,000 men.

My health is much improved since my trip to Jerusalem. It has, I think, placed my cough where it cannot endanger me.

June 27
Beirut

Friends of several of the officers have written that we are to be called home this summer. I hope this is so, for since receiving the letter from Edward I am more anxious than ever to be there.

This is a hot day, but the climate here is preferable to that of Egypt. It is not sickly here now.

June 28
Damascus

In courtesy to the British ships in port we dress ship in honor of the coronation of Queen Victoria. At noon we fire a national salute.

A mutiny is reported to have taken place on a British frigate which recently put into Malta. Most of the officers were killed. The Captain was thrown overboard, but in some way was saved. Forty of the mutineers left in boats with arms.

June 29
Beirut

The Captain, his son and Assistant Surgeon Clark started today for Damascus.

The Paymaster is trying to get up another party to go to Balbeck.

In the afternoon I went on shore. Finding it too hot to travel about I took refuge in a smoking house. In such places, which are constructed of poles covered with mats the Turks spend much of their time in the heat of the day, smoking their "hubble bubbles," drinking coffee and playing cards.

It was cool and comfortable there and I smoked four pipes of tobacco without feeling dizzy.

I failed to find my old friend S. Sarkies. On returning to the ship I learned that he had sent his brother to invite me to take dinner with him.

Chapter Six
July 1864 to December 1864

July 1

Very warm. I am staying on board because it is more comfortable here than on shore. I am occupied making my quarter returns. A strong wind is blowing from the sea and the ship is rolling considerably.

Dispatches from the United States say that General Grant is driving General Lee before him.[1]

Notice has been received from the Italian Government to remove our stores from Spezia, for what reason I do not know. A place has been offered to our Government for a depot on the Island of Sardinia and a request is made to have an officer sent there immediately to look over the proposed location.

July 3
Beirut

The sea is very rough. In the afternoon I went on shore with Cox. The sea was breaking just outside the landing and across the entrance, but after waiting for a while we found a chance to pass over.

The landing was crowded with hundreds of people waiting for some important official to come on shore from a steamer. Baggage of all sorts was being landed from boats, much of it falling overboard from the tossing boats before it reached the shore. We pushed our way through a crowd of naked men and boys and finally succeeded in reaching the street. I wish I had a photograph of that crowd.

In the street we found a military company drawn up to receive the distinguished man. We saw him arrive. He was followed by five or six others, presumably his guard or members of his units. None were in uniform. The man saluted was a short rough looking man. I was unable to get a good look at his face. Turkish officials do not usually make much of a personal show. They do not seem to be a vain people.

We took a stroll toward the western part of the city. It contains many pretty residences, belonging to Englishmen and Frenchmen located here as well as to natives. We went into a smoking house and smoked and took lemonade and coffee in the Turkish fashion. Here we met a Turkish officer who speaks some English and accepted his invitation to accompany him to his barracks. They are in a healthy locality, on an eminence which overlooks the city. They were comfortable and well equipped in every way. We were shown the hospital and the men's and officer's quarters and were received with the greatest cordiality.

After having a luncheon at the hotel we walked a little, although really the most comfortable part of the day, on shore and then to the landing to return to the ship in the sunset boat.

On leaving the landing several men started a row in the boat. The coxswain broke his tiller on the head of one of them. Oars were used on the heads of others with good effect. Fists were employed freely. One man jumped overboard to get clear. The affair started just at the entrance where the seas were breaking and for a while the boat was drifting about in imminent danger of being filled, but fortunately we had the trouble quieted down and the men fished out of the water and back in the boat before anything serious happened. Such scenes are disgusting to <u>any one</u> who is sober.

July 4
Beirut

At eight bells our ship is dressed with flags and the French frigate also. The British war ships dress their mast heads only. Since this is all that we did a few days ago on the occasion of the anniversary coronation of the Queen it is all that we can expect from them.

The day is delightful and quite comfortable. At noon we fire the customary national salute in which the French and British ships and a Turkish battery on shore join.

The U.S. Consul invited the officers of the ship to his house to celebrate the day. During one of the later stages of the affair a man from the ship, Riley by name, who was on liberty and drunk invaded the Consul's house, passed into the dining room and with a club swept china, champagne glasses, etc., off the table. Complaint is also made that the same fellow wantonly slashed with a knife an ass that was standing in the street.

Riley is an Englishman who was shipped on this station and should be discharged here after paying for the damage.

I went on shore and walked about. In many parts the city might be said to be entirely built over, as the streets are nothing more than archways beneath buildings which are masses of stone.

All shops are small. A room 12 by 14 feet without shelves or counter suffice for a dry-goods merchant. The goods are piled up promiscuously and the dealer sits on the floor which usually reminds me of a coal-bin. Some shops under the control of the French or other foreigners are a little more after the European style. The dry goods are of both French and English manufacture. Cutlery and crockery are mostly English and fancy articles French.

A blacksmith shop is a place ten feet square with the tools scattered over the floor around the fire and forge. The smith sits cross-legged while he works.

Carpenter shops, tinners' shops and mechanic's shops would be looked upon by our mechanics as mere "lockers" rather than places in which to work. All such places are virtually archways lighted by the entrance which is usually the full size of the arch.

Men carry around water and a drink made from the juice of raisins in a pig skin slung on their backs by straps. A receptacle on the right side of the pouch holds the glasses. If you wish a drink the carrier removes his thumb and out comes the liquor, squirt-to such a distance that the man seems to be dextrous to be able to fill the glass without spilling any of the liquor.

The common mode of carrying water in this country is in the skins of hogs or of other animals on the backs of asses. Watering is a great business here and many persons live by it entirely.

In every business and under all circumstances the men here may be seen smoking. Even the men on horseback will have a pipe with all its appendages.

The Turkish tradesman seldom shows any interest when you enter his shop—or call, for it is not necessary to step inside—and if you go away without buying anything it appears to be the same to him as though you purchased. He will not try to induce you to buy, nor will he abuse you if you do not.

I notice that in the shady streets the women wear, in many instances, veils which reveal their faces and in this way I observed many pretty faces. The majority of the women however whose faces I saw had no need to hide them. A man would not look at them more than once.

I have seen some very fine looking young women with their faces exposed and their breasts also, but I presume that they are not Muhammadans. The breasts of the veiled Mohammedan women are frequently to be seen.

I think that the custom of covering the face will gradually disappear. Even now there appears to be a tendency to meet this custom by merely passing a portion of the dress across the chin.

I leave my companions Jones and Fletcher who go to the Consul's and I walk around alone until I become weary and return to the ship in a shore boat.

At the landing I saw a man who had just murdered a Frenchman and his wife and child brought to the landing in the company of an officer and two soldiers, put into a boat and taken away together with several others who were being held as witnesses or accessories to the crime.

Some of these natives are as bad as they look and a very little money is a sufficient incentive to murder.

July 5
Beirut

We are taking on wood and water and preparing to go to sea. Most of the forenoon was occupied in target practice. Over fifty shells were fired. My station in charge of the magazine never permits me to watch the shooting. It was said to be very good today.

The Captain, his son and Doctor Clark returned today from Damascus.

We learn today that the report which we heard on June 29 with various details of a mutiny on a British frigate was not only false, but without the slightest foundation. How such a complete fabrication could start is more than I can understand.

July 7
Beirut

The principal event of the day is the visit of the Bashaw of Beirut to our ship. He is received with a salute of 19 guns. He does not speak English and his private secretary who accompanied him acted as interpreter. He looks more like a European than a Turk. He has the appearance of an intelligent man whose business affairs occupy his attention.

July 8
Beirut

We receive on board a quantity of bread and prepare to sail, but the wind dies out. Riley is being court-martialed. He did over $100 damage at the Consul's—more money than is due him on the Paymaster's books.

News is received of the sinking of the Confederate steamer *Alabama* by the Federal sloop *Kearsarge* off Cherbourg. The Commander of the *Kearsarge* sent a challenge to Semmes who accepted and came out in company with a British and a French ship and some pleasure yachts to witness the fight. The fight lasted an hour and twenty minutes and resulted in the sinking of the *Alabama*. Semmes was picked up in the water by a yacht and escaped, according to the report.[2]

The *Kearsarge* is reported to have had chain cables fastened to her sides which lessened the effect of shots upon her. It is said that Captain Semmes made his will and left a large sum of money and several chronometers with the Brazilian Consul. Nothing is said of the casualties of the fight.

The *Kearsarge* was built and fitted out at Kittery and I know many on her, including Mr. Thornton the executive officer, for whom I have a high regard. I also knew Semmes as a lieutenant. From all accounts he has proved to be a different kind of a man than I thought he was.

July 9
Beirut and the sea

After waiting for mail from the French steamer which arrived last night we weigh anchor and sail. There was no mail for us. The report of the sinking of the *Alabama* is confirmed. Nobody knows where we are going. The Captain is keeping our destination a secret.

July 10
At sea

This morning we make a sail ahead, supposed to be the British ship of war *Chanticleer* which left port six hours ahead of us. She is far to the windward. In the afternoon we make the Island of Cyprus, stand clear and tack ship, the wind being ahead. We see the British ship just before sunset far to the windward. We have gained little if any on her.

A fine breeze all day. We take in royals at sunset and in the evening double reef the topsails according to Naval custom when cruising.

At muster an account of the sinking of the *Alabama* was read by the Captain's clerk. It appears that Semmes lost his ship, but not his honor, according to the account. The *Alabama* had nine men killed and twenty one wounded. She attempted to run away when the fight was going against her and Semmes complains that five shots, wounding several of his crew, were fired at his ship after her flag was struck. This is an English account. We hear nothing about casualties on the *Kearsarge*.

I feel quite well these days and have a great appetite—a great improvement over my condition a short time ago.

July 12
At sea

The wind is light. The ship heads within two points of her course and goes along at the rate of five or six knots, pitching heavily into an old head sea. I notice that some of the men have watermelons, eggs, herring and other edibles in their bags. They provide themselves with something to eat out of their own funds. Potatoes the mainstay of the regular ration were too dear to purchase at Beirut and were not to be had in a large quantity at any price.

We have gained little in the last two days and there is every prospect of a long passage. At eight bells we reef topsails as usual. The wind continues fresh.

July 13
At sea

The wind is the same. The royals were furled all day but the sea is smoother. I am working on my accounts. Quite dull these days.

Unaccustomed to a seafaring life, the poor sheep bleat, the pigs squeal and the cocks crow so that we have a variety of music on board.

Old Sergeant Robbins is again giving an exhibition of his peculiar passion for having men confined for nothing. He usually begins by making some unfounded and anger provoking accusation which leads a man to make an indignant reply and then Robbins has a tantrum and reports the man for impudence and insubordination. No questions are asked. No investigation is held. One side of the case, Robbin's complaint, is sufficient. Down goes the man for from three to five days. Martin, a private, has just received three days for no reason whatever.

I suppose that the executive officer feels that he must uphold an incompetent in a position of subordinate authority or get rid of him and that in Robbin's case it is better to do the former although it may be hard on the marines.

July 19
At sea

Last night about sunset we made the Island of Crete. It has been in sight all day.

The old topgallant sails and royals which have been used until large holes appeared in them were unbent today and new ones bent in their places.

July 21
At sea

Last night after trying all day to double the point of the Island of Crete to the windward, we took a long tack of eight hours off shore. It was unfortunate for the wind changed the wrong way and headed us and all day today we are trying to make up for what we have lost.

We have approached quite close to the Island of Crete about twenty five miles from Cape St. John. The land is high and has a barren appearance. The shore is steep and rocky. The Sphakia mountains tower above us. The hill slopes are scantily covered with stunted trees. These are the only sign of life or vegetation that we can see.

July 22
At sea

This morning we were off Cape St. Mark with a light wind. At noon the wind sprang up and we passed the westernmost end of the Island of Candia. A bay apparently about ten miles deep makes into the Island between capes St. Mark and Spada. A large high rock stands out in the sea some distance from the mainland near the westernmost end. Although no signs of civilization are to be seen on the side of the Island which we have just passed there is a large population on the Island, most of it being on the northern side.

The wind continues to haul to the West until at two bells p.m. we brace the yards—the ship is going free and on her course for the first time in many days! Every one is made more cheerful by the fair wind. Never before has a favorable breeze been so long lacking during the cruise.

July 23
Grecian Archipelago

We came in sight of the Ionian Islands before sunset yesterday. Soon afterward the wind died away and the evening was calm and most delightful. I spent a portion of it on deck. The sea was as smooth as a mirror. The moon shone brightly and the dark outline of the islands seemed to serve to bring out more strikingly the beauty of the moonlit sea.

Today the wind is light and the sea smooth. The sun shines warmly on deck, but below it is quite comfortable.

I overhaul lockers and air my clothing. I feel very well these days, but the salt "grub" is not so palatable after having lived on fresh provisions so long.

From Beirut to here has been the longest passage counted in days that we have made since we crossed the Atlantic.

We have come more than 700 miles against a wind that was "dead ahead" continuously for two weeks. Considering this fact we have made good progress.

It is rumored that the Captain has not decided whether to go to Athens or to Smyrna. The Captain has a boil on his back which makes him irritable. Perhaps he would prefer to be well before he goes to Athens. "Tom," his son is the ruling genius that guides the ship and if <u>his</u> fancy leads in the direction of the Ottoman Empire thither we will go. Considerable complaint is made of his influence on his father, real or supposed, and Mr. Abbot does not hesitate to let himself be heard to say that he hopes that if we attempt to go through the Dora Passage it will blow a gale ahead for six weeks. Everyone desires to be back in Spezia as soon as possible so that we shall lose no time in getting started for home if orders come for us to do so.

July 25
Athens

Until 3 p.m. today we were in doubt as to where we were really bound. During the forenoon we were beating against a strong head wind blowing directly from the Dora Passage. That suggested Smyrna. It was not until we had weathered "St. George's" Island and headed into the Bay of Athens that any one felt confident of no further contention with the North wind of this wild Archipelago.

We passed the Island of Sea upon which are the ruins of a temple dedicated to some Grecian deity whose name is unknown to me. These massive stones, the lofty columns of time-worn marble, on this barren and uninhabited place bear witness to architectural proficiency of the ancient Greeks and to a wealth and culture long since faded and gone.

Nelson, our Greek, was sent to a craft near the ship and secured a pilot who brought us to anchor in the evening just outside the Piraeus. Our anchorage is near the British ship-of-the-line *Gibraltar*. She has been stationed here for the past six months and is soon to be relieved.

Sailing up the bay we saw the ancient Acropolis and Mount Lycabettus standing like sentinels over the city which was hidden from our view. The bay where we anchored has been the scene of ancient naval battles of the greatest import to the world. Socrates, Plato, even St. Paul, and a host of other men whose influence is still felt in the world today once looked upon the hills and valleys as I am now doing. I am surely glad to have this opportunity to visit this place and see its reminders of its ancient glory.

July 26
Athens

The morning finds around the ship many boats, manned by bright eyed active Greeks. Some expect to take passengers ashore. Others offer fruit for sale. There appears on board a washerwoman of gigantic proportions who brings with her correspondingly voluminous recommendations attesting her proficiency as a laundress. She is one of the ubiquitous Maltese to be found everywhere on the shores of the Mediterranean and dangerously shrewd like the rest of them.

Boy McLaughlin who has been studious in learning to read and lately serious on matters of religion was taken in the sick bay this morning as a lunatic. For a few days he has kept from meals, avoided company and read religious books. Today the Doctor noticed the boy's conduct and recognized him as a fit subject for a doctor's care. He seems to be in a trance-state sometimes, and performs singular acts of devotion, such as holding a piece of bread before him, closing his eyes and repeating, "The bread of life, I have found it," etc., etc.

Nelson, our Greek, has permission to visit his relatives who he has not seen for eighteen years. During this time he has traveled much and has had many occupations and experiences. At one time he found employment in guiding caravans across the Sahara Desert. In his wanderings he reached America and eventually became a seaman in our Navy and as such joined our ship at Portsmouth.

July 27
Athens

We are painting ship. We fired a salute for the Greeks and have been receiving visitors from the British, French and Russian war ships.

The Russians very courteously offered to assist us in watering ship. Their men are hardy looking and are said to be the smartest sailors in drill to be found in any Navy afloat.

The Russian ship-of-the-line in port has on board 1,400 men and I am informed that the French Admiral is watching their movements. It is suspected that they intend to land a force somewhere.

Besides the Russian there are two Greek, two British, one French and one Austrian ships of war in port.

Boy McLaughlin had a mad fit this morning and was placed in the "brig" under charge of the sentry. He was also guarded last night in the "sick-bay" where he disturbed the rest of the occupants by his loud noises. He is a Roman Catholic. He says that he is ready to be sacrificed. It would appear that he does not sufficiently understand any book from his own reading to produce this unexplained state of mind. It is a singular kind of frenzy.

It is reported that the Confederate steamer *Florida* has been in an engagement with a Federal cruiser which was disabled. Its name is not given.[3]

July 28
Athens

This morning in company with Messrs. Philbrick, Jones and Fletcher I went on shore at the Piraeus, or port of Athens, where we hired a carriage to take us to the city. We encountered here the same kind of people to be met in all places that strangers visit. After considerable bargaining we induce a driver to take us to Athens at a reasonable price and leave us there. Four glasses of lemonade at a half-way house costs us a half a dollar.

A ride of five or six miles over a level road brings us to Athens. We mail letters, visit some book stores and some places where photographs are sold, at one of which we meet a Maltese whom we employ as a guide for the day.

We proceed to the "Great Britain Hotel," a new and elegant building nearly opposite the King's Palace, but it is full and no rooms can be obtained. We then go to the "Grand Hôtel des Etrangers," French, where ample accommodations are secured. After resting we have luncheon and then start out to see the ruins of ancient Athens.

We come to a plain in the southeast quarter of the city. It has the appearance of a parade ground. It is level and free from rocks or stones until we reach the remains of the Temple of Jupiter Olympius. Here are sixteen columns of stupendous size. One is fallen. It lies in the same position as when it fell, its various sections being slightly separated. Their circumference I should judge to be about twenty five feet. To the west and on a line with the Acropolis is the gateway leading to the temple. This is in a very good state of preservation and part of the superstructure is intact. The fact that the ruins of this temple stand alone upon a plain away from any other building makes their massive construction and their fine proportions more impressive.

We next turn our steps toward the Acropolis. Ascending the southern slope we come on to the Theater of Bacchus which has been lately excavated. The examples of ancient art which once adorned this structure are strewn about. Parts of statues of all sizes, fragments of columns and of marble pillars are piled up promiscuously over the entire area.

The form of the theater is circular, the stage being in the southern part and facing the Acropolis, in the direction of which the rows of seats gradually rise. In the rear of the stage are several statues, the largest of which has the legs broken off. The first row of seats which were reserved for the Senators are carved from solid marble, six seats, together with their backs being carved from a single piece of marble. Each seat is concaved slightly and has a hole in front to let the water run off, hence I infer that this theater had no permanent roof as the amphitheater at Pompei had.

Passing around toward the western slope of the Acropolis we look down upon the Theater of Heredes whose arches and columns have suffered severely from the missiles and other destructive agencies of many vandals. In the center of the pit is a well from which I see men drawing water. The southern wall of this building is almost entirely preserved, but some of the arches on top are destroyed.

We now approach the colossal white marble Propylaea. In the center of this structure is a portico about sixty feet broad. It contains six Doric columns raised on four steps. Through it runs a magnificently paved road about thirty feet wide. From the portico two wings extend about thirty feet to the west, each having three columns on the side toward the portico. The left wing contains numerous pieces of statuary, but scarcely one remains whole. I have been nowhere where I regretted more the destructive acts of vandalism.

Before passing into the citadel we step aside to view the Temple of Victory which stands near the right wing. There are four Ionic columns on the eastern and western ends. Its frieze is sculptured with figures of Greeks and Persians fighting on the plains of Marathon.

We again enter the Propylaea and passing through it with the three Ionic columns on either hand we come to where the bronze doors stood which led into the interior of the citadel. This building was begun in the year 473 B.C. and was completed by the architect, Mnesicles in five years, so we are told.

We are now fairly within the citadel. Everywhere around us we see the marks of vandalism. The Turks, whose forte has been to destroy the art and beauty that others have created, destroyed during their attack on Athens in 1826, everything that their patience and industry made possible. The columns of the Parthenon are battered and chipped by the shots from the Turkish battery which had been placed on the Museum. It is really distressing to look at the effects of their shots on this noble building.[4]

On entering it one cannot fail to be impressed with the superiority of the workmanship. The blocks of marble composing the walls fit so perfectly that I judge them to have been water tight. Every surface is perfectly level and smooth. The floor is of marble slabs about four feet square and likewise perfectly fitted.

Numerous sculptured friezes are to be seen, but the best specimens were taken to England by Lord Elgin. Those which remain have been so badly defaced by the hands of vandals scarcely a figure remains perfect.

The Parthenon occupies the highest part of the Acropolis. From its floor one may now look through the breeches in its once lofty sides upon the sea toward the South and the city to the North. The Parthenon or Temple of Minerva was a peripteral octostyle of the Doric order. The columns on the sides were each six feet two inches in diameter at the base and thirty four feet in height. They rested on three steps.

Within the peristyle at each end stood six columns, each five and a half feet in diameter forming a vestibule to the part which stood two steps above the peristyle level. This part consisted of two chambers about sixty feet in width and one forty three and the other ninety eight feet long, the roof of the former being supported by four columns four feet in diameter, and the latter by sixteen three feet in diameter. The height of the temple was fifty six feet and the area which it covered 228 feet by 108.

The Parthenon was converted into a church by the Christians and into a mosque by the Turks. In 1776 it was considered the finest mosque in the world.

The Erectheium is about 160 feet north of the Parthenon. It contained the united temples of Minerva, Pallas, Pandroses and Neptune. It was an irregular architectural structure. It was a beautiful structure, but comparatively small, its entire area not exceeding 63 by 36 feet. It was about 28 feet high.

Here was preserved the trident of Neptune which struck when the horse issued forth; also the olive tree of Minerva and an image of the goddess which fell from heaven. Before the image was suspended a golden lamp which requires oil but once a year. The wick being of Carpathian flax which was never consumed. A brass palm tree above carried off the smoke. Here too were kept the wooden Hermes presented by Cecrops; the chair of Daedalus; the scimitar of Mardonius; the breast-plate of Masistrus who commanded the Medes at Plataea, and numerous groups of statues. The portico of this temple was used by the Turks as a powder magazine.

About the Acropolis are to be seen some rude specimens of ancient architecture supposed to be the work of the Pelasgi who fortified this place before the Persian invasion. To the north of the Propylaea is still to be seen the ancient grotto dedicated to Apollo and Pan. It is reached by a flight of steps. Some of the other temples which we inspected were those of

Aesculapius, Themis, Venus, Tellus and Ceres.

On leaving the Acropolis we visit the prison of Socrates. It is near the Museum. It is cut out of the solid rock and is lighted and ventilated by means of a conical opening through the top. It is entered through a rude gate apparently used chiefly to prevent the egress of asses and other animals which evidently are sometimes kept there.

I next stand on the site of the ancient Agora where the people assembled to listen to their still famous orators. It is to the west of the Acropolis and is now a barren place.

On the way to Mars Hill we pass on the left near the Areopagus a lodge down which it has been the custom from time immemorial for women who bear no children, to slide. The descent is about twelve feet and the rock is highly polished. I am informed that the practice is as common now as ever and the condition of the rock attests it.

Leaving the Agora after attempting to imagine this barren spot to be covered with trees and artistically divided into markets, streets and public halls and to be surrounded with altars to twelve gods, we come to the beautiful plain where stood the Temple of Theseus. It must have been a magnificent structure to judge from its ruins. It is a periptoral hexastyle. On its sides are thirteen Doric columns, each about thirty feet high. The cell is thirty by forty feet. Near the Theseum were the Gymnasium of Ptolmy and the Temple of the Dioscuri (Castor and Pollux).

To the southeast stood the ancient Senate House from which the street led to the theater of Bacchus, one of the notable thoroughfares of ancient Athens.

The Temple of Theseus is used as a museum at present and contains numerous statues and other specimens of carved marble of great interest. About the Temple we saw recruits drilling and heard apprentice buglers practicing the calls. As I stood upon the steps of the Temple and looked out on the pleasant plain before me and saw this evidence of the military effort of a feeble modern nation I could not help but think what scenes this same plain must have presented in the way of martial pomp when Greece was at the height of its military glory.

We visit the Temple of Aeolus and the market place. One of the archways, or gate, is still standing. The Temple is small, circular is shape and surrounded by a wall. We next visit the principal church of the city. It is a neat edifice containing some very fine paintings. Those of the twelve apostles above the principal altar are especially noteworthy.

Our dinners were to be ready at 5 o'clock and it is nearly seven, so we hasten to the hotel. After washing and removing some of the Athenian soil which we have accumulated we give our attention to the most excellent dinner which has been provided for us.

While we are dining our attention is called to the fact that the King is passing the hotel in his buggy. We can see him plainly from the dining room windows. He is a very youthful looking King, apparently about eighteen years old.[5]

After dining we go to our sitting room the windows of which give us a good view of the city in the vicinity of the hotel and we are thus led to make a mental contrast of modern Athens with what the ruins we have seen have suggested of the past.

Everything is as lovely as a summer sky can make it. The royal gardens spread out their green foliage beneath us. The neat buildings and the clean streets invite us to a walk. We pass the Royal stables, the Mint and the Military Academy and see other points of interest of the city in a most agreeable way.

A carriage is procured after some difficulty because at this hour most of them have been hired to take people to the baths at the Piraeus. We drive to the Hotel, take leave of our host and our Guide and turn toward the Piraeus.

We have an excellent carriage—I must compliment the Athenians on their good taste in this matter—and the ride is most enjoyable. I am the only one in our company who has the confidence to start the singing and while I am not complimented on my musical attainments everybody feels like singing and all join in. Before we realize it we are at the Piraeus. After a short tarry at a Café where we meet some of our officers and drink some "pop" beer we return on board with the pleasantest memories of our day's visit in the classic land of Attica.

July 29
Athens

We salute the Greek flag.

Several Russian officers visited the ship; also some Austrian officers. The latter were justifiably offended because our Italian bandsmen played Garibaldi's March.[6] Our Captain ordered this stopped and then they started up Kossuth's March. The Captain has put the whole band on the "black list." I wish he would put them all on shore to do as they please.

The Italians show great enmity toward the Austrians. One of our bandsmen spat in the face of an Austrian sailor who came on deck and we learned afterwards that our Italians had been spitting out of a gun port onto the crew of the boat of the Austrian war ship which brought the Austrian officers to our ship and was waiting alongside for them to return.

The boy McLaughlin is growing more violent every day. A sentry and another man are required to attend to him day and night.

The British Vice Consul visited the ship and received the customary salute.

July 30
Athens

Visitors from the British and the Russian ships are on board during the day.

The *Gibraltar* was relieved by the frigate *Liffey* yesterday. The former has sailed for Malta.

The noise of the insane boy which continues through the greater part of the day and night is most annoying to every one, especially to those near the hospital who are deprived of their sleep on account of it. If we are to be subject to his harangues every day and night during the remainder of this cruise the whole ship's company will become crazy.

July 31
Athens

After listening to a fine sermon by the Rev. Doctor Hall I went on shore with Messrs. Hunter, Wilson and Smith. Before we landed we sailed around to the Piraeus. In the harbor there are the Russian, French and Greek frigates besides several smaller vessels of war. The Russian ship is a noble looking craft, very much like an American in build.

On shore we meet several Englishmen with whom we spend some time and discussed international affairs in good humor. At sunset Smith and I returned to the ship.

Some of our men have permission to visit the Russian frigate. Tonight there is to be a grand ball on board. The King of Greece will be present. Our officers will attend.

August 1
Athens

The ball on the Russian frigate was attended by 600 people. Our officers say that it was a grand affair.

The boy McLaughlin took charge of the "sick-bay" this morning and required force to quiet him. A "strait-jacket" has been fitted for him and the first outbreak that again occurs it will be put on him.[7]

It is reported that Gen. Fremont has received the nomination of the Republican Convention at Chicago.[8] It is also reported that Governor Seymour of New York and the Federal Government are at loggerheads on account of the release by the latter of certain New York newspaper editors who were arrested by order of the President and taken into custody by General Dix. It is said that his act is now being upheld by the Governor. We also hear that 30,000 Confederates are marching on Baltimore.[9]

If accounts be true, affairs at home are in no better condition than they were a year ago. When I think of my country I tremble for her fate.

August 2
Athens

The wind is drier here than in Egypt or Syria and while the sun is very hot today there is a good breeze and the ship is very comfortable.

Several Russian officers are visiting the ship. They and our officers have become very friendly. At the ball a few evenings ago a Frenchman was heard to remark that in the estimation of the Russians the Americans were the only people of consequence in the world.

August 3
Athens

The Russians make their last visit to the ship and are entertained agreeably in the Ward Room.

Our officers and crew have an invitation from the officers of H.M. Ship *Liffey* to attend a dramatic performance on board this evening. Several officers and about 80 men attend. The performance was very good. It was called "Luke the Labourer." This was followed by the presentation of a regular plantation concert and then came a short well presented farce "Slasher and Crasher." It was laughable. Both the officers and men of the ship took special pains to provide for our comfort and to entertain us.

I may say that this is the first time that I have met anybody from a British war ship who was not in favor of the Southern Confederacy. Perhaps this might be called an "Irish man-of-war." Not only is its name Irish, but the Captain and a large portion of the crew are Irishmen. She is a screw frigate of the older type, yet a fine ship. I may say too that this is the first foreign ship of war on which I have set foot since the cruise began.

As might be expected our men are having a good time with the "British tars" who are finding old acquaintances and neighbors among our crew.

August 4
Athens

In the afternoon Thomas O'Brien, the Master-at-Arms of the *Liffey*, with several other petty officers and seamen came on board to visit our ship. I undertook to entertain them and managed to do so in a very acceptable manner. In the evening I left the ship with four of them who took tea with me ashore.

Tomorrow we sail and I took the last opportunity to do some more sightseeing here. We had a bath at the bathing place of the Athenians. Hundreds come here every evening for this purpose. A restaurant nearby is crowded until midnight.

After a refreshing bath we walked to an eminence on the south side of the Piraeus where the French band was playing. The place was illuminated by bon-fires and was filled with promenaders.

Stopping for some refreshments at a Café on the Square we proceeded to the "Queen's Café" where we spent the time very pleasantly until ten o'clock, the hour of my return to the ship.

On arriving at the landing we found most of the officers of our ship and the Russian officers and the American Consul[10] having a parting jubilee, a jollification of the old sort. Champagne was being tossed about like water and mingled with wild cries of, "vive l'Amerique" and "vive la Russe." The time that we were due on board passed. Cheers were rending the midnight air before a parting was effected and then the Russians actually carried our Paymaster on their shoulders and put him in the boat. As the festivities at the Café were subsequent to an evening of generous hospitality on the Russian ship it is needless to say that our officers were pretty well "saturated." The greatest friendship has developed between them and the Russians. This parting scene "capped the climax."

When we reached the ship we found that the few officers who remained on board had been entertaining British officers in a very similar manner and were in a charitable mood for receiving our shore party. This day will do for a while. Entertainments of this sort are sometimes unavoidable, but not often.

August 5
Athens and the Archipelago
A strong north wind is raising a cloud of dust over the Piraeus and the city of Athens.

We were ready to sail from the City of the Philosophers at one bell this morning, but the smashing of the Consul's boat alongside our ship while waiting to take him ashore delayed our departure because we had to send him on shore in one of our boats and wait for its return. We then stood out toward the Dora Passage under single reefed topsails. When just off the eastern point of the bay the wind came down on us with perfect fury. All hands were called to shorten sail, but the Captain came on deck and gave orders to keep the ship off for Milo. We went along, by Anti Gozo and soon passed Milo, when the course was again changed, more to the westward and we finally knew that we are not going to Smyrna.

The wind is blowing down through the passage with all the force of a winter gale. We saw many eastward bound ships lying under the land waiting for a chance and I think that the Captain decided that he would not waste time in contending with a head gale even though he wanted to go to Smyrna.

We receive news of the capture of Petersburg by General Grant and 15,000 prisoners. Lee is retreating towards Richmond and Grant pursuing. The inhabitants of Petersburg saw that Grant was placing siege guns about the town and did not want it bombarded.[11] This is the most rapid fall that I have known since the war started.

If these reports be true even more favorable news is to be expected soon. At sunset we are off Cape St. Angelo of the Elos peninsula.

August 6
At sea
This morning when I came on deck we were in the Corvi Channel, a narrow passage

between the island of Cerigo and the peninsula, by going through which we save a distance of 70 miles. The wind is blowing furiously and we are under very short sail. It usually blows hard here, the wind taking up the water as it is doing this morning. On entering the Gulf of Kolokythia we meet with a number of brigs and barks which have passed outside of Cerigo. Soon after we lose the wind of the channel and meet vessels coming toward us with a fair wind, then we encounter light variable winds so that we see vessels going in all directions with a fair wind. In the afternoon we pass Cape Matapan and enter the Gulf of Halamata.

August 7
At sea

Our course is NW by W. We are having light variable winds.

At general muster today the Captain stated that our crew is the most thievish of any that he has known during his forty years at sea. The particular reason for this remark was the disappearance of a coat belonging to his son "Tom" and another belonging to an officer, both having been left somewhere on the quarter deck. He says that he will refuse an honorable discharge to anyone who has been detected stealing.

After master "Tom's" coat was found to be in possession of a Ward Room steward who put it away for Dr. Clark to whom the steward thought it belonged. Very likely the other will turn up in a similar way. I do not doubt that our crew deserves the reputation which he gives them, but these coats were rubber coats and sailors are not likely to steal coats or anything else which they can neither use nor successfully conceal.[12] If more attention were paid to the reports of thefts from sailors bags and effort made to identify the thieves and punish them there would be less justification for the Captain's remarks. In final analysis he himself is responsible for the condition of which he complains.

August 8
At sea

The wind has been ahead all day. We have met with several ships bound in the same direction as we. We have passed them all, but our ship is not in trim to do her best. It is a pleasant sail, but as we are looking forward to arrival at a new port we are naturally a little impatient.

August 9
At sea

The wind is light. We are heading within two points of our course. At noon we were 190 miles from Messina.

I am attending to my duties and reading *Carthage and her Domains*. I am very well and as happy as I can be in present circumstances, but am anxious to reach port and find out what orders are awaiting our ship.

Mr. Abbot observed today as the anniversary of the birth of his wife by opening two dozen bottles of champagne in the Ward Room.

August 11
At sea

When I came on deck the ship was heading NW by W, the wind light. At noon we made land—the coast of Calabria and at two bells were close in.

All divisions were called to quarters and all bags were searched to discover lost articles. The Paymaster is said to have lost a bale of cloth pants and I hear also that he finds himself short in his clothing account some $2,100. It may be that the Paymaster has trusted to those to whom he should not. Attention to business is the only safeguard against such surprises.

At sunset we are about forty miles from Messina.

August 12
Syracuse, Sicily
This morning I was surprised to find that we were off Syracuse instead of Messina. It appears the wind becoming unfavorable during the night to go to Messina advantage was taken of a fair wind to come here, especially, as it is said, since the Captain's son "Tom" wanted to see this ancient place. At daylight we squared away for the port and when within a mile of the entrance took on a pilot.

The coast about here is comparatively low. The city is on an island. At a distance there appears to be no harbor, but as we approached a passage opened up at the left near the fortifications. On entering this passage near the battery and hauling around close to the point a beautiful and spacious harbor comes into view.

The appearance of the city from the harbor is ancient and rather dilapidated, but a row of ornamental trees which skirt its western border outside the wall and the country toward the water on the west, with its green foliage and pleasant landscape combine to make this one of the prettiest ports in Italy.

In the afternoon I went on shore alone. Meeting Smith at the Hotel we proceeded together to look over the remains of the ancient city.

The only guide that we could obtain was a coachman who spoke only what he called "Italian." The present city is a fortified so-called "episcopal" city of 16,000 inhabitants. It contains a Royal College, two seminaries, a Library, a Museum and several other public buildings. The modern city stands amidst the ruins of the ancient Syracuse which extend over a space twenty miles in circumference. Of the five once magnificent populous districts, the Island of Ortygia is the only one now inhabited. The famous fountain of Arethusa flows through the town. It is a muddy stream about four feet deep and its water is used for washing purposes.

We pass over two canals commanded by what were once strong fortifications. Now no guns are mounted on them and they are overgrown with grass. We then approach a plain, the site of one quarter of the ancient city.

We first inspect the old Greek theater. It is hewn out of the solid rock. It was referred to by Cicero as "maximum," and regarded by Diodorous to be the most beautiful edifice of the kind in Sicily. The view from its top is attractive and must have been magnificent when Syracuse was in its glory.

The theater is semicircular is shape. Its diameter is nearly 120 feet and it held 40,000 spectators. Two corridors remain, as do many of the seats. Little however remains of the part where the stage once was.

Near the Theater are the famous stone quarry and the "Ear of Dionysius." The latter is 58 feet high at the entrance, 17 feet wide and 210 feet long. Its sides slope gradually to the summit along which runs a small channel terminating in a chamber near the entrance. Dionysius spent his leisure hours in a private apartment in this chamber listening to the conversation of the prisoners in the cave. The tearing of a piece of paper is distinctly heard the entire extent of the cave and a pistol shot sounds like a cannon. A curious feature of the cave is a single stone bath, just large enough for one person. Antiquarians are unable to explain its presence here. It is said that at one time Dionysius had 6,600 political prisoners confined here. This artificial cave is the most stupendous work in stone that I ever saw.

Nearby is the amphitheater. It had four entrances. It was partly of masonry and partly hewn out of the solid rock. This and the Theater are the most interesting of the ruins. We next go to the Catacombs, now called "La Grètta di S. Giovanni." They are well constructed and so extensive as to resemble an underground city. The entrance is about six feet high and eight feet wide. It is at right angles to the principal underground passageway, above which are openings admitting light and air. Other passageways branch off in various directions for entire families and others for a single individual.

We return to the modern city, passing a column once forming a part of a gateway of the ancient district. We come to the Museum. There we note particularly a statue of Venus without the head—a fine piece of sculpture; some colored glass vases and inscriptions taken from the street of the Tombs.

Ancient Syracuse contained within its walls five cities, or districts. It was founded 700 years before Christ by Archias of Corinth and at its most flourishing stage contained 120,000 inhabitants. It is said to have maintained an army of 1,000,000 infantry and 10,000 cavalry and a Navy of 500 covered vessels. Syracuse was taken by Marcellus, 202 B.C., and came under Roman rule. Archimedes, the mathematician lived and died here. His tomb which was discovered by Cicero during his tour of the island is still shown.

We are notified by the local officials that the Italian Government has adopted the policy of the British and French with respect to the war vessels of the Federal and Confederate "powers." We are politely informed that we may remain in port twenty four hours.

The rule does not apply to "scientific expeditions" and it is said that the Captain is going to claim that we are to be reckoned in this category, some of our officers asserting that he might do so without compromising his reputation for honesty. They say that all that is necessary is to designate the members of the ship's company to fill positions in an organized "scientific corps." Paymaster Pangborn says that in view of this latest European official emanation he suggests that we organize to study "gas," and that we would probably find it light.

Notwithstanding this official warning we will probably remain here until Monday. The people do not know of this action of the Government with respect to American war ships. It certainly would not be popular. It has not been published. There is no doubt that it has been dictated by the French and is a reflection of the relations of the French Empire with the Confederacy.

The Paymaster has telegraphed to Spezia to ascertain what news is to be had. I spend the evening with Messrs. Grainger, Ryder and Kempton and return on board with them at eight bells.

August 13
Syracuse

A dispatch from our Consul at Messina states that he has a large mail for us, including an important official document, and thus intimating that orders to return home are awaiting us there.

The consul at Alexandria has had a difficulty with the Egyptian Government in relation to a pump which he had in operation and which was destroyed or rendered unserviceable by the authorities. He gave notice that if an apology was not made within three days he would terminate all official communication with the government.

No apology was made and he accordingly took down his sign and flag and closed the Consulate. He has sent for all the ships of war which our government has in European waters. Our Captain received a dispatch from the Consul today, but we will not go anywhere until we have been to Messina and received our mail.

It is reported that General Sherman has captured Atlanta and taken many prisoners.[13]

August 14
Syracuse

I went on shore at noon, but the dust of the streets, whirled about by a strong breeze, was so annoying that I spent most of the day at the "Trattoria all'Alberco" in company with the Paymaster and the lieutenant of Marines. I dined with Messrs. Philbrick and Cox, after which we took an evening promenade and returned on board at ten o'clock.

Our host at the "Alberco" has some very good wine which he has kept for fourteen years. This wine recommends itself to everyone who has tasted it. Since the American squadron has ceased to make any protracted visits here he has had little sale for his large stock which he says that he put in expressly for the Americans. To judge from appearances some of our officers who took dinner there Friday night sampled it "not wisely but too well."

Return on board at 10 p.m. and find that visiting officers from an Italian Mail Ship are being entertained in the Ward Room in a very convivial manner and I suspect that the "Alberco" wine has been an important adjunct to the dinner.

August 15
Syracuse and Catania

This morning we got under way with a good breeze at 8 o'clock and stood out of the harbor and then hove to set on shore in one of our boats the Consul who had accompanied us outside. On the return of the boat we squared away for Catania where we are to stop to gratify the curiosity of those who desire to visit this ancient place. We arrive at 3 p.m. It is only a small party of us who accept the invitation of the Captain to accompany him and go on shore. A strong wind is blowing and this ostensibly serves as an excuse, but back of it there is impatience at any delay in reaching Messina and finding out what orders are awaiting the ship there. Only three Ward Room officers come with us.

Catania is situated at the foot of Mount Aetna on a fertile slope facing the sea. It is about 25 miles from Syracuse. It has a population of about 56,000. The city was founded 753 years B.C. It has the only university on the island and is seat of a Bishop whose revenues are considerable owing in a great measure to the trade in snow from Mount Aetna. This mountain supplies frozen snow for Malta as well as Sicily. The city was badly damaged by the eruption of 669 and almost entirely destroyed by that of 1695 when a great part of the inhabitants were buried in its ruins. Phoenix like it arose from the ruins so much increased in importance and in beauty as to rival every other city on the island.

The Cathedral contains several splendid paintings and some fine specimens of (?) and alabaster. The Museum of the Monastery has a large collection of ancient Sicilian vases, many of them exquisitely carved and colored, a still larger collection of ancient medallions and many other interesting objects of antiquity.

The remains of the ancient town are mostly underground. The lava buried the ancient mole and filled the harbor to some extent. Down sixty steps cut in the lava one is shown a living spring of clear water. It is said that the Greek Theater over which modern buildings now stand was larger than that of Marcellus at Rome.

When bringing the ship to on our arrival at this place today Spinny, my assistant, nearly lost his arm by having it caught in the block while overhauling the topsail sheet. His hand is considerably injured.

August 16
Strait of Messina
The wind was ahead until afternoon when it changed as it frequently does after noonday in this region. As we sail along the shore the beautiful scenery serves to ease somewhat the nervous tension which everybody feels regarding the mail which awaits us at Messina. We see many pretty little towns and villages nestled among the hills and in the ravines of this rough volcanic country. It looks as though Nature had tried to upturn the foundation of the Island. Aetna which from time to time has laid waste cities and towns and buried their inhabitants is quiet now, but the smoky breath from its nostrils suggests an impatience to start its work of destruction again.

At sunset we are just within the mouth of the strait. The tide is against us and all prospect of our reaching Messina tonight is gone. The ship is put under easy sail for the night with the main top-sail aback.

August 17
Messina
This morning found us working through the Strait with the wind and tide against us. A pilot was taken aboard, but it was noon before we reached the harbor. The Consul, Mr. Bhen sent the mail to us outside. Soon everybody is devouring the news. Some have a dozen letters. All are interested in or have one. Some officers are notified that their pay is raised. Others have assurances that the ship's orders for home have been issued by the Department. Nobody knows however whether they have been received on board.

Soon the Surgeon, Dr. Messersmith, reads in the Ward room a part of a letter which he has received from his wife. She writes, "Hurrah! The *Constellation* has been ordered home!" She then goes on to say by what good authority she has been so informed. This is sufficient. The captain soon learns about the Doctor's information and its source and admits that it is correct.

The news spreads like wild fire through the ship. In an incredibly short time it is known to the entire crew and the cheers from three hundred and fifty throats can be heard for miles. It certainly is happy news for all.

We are notified that the 24 hours rule respecting our tarry in port is in force at Messina, but a dispatch is sent to Turin requesting permission to delay our departure somewhat. This seems to me to be too much like begging. A reply grants us permission to remain two days!

I went on shore in the evening and made some purchases and returned with Messrs. Cox and Philbrick at six bells.

August 18
Messina
Further permission to remain has been granted. I understand that we now have a general permit to visit without limit any ports in Italy.

In the afternoon I went on shore with some of my shipmates to purchase dry goods.

Following the example of some of the others who said it was cheap, I bought a silk dress pattern, thus disregarding Benjamin Franklin's maxim. Perhaps it may be of some service to some one.

The bark *Money Nick*, of Boston, is here. The Captain came to visit us today and I had a talk with this New Englander. His craft was here with us twenty two months ago and during this time he has been very successful in the fruit trade between this port and the United States.

In the evening I visited the park and listened to a fine band. Messina is a thrifty business city and seems to be improving.

Our officers are buying all kinds of clothing for themselves and their wives.

August 19
Messina and the sea

At 4 a.m. we are again under way, standing out of Messina for the last time this cruise. It is almost a calm, but we have the current to assist us on our way. Thus drifting, sometimes sideways and even stern first we pass between Scylla and Charybdis without observing any cause for anxiety.

The *Money Nick* is in company with us and likewise safely drifting. She is bound to Sardinia. We are bound to Spezia.

In the afternoon we make less progress as the current turns against us and the wind continues light. We however outsail the clipper bark which has the reputation of being fast and which being light, in ballast, should go faster than we in this wind if she deserves her reputation. Our course brings us close to Stromboli on the windward side and at 9 p.m. we are just abreast of the volcano.

While busy writing in the Store Room I am informed that Stromboli is emitting fire. On reaching the deck I see bright red fire on the side of the crater, but the spouting has ceased. In a few moments a jet of fire shoots up in the air, lasts about a half a minute and then dies away. Those ejections are accompanied by a sound like distant thunder, reaching us a few seconds after the eruption.

A half an hour later I have the benefit of another fire shooting exhibition from Stromboli much longer than the first, thus making three different discharges within three hours.

Notwithstanding the activity of this volcano human habitations are to be seen on the lower slopes of the mountain. The residents are probably fishermen as I noticed numerous lights around the base of the mountain such as are used by fishermen on this coast. How few places are so dangerous that men will not try to live there!

August 20
At sea

Light fair wind. Excessively hot. I have never felt more uncomfortable from the heat since we have been in the Mediterranean. We have made 140 miles up to noon.

It is reported that the ship is ordered to "New Orleans where she is to be used as a Receiving Ship." I do not credit this story—although it may be true.

August 21
At sea

The heavy swell which accompanies a light southwest wind operates to shake most of the wind out of the sails and partly in consequence we are averaging less than four knots. At

8 bells p.m. the wind heads us off our course. It is quite as hot as yesterday—too hot even to read. Everyone is lying about the deck and trying to make himself as comfortable as possible.

At general muster today the Department circular stating the increases in pay of petty officers and seamen was read. My pay is now $40 a month besides the ration which makes it $49.50.

The name of Richard H. Seaward of Kittery is mentioned in the reading of the list of those who have been promoted for meritorious conduct and entitled to a gratuity. He is made a Master's Mate. It is stated that outside his line of duty and on his own initiative he displayed great personal bravery by going under fire during an action and dragging wounded soldiers to safety.

August 22
At sea

A light breeze all day, the ship making about five knots. Warm as ever.

I break out the Boatswain's store room to take an account of stock and make it clean. I provide a warm job for some ten men during the two watches below. The rats are set in motion and their homes destroyed. The numerous cats on board have reduced the stock somewhat, but I think that about 2,000 congregate in my quarters every night. I find my stock of cordage on hand to be all right, checking up with my account of cordage received and issued.

At 2 bells p.m. we make the Island of Monte Christo.

August 23
At sea

Last night all studding sails were taken in and consequently the ship's progress was much lessened as the wind was light.

This noon the Island of Monte Christo was on the starboard quarter. At noon we were passing Elba. At 8 bells p.m. the wind hauled to the west and headed us off our course 1/4 of a point. We were then 55 miles from Spezia. This is probably the last time that I shall pass this way.

August 24
Spezia

At ten o'clock last night the wind came fair again and so we have to shorten sail. Soon after 4 a.m. today we made the light of Spezia through a cloud of mist which is characteristic of this place. Morning brought a fine clear sky and the green hills and the pretty villages of this old Italian home of ours appear as attractive as ever. Since the hope of once again enjoying our homes in a America has revived our fondness for old Spezia has, however, abated somewhat.

A large bark is lying here with Government stores on board. The bark will take them to a new place as soon as we receive our supply. There is much for us to do in the one week in which we are expected to prepare for our homeward voyage.

Andy Wilson, a seaman and a native of Sweden whom we left here sick with a consumption, died June 4, lamenting his only wish could not be gratified—that he could not be borne by his shipmates to the grave. He was a kind and agreeable shipmate and of good deportment.

Charles D. Bellows who was left here with the same complaint though of a less dangerous stage, has improved in health.

Two Italian ships of war lie here, the *Partenope* and the *Formidable*, an ironclad. Many improvements have been made in the government works here since we left.

August 25
Spezia

At daylight all hands are at work on the ship's rigging, "rattling down" and tarring it. The hold was broken out yesterday and is now ready to receive stores. I have received some stores in the Boatswain's and the Carpenter's departments.

In the afternoon I went on shore at the Store House and walked to Spezia, had supper, spent the evening walking about this beautiful summer retreat and returned to the ship with the officers at 10 o'clock.

It is reported that Admiral Farragut has achieved a victory at Mobile.[14]

August 26
Spezia

It is reported that Secretary of War Stanton has resigned.[15] Wm. E. Smith receives a sentence of a court-martial for assaulting Michael Gaul, marine. Smith is to be confined 30 days in the "Brig" with three days a week on bread and water and is to forfeit three months pay. He is a hard case and there is little prospect of his being better. He has already served several terms in the penitentiary. He was sent on board the *Massachusetts* school ship on promise to reform, from which place he was transferred to our ship. There are others on board similar to him, but not so bold.

August 28
Spezia

At general muster today there was announced the court-martial of Michael E. Gaul for assaulting Wm. E. Smith. He is to forfeit one month's pay, to be imprisoned thirty days and to perform one month's extra police duty. He is another of those hopeless characters, to be found in every community as well as on our ship, who might be hung at the yard arm with benefit to their shipmates as well as to the communities that they are going to afflict after they have received dishonorable discharges from the Navy. But have we the right to say that there is no reason for their creation?

At one o'clock I go on shore with Smith, the Surgeon's Steward. We walk around to the Lazaretto. Returning we lie down for a while on the bank in the shade of the olive and fig trees. I enjoy these quiet rambles about the shores and coves of this beautiful bay where the rippling of the water mingles with the songs of the birds, the voices of the peasants and distant bugle calls. This melody causes me to fall asleep. I dream of my distant home and friends that have so much engaged my thoughts lately, but on awakening it is with regret that I realize how brief the time now is before I shall leave forever these sunny skies, these delightful landscapes and balmy zephyrs. I shall never forget them and doubtless will often wish that I might see them again. Attractive Italy! How I wish your political and social condition were in keeping with your beauty which meets the eye!

August 29
Spezia

Mr. Laurence, our Consul-General for Italy, Mr. Rice the Consul at Spezia,[16] Mr. Gould, the artist, and several other gentlemen visit the ship. They receive the customary salute.

The taking of Mobile by Admiral Faragut is confirmed. It is also reported that the *Niagara* has captured a rebel ship.[17]

I receive a letter from my brother Edward giving me cheering news of the recovery of his health.

The dreaded yellow fever from which so many of my fellow townsmen have died in the Tropics has visited Kittery and a good many have died. It was brought to the Navy Yard by the ship *Esota* and the disease caused the suspension of work at the Yard for a while. The ship was taken down the harbor and anchored. Two watchmen on board died. After the ship's bilges were pumped out many people living on the neighboring shore came down with the yellow fever and one entire family died.

September 1
Spezia

The bandsmen are discharged. Yesterday they played for the last time, concluding with *Auld Lang Syne*.

The Captain entertained a party on board last night. It had as a sequel a row among some of our officers on shore. I learn this morning that for some reason, unknown to me, Surgeon Messersmith smashed his cane over the head of Acting Master Kempton. The Lieutenant of Marines followed with his fist in the direction of Kempton's jaw, knocking him down, whereupon Kempton drew his sword, but before he could do any damage the Paymaster caught Kempton by the throat, "got the heave on him" and made him give up his sword. All this, I understand, took place in the street. The Surgeon today reported Mr. Kempton and he is confined in his room under arrest. This is too often the conclusion of a happy affair in which drink has been the exhilarating feature.

At the dinner Colonel Long and Mrs. Rice, the wife of the Consul were each presented with a gold chain worth $50. The chains were the gifts of the Captain and officers of the ship.

I am sorry that the affair afterwards took such a wild turn on shore. I hope that the Consul General will not hear about the affray.

I have received four paintings from Sardinia of Naples which I ordered last spring. I had given them up long ago as they were not sent when promised. They are, a view of Naples from Pausilippo, (?) a view showing the ancient Greek Temples at Paestrum, a Ste. Agatha and a Zingarella.

We are taking in stores and caulking ship, etc. The ship is found to be quite rotten in the upper sides and in need of some new planking. Our firewood has come from Leghorn.

September 2
Spezia

The provisions are all on board. The boats are being taken in for the last time, I hope. We expect to be ready to sail tomorrow.

The shoemakers have been doing a great business with our men who are providing themselves with sea boots. When a pair is brought on board to deliver to a sailor a crowd of his shipmates gather around to inspect and criticize the boots.

The bandsmen have been on board all day waiting for pay due them. It has been amusing to see them when they think that they hear coins jingling in the Ward Room, rush to the skylight, look down and then turn away with disappointment depicted in their faces. I remit Scardinia the amount of his bill by Post Office Order.

September 3
Spezia

The caulking is completed, the messenger is brought up and the chafing gear put on. This looks like going to sea.

The old bum-boat woman had a fight this evening with a gentleman competitor. She threw thirty or forty eggs at him, but her shots went wild. Then her oarsman took a hand in the affair. After several jabs with an oar on both sides, directed to the abdominal region of each other, the bum-boat woman's oarsman landed one which put their competitor overboard. The old lady received a few raps over the head with an oar, but they did not put her hors de combat or even interrupt her flow of language.

September 4
Spezia

The ship is crowded with tailors, shoemakers and other trades-people making their last efforts to separate us from our money. The men are running to the Paymaster for money faster than he can make provision to meet their demands.

At 5 o'clock I went on shore. I called on Colonel Long, Mr. Rice, the Consul and bade them and my other friends "good bye." Then Messrs. Grainger, Cox, Drew, Brown, Smith, Hunter and I paid our respects to Mr. Lucas whom we familiarly call "Peter." He entertained us royally and then we bade adieu to him and this "sunny Land."

September 5
Spezia and the sea

A clear sky and a fine breeze from the north. Colonel Long and Mr. Rice come to the ship to bid us farewell. The partings over, the capstan flies around rapidly and the chain is "short" in a few minutes. Two salutes are fired in honor of Colonel Long and the Consul and at two thirty p.m. the ship's head has swung off and we are sailing out of the Bay of Spezia for the last time.

I noticed that the eyes of many were moist as they bade adieu to their old friends in Spezia. We waved our handkerchiefs long in the wind as we strained our eyes to follow the boat that bore our friends to the shore.

A fine breeze fills the sails and we rapidly glide out of this delightful bay—our Italian home. The town of Spezia with its old fortifications disappear in the distance. La Polla and Lerici in their turn are hidden by the shadows of the mountains until nothing but the old town of Porto Venire and the sublime scenery of the outer portions of the Gulf are left to bid us their farewell.

Adieu verdant hills of Italy! The Land whose sunny smiles have cheered my heart for more than two years and have relieved the tedious and soul-destroying monotony of that life from which thy receding shores tell me that I am soon to be delivered, I bid thee farewell!

Had my birth been here it is here that I would prefer to remain with the patriots who are willing to sacrifice their lives and all to see Italy united and free. May that event not be long delayed.

September 6
At sea

A calm prevails all day. We are between Corsica and Genoa and the tide is taking us toward the latter place.

Alexander Carter is made Paymaster's Steward in place of Mr. Ferrell and he becomes our messmate.

I witness one of the most beautiful sunsets that I ever beheld.

September 9
At sea

Still calm. This is tedious. Corsica is still in sight. The sailors say that lack of wind is due to the Paymaster's failure to serve out "Monthly money" and he has been so informed by the old signal quartermaster, May. This calm is evidently "getting on the nerves" of the Captain as well as on those of the rest of us. Today he became so exasperated over the noise on the gun-deck that he threatened to court-martial the offenders. Nobody else had observed any unusual noises or sounds there.

Several whales have been near the ship during the calm. Whales are said not to be residents of the Mediterranean. Porpoises and blackfish in great numbers are seen playing around us every morning.

The Captain's Clerk ("Tom," his son) tried the experiment of lowering corked bottles to a depth of 150 fathoms. One which was in a bag was crushed to pieces. Another had the stopper forced in. Another in which the cork was retained in place came up partly filled with salt water.

By astronomical observation and mathematical computation our progress for the twenty four hours preceding noon today was three quarters of a mile.

September 12
At sea

The calm has continued up to today. Last night Corsica was still close at hand. In eight days we have gone less than 100 miles. During these calm days I have noticed in the water a sort of sea-serpent, or rather several of them. They were jointed things with a red spot on each joint. They moved just under water and projected their heads a little above occasionally. They are new to me.

The weather has changed today. The sky has become cloudy. The wind this afternoon came from the northwest, out of the Gulf of Lyons. At 5 p.m. we are going eight knots and on our course.

September 13
At sea

Today we have wind enough to satisfy everybody. Last night the wind came from the NNW and increased so that the topsails were close reefed and the foresail and mainsail taken in. At 5 bells this morning the royal and topgallant yards were sent down.

I left my hammock at 4 a.m. to see in what condition things were in the Store Room. I found everything movable distributed over the floor. Planes, cooper's jointers, tinners' shears, paint brushes, wrenches, balances, etc., were all mixed together.

On the berth deck we were nearly afloat. Water was running across the deck. It came through the sides of the ship. The Gunner and the Boatswain were turned out of their berths by the flood and rigged up spouts over them to protect themselves.

It was amusing to see the maneuvers to get hammocks in the nettings when they were piped up. An Italian, lately shipped, who had the last turn on his hammock lost the end of the lashing when the ship made a heavy lurch to the leeward and he sat in a pan of flour which arose in a cloud above his head. Extricating himself from this he brought up in a mess chest among the tin ware. Then starting again for the deck he came in collision with another man and barely escaped being knocked into the fore-hold. What further misfortunes he encountered before he reached the spar-deck I was unable to observe.

No tables were spread today. Everybody took his food between his knees. Nor did all the food which was cooked reach those for whom it had been prepared. Everyone had his misfortunes and a cook or steward not the least. A darkey with a plateful of omelettes would be thrown on the steps by a roll of the ship and the contents of the dish go flying over his head and light on the steps or deck to be quickly scraped up by some sailor standing by with a dish and knife waiting for just such an accident. Probably three pots of tea were made before one reached its destination.

I felt somewhat sick in the morning, but eat my allowance of cold pork three times during the day.

This is the most disagreeable day which we have spent in the ship. There is no place that is not soaking wet. One needs sea boots even on the berth deck.

The Captain lost his soup for dinner and we our stew at the same galley. Our table turned bottom up the first thing this morning and then our mess chest got adrift. As I was going up forward a spit kid which came from somewhere caromed against the sheet-chain throwing its contents of tobacco juice to the leeward and giving me a shower.

Old Blucher got mixed up with a coil of rope on the quarter deck and was carried across the deck rope and all with his feet in the air and brought up in the lee scuppers.

September 14
Mahon

This morning the wind has abated and the sea gone down. The topgallant and royal yards are sent aloft and all sail is set. Mount Toro the first land to be seen from the sea is in sight and we will soon be able to make out the city of Mahon.

At three thirty the pilot comes on board. He is the same old fat jolly fellow that we left here. Before boarding us he inquires if we have a bill of health from a Spanish Consul. Once before he was quarantined with us for five days, hence his caution.

Mr. Robinson, our Consul, is on hand in his sail boat and the people of sleepy Georgetown flock to the battery to see the ship sail into port. The arrival of a man-of-war creates as much excitement here as an eruption of Vesuvius would cause in Naples.

Here is old Pratz who has visited our ships from times beyond memory. He wears the same hat, coat and "dickey" that he wore thirty years ago. I presume that he has recovered from the ruinous soap speculation which he undertook some years ago—just at the time when the Navy began supplying its ships with soap by contract at home. Here too, is old "Nancy Brandywine" and the usual delegation of female Mahones' who are accustomed to meet our ships.

September 15
Mahon

An examination of the ship shows that she needs more caulking and some more planking.

It is estimated that the work which will be done here will take about ten days.

In the evening I went on shore with Hunter and Jones, landing at Georgetown. We called on our old friend Señor Raphael with whom we spent about an hour and then rode to Mahon where we remained until 10 o'clock. Mahon has the same lonesome and forlorn appearance now that it did when we left it last. Frank Losano, the proprietor of the "Golden Lion" has died and the house is closed. This was our favorite resort.

September 16
Mahon

The usual number of Mahon females are on board during meal hours. It is reported that General Grant is besieging Richmond and Petersburg.[18]

A discovery of an extensive Rebel League has been made. Some of General Grant's staff officers and many prominent men of the country have been found to belong. George Law of New York is named as one of them. I believe that they are reputed to be of the order of the "Knights of the Golden Cyrcle." The records of the order are said to have been found and to be in the possession of the Government.[19]

September 21
Mahon

The work on the ship is progressing well. Some of our officers have been finding a welcome diversion in yachting. The competition among the boats is very keen and there have been some really exciting races.

A subscription is started on the ship to defray the expense of the passage of the widow and children of Frank Lozano to the United States.

Last night Orderly Sergeant Robbins when attempting to board the gig to come to the ship stepped upon some floating straw which was once a soldier's bed and to his astonishment found that he was not on *terra firma*. After much scrambling and some help he landed in the boat, bringing much straw with him.

September 22
Mahon

Robert Mulligan, a colored man, died this morning from a bronchial consumption after a brief sickness.

The Governor of Mahon and his Lady visited the ship this forenoon in company with the Governor's secretary and our Consul.

At two thirty p.m. all hands were called to bury the dead. The body of Mulligan, who was the best specimen of the Negro race on board, was placed into one of the cutters and was followed by several officers and the Consul to its last resting place near the "Golden Farm."

Mulligan was probably about twenty years old, but his age and place of birth were not known and a simple planed board with R.M. painted in black upon it is all that we leave upon the barren shore of this harbor to record the fact that this jolly active Negro once lived.

In the evening I went on shore with Mr. Jones, said good bye to friends and met some of our shipmates at the Hotel Castell, returning on board at seven bells.

Reports of the taking of Mobile and Atlanta have been confirmed. Gold has fallen to $1.10. Morgan, the Guerilla, has been killed.[20] If recent reports hold good a more favorable situation has developed on the Federal front.

September 23
Mahon and the sea

At five thirty this morning, "All hands up anchor" resounded through the ship.

The usual number of persons who have bills to collect from the officers and crew are scattered among the ship's company and boats filled with females surround the ship who have approached to pay their respects to their late hosts.

We are soon underway with a very light wind, but with the help of the ship's boats we are out of port in about an hour. We are followed by several shore boats in which I notice women with handkerchiefs at their eyes. Whether they really do feel bad at parting with some one I do not know, but I believe that they would not feel quite so bad if they did not realize that their free rations were gliding away.

At sunset we are in sight of Majorca. At 8 o'clock we are clear of Cape Mola with a fair wind which is giving us a fine start. Mahon is now left for the last time this cruise, I trust.

September 26
At sea

This morning finds us still sailing on our course with a light breeze. At 3 p.m. we are at Cape de Gata going about 8 knots with studding sails set on both sides. We pass an Italian bark and several steamers in shore.

A court-martial is in session. Several men are to be tried before it adjourns.

September 28
Gibraltar Bay

This morning at 6 o'clock we are close to Europa Point with a strong breeze from the east. The topgallant and light sails were taken in several hours ago and we enter the bay under easy sail and anchor on the Spanish side. A Russian frigate lies at the head of the bay.

The USS *St. Louis* sailed for home two weeks ago.

The American Consul at Algeciras has been deposed for charging the government for postage on letters of ships' crews on which he paid no postage. Serves him right. Should all who do the same thing be similarly dealt with there would be more out of offices which they are now filling.

This is the anniversary of my birth, being the third which I have seen in this ship. How swiftly the years roll on!

It was the intention of the Captain to remain here three days, but now orders are given to have the ship ready for sea tonight. An official dispatch has been received here which doubtless determines this action.

A strong breeze has prevailed all day. Heavy clouds hang over the Rock, indications of wet weather.

Accounts are being signed. This event always creates a discussion among the men who think that they find mistakes in the Paymaster's accounts with them. Sometimes they do, but not frequently.

September 29
At sea

Last night after dark a boat with stores for the officers' messes came to the ship from Gibraltar. There followed a scene of confusion which was unusual and which had some amusing features. A barrel of flour came down the main hatchway narrowly missing our old

Orderly sergeant and giving him a bad fright. The head came out of the barrel and the deck was covered with flour. One mess missed a barrel of flour, a barrel of ale, a jar of tripe and a tub of butter; another a bottle of mustard, a package of coffee and some red herring. The Master-at-Arms is called to assist in the hunt. A barrel of flour belonging to the Ward Room mess is found in the starboard steerage room. It is hinted that there may be found in the port steerage store room articles belonging to the Ward Room and starboard steerage messes. Jones who purchased the stores for both messes and came off with them pretty "tight" does not see the need of checking up the articles received with the bills. He takes the cheerful view that "they are all on board the ship somewhere" and that "everything will come out all right." This optimism is hardly consistent with remarks which one overhears such as, "where is our jam? We are in a ham." The Executive Officer gives the Master-at-Arms orders to examine the port steerage and take an account of stock. Somehow a contention arises that $15 worth of goods have not been delivered as per bill. This gives rise to a dispute with the man who bought them. The Captain asks the Executive Officer repeatedly why the strangers have not been sent from the ship. Meanwhile the gale continues to increase and loud calls come to the grocery man from his men in his waiting boat telling him that if they do not start before the sea gets worse they will never reach shore at all.

As the scene closes "Pop" Allen, already exhilarated by his visit to the Rock, comes up to take the deck fortified for further needs with a bottle of wine and a bottle of ale in his pockets. Just as he is going up the ladder one bottle slips out and smashes in the fall and its pieces fly in all directions. "Pop" keeps on going paying no attention to his loss.

This morning the wind has moderated somewhat. At daylight we get under way and were soon sailing through the strait with a fair strong breeze. Soon Tarife light is passed. We fly swiftly past Cape Spartel and soon pass onto the broad Atlantic going at the rate of twelve knots.

We take a farewell look at the avenue which has admitted us to the scenes of our troubles and our joys for the past two and a half years and then we turn our heads to the westward to the shores of the New World where old homes and friends and new experiences await us.

October 1
At sea

Last night all berth deck ports were closed and covered at quarters. This precaution against a surprise is henceforth to be observed as we are now in the cruising grounds of the Rebel war ships.

Today as yesterday we have light westerly winds, varied today with occasional rain squalls.

October 3
At sea

This is tedious for us who are so impatient to be across the Atlantic. All day we have a strong breeze from the same direction—dead ahead. In five days we have made 225 miles.

October 5
At sea

The wind is light. The ship has been heading SW by S and sometimes W. At 7 bells p.m. the wind dies away and it becomes calm again.

I spent most of the afternoon on the spritsail yard fishing. This has been quite a diversion.

I caught five "skip-jacks." They are plump handsome fish weighing on an average about eight pounds. They have a tail like mackerel. They are "gamy" when hooked. A white rag is used as bait. It is kept in motion near the surface of the water and the fish jump for it.

October 7
At sea
This morning when I came on deck the wind was blowing a strong breeze. The topgallant yards were sent down and the mizzen topsail furled. The ship was put under treble reefed topsails and double reefed foresail. The wind is SE. We are bound for Teneriffe. Soon the wind hauls to the NE and diminishes, but the sea continues rough and irregular. We shake out one reef in the topsails and the reef in the foresail. At 4 p.m. we are 420 miles from Teneriffe.

In the afternoon the inner bulkhead of the cabin is removed and a 32 pdr. gun is pointed out of the cabin window and tried both with shot and shell. The same kind of a gun is tried out of the bow port on the same side. Other preparations are now being made which indicate war more than yachting. A good opportunity now offers for putting the ship in her most effective fighting condition which at the best does not make her very formidable.

October 10
At sea
This morning we were going about 5 knots with a light southerly breeze.

At 10 a.m. we beat to quarters and started target practice with the big guns. We fired four rounds from the port battery. The Captain was present on the gun deck and superintended the pointing of some guns. Most of the firing was rather bad I am told. I was in charge of the magazine as usual and therefore did not see anything.

October 12
Santa Cruz, Teneriffe
A good breeze enabled us to beat up to the Island by noon and at three thirty we dropped anchor in port. We learn that the Confederate cruiser *Florida* left here a month ago.

We fire a salute and receive one in return. This is the place where Lord Nelson lost an eye in an unsuccessful attack on the fortifications. The American Consul visited the ship. He received the customary salute. We will take wood and water on board tomorrow.

October 14
Santa Cruz
In the afternoon I went on shore to see the city. The buildings are decidedly Spanish as to construction, shape and color being white-washed or painted white. The streets are tolerably clean. To judge from appearances a large proportion of the population are in indigent circumstances.

There is a considerable trade with England, a regular line of steamers running here. Quantities of coal are also brought here from Great Britain in small sailing vessels which take back fruit from here and St. Michaels and other ports in the Azores. Sugar, tobacco and cigars are imported from Cuba.

The chief feature of interest here is the physical character of the Island. The peak of Teneriffe is 12,180 feet high. When not hidden by clouds it can be seen from the deck of a ship 120 miles at sea.

The same sort of extortions and impositions are practiced on visitors here as at all other Spanish ports which I have visited. When one engages a boat here to take him to his ship, it means a disagreeable row. The other boatman will threaten and abase the one whom you engage and there will be a great noise and such loud profanity in any event. I dislike these Spanish places very much and am always glad to leave them.

I took luncheon at "Richardson's Hotel," visited some English importing houses and returned on board at 4 p.m.

October 15
Santa Cruz and the sea
Last evening Benjamin O. Van Tassel, a colored man died. He had been sick a long time with dropsy.

We got under way at 8 a.m., but owing to the light wind it was noon before we wore clear off the land. We take the body of the dead Negro to sea with us.

Two of my mess-mates who went on shore yesterday for supplies obtained some Teneriffe wine, the effects of which on them were somewhat obvious yesterday and have been all day today.

The variable winds do not enable us to clear the western point of the Island and at sunset a strong wind strikes us dead ahead causing us to reef top-sail. At the same time all hands are called to "bury the dead" and the body of Van Tassel was "committed to the deep" there to remain with the countless others who sleep in an ocean grave. The reading of the burial service, the sober faces of shipmates standing at attention and balancing themselves on the rolling and pitching deck of the ship and the thought which always comes, "whose turn will it be next," all contribute to make a burial at sea a most impressive affair. As is customary, as a mark of respect to the dead, the headway of a ship is checked for a moment by allowing her to "come to," as the body is slid off into the sea.

Topsails had been reefed and the men were off the yards as this maneuver was carried out on this occasion, but halliards, clewlines, etc. had not been coiled down and in a voice which was audible on deck Jack Ripley, the captain of the main top, who was there attending to his duties there, expressed his opinion of the propriety of "making such a fuss over a damned nigger."

October 20
At sea
This morning there are five or six ships and barks in sight. We outsail them all.

We are now in the tropics in the trade winds at last, and going along under a six knot breeze. The air is mild and the soft wind feels like the summer zephyrs of my home climate. The little trade clouds rise and scatter themselves over the sky and then give rise to others. We are now sure of a fair wind to St. Thomas.

October 22
At sea
The ship is averaging between four and five knots. Slowly we are lessening the distance between us and the western world, but it does not seem like a homeward bound passage, merely an extension of the cruise.

Everyone is happy and things are going pleasantly, a few family jars excepted.

At general muster this morning the Captain read several articles of war and explained them. They related to destroying or disabling the property of the United States and to other crimes which have been committed on this ship. He referred to the cutting of gun-breechings and train-tackles about a week ago and to the robbing of the Paymaster's store rooms and other depredations. He stated that it was his duty to report these acts to the Department and that none of the crew would probably be discharged until the Department's investigation was made. He referred to the possibility that nobody might receive an honorable discharge unless the perpetrators of these acts were identified. The Captain does not exaggerate. This ship's company has acquired the reputation of being a set of outlaws and doubtless will receive official attention as soon as the ship joins a squadron. There are a comparatively few men on board who are capable of committing these acts and while such men are known it seems impossible to discover which one or ones have committed a particular act and hence all have to suffer.

October 28
At sea
A fine breeze. During the last 24 hours we have made 191 miles. Pleasant sailing, but it is very warm. I look for hours at our able ship as she sails along and admire the sight of the parting water at the bows.

The British ship *Coldstream* made signals to us as she passed close under our stern standing to the northwest through the trade winds probably bound to England. Not having the signal code used by British merchant ships we could not read nor answer her signals. It would seem that a man-of-war should have the signals and signal codes in general use among merchantmen as valuable information might be obtained or conveyed by this means.

Last evening while the watch on deck was engaged in a musical performance the drum beat to "general quarters." This was a complete surprise for no one except the Executive officer knew that the call was to be given until the drum commenced to beat.

October 29
At sea
The same pleasant wind and weather.

The Captain sent for me today and inquired of me of certain monies by me kept for some of the ship's company. His object is to try to discover some clue to the identity of the persons who have been committing the depredations on the ship, and in this I hope that he may succeed.

From time to time sailors have given me money for safe keeping or to remit home to someone because of their belief in my honesty and reliability. We went over my entire record of such transactions, but found nothing to indicate that a man had more money than he ought to have nor anything else which seemed suspicious.

The present uncertainty as to the identity of these scoundrels tends to throw suspicion unjustly and is disturbing to the morale of the whole crew. It is the duty of everyone to aid by all honorable means to bring those guilty to punishment. We are 1,100 miles from St. Thomas.

October 30
At sea
Less wind today. The ship is making about six knots.

It is understood that the Paymaster has evidence pointing to the identity of a certain person who robbed his store room. I hope that this is so and that the guilty parties will be detected and properly punished—every one of them.

It is a matter of great satisfaction to me to know that I have been extremely scrupulous in protecting and in demanding from others a strict accounting for property for which I am supposed to be responsible and that I have been referred to as "tight fisted, a tough Down-East mate," and by other more uncomplimentary terms, but I am respected and by no means unpopular on the ship, and at a time like this when everybody is looked upon as guilty of neglect of duty if nothing worse it is a source of more happiness to me then the possession of money to the value of the ship and its whole equipment would be that no suspicion of dishonesty or neglect of duty is directed toward me.

The old adage, "Honesty is the best policy," is well worth keeping in mind and is to be observed by those whose duty it is to prevent dishonesty in others.

November 2
At sea

Very warm. It is almost suffocating in the Store Room. The wind is light. I feel rather weak. Salt provisions are beginning to affect me, I fear.

At noon today we are 755 miles from St. Thomas. A few dolphins are sporting around and gulf-weed begins to make its appearance.

The Paymaster and the Captain's Clerk are very anxious to read my journal of the trip to Jerusalem, but I do not deem it proper to let my private record go out of my hands, especially as I think that the trip to Jerusalem is not all that they would like to read.

A request from a Paymaster or a Captain's Clerk to see my diary is a different proposition from a singular request from the Captain or the Executive Officer who are responsible for the discipline of the ship. Although I might meet a request from the latter as I have this it would carry with it an implication that I might be withholding some information of value in tending to identify the men who are guilty of the crimes and misdemeanors committed on the ship. I do not want to be placed in this position.

As the mate of vessels it has been my duty to keep the log and probably this habit is responsible for starting a diary on this cruise. From the first however I thought it would be interesting to have a diary to refer to after the cruise was over.

As time has gone on the writing up of the diary has given me something of interest to look forward to every day. Occasionally there has been a delay of a day or two in writing it up, but except when in the sick bay after my operation and while at Jerusalem where I took frequent notes which were afterwards written up, the diary has methodically claimed my daily attention. The effort to describe events and to record my thoughts has given me needed practice in English composition and has tended to prevent me from going astern mentally in the position which I occupy on this ship.

I have expressed my opinions and criticized our officers and others on the ship and have recorded events reflecting unfavorably on them. It has seemed to me that after having tried to give vent to my feelings by committing them to writing I am less inclined to think about disagreeable matters afterwards.

I have, however, never written anything with the idea that it might be used as testimony against anybody afterwards and I do not believe that I have recorded anything or expressed any opinions that could really be used to harm anybody except myself. I have made no secret of the fact that I have been keeping a diary. Those who have come into the Store Room have often found me writing my diary. The Captain and others with whom I went on the

Jerusalem trip saw me taking notes for my diary. This request to see the diary, however, and the situation which recent depredations have created on the ship have decided me to keep the foolscap sheets of my diary where they cannot be found by others and in such shape that they can quickly be given a sea burial should such action ever seem advisable.

November 3
At sea

As we are running with the wind there is little circulation of air through the ship, moreover it is actually <u>hot</u>. Everybody is complaining of the heat. The crew however have energy enough left to continue their gossip as to the identity of the men who are guilty of the acts which have caused the present prospect of delay in the discharge of the crew of the ship and in difficulty in obtaining honorable discharges. One day I hear of evidence against certain men and the next day gossip directs suspicion towards others.

Today Orderly Sergeant Robbins furnished us another diversion. He reported the Larceny of a coat and pants from his store room. They were found in the cock-pit behind some gratings. An investigation brought out some very circumstantial evidence that the sergeant had placed them there himself to show neglect of duty on the part of a sentry. In addition old "Billy" May the Quartermaster says that he saw Robbins put the clothing there. May supplements his testimony with the statement that he sailed with Robbins years ago when he was a private marine and that he was a "damned scoundrel" even then. It is brought out however that since the hatch covers have been put on at quarters every night Billy has been deprived of a comfortable place in the cock-pit where he used to sleep and that he blames Robbins for not arranging somehow for the continuation of the privilege and those who know Billy suspect that he is talking "rather freely," to say the least. In a contest of this sort I would not know whom to believe. The Master-at-Arms has gone on the "sick-list." He has been complaining for several days.

I spend the night on deck in the comfortable breeze until 12 o'clock. These moonlight nights are delightful. I shall never forget them.

November 4
At sea

A good breeze and we are fast shortening the distance to St. Thomas.

In the evening Mr. Fletcher, officer of the forecastle, went below for a tin pot in which he was to prepare a drink for himself and the officer of the deck, but so vigilant are some of the ship's company that he was reported and called on to tell what the pot contained. This was easy. It contained nothing. The object in reporting him he could not understand as he is a strictly temperate man—"a total abstainer" and known to be in fact. I am in doubt myself as to the object.

This morning we made a sail on the starboard bow which proved to be the brig *Mersey* of Liverpool, Nova Scotia bound from New York to Surinam. Boats, jib-boom and everything on deck are gone. They say everything in the cabin has been destroyed. She has jury masts rigged with very small sails set upon them. She sailed from New York September 29, loaded with flour. On October 9, then off Bermuda, a gale was encountered which increased to a hurricane and hove the brig on her beam ends. We saw the masts were cut away and when she righted there were nine feet of water in the hold. The cabin had filled and everything washed out. Compasses, chronometer and other navigating instruments were lost. The Captain lost all his clothes. The cooking apparatus was swept away.

One man was washed overboard and disappeared while clearing the wreck. Another man coming up the companion way with a lamp filled with kerosene oil in his hand had the contents knocked down his throat and was crazy for several days. The Captain and the mate are North Americans and the crew "Dutchmen."

The Captain was asked to come to our ship and to bring his log. His entire clothing consisted of a straw hat and coat and pants of a blue cotton material. He wore slippers. We sent him back to his vessel with a topmast studdingsail and spars to spread it; a time piece, quadrant and compass; some water, bread, beef and coffee; and tobacco and pipes as luxuries. Even though dependent solely on dead reckoning for nearly a month his longitude actually checked up within two miles of ours![21]

It was ten a.m. when we hove to alongside the brig and 2 p.m. when we kept off on our course again. The brig with our studdingsail spread followed soon after. The mate of the brig has been in our Navy and was on the *Brooklyn* at the capture of Mobile.[22]

The sight of a wreck at sea is most distressing and when assistance cannot be given it is horrible, yet the Captain says that two vessels passed him and paid no attention to him. Such conduct among civilized people is inexplicable.

November 5
At sea

At noon we were 250 miles from St. Thomas and going towards it at the rate of 8 knots. Our little protégé was not in sight this morning, but this fine wind will soon bring her to St. Thomas.

Today the Surgeon cut a small protuberance off the side of my head near the ear. It has been a sort of identification mark for several years. It was not bothering me—just useless.

November 7
At sea

At daylight we made the Island of Sombrero and at 7 a.m. passed it, leaving it on the starboard.

We showed our flag and the British was hoisted at a staff on the shore and an American bark at anchor hoisted the stars and stripes at her mizzen. The island belongs to the British, but its only product, guano deposits, are being worked at presently by an American company. Several vessels are usually to be seen loading here. All that could be made out of the island from our ship are some huts and numerous derricks used for hoisting the guano into lighters. The island is about 90 miles from St. Thomas.

At 10 a.m. we make the island of Virgin Gorda and by noon we are abreast of it. It is a fine breeze and pleasant sailing.

The land on the starboard hand is called the "Virgin Islands." Even from the distance it looks green. What we see is chiefly conical peaks and rough headlands. Although I have never approached it before from this direction it is a familiar sight. It was father's practice to sketch the land-falls in his log book when he made land. Those sketches gave his old log books an interest to me as a boy and one such sketch, labeled, "the Virgin Islands," for some reason appealed to my childish fancy and has remained pictured in my memory. It is what I see when I look toward the land. At four thirty p.m. we pass "Frenchman's Gap," a small conical rock about 8 miles of St. Thomas lighthouse and make what is called the "Sail-Rock," a rock resembling, from our point of view, a schooner standing into port.

At 5 p.m. we anchor in the harbor of St. Thomas.

Our pilot tells us of the capture of the Rebel steamer *Florida* by the USS *Wachusett*. The San *Jacinto* and the *Wachusett* left here a fortnight ago.

I like St. Thomas. Perhaps it is because it furnished the one bright spot in a very trying experience for a boy. It was ten years ago that I brought into this port for a cargo a bark the command of which I had practically usurped.

It is a fine snug little harbor surrounded by high land clothed with green foliage, the fragrance of which is most refreshing after so many days at sea. The city is built on three hills. The buildings are neat and present a very attractive appearance from the water.

November 8
St. Thomas

The *Florida* was "cut out" of the harbor of Bahia, Brazil on October 7. At the time of her capture, several officers and 74 men were on shore. Her guns were run in and unshotted. The *Wachusett* ran down on her quarter knocking the mainmast out of her. She was towed to sea in the face of the fortifications, a Brazilian sailing and a Brazilian steam ship of war.[23]

This is the day of the Presidential election in the United States. It will undoubtedly be close. Important results will follow in any event. If Abraham Lincoln be re-elected the homes of many a rebel will die. I judge from a speech of Jeff. Davis that his affairs are becoming desperate. He is making an appeal for the return of deserters to the ranks stating that if they do not so return he cannot see success ahead.

The steamer *Trent* of international notoriety and other British steamers are in port here. The USS *St. Louis* has been here and has sailed for Port Royal.

Fruit and washer-women are being offered us in abundance. Both are tall in price, the latter are also slender.

November 9
St. Thomas

This morning our protégé, the *Mersey*, came in port. She has done admirably well. As the brig passed our stern the Captain dipped his flag to us. No doubt his heart feels lighter as he drops his anchor safe in port at last.

In the afternoon I went on shore with Mr. Jones to show him the town. At the landing we encountered the usual crowd of darkies that one meets in a West Indian port, and the same bantering talk and the characteristic Negro laugh.

St. Thomas seems to be a much livelier place than I remember it ten years ago. English, French, and Danish shops are well stocked with goods. Everyone seems to have money and the "sharpers" are everywhere on the alert to get more. American gold is abundant here and as soon as we dropped anchor it began to be brought on board to exchange for our French gold. The ship is a broker's office. Every sailor is trying his hand at the exchange business.

As we passed a house we were accosted by a colored man who recognized Jones and myself as among those who had given her some clothes to wash when she was on the ship. She told us that her name was "Arabella Martin." She invited us in and as she added, "All de 'merican ossifers come here," we felt that we could hardly decline without reflecting on American officers. She apologized for the appearance of the interior of her dwelling, excusing it on the ground of a rush of laundry work and her duties in connection with arrangements for a "Dignity Ball." She brought forth some ale and insisted that we all drink to the "Stars and Stripes."

These people have too much effrontery to suit me, yet in some ways they are amusing. There is one character known as "Aunty" who trades with ships and excels them all in tactful ways of securing business. "Law," she says, "talk about de *Ticonderoga*, de *Kearsarge* an' de *Wachusett*, day ainít nowhere for de money; dis ship comes right straight from de place where dey makes it."

The ship merchants and agents here are prosperous and are affable and honorable men. I took Jones with me to call on G.W. Smith & Co. and Abbott, Phillips & Co. The latter secured the cargo for me for the bark when I was here ten years ago. Those connected with both of these concerns are well acquainted with New England men with whom they have been doing business for a half a century.

November 11
St. Thomas

An engineer on a British steamer in the harbor cut his throat this morning after attempting to drown himself.

Several American vessels arrived in port today; also some flying the British and the Dutch flags.

This afternoon I went on shore and made a visit to "Blue Beard's Castle." It is on a hill at the eastern end of the harbor. From it one has a good view of the sea, the harbor and the town. The castle itself has been repaired since I was here before and is now in very good condition. It is elliptical in shape and about 50 feet high.

In front of the castle is a statue which is said to be an exact likeness of Blue Beard. He is represented as ferocious looking being armed with to the teeth besides carrying a musket in his hand. Eight guns which formerly commanded the hill against approach from the city are to be seen lying on the ground where they were once mounted. They are 6 or 8 pdrs., of iron and quite long for their bore.

I had a stroll around the hill to see how the local Negroes live. They seem to be poor and those here outside the city indolent. I saw two Negroes building a house. I learned that they do not get the pitch pine lumber as formerly but use the local soft wood which is not durable. This common lumber costs $35 per thousand feet. A house of two rooms costs $250. This does not seem dear, but they are disposed to complain. The colored people here are prejudiced against the North and are ardent secessionists. The only possible reason which I can discover is that they like the English better than us.

I met old Captain Berry with whom I became acquainted in Palermo a year and a half ago. I also spent some time pleasantly with Dr. Geo. K. Field of New York and his son whom I met with some of our officers. They are here for a few days in their yacht in which they are around the guano islands. The Doctor has recently disposed of his interests in the Island of Sombrero. He is a very wealthy man, a great story teller and otherwise an entertaining gentleman. The Captain of his yacht who belongs at San Juan, Porto Rico is also good company.

With regret I parted from them at 4 o'clock when they left for their yacht to sail for an adjoining island. The Doctor has had agents for medicines in every New England town and he has acquaintances there whose names are familiar to every New Englander. I returned on board at 10 p.m. with Messrs. Mallet, Philbrick, Drew, Fletcher and Cox.

November 12
St. Thomas and the sea

We wait until 2 p.m. for the small boat and then take leave of St. Thomas. At sunset the Island of Porto Rico is in sight.

It is reported that we are going to New Orleans to be a receiving ship. Another report is that it is not New Orleans, but Pensacola; another that it is Port Royal. It is also said that we are going to Ship Island to be a hospital ship. From my information however I am satisfied that the Navy Department has not yet considered the ultimate disposition of our ship and that in the meantime we are to cruise about the West Indies and the Gulf trying to capture or destroy Rebel privateers and cruisers and blockade runners. The process of reasoning attempting to use an old sailing frigate for this purpose seems to be that our ship is supposed to be in European waters and there is no United States warship cruising about here and consequently she might approach closely to a rebel vessel or blockade runner without exciting suspicion. As it is the practice of such vessels when off shore to move under sail or to lie with their fires banked and down it is conceived that we might surprise such vessels and capture or sink them. Perhaps it has been considered also that should we "catch a Tarter" and be sent to the bottom ourselves it would not be a serious loss and would save the trouble of thinking how to dispose of this old ship.

I spend the evening on deck in the bright moonlight in the breeze which is carrying us along—6½ knots over a smooth sea. Many would try to enjoy such an excursion as this.

November 13
At sea

The wind is the same and Puerto Rico is still in sight. It is a beautiful day, but quite warm. I always like a quiet Sabbath at sea and as we approach the United States they seem even pleasanter.

November 15
At sea

The Island of San Domingo is in sight all day, but too far away for me to recognize any familiar landmarks.

At noon we hove to a French brig by firing away a little powder, boarded her and found her loaded with coffee, bound to Bordeaux. Henceforth we will board all vessels which we meet during the day.

November 18
Caribbean Sea

After having the Island of Jamaica in sight all day yesterday we passed the western end this morning. The wind is light.

I am busy taking account of my stores although it is very hot below deck. My purpose is to have all my accounts balanced whenever I am called on to deliver the stores or account for them.

November 19
Caribbean Sea

Moving along at 4½ knots. At noon we make the Island of Grand Cayman. At 4 p.m. boats come off to the ship from the island with turtles, fruit and parrots to sell. The men in charge of the boats are English or Scotch. The Negroes with them speak English.

The island is low and appears to be about twenty miles long. It looks green. Only a few houses are to be seen.

November 21
Caribbean Sea

This morning we have fresh breeze from the SSE. It seems that we have passed out of the "trade winds." We are making 11 knots. A pleasant sail. At noon we are past Cape St. Antonio and are flying into the Gulf of Mexico. Am still busy taking an account of my stores.

This afternoon we had showers, then the wind changed to the NW. One reef after another has been put in the topsails and now we are contending with a regular NW gale.

November 22
Gulf of Mexico

The topsails are close reefed. A new main-topsail has been bent and other reparations made to receive a continuation of this tempest. We sight a brig and a ship to the windward. The ship is a vessel of war, but we cannot make out her nationality. In the afternoon we wear our ship and stand on the same tack as the other and gradually draw closer to her.

A sea struck the ship's bow sending solid water over the fore yard, wetting the sails thoroughly, drenching the men in the fore top and sending things in all directions in my Store Room. My heavy water keg broke adrift and gave me a lively time for a while. A man-of-war in a gale is one of the most dangerous places in the world that a person could find to dwell in.

Such an introduction to the Gulf so early in the season and especially after pleasant sailing with an uninterrupted fair wind for a month makes us dread the more northern coast which we are probably soon destined to see.

November 23
Gulf of Mexico

The wind is not so heavy but the gale does not seem to be over and we are carrying the same sail except that the main stay-sail has been set. We see a ship to the leeward, probably the same that we saw yesterday. It has grown colder and we are putting on more clothing.

November 24
Gulf of Mexico

Cloudy and unpleasant. The sky looks like a northern one. We have shaken one reef out of our topsails and have bent a new mainsail. We have been making 7 or 8 knots.

At night the turbulent sea takes on a phosphorescent character which makes it appear to be a sea of liquid fire. It looks sublime! The wild appearance of the sky and water serves as a reason for shortening sail and putting the ship close to the wind although we might stand on our course.

November 25
Gulf of Mexico

The reefs are turned out of the fore and mainsails and one out of each topsail and we keep off a little. The ship has quite enough sail for comfort, but some wish that more was on her. I am tumbling around while trying to balance my accounts and to answer frequent demands which are being made on me in the Boatswain's department.

The studdingsail booms are taken down and the gear is stowed away. It is a safe bet that they will not be wanted any more this cruise.

November 26
Gulf of Mexico

The sea and wind have gone down. Reefs are shaken out. The topgallant and royal yards are sent aloft and the sails set. The anchors are unlashed and the usual preparations are made when nearing land. After the shake up of several days past it is quite a relief to be able to stand still for a moment, or being in motion to go in the right direction.

I am three years in the Navy today.

November 27
Mobile Bay

At noon we approach forts Gaines and Morgan and soon after come to anchor. Our ship's number is hoisted, but no response comes from the fleet up the bay until three p.m. when the *Bermuda* and a tug-boat start down toward us.

We are soon informed that "Old Abe" is reelected President, that Rear Admiral Farragut is to leave Mobile tomorrow to become Secretary of the Navy and that Ben Butler is to be Secretary of War.[24]

Orders were brought to us to proceed immediately to the Pensacola Navy Yard and after a few turns of the capstan we were again under way.

November 28
Pensacola

At daylight we are off Pensacola and make the USS *Kennebec* at anchor. We also anchor and wait for the tide to rise to enable us to pass over the bar. Soon we are under way and pass the forts and then take a turn in the crooked channel around Santa Rosa Island brings into view a fleet of Naval vessels, the steamships and the Navy Yard. We are in a truly naval place, warlike but silent. The stars and stripes are flying everywhere, but the low sandy shores and the background of scrub pines do not suggest the United States but rather some wild region beyond the influence of civilization.

We are really in what until recently has been within the realm of the Confederacy and Confederates still hold possession of territory within ten miles of us. A short time ago they made a <u>sortie</u> and nearly succeeded in releasing Admiral Buchanan who is being held a prisoner here.[25]

Mr. Abbot, our Executive Officer has been ordered to the *Kennebec*.

After dinner the *Hartford* with Admiral Farragut aboard steamed into the harbor. She is a splendid ship.

At nine o'clock tonight I learn our fate. We are to be sent North. Being sent North even in winter is preferable to being anchored as a hospital ship at Ship Island or being used in some of the other ways that rumor or imagination has suggested.

November 29
Pensacola

The usual amount of scrubbing and scraping has been going on in anticipation of a visit from Rear Admiral Farragut. At 11 o'clock he arrived accompanied by several officers.

All hands were called to quarters for inspection and in regular course Admiral Farragut comes into my Store Room. He commended the appearance of the ship generally and gave us praise for a fine, neat and well kept Store Room. He looked somewhat older than when I last saw him about eight years ago, but perhaps this is because I was closer to him today. He does not however look old. He must be approaching seventy, but would pass for fifty.[26] He has a quiet dignity that is suggestive of kindliness, nevertheless he is a strict disciplinarian, if he has not changed, but he is just and is thoughtful of his officers and men and tries to see that they receive proper recognition for meritorious conduct. Although I understand that there are some higher officers who are "trying to steal his thunder" the general feeling in the Navy appears to be that he deserves all the glory that he is getting and that they are glad to see him get it.

Mr. Sylvanus Bacchus our second Lieutenant is now the Executive Officer of our ship. Mr. Abbot takes command of the *Kennebec* tomorrow.

November 30
Pensacola

We are receiving wood and water preparatory to going to sea. About 1 p.m. the Admiral passed us in the *Hartford*, bound North, and received our cheers.

Smith and I went on shore to visit the Navy Yard. Here we see the cruel work of war. The Yard is level and well laid out and to judge from the ruins of the buildings which have been razed and the remnants of property which have survived the fire a well equipped Navy Yard once existed here.[27] The damaged dock basin is a receptacle for all sorts of small craft and a place for watering ships. I noticed a pile of guns of various sizes, patterns and bores, which have been captured from the Rebels.

We passed out of the Gate and entered Warrington. It is a town of small unpainted wooden cottages and shops. It is wholly uninteresting and to me disgusting. The sand is ankle deep and nothing is to be seen growing except pine trees. I soon am satisfied to turn back to the Navy Yard thankful that I do not have to live here.

Everyone whom we meet about the Navy Yard appeared indifferent, churlish and morose. It was a pleasure to be once more on the deck of my old ship, and home. I found waiting for me Mr. Adams, Gunner of the *Ossipee*, an old friend whom I have not seen for more than ten years. Soon Mr. Dixon, Carpenter of the *Hartford*, appeared and took us by surprise. As they mentioned the Kittery and Portsmouth men whom I know and who are in the fleet it seemed to me that they had named every able bodied man in Kittery until we went on and recalled men from both places who are with the Atlantic fleet and on our ships and the *Kearsarge* and other ships and in the Army. Now the peaceful pursuits in the towns about the Piscataqua have been depleted of able young men to take part in this war!

December 1
Pensacola

In the afternoon I visited the brig *Fidelia* of Bangor and had a talk with Captain Stone. He gave me some news regarding my friends in Bangor. On my return I find an invitation from a Mr. Bennett to visit him on the Steamer *Cow Slip*. I discover that the steamer *Cow Slip* is a Revenue Cutter attached to the Navy and that Mr. Bennett is an old acquaintance and fellow-townsman. I had a very pleasant interview with him even though saddened by the news that this or that one of our mutual friends was no more, often that he was a victim of the war.

One of our men who was just outside the Navy Yard this evening was knocked down by two men who attempted to rob him. His yell of "murder" which could have been heard at Fort Pickens brought the picket and our Master to the spot at the same time. They captured one of the men but the other escaped. Such occurrences occur here every day. Old "Buck" the quartermaster was robbed this evening.

Night before last an officer who left his horse to take a drink found on coming out of the building that a drunken soldier had mounted his horse. The officer drew his pistol and the man was hove to with a shot through his body which will probably prove fatal. Any man who is outside the Navy Yard alone after dark is in danger and there is new nonsense when danger seems to threaten.

Henry Deering, an assistant Surgeon in the Navy, a companion of my childhood died here a short time ago.

December 2
Pensacola

The first thing this morning is the transfer of 26 men from our ship to the *Kennebec*. These are all men who were shipped on the station and comprise a lot of good active men. I feel sorry to separate from them before the end of the cruise—but such is life! I shall probably never see them again. War separates the dearest friends.

December 3
Pensacola

We are hearing of feats which are being performed by the 2nd Maine Cavalry, stationed here. One of the latest is the capture of some Rebels who have been making raids on Pensacola and the vicinity. These fellows had pickets posted in advance who were surprised and captured as the result of information given by a Negro. The men of the 2nd Maine Cavalry then put on the clothing of the captured pickets and when their reliefs came they too were surprised and captured. After thus being deprived of the warning protection of their pickets the 2nd Maine Cavalry was able to surround the main body of the Rebels and take them all prisoners.

We expected to sail this morning but were delayed by the court-martial of a sergeant whom old "Buck," the Quartermaster, has accused and identified as the man who robbed him when on shore two nights ago. The court-martial found the sergeant not guilty, a verdict which our men say was entirely contrary to the evidence. If so it would seem that Army men were inclined to stand by each other.

At 4 p.m. we were ready to sail, but the tug *Penguin* which was to tow us out broke down.

The men who were transferred to the *Kennebec* came back to visit us while on liberty today. They appear to be much better contented with their new ship than I thought that they would.

The flags of all the merchant ships are at half mast on account of the death of the Captain of one of them.

December 4
Pensacola and the sea

Soon after daylight the anchor was up and we hauled away and sailed down the harbor without the assistance of the steam-tug which stood by to help us. Mr. Abbot, our late

Executive accompanied us and when he took leave of us just outside the harbor all hands went into the rigging and we gave him rousing cheers as he went aboard the tug to return up the harbor to his own ship. We have lost an Executive who is truly an <u>officer</u> and as well a <u>gentleman</u> honorable and considerate. He carries with him the good will of the whole ship's company—may good success attend him.

It is the coolest day of the season, but the sky is as pleasant as that of Italy. We are to cruise from here to Cuba, touch at Havana and then proceed North along the Atlantic Coast to Hampton Roads.

December 5
At sea
A light wind from the southwest all day. Pleasant and warm. I am amusing myself writing. I feel very well since the weather has become cooler and am only wishing for a good breeze to speed us on our way.

December 6
At sea
This morning we made a brig on our weather quarter. She appears to be sailing as fast as our ship. She shows no flag. We tack and stand after her. She again tacks and so do we. All the afternoon we have gained but little on her. She again tacks as the wind hauls, standing on the starboard tack. We do the same. As night comes on we lose sight of her.

December 11
At sea
Last night I had a peculiar and impressive dream from which I was awakened by the striking of "eight bells."

After days of head wind a light breeze from the northeast strikes us after noon and we soon sight Cuba.

We heave to a vessel by firing a gun. She sends a boat to us. The officer who comes on our ship says that they did not suppose that we were an American man-of-war. The men in the boat said that they did not know of such a ship as ours in the Navy. The vessel is the *Non Parillis* (?), a store ship bound to Pensacola, 18 days out from New York. She is a clipper built vessel with three masts and square-rigged on the foremast only. She is a good sailer.

At nine p.m. the wind increases to a gale. The topsails are reefed and the upper yards sent down. The lights of Havana are in sight.

December 12
Havana
This morning we made a sail to the windward which proved to be a vessel loaded with cotton. She showed the British flag and when we wore ship and stood toward her she crowded on sail and ran for port. We tried to head her off, but did not succeed in doing so.

We then hauled on the wind and kept standing off and on until afternoon, the Captain deeming the sea too rough to enter port. Finally the Captain yielded to the persuasion of Mr. Mallett, our Master, who is familiar with the entrance to Havana and he took us in.

The American flag flies on several steamers here and I see one Rebel flag on a blockade runner. Here are the *Fanny* and the *Erin* which have been so successful in this business. We salute the Spanish flag and receive a salute in return.

December 14
Havana

Very hot. The U.S. Schooner *Sea Bird* arrived from Key West for the mail.

At 10 a.m. I went on shore. I walked around a while alone and then met some of our officers with whom I spent most of the day.

This is a hot-bed of Secession. Every man whom you meet except perhaps a few in command of vessels flying the American flag, is a bitter and rabid Secessionist. Soon after I went on shore a steamer from Galveston, loaded with cotton entered port. She steered as close to the stern of our ship as she could and the crew took handfuls of cotton from the bales and shook it at our ship, at the same time cheering and making insulting noises and yelling abusive epithets. This is a disgrace to the British flag under the cover of which it is done.

The schooner that gave us the slip the day before yesterday was a blockade runner, am informed on good authority.

One sees on shore plenty of Confederate and Yankee refugees from conscription draft and I judge that they are very much alike in political sentiments and conceptions of duty.

Our ship is lying near the track of ferry boats and every time one passes our ship is the object of a noisy and insulting demonstration. Even on the street people turn their noses at us and make insulting remarks.

In my judgement it would be good policy to keep our war ships away from this port until we are ready to come here and meet insults with loaded shells. Old Moro Castle stands out as an inviting target. I never could understand how it got its reputation. Its position is picturesque, but I judge that with modern naval armaments and means of protection it might easily be passed.

Havana is a large and active city. It seems to be busier than when I have been here before. The streets are not improved. They are narrow and inconvenient, even for pedestrians. The restaurants and public houses are well appointed and offer one the luxuries of every climate. There is still the music in the square before the Captain-General's Palace and the same evening parade of the fashionables. The cost of living is very high here, especially for a visitor.

When I went on shore alone I had intended to call on my Spanish relatives here. I do not know however what their political beliefs and sympathies are in regard to the war and as I began to realize that I was being treated to about all the Secession I could stand I concluded that it might be pleasanter for me to keep away from any local relatives and I accordingly did so.

I bought some "Carabaga" cigars and returned on board at sunset.

December 15
Havana and the sea

All hands were called at daylight to prepare the ship for sea. At 7 o'clock came the words that the men so long desired to hear. "All hands up anchor for the United States," was piped by the Boatswain and his mates. It comes however too late to have its usual effect upon a man-of-war's crew because our men feel that they have already been in the United States. It is true that they have seen there little to suggest "united" or "union" except among those who are fighting to establish it, but they have been in what was <u>once</u> a part of the United States and I hope that it may be again.

It is a delightful day and as we pass out of the harbor the music of the bands and the thought that we are really homeward bound makes the day seem still pleasanter.

Off the entrance we meet an American brig and schooner waiting for wind to change to enable them to enter. We send a boat to board the brig and speak the other vessel. It will be many months before we see another day as warm as this. Cuba with its rich foliage and sunny sky is fading in the distance and we will soon be occupied with our friends in a colder climate—if Providence permits.

December 16
At sea

Strong breeze from the ENE. Topsails are reefed all day. We made Sand Key light last night and stood off shore with the bark *Atlanta* of New York. She was ahead this morning but we overtook her during the day. Soon after dark we made the light on Sombrero Key and before midnight are past the southern extremity of Florida.

December 17
At sea

Wind free and a good breeze all day. We are making 8 knots by the log and probably 11, taking the current into account.

At noon we make a schooner to the leeward and start after her but on seeing that she is standing north we return to our course.

One of my messmates, the Paymaster's Steward (Alexander Carter) who has been under the influence of spirit for the past two days has supplied us with what corresponds to a family jar. Like all men he is much better when sober. I make this note to remember some aspersions which he made regarding me yesterday and this morning.

December 18
At sea

Wind light and from the E all day. We speak the ship *New England* from Pensacola for Philadelphia. The Captain and some officers send things aboard to be taken home. The band plays a few familiar and patriotic airs, we dip our ensigns and separate.

It is very hot and uncomfortable on the lower deck.

Gaul, the marine, is again sentenced by a court-martial. This time for disobedience of orders. His sentence was one month's confinement in double irons and three months of loss of pay, but the Captain reduced the loss of pay to one month.

December 19
At sea

Last evening the wind changed to SW with rain. Before midnight the topsails were double reefed. Soon after the topgallant sails were set over them and we made great progress all night—going 10 knots some times.

This morning we had a little excitement. At daylight the lookout at the masthead descried a vessel. It proved to be a typical blockade runner—painted white, very low and sharply built. When first sighted she appeared to be waiting with fires banked for the assurance from shore that the coast was clear to run in. When however our ship headed in her direction smoke began to come out of her funnel and she made off to the windward at good speed.

The wind was light at the time, having just died down, but we kept after her with all our sail and fired a gun to heave her to. She did not accept the invitation—or heed the warning.

Our ship was kept as close to the wind as she could go and the 30 pdr. Parrott was brought into use. The distance was about four miles I should judge, and the Parrott at its extreme elevation could hardly make that distance. Several shots however came so close to her that she began to zig-zag her course. The 32 pdr. was tried twice, but fell far short. About twenty shots were fired in all and they at least had the effect of making the smoke come blacker and blacker out of his stack.

Our object in firing was partly to attract the attention of our steam war ships which might be in the vicinity. This seemed to be successful. A steamer appeared in pursuit and perhaps its crew will get the prize money which saw slip away from us. If not the men on the blockade runner probably enjoyed the excitement as much as we did. It doubtless served to break the monotony of their sea life as it did ours.

December 20
At sea
Last night the wind came heavy from the NW. All hands were called to reef topsails and then there was a storm of voices on deck. Mr. Mallett, the Master, took the deck and had one of his wild freaks which would frighten anyone but experienced sailors and make him think that the ship was going to bottom immediately. It was one of those merchant ship performances which used to be so disgusting to my father.

We were put under close reefed topsails and storm staysails which we have been wearing all day. Near noon the wind hauled more to the NE and we stood in showing our heading NW. The sky is cloudy and the wind chilly. Everybody begins to look blue about the face and overcoats are brought into requisition generally.

It really looks as well as feels like the <u>North</u>. This is the first smell of the icy breath of a northern winter that I have had for three years.

At 4 p.m. we sound and get 85 fathoms. We are supposed to be off Cape Hatteras. I judge that we are a little north of it and that if the wind should head a little that we can go on in the morning.

December 21
Off Cape Hatteras
The wind changed to the SW this morning and we have had a regular old fashioned gale all day. The ship is under close reefed fore and main topsails and fore-topmast staysail. No observation could be obtained and the land was frequently used during the night. At 8 a.m. the ship's helm was put to the NW and was kept so until 11 o'clock when it was changed to E. A noon observation of the sun showed us to be south of the Cape. Soon after the cry of "breakers abeam" from the lookout aloft sent shivers down the spines of everybody who heard it. Breakers had been made out on the lee beam. Like the pilot who knew where he was by hitting the rocks we recognized the spuming mess of breaking seas close at hand to the northward of us as the treacherous shifting Diamond Shoals and we knew that we were about eight miles southeast of the extremity of Cape Hatteras and that we could have not been far from the shore which, on account of the weather, was not made out when we changed our course from NW to E at 11 o'clock. The wind is blowing with such fury that it takes up water from the surface and makes seeing difficult.

However the direction of the wind enables us easily to stand off clear of the shoals and we are not added to the long list of ships which have been lost with all hands near the end of a voyage,

I do not know what excuse can be made for being in where we were. Captain Stellwagen has surveyed this region and probably knows it better than any living man. It may be that he trusted to this acquaintance and to his memory more than he should in dictating the navigation of the ship the past two days. I was wrong of course in judging that we were north of Hatteras last night, but I am at a loss to understand how we could have had <u>85</u> fathoms where we must have been.

The wind increases. The topgallant yards are sent down. The topgallant yards soon follow. The howitzers are put in the hold and all superfluous gear. Hatches are battened down and everything is prepared so far as possible for still worse weather conditions. The Ward Room is afloat and the excessive rolling of the ship tries the lashings of everything not strongly secured.

At dinner I saved the table and the table ware from going into the main hatchway. Our table caster went down but was retrieved not seriously damaged. It is a lucky thing and has stood many knocks.

"Who would not sell a farm and go to sea?"

December 22
At sea

Last evening the wind came from the W, as the sailors say, "butt end first," and made our good old ship tremble and career like a reed. The foresail and main staysail had just been set but soon all hands were called to shorten sail. The foretopsail was furled and all that we had left on the ship was the maintopsail and the foretopmast staysail.

I never saw it blow much harder than it did for a short time.

All day today we have been lying to under short sail. The ship is rolling and pitching heavily. It is wet everywhere and cold except on the berth deck. Here it is so unhealthy from the foul air which has only two small means of escape through the battened hatches that the spar deck is preferable on many accounts.

A dismal day. A hard gale and poor diet—enough to make one unhappy. I have been balancing my ledger all day, so have kept myself employed.

One sea came over the ship this afternoon flooding the decks and causing quite a commotion, but because she was not knocked down in the squall last evening everyone is ready to acknowledge her merits. She <u>is</u> a good sea-boat.

What will come next I do not know—perhaps a north-easter.

December 23
At sea

The wind blew a terrific gale all night. It was cold also and the most disagreeable night spent in the ship during the whole cruise. The changing of the wind to the north made the ship labor more heavily and the creaking of the deck frame and the occasional shifting to the leeward of things which had broken adrift made a great racket.

Last night and all day the Captain has had the quartergunners heating shot for him to keep him warm.

At noon it was evident that the gale was abating and the motion of the ship was becoming less violent. The observation at that time placed us 80 miles from Cape Henry and 7 miles south of its latitude.

At 3 p.m. we get up the stump topgallant masts and make more sail. We head W by S and go along slowly. We may reach port by Christmas.

December 24
At sea
The wind is still ahead, but we are gaining something by standing north.

It was very cold last night and all hands were called to reef topsails. They are still reefed. It seems that anything but a close reef is out of the question now. In the afternoon the wind becomes more favorable. At noon we were 55 miles from Cape Henry.

Brown, a colored man, steward of the Forward Officers mess, died just before noon. His sickness was rather mysterious. Soon after leaving Havana he was taken with severe vomiting as were the cook of the mess and one other man. Brown has remained since that time in the sick bay without attracting any special attention until yesterday when his symptoms assumed a different aspect and the Surgeon came out with the Assistant Surgeon to see him. Brown had had typhoid symptoms and only last evening was he treated for this disease and today he is dead! He was a strong and robust man and has been healthy all the cruise. Fatality seems to attend the Negroes who go in the sick-bay. All have died thus far. Brown is the third since about the middle of September.

He was a likable fellow and a faithful servant. Before he went in the sick-bay he came to me, sick and miserable, as other men in the ship have done when in trouble. I advised him to report to the Doctor. He reminded me that no colored man who had gone in the sick-bay during the cruise had come out alive. He was a married man and he told me about his wife and children to whom he was much attached. He had bought many little things for them here and there during the cruise. He had had their pictures painted from photographs at Naples and was looking forward to being with them in a few weeks. All these mementoes and trinkets he brought to me and asked me to see that they reached his family if his illness terminated as he expected.

After being brought so near their door by the husband and father they must now be delivered by another. Such is life! How uncertain are all our hopes!

I cannot help being fearful of this emancipation business. Few if any Negroes are capable looking out for themselves. They are dependent upon white men to protect their interests if their interests are to be protected at all.[28] From the class of whites with whom they come in competition the Negroes will encounter enmity and prejudice. Who will there be to protect them? What is to prevent them from being abused and exploited in a wholesale way by cruel and unscrupulous men?

At 4 p.m. a cast of the lead gives us 17 fathoms. We must be within twenty five miles of land. If not blown off shore again we should arrive tomorrow.

December 25
Hampton Roads
This morning we took a pilot off Cape Henry. A light breeze brought us nearly to the Rip-Raps, then meeting a head tide we anchored. The *Dictator* came down on a trial trip accompanied by two steamers. This is the first "monitor" that I ever saw. They appear very low—too much so to please me as a sea-going craft, or even as a home in port.

Brown, the steward who died yesterday was examined by the doctors last evening. He was found to have an ulceration of the bowels produced by an inflammation. I witnessed the dissection.

This is Christmas, but we have rather a hard fare for the occasion. Some sardines are the only luxuries which we can obtain.

I have grown quite thin on the ship's rations from which we have few changes since we left Gibraltar September 29.

At sunset we move up and anchor off Fortress Monroe among the numerous other vessels here in the employ of "Uncle Sam." It looks like a lighted city around us in the evening. Savannah is reported to have been taken, General Hood to have been defeated by General Thomas, and other victories. They may be true or may be otherwise.

Everybody on board is anxiously awaiting information as to where we are going from here or what is to be done with us.

December 26
Off Fortress Monroe
Brown was buried this morning. Officers and others are shipping away their personal effects and articles purchased in Europe.

The reported capture of Savannah is confirmed. We hear also that Fort Fisher at Wilmington has been taken by the combined forces of Porter and Butler.[29]

December 28
Off Fortress Monroe
The Captain returned from Norfolk last night and it is understood that our ship is to go to the Navy Yard there, but there are no signs of starting.

The Captain has asked for a Court-of-Inquiry regarding the depredations, loss of property or thefts which occurred on the ship and I presume that his request will be granted.

Sailors from the British ship of war *Buzzard*, lying here, had some trouble at a theater in Norfolk a few evenings ago, thereupon liberty was given to about 50 of the ship's company. They went ashore evidently looking for trouble and they found it. In view of the challenge men were allowed ashore from some of our ships. A general row in this theater followed. The British sailors were thrown from the galleries down into the pit. One was killed and several badly injured. The soldiers were called out to quell the affray.[30]

December 29
Off Fortress Monroe
I ship a case of paintings, books and other personal effects to Portsmouth, N.H. by Adams Express.

The steamer, *Fort Jackson*, Captain Sands in command, has arrived from Fort Fisher with 45 wounded men. The bombardment is reported to have been a success. Our former Lieutenant R.R. Wallace is the Executive Officer of the *Fort Jackson*. He makes us a visit this evening.

December 31
Off Fortress Monroe
The arrival of the *Baltic* and other large steamers with troops aboard and their transfer up the river indicate an important military movement in this vicinity.

The steamship *North America* from New Orleans for New York was lost off Cape Hatteras with 197 sick soldiers the 22nd inst. 62 persons including the Captain and crew were saved. Accounts from Wilmington state that the bombardment of Fort Fisher was terrific, 115 shells a minute being thrown into the fort. A newspaper controversy regarding the feasibility of capturing the fort has been started by the friends and enemies of the Admiral and General Butler.

Chapter Seven
January 1865 to
February 1865

January 1, 1865
Off Fortress Monroe

Another year has overtaken me in my prison-house—how soon it has arrived. This is the third "New Year's Day" that I have spent on board this ship and during this time war has caused the land to mourn the loss of many of its bravest and best and has brought affliction and sadness to every home. Although as it has happened I have not been exposed to the shots of an enemy on the field of battle nevertheless I have reason to be thankful to Him "who marks the sparrow's fall" for my preservation from the dangers of the sea and from disease in the many unhealthy places that we have visited.

The New Year was ushered in by a call, shortly after midnight, of "all hands" to prepare to let go the sheet anchors.

I shook like an aspen leaf when I turned out of my hammock to attend to my duties in connection with this call. It seemed colder than I ever knew it to be and I was surprised to see at 8 o'clock that the thermometer was 35 degrees—not cold at all, as compared with a New England winter day. My absence from northern winters has evidently unfitted me for this climate.

January 3
Off Fortress Monroe

The Navy Department has asked the Paymaster for a muster-roll. This would indicate that the Department has not entirely overlooked the existence of this ship.

Gen. Butler is at his headquarters, having returned with his troops from Wilmington. The fleet is still pegging away at the fort. A Division was sent down yesterday to assist the land forces.

Several steamers have arrived, filling the Roads.

The British corvette *Buzzard* came down from Norfolk today and the French ship of war has sailed.

January 5
Off Fortress Monroe

Ice is interfering with steamboat navigation between here and Washington and Baltimore. The transport steamers have been filling up all day, presumably for Wilmington. It is reported that Gen. Grant is here and has been going around the fleet.

One of our Italian musicians remarked that the "iron-clad" lying close by has been here doing nothing ever since we have been here and asked why it did not go and fight. On being asked where he saw an "iron-clad," he pointed to the fort on the Rip-Raps.

Sausages sell readily among the sailors. Today two pieces of block strap cut the proper length and wrapped in greasy paper were sold to seaman Cripps. He stuck the package in his pocket while he reached for his money to pay for his purchase. There were vocal fireworks later when his appetite led him to take out the package.

January 6
Off Fortress Monroe

Orders came today for the ship to proceed to Norfolk. We understand also that a Court of Inquiry will be held on board.

I join with his other friends in drinking a glass of wine to the health of our Paymaster, Mr. Pangborn, who is celebrating today the 26th anniversary of his birth.

I went ashore at Fortress Monroe today. It was stormy and wet navigating in a small boat. Fortress Monroe is a lively place now if never before. Steamboats are constant—arriving and departing. Army and Navy officers are jumbled together with soldiers, white and black and in all varieties of uniforms, all branches of the service being represented in the crowds that are in continual motion and seem to be doing nothing and getting nowhere.

January 8
Norfolk

A gale has delayed our departure for Norfolk until this morning.

January 10
Norfolk

The Baltimore boat, the *Georgiana*, came in this morning with her upper works badly stove as the result of a collision in the bay. Several persons were lost overboard and drowned, having been torn from their berths by the protruding parts of the other vessel. One bridal couple occupied a stateroom with friends in rooms on either side. The bridegroom was torn from the room, but the bride caught him by the ankle and hung onto him until he was rescued. He was put on shore at Fortress Monroe in a critical condition. The couple and their friends lost most of their effects. Many others were left with nothing but their night clothes, the salon having been completely swept away in some places.

This is the first accident that the Steamboat Line has had since it has been in existence.

The Court of Inquiry convened today. Men in the Paymaster's Department were called on shore to be examined.

Commodore Bell and Paymaster Washington Irving are on the board. It has many cases to investigate at this station. I am also informed that they regard this as the least serious case which they will have to consider. If this be so it suggests a pitiable state of depravity in the Navy at present.

January 11
Norfolk

Ensign Brown has been detached and ordered to the *Cambridge*. The Court of Inquiry is in session.

General Butler has been removed from command here and ordered to Tennessee after he visits his home in Lowell, Mass. This looks like getting him out of the way.[1]

January 12
Norfolk

The sun is quite warm, but I am too busy with my accounts to enjoy it.

In the afternoon 250 men were put on board from the *Lady Lang* and we are in a queer mess. More than 60 can find no place to hang their hammocks and it is difficult to move about the decks. We are now a regular old "Guardo." The *Julia*, a blockade runner, was brought in today. She was in Havana when we were there. I have learned that the blockade runner which we chased on December 18 was captured and brought in here before we arrived. She was presumably taken by the vessel which we started in pursuit. She was a rich prize. From what I am told about her value I figure that my share in the prize money would have been about $100 had we captured her as I believe we might have done had we run up the British or French flag.[2]

January 13
Norfolk

The Court of Inquiry is in Session on board and witnesses are being heard, but no information regarding the proceedings is obtainable from them. Our ship is filled to overflowing with all sorts of "bounty men."[3]

January 14
Norfolk

With the Captain's permission some of the ship's company addressed a letter to the Secretary of the Navy in regard to their discharge from the Service. I understand however that orders have already been received to pay off the men whose enlistment has expired as soon as the Court of Inquiry has adjourned. A draft of men from Portsmouth N.H. came alongside, but the ship is too full to accommodate them. I am told that they are from some ship which has gone out of commission there.

January 15
Norfolk

The draft of men from Boston and New York which we have had on board left this morning to go up the James River. The ship seems like home again to be free from such a crowd of dirty recruits.

I have closed up my ledger account.

January 16
Norfolk

The Court of Inquiry adjourned today. The Paymaster seems to be much elated by his expectation of a favorable report from the Court so far as he will be personally affected thereby.

Mr. Cox, Carpenter of the *Sabine*, was on board today. My old fellow townsman seems to be as smart as ever.

Negroes are bringing fresh vegetables and other foodstuff on board and our men are now abundantly supplied, as if they have not been for months.

January 17
Norfolk

We learn of the death of the Hon. Edward Everett who died on the 15th inst.[4]

Fort Fisher has been taken. Some of the wounded men from the fleet have just passed us in a steamer. Doubtless friends and fellow townsmen are among them. Our losses were heavy I hear.

January 18
Norfolk

This morning the *Santiago de Cuba* and the *Fort Jackson* came up from Wilmington with wounded men. Our boats have been employed all day in assisting in their removal to the hospital.

We are told that Fort Fisher was taken by assault and that the fighting was most desperate.[5] The sailors and marines attacked from the water front, the sailors being armed only with cutlasses and pistols. They were driven back at first, but while the garrison was fighting with the sailors the soldiers gained the inside the of the fort from the land side. There was bloody hand to hand fighting inside the fort in which the sailors took part after they had rallied from their first repulse. They say that the sailors fought like demons with their cutlasses. Soon after our forces entered the fort the magazine blew up killing, some say, 700 of our men, but I think that this must be an exaggeration.

The number of wounded placed in hospital here today was 150.

This afternoon I visited Portsmouth, the Navy Yard, and Norfolk. I was unable to get any information regarding the names of the wounded men.

Everything has an appearance of decay and neglect in the once happy towns about here. The destructive work of war is also in evidence.

January 19
Norfolk

The total Federal loss at Fort Fisher appears to be about 1,200 men, most being from the Navy. The number killed in the explosion is now stated to be 200. The garrison of the Fort consisted of about 2,500 men of whom 500 were killed it is said. I am told that about 2,000 sailors and marines were landed. I cannot learn how many soldiers were engaged in the attack.

The USS *Saugus* came in last evening and several other ships from Wilmington. I wrote the 4th Auditor respecting my pay and visited the Navy Yard.

January 21
Norfolk

This morning the *Susquehanna* and the *New Ironsides* came up. The *Colorado*, Commodore Thatcher's ship, and other large wooden ships are at Hampton Roads. The *New Ironsides* was struck four times at Fort Fisher. She shows no sign of damage.

January 22
Norfolk

A tug came alongside this morning and took our ship up to the Navy Yard where we moored. Everything is in confusion on the ship as the hold was broken out to the bottom to obtain some anchor stocks for the mooring anchors.

My townsman Geo. W. Mitchell came on board to take me to dine with him but I was too busy to go. The men's times will be extended on the accounts until Wednesday next when all whose terms of service expire on or before February 1 will be discharged.

January 24
Norfolk

Stores and equipment of the ship are going on shore. All sorts of stores are moving at once. Each Warrant Officer seems anxious to be rid of his property first. By 4 p.m. the Store Room is clear of everything except the lamp oil—empty and swept clean.

January 26
Norfolk

I spent last evening on shore with Geo. W. Mitchell. I have just learned of the death yesterday of Mrs. Hanscom, an old lady friend and the wife of Naval Constructor Hanscom of this Station.

The procedure of "paying off" our crew is in progress. About 40 of the crew whose terms of service have not expired are transferred on board the USS *Lawrence*.

After the men have left the ship seems gloomy and desolate. The decks are strewn with the contents of mess-chests and articles of a sailor's wardrobe. Small boys are swarming onto the ship and carrying off everything that is left unprotected.

The Captain, Paymaster and some of the officers still remain on the ship; also the bandsmen who gave us some good music.

I sleep on a mess-chest near the Captain's galley stove in which I keep a good fire. The gig's crew who are still with us invite me to share their coffee.

During the evening the Italian musicians started making a noise on the gun deck. The Master-at-Arms who was intoxicated got the idea in his befuddled head that they were ghosts and on going up to investigate ran into one of the Italians in the dark who was carrying an armful of wood to the Captain's Cabin. Thereupon the Master-at-Arms struck the poor fellow, knocking him down, scattering his wood in all directions and frightening him so that his yells of "murder" resounded all over the empty ship.

January 27
Norfolk

At noon today the ship formally went out of commission and is placed in charge of an Acting Master.

A steam tug came alongside to take baggage. I accompanied the officers to Norfolk where I took leave of them, probably for the last time.

In parting with me Mr. Bachus, the Executive Officer, said that he hoped that I would not yield to a temptation to remain in the Navy and informed me that, "a man-of-war was no place for a man of my stamp." I told him that I considered this quite complimentary. Thereupon he added with a serious nose which was almost amusing in him, "you have no right to waste the brains and ability which God has given you in any position which the

Navy has to offer you." This evidence of his friendship and respect touched me deeply and I told him so. I said that I had no intention other than to resume the practice of law which I had left, and assured him of my heartfelt wishes for his own future success and happiness.

I remained in Norfolk with my friend Mitchell. I also met another native of my town, Joseph Lewis.

January 28
Norfolk

I called on the Commandant to obtain my discharge. It is promised when I secure a certain certificate from the Naval Store Keeper.

I dined with Mr. Swift, the Gunner, whose home is on St. Helena. After going back on board to pack my baggage I return to Norfolk and spend the evening in Mr. Pangborn's room where they are working on his accounts and then go to the Atlantic Hotel for the night.

January 29
Norfolk

A cold room and a cold breakfast. My hotel offers scanty comforts in either respects also.

I visited Portsmouth with Lieutenant Ford. On the ferry I met Boatswain Hingerty, late of the Portsmouth, N.H. Yard. He has been detached and has come to his old home here to live with his family. I dined with Mitchell and made arrangements to board with him for which privilege I am very grateful.

January 30
Norfolk

This morning I obtained a transfer of my account from the ship to the Navy Yard. I met an old citizen of Kittery and an acquaintance, Mr. John Brown. He now resides in Baltimore.

January 31
Norfolk

I found Mr. Hunter on the ship this morning. At my persuasion he is to take a new start in shore life.

I visited Norfolk with Ensign Brown and dined with him and then accompanied him to the *Cambridge* to which he is attached.

I also visited Ed. Lane, a relative of mine, on the *Agawam*.

Captain Berrien,[6] the Commandant, assures me that he will give me a discharge from the Yard tomorrow, but not one from the ship owing to the neglect of the officer of the ship whose duty it was to attend to this matter.

I visited Hunter at the New York Hotel in the evening. I am glad that Hunter has located himself for he has been adrift ever since he came on shore.[7]

February 1
Norfolk

Visited the Paymaster to see about my discharge and learned that delay in obtaining it is due to neglect on his part and the Captain's. I again visit the Commandant who orders my discharge, but am obliged to wait until tomorrow for it and for my pay.

February 2
Norfolk and afloat

I settle with the Paymaster and pay my bills. Hunter accompanies me to the steamer *Louisiana* on which I leave for Baltimore at 8 p.m. We arrive at Fortress Monroe at 4 p.m. We lie alongside the steamer *River Queen* on which I see President Lincoln and Secretary of State Seward who have come here to meet the Confederate Commissioners with propositions respecting peace.

February 3
Baltimore

This morning we found the channel so blocked with ice that we kept off for Annapolis, but then saw an opening and managed to make our way through to Baltimore.

Some sick soldiers are passengers with us and their pitiable condition bespeaks the cruel effects of war.

I leave for New York at one thirty p.m. arriving in New York at 11 p.m. Two of our men, Veasey and Connor are traveling with me.

I go to the "Bay Street House."

February 4
New York

Spend the day going about New York. It is indeed a great city and its fine harbor and surroundings compare favorably with any city which I have seen in Europe.

At 4 p.m. I take the Sound steamer *Commonwealth* for Stonnington where I board the train for Boston. Slow progress is made because the engine breaks down twice.

February 5
Boston

I arrive in Boston at 8 a.m. and go to the Commercial House where a snow storm keeps me confined most of the day.

I meet Engineer Louis d'Arville of the USS *Fort Donaldson*. He came to New York in the prize steamer *Blenheim* captured at Wilmington.

February 6
Boston

I called on Mr. Stillman B. Allen and met at his office his father-in-law Mr. Seaward and Miss Kate B—— with whom I have been corresponding.

I visited the Navy Yard and saw there among other friends J.H. Bellamy and his brother Elisha and took dinner with them.

When walking along Tremont Street I caught a glimpse, some distance ahead of me, of a stiff-necked high collared figure that turned out of the crowd with a military stride into one of the blind end "courts" or alleys to be found in Boston. I thought that I recognized Commodore Thatcher and I suspected that he had gone into the blind alley with the idea that it offered a short cut to another main thoroughfare. On reaching the place I turned off also to satisfy my curiosity and I found myself face to face with Commodore Thatcher coming out. He recognized me at once and greeted as though he were really glad to see me. He asked me about myself and my plans for the future and inquired regarding Captain Stellwagen's health.

I congratulated the Commodore on his distinguished services to our country since he had left us. He thanked me and said, "I have, as always, tried to do my duty." He then added that he was inclined to feel better satisfied with his career than when we last met and "talked over our future prospects;" that he hoped to have a better opportunity in the future "to show what he could do," leading me to infer that he is expecting some important command.

After I had assured him of my sincere wishes for his success he replied with an approach to a smile, "I was not built for a naval hero. If the writers tried to make one out of me I fear that I would do something or fail to do something that would spoil their plans. I will just go on doing my duty."

In leaving me he said, "They will be retiring me soon. When they do I am going to live in Boston and I hope that you will come to see me for I am afraid that I will be very lonesome." Whether he is in Boston on an official mission or on leave I did not learn.

I took the train from Boston which arrived at Portsmouth at 5 p.m. and happened to meet at the station there my brother Edward who had just come from Portland.

In a short time I am again in Kittery—again among my childhood scenes and in my home. This is truly a great pleasure and that for which I have good reason to be grateful. I have been absent from my home two years and eleven months less four days. I have spent three years two months and five days in the service of the United States Navy.

February 10
Kittery Point
I am glad and thankful to be home again "amid the scenes of my childhood." It is what I have been longing for and looking forward to for nearly three years, but somehow I do not find here the "peace of mind" which I expected. It seems unreal. I feel bewildered.

In the past three days I have been greeting old friends. I have an opportunity to go into a law office, but I am wondering what is going to keep this town alive when its war time activity is passed. Shipbuilding is practically dead. Only a more remnant of the fishing fleet remains. There is no manufacturing industry. Is Kittery destined to become another Georgetown and Portsmouth another Mahon?

Today has been a miserable day. I have been tramping in slush and mud. Soft snowflakes have mingled with the cold Maine winter fog.

As I sit alone tonight in the old home, in a room endeared to me by its memories of my father and mother, arranging the foolscap sheets of this diary to put them away, my thoughts turn to the old ship that I have left.

I see the familiar faces of my shipmates. I look across the sparkling waters of the beautiful Spezia Bay and see the sun shining down on the villages nestled among the green mountain slopes beyond.

I am back in the foretop of the ship, where I liked to go. I feel the sway of the masts as the gusts strike the royals. I hear the hum of the back-stays in the swish of the wind and the creaking of the ship. I am watching once more the tumbling ridges of fear widen out from the bows as she jumps into the seas.

Now I am on St. Thomas. It is moonlight. I am looking down on the glistening roofs and the tropical verdure of the town. In the distance I see the ships with their spars standing above the trees. I make out my old ship with the lights from her ports dancing on the moonlit waters of that splendid harbor.

As the events of the three years' cruise begin to pass again before me the notes of a real bugle come to my ears through the fog of this dismal winter night. It is bed time at the Navy Yard across the river. First it was "tattoo." Now it is "taps."

All my life I have listened to the soothing notes of that "call," but it seems to have taken on a new meaning as it comes across the water to me tonight. The bugle tells me that the time has come to lay at rest forever these thoughts of the sea to which I have yielded as a boy. It reminds me that I am now over thirty years old and that I must go to work; that I must get back to the practice of law and try to make up for lost time if I am to expect to accomplish anything before "taps" are sounded for me.

★   ★   ★

No photograph is known of the *Constellation* until the 1870s. However, in 1856, Italian artist, Tomaso de Simone painted this image while the ship was in Naples. *USS* Constellation *Museum, Baltimore, MD*

Despite being one of Moses Safford's closest friends, William Cox is only referred to in the diary by his last name. He served the position of paymaster's clerk. Moses retained his friendship with Cox well into the twentieth century. He is pictured here wearing his summer service white trousers. *USS* Constellation *Museum, Baltimore, MD*

The five-gun, 437-ton cruiser CSS *Sumter* was the first Confederate commerce raider of renown. Captained by Raphael Semmes, the mere mention of her name caused dread in the American merchant fleet. Her crew captured eighteen ships between July 1861 and January 1862. Listed as a "Pirate," her image in *Harper's Weekly* is depicted above. To avoid her capture by the U.S. Navy, she was sold by the Confederacy in December 1862. She was later put to use as a blockade runner, bearing the name *Gibraltar*. *U.S. Naval Historical Center*

In spite of the domestic military needs at home, the U.S. Navy maintained a presence all over the world during the Civil War. Various ships rotated in and out of European waters. Seen here, USS *Kearsarge*, which later won fame for defeating the CSS *Alabama* off the coast of France, participated in patrols and cooperated with USS *Constellation* in the Mediterranean. *U.S. Naval Historical Center*

Posing for his portrait is an unknown sailor from *Constellation*'s Civil War years. His rank is identified by the embroidered star on his sleeve. "*Constellation*" can just barely be made out on his hatband. *USS* Constellation *Museum, Baltimore, MD*

Executive Officer Lieutenant Commander William W. Low served as *Constellation*'s executive officer, or second in command, from the beginning of the war until he and Thatcher were transferred stateside. He was ordered to command the ten-gun side-wheel gunboat USS *Octarara* in the West Gulf Blockading Squadron. His authoritarian style of command caused the news of his transfer to be joyously received by the crew of *Constellation*. Low received recognition for his command of USS *Octarara* during the Battle of Mobile Bay and the attack on Fort Morgan. *Courtesy of Earl Sheck and Lawrence Bopp*

Moses Safford as he appeared at the height of his career in 1880 as a local attorney in Kittery, Maine. *Courtesy of Joseph Frost*

Commander Henry Knox Thatcher (1806–1880) took command of *Constellation* in late 1861. Bypassing the rank of captain, he was promoted to commodore in early 1862. Ordered to return to the States in July 1863, Thatcher ultimately earned the rank of rear admiral and earned accolades for his command of a division of ships in the assault on Fort Fisher, North Carolina, in January 1865. When Admiral Farragut was ordered to Washington at the war's end, Thatcher was his replacement as commander of the Gulf Squadron. *Courtesy of descendents of Edwin Harrison Miller*

When USS *Constellation* arrived at Gibraltar in April of 1862, Commodore Thatcher found USS *Tuscarora* (pictured) blockading CSS *Sumter* in port. Employing the authority of his newly received promotion, Thatcher left *Tuscarora* to the sedentary duty of guarding *Sumter*, thus freeing *Constellation* to continue its patrol in the Mediterranean. *U.S. Naval Historical Center*

His name lost to history, this "old salt" is representative of the 240+ sailors who crewed *Constellation* during the Civil War. Note the ship's name prominently displayed on his hatband. The telescope is most likely a photographer's prop being misused for a humorous impression. *Courtesy of descendents of Edwin Harrison Miller*

Private Manning Waldron served in the 27th Maine Infantry Regiment. A childhood friend of Safford's, Waldron died of disease at an army hospital near Arlington, Virginia, on December 3, 1862. The members of his regiment held a lottery to raise funds to have his remains returned to Kittery for burial at the First Baptist Church Cemetery. Waldron was laid to rest in a plot immediately adjacent to where Safford would join him over fifty years later. *Courtesy of Joseph Frost and Lawrence Bopp*

Following his death on May 8, 1914, Moses Safford was laid to rest next to his wife in the family plot at the First Baptist Church on Pepperrell Road, east of Kittery, Maine. Very close by is the grave of his childhood friend, Manning Waldron, whose death from disease while serving in the 27th Maine Infantry during the Civil War was noted by Safford in his diary. *Courtesy of Lawrence Bopp*

Robert O'Neil Ford (1838–1913) served briefly in the elite 7th New York National Guard Regiment before receiving his commission as a second lieutenant in the Marine Corps in August 1861. After four months of service at Marine Barracks, Washington, he reported to *Constellation* to command her marine guard. While at sea, Ford had advanced through the schedule of promotions and was elevated to first lieutenant in mid-1863. In 1865, he was ordered to the Brooklyn Navy Yard. Lieutenant Ford resigned his commission in 1868. *Civil War Library of Philadelphia*

Although not specifically cited in the diary, Seaman Barnes was one of the crew who joined Safford in purchasing civilian clothes from an Italian tailor. *USS* Constellation *Museum, Baltimore, MD*

When *Constellation* put into Norfolk Navy Yard in December 1864, much of the complex was still in the devastated condition pictured here. The navy yard was burned by the U.S. Navy when it evacuated the facility in April, 1861. After having spent almost three years overseas, the crew of *Constellation* returned to an America hardened and wearied by war. The crew's observations of activities at the navy yard caused many to realize how fortunate they had been to be assigned overseas. *Library of Congress*

Shown here at the beginning of the twentieth century (*c.* 1926), USS *Constellation* still retains her nineteenth-century appearance. *Courtesy of Stephen Bockmiller*

John Hunter was successful in becoming a boatswain thanks to the assistance of his friend and shipmate, Moses Safford. Unfortunately, after Safford's departure from the navy, Hunter regained his fondness for alcohol and would eventually retire as a boatswain's mate. *Courtesy of descendents of Edwin Harrison Miller*

The diarist, photographed in Italy in 1863, sporting his newly tailored civilian suit of clothes. Then, as now, American sailors traveling abroad seized the opportunity to purchase souvenirs and products that may have cost more back home. Safford tells in his diary of such cumbersome purchases as paintings that were obtained by the officers and crew having to be stored in the hold pending the end of their patrol and return home. *Courtesy of descendents of Edwin Harrison Miller*

Serving as acting lieutenant during his service aboard *Constellation*, Edwin Miller was one of many of Safford's companions on excursions ashore. *USS* Constellation *Museum, Baltimore, MD*

Philadelphia native Captain Henry S. Stellwagen (1810–1866) was ordered to take command of *Constellation* upon the reassignment of Commodore Thatcher in July 1863. After his controversial near-loss of the steamer USS *Mercedita* to the Confederate ram CSS *Palmetto State* near Charleston Harbor, his reassignment to a sailing vessel greatly removed from the scene of battle can only be interpreted as a "punishment tour." He was an inventor and renowned oceanographer; Stellwagen Bank off the coast of Cape Cod is named for him. *USS* Constellation *Museum, Baltimore, MD*

Thomas Stellwagen was the son of Captain Henry Stellwagen, who assumed command of *Constellation* in July 1863. Thomas came aboard in Italy with his father to serve as his personal secretary and held the position of captain's clerk. *Courtesy of descendents of Edwin Harrison Miller*

Safford's close friend from Maine before the war, navigation officer and acting master Eugene Mallett was also a traveling companion ashore. *Courtesy of descendents of Edwin Harrison Miller*

Assistant Surgeon Stephen J. Clark (1839–1901) was a native of New York City and an 1861 graduate of the New York University School of Medicine. After brief service at the renowned Bellevue Hospital, he was appointed assistant surgeon in the navy on January 24, 1862. Clark served aboard *Constellation* until January 1865. He was then ordered to New Orleans where he served aboard USS *Portsmouth* until his resignation on May 20, 1865, after which he entered private practice. Notice his unorthodox use of a marine officer's epaulettes, sword and sword belt for this photo. *Courtesy of descendents of Edwin Harrison Miller*

The diarist is pictured here, sitting for a portrait in 1906 at the age of seventy-three. At this time, he held a civil service position at the Portsmouth Navy Yard in Kittery. *Courtesy of Joseph Frost*

Surgeon John S. Messersmith (1810–1891) was appointed assistant surgeon in the navy in 1837. Serving aboard USS *Truxtun* in 1846, he became a prisoner of war when the ship was driven aground in a storm and the crew was forced to surrender to Mexican authorities. After his release, he participated in Commodore Perry's capture of Tabasco and established a naval hospital there, which he managed until war's end. From 1850 to 1855 he served in the Pacific Squadron. Messersmith was ordered to USS *San Jacinto* in the African Squadron in 1860, but was soon transferred to *Constellation*, where he remained through the end of the Civil War. Messersmith retired in 1872 with the rank of medical director and maintained a private practice in Lancaster until his death in 1891. *Courtesy of Descendents of Edwin Harrison Miller*

In 1868, Miss Arabella Rice bequeathed $30,000 to create a free public library in Kittery. A small library was quickly established. In the 1880s, Moses Safford served on the board that oversaw the construction of this Queen Anne-style library building. The Rice Library was opened in 1888, and is still in use today. Safford's name appears on a large dedication plaque in the lobby of the building. *Courtesy of Lawrence Bopp*

Moses Safford's home was located at the corner of Walker and Wentworth Streets in Kittery. For many years, his next-door neighbor was Brevet Brigadier General Mark F. Wentworth (former colonel of the 27th Maine Infantry Regiment) whose home (pictured) is listed on the National Register of Historic Places. Safford's house was located to the left, where a children's library now stands. *Courtesy of Lawrence Bopp*

John Grainger served as the ship's gunner during the Civil War. The gunner was the ship's senior non-commissioned gunnery officer. He was widely respected for his mastery of the thirty-pound Parrott Rifle on the spar deck. Grainger was still serving the navy at the Portsmouth Navy Yard in his seventies. *Courtesy of descendents of Edwin Harrison Miller*

USS *Constellation* still exists today, thanks to the devotion of Americans who refuse to allow their history to be lost. The ship is open year round to visitors and is constantly undergoing careful historic restoration to her Civil War appearance. *Courtesy of Katie Bopp*

A Ship, A Man and a Legacy: Part Two

*U*PON HIS DISCHARGE FROM THE navy, Safford returned to both his practice of law as well as his political appointments. His mother would belatedly get her wish to see her son pursue a much safer career now that Moses's nautical wanderlust appeared to be at last fully sated. He also pursued his courtship of Mary Catherine Bellamy (1830–1907), who became his wife on November 29, 1866. His beloved Kate was the half sister of John Haley Bellamy, who was well known for his woodcarving skills, particularly of spread eagles in which the narrow head emerged three-dimensionally from the body. Moses and Kate's marriage proved to be a happy relationship that would be blessed with four children: Moses Victor [who went by his middle name] (1867-1947), Mary Bellamy [Wildes] (1869-1951), Edward Hart (1871-1898), and Stanley (1872-1873). Victor went on to become a medical doctor, Mary graduated from a seminary and later married lawyer Alonzo Wildes, and Edward became a lawyer. The reason for the early demise of their last child, Stanley, is unknown.

Moses became quite involved in his community through civic and patriotic activities. He helped to initiate and organize the Edward G. Parker Post, #99 of the Grand Army of the Republic, in which he became a commander. (Edward G. Parker was a member of the 17th Maine Infantry and was wounded at Chancellorsville in 1863. That year he was promoted to corporal, then sergeant in 1864 and later possibly lieutenant. He was killed at Spotsylvania Court House, in Virginia on May 12, 1864.) Moses became a Freemason and was the first senior warden of the newly formed Naval Lodge #184, which still exists today. He was very active in the Episcopal Church, an important member of the Maine Historical Society and he promoted the interests of the Navy League. He served Kittery as registrar of probate, selectman, town agent and superintendent of schools. His proudest accomplishment was the founding of the Rice Public Library in Kittery. He spent four years as chairman of the building committee to see that the Rice donation went to develop a library of which the town would be most proud. Completed in 1889, this beautiful building still stands and is in continual use today as a testimonial to his efforts.

Moses became a diarist a second time in his later life. Perhaps lonely after Kate's death in

1907, he took up the pen again and kept a daily record of his life for the next three years. At the time in his seventies, most entries reveal his suffering with the pains and infirmities consequent of old age. He relished visits from Victor and his wife and was thankful that he had his daughter Mary there to look after him. Winters were particularly hard on Moses, but summers would see his spirits rise and he would often take to the road. In 1910, he visited his old shipmates William E. Cox and John R. Grainger. These septuagenarians were still quite active men, as Cox was involved in town affairs while Grainger was still working at the navy yard.

The second diary ends a few days after Moses's seventy-seventh birthday, but his story does not end here. From correspondence taken from his legal files, it seems that his shipboard diary was known by his shipmates. Several letters were found in which widows were seeking help in receiving their husbands' pensions and were asking Moses to help verify their men's service aboard *Constellation*. Moses's responses were kind and honest in dealing with these heartwarming entreaties. The diary may not have been published but its importance was established.

Moses carried on the remainder of his life enjoying his church, his fraternities and his family. He continued to go to patriotic affairs and was often the guest speaker. He noted once how he had stood next to Admiral George Dewey at an annual observance in 1908 of the death of Admiral David G. Farragut. He continued his enjoyment of the arts and music. Moses often reflected upon his amusement with the new "talking machine"(an early phonograph) Victor had brought him that allowed him to listen to music to wile away his time. Moses never lost his love of the sea and even a few days before his end he traveled to Boston just to see a new "knockabout" schooner he had read about in the newspaper. He cut out poetry and news articles about former Union men and kept them in his files.

On May 8, 1914, Moses Safford took his final voyage at the age of eighty-one. As a token of their respect and esteem, the local townsmen closed their places of business for his funeral service. This old mariner had not only been an able attorney handling probate and settling estates amicably, but also a close friend, a good talker and one who always offered wise words of guidance and comfort. He was buried in the family plot in the First Baptist Church Cemetery in Kittery Point.

But Moses Safford would live on, not just in the memories of his friends and family but also through the diary he had kept so long before his passing. At some unknown time in his later years, Moses had the pages of foolscap that had made up his diary bound as a book and put aside as a personal keepsake of his naval service. Moses's son Victor was enamored of his father's account and ventured to preserve his father's diary in the 1930s by painstakingly typing the original manuscript. His typing was very poor, with numerous errors and typeovers, which reveal it to be a primary effort that he intended to recopy at some future time. Victor deliberately omitted his father's name in the typewritten copy, referring to him only as "our Diarist." He also omitted all the logbook references to winds, sails and navigation. He abridged to a great deal the details of the side trips his father had taken, believing that many of the "facts" were erroneous information given by his father's tour guides. Victor also dismissed some of his father's poetic musings as "the sometimes quaint and often somewhat stilted language which was characteristic of the time when our Diarist wrote."

In his personal commentary on the diary, Victor reveals how he too believed *Constellation* was the original frigate and he derides the navy for keeping such an ancient vessel in use during an age of steam. Despite his mistaken belief and good intentions, Victor failed to pursue publishing the diary and the idea died with him in 1947. None of Moses's children had offspring of their own and widowed Mary was the only child left. Mary was rather quiet and was not as outgoing as the male members of her family had been. Somewhere along the line, she crossed paths with aspiring historian and Kittery native, Joseph Frost. They got along well and she shared her father's writings and research with Joe to help him in his own local historical investigations. At one point Mary agreed to turn over all of her father's papers to her closest friend Joe and even finalize the gift in writing. Unfortunately, lacking the probate skills of her father, she failed to get a lawyer to verify this will. When she died in 1951, the new will did not stand up to probate and the estate reverted back to the will of Moses Safford, which stated that if no heirs existed, all his possessions would go to the state. Since his house, in which one room was used as his law office, was a bit rundown and in the way of development, the state had it razed. In a sad twist of irony, Safford's legal will would nearly destroy the history he had tried to preserve.

Joe Frost's begging to save the historical records fell on deaf ears and he was forced to literally root through the construction dumpsters to save what he could. He managed to find the typed copy and the later-written diary as well as other personal papers belonging to the family but the original manuscript was destroyed. Joe, who was a retired paymaster from the Portsmouth Navy Yard, donated a copy of the diary to their museum, where it still resides. Somehow a copy of the diary found its way to a gun show, was purchased by a *Constellation* supporter, and donated to the USF *Constellation* Foundation.

Meanwhile, the citizens of Baltimore, Maryland, believing the ruins of *Constellation* deteriorating quickly in Boston Harbor were the remains of the original frigate, mounted a strong campaign imploring government authorities to allow them to have the vessel returned to its home city. In 1955, the U.S. Navy agreed to allow the citizens of Baltimore to have the barely recognizable *Constellation*. Still believing her to be the original frigate, the foundation spent its time and efforts in restoring the ship to a 1797 appearance. Their dream was to revitalize the newly developed Inner Harbor of Baltimore with the ship as its focal point and as a historic draw for visitors. By the late 1970s their dream became a reality as Harbor Place in Baltimore's Inner Harbor became a tourist magnet and showed how fruitful revitalization efforts could be for old cities. Millions flocked to the new project with *Constellation* as its centerpiece.

Unmindful of the large visitation the ship and the Inner Harbor project drew, historians of note battled with one another in a very protracted argument as to whether this *Constellation* was or was not the original frigate. Dana Wegner, in his book *Fouled Anchors: The* Constellation *Question Answered*, provides a detailed accounting of these arguments and the findings thereof. With all argument centered on the Federalist Period, any Civil War history of the ship was ignored. Consequently, the Civil War diary of Moses Safford was relegated to a file cabinet, considered to be useless in relevance to the current restoration effort and forgotten.

After numerous restorations and a concession to the argument that the ship was not the original frigate, the ship began to have severe problems. In 1993, the U.S. Navy became concerned with a noticeable deterioration of the ship that was causing it to "hog up" in the middle. This developing hump indicated that the ship was in danger of breaking. Coupled with general deterioration of the added superstructure, the ship was condemned and closed to visitation. Arguments to either preserve the ship or destroy it raged through the Maryland State House and the newspapers. A compromise was reached in which the state and Baltimore City would match private donations to restore the vessel, but only to her proper historical appearance as an 1854 sloop of war and not as the 1797 frigate. In 1996 this major restoration process began.

While breaking down the ship to her original fabric, laser surveys as well as archeological evidence definitely proved her 1850s origins. The ship had seen active service from 1855 until 1947 and had numerous embellishments and additions to make her useful to more modern needs. Now the trick was deciding how to restore her without copying any of these later changes. Suddenly, the Safford diary became most important. Using the details Moses gave in his account, along with the found original plans of *Constellation's* designer, John Lenthall, the ship was restored to her former glory. One major detail the diary provided was the installment of the ship's portholes. Restorers were not sure if these originally existed or were added in the 1870s, but the diary noted on September 13, 1863: "The berth deck air ports were open as is customary in port. As it became rough and the ship began to tumble about Boatswain Hunter was awakened by a stream of water the full size of the air port which came in and struck him in the chest and face." After over one hundred and thirty years, Moses Safford's diary had spoken again.

On July 2, 1999, the newly restored *Constellation* returned to her rightful place as the centerpiece for Harbor Place. Her role as a historic representative of Baltimore's maritime heritage was now heightened with her greater distinction as the sole surviving Civil War era ship afloat. Slowly but surely, each year the ship underwent more and more restoration work to bring her back to her full Civil War period glory. Now it came time to get the diary published as well.

Having only a typed copy of the manuscript, ownership of the diary had to be first determined. While on a visit to Kittery, Maine, for research, one of the future editors was directed by the local librarian to see local historian Joe Frost. The visit turned out to be most fruitful as Joe gave his permission for publication and added numerous historic details to the story. Joe had several pictures of Moses, as well as his cane and a ring that Moses had purchased in the Holy Lands during his visit. The ring had his initials in Hebrew engraved into a black stone, most probably onyx. Various pieces of correspondence that Joe had saved rounded out the background of the diarist. At long last, the full story could be told, and the legacy of Moses Safford would now be complete.

At first the diary may have served to refresh Moses's memories of times good and bad when he had served his country during a time of crisis. It may have brought him some solace during his times of reflection. He may have kept it only for his own remembrance, but the diary had become a living document over the years. It served to assist others in gaining pension payments to aid dependents in living a more secure life. It provided a sense of pride and history to the children of Moses Safford and preserved a proud memory of the father whom they adored. It served as a defining artifact in restoring a vessel that proudly served its nation in ending the abominable slave trade and did its part in winning a devastating civil war.

And now the diary lives on, providing new readers a glimpse of life aboard a sailing ship at a time when the fate of our very nation was at stake. It allows us to see the hardships, the good times, the grief and the happiness that our servicemen went through to secure our liberties at the expense of their own. It shows the efforts of those whom opportunity failed to call to glory in history, but who served with honor nonetheless. It serves as a living reminder to the sacrifice of life and time that our servicemen give to maintain our freedom. It lives on by assisting in the preservation of a historic vessel to carry on the lessons of the cost of liberty to generations yet to come, as USS *Constellation* continues to "show the flag."

Captain Henry S. Stellwagen, USN
13 October 1809–15 July 1866

IN THE EARLY YEARS OF our nation, some families developed traditions of serving the country in specific ways. There are some, such as the Lees of Virginia and their service in the army, and the Rodgers of Maryland and their service in the navy, that come to mind immediately. There were others with shorter histories, however, which have escaped notoriety. One of these families was the Stellwagen family of Philadelphia, Pennsylvania.

Daniel Steinmetz Stellwagen, a merchant sea captain and the son of a Revolutionary War militiaman, and his wife Mary Perott Fischer Stellwagen became the parents of a son on October 13, 1809. The child was named Henry Schreiner Stellwagen. While the child was a toddler, America became embroiled in its second war with Great Britain (1812–1815). Captain Daniel Stellwagen's ship, the *Concord*, was captured by the Royal Navy when trying to run the British blockade in the Delaware Bay. A prisoner of the prize crew that was placed aboard *Concord*, Captain Stellwagen led a heroic revolt by his crew, which overpowered the prize crew and delivered the British personnel to American authorities in Philadelphia. Stellwagen then joined the U.S. Navy as a sailing master, serving with Commodore Thomas McDonough's squadron on Lake Champlain in New York. On September 11, 1814, Stellwagen participated in the Battle of Plattsburgh, which was a significant naval victory for the United States, and he received commendation and a sword from Congress for bravery. Upon the conclusion of the war, Sailing Master Stellwagen returned to Philadelphia and plied his trade until his death in 1828.

Henry S., one of the Stellwagen's five children, followed in his father's footsteps and entered the navy after a single sail on a merchantman as a teenager that took him to the East Indies. Young Henry obtained a warrant as a midshipman in the U.S. Navy effective April 1, 1828. After briefly serving at the Philadelphia Navy Yard, Midshipman Stellwagen reported to the eighteen-gun sailing sloop USS *Vandalia* for three years of service in the Brazil Squadron, returning in late 1831. In 1834, Stellwagen passed his lieutenant's examination and was elevated to "passed midshipman" (roughly equivalent to the rank of ensign today). He continued to serve in the navy in a number of posts up to the start of the Mexican War, obtaining promotion to lieutenant in 1840. In 1839, he married Mary Ann Cook. The Stellwagens had three children, two daughters and a son, Thomas Cook Stellwagen, who later became a prominent dental surgeon in Philadelphia.

Stellwagen's principal contribution to the navy and the maritime sciences was as a hydrographer, or mapper of submarine topography. In 1841, Lieutenant Stellwagen's services were lent to the U.S. Coastal Survey, the first of two stints with that agency. During his service, he was an innovator, creating a device for retrieving sediment samples from the ocean floor, which became known as the Stellwagen Cup. For this invention, Lieutenant Stellwagen was awarded the John Scott Premium and Medal from the Franklin Institute in 1849.

Lieutenant Stellwagen was recalled to the navy in 1842 and assigned to the ten-gun brig USS *Porpoise*, which was shipping out for service in the southeast Atlantic. The *Porpoise* was ordered to participate in the first U.S. naval squadron assigned to patrol the west coast of Africa with forces from the Royal Navy. Their mission was to disrupt the international slave trade that was originating from the Congo River delta and exporting its human cargo to the Western Hemisphere. While on station, Stellwagen was temporarily assigned in late 1843 to USS *Saratoga*, Commodore Matthew Perry's flagship, during negotiations between local Liberian tribes intended to end hostilities and protect American interests. Lieutenant Stellwagen returned to his assignment aboard *Porpoise*, serving until the end of the cruise in late 1844.

The outbreak of the Mexican War in 1846 occurred while Lieutenant Stellwagen was assigned to the fifty-gun sailing frigate USS *Potomac*, patrolling the Caribbean and Gulf of Mexico. In 1847, *Potomac* aided in the invasion of Vera Cruz by General Winfield Scott's troops. Later in 1847, the fleet attacked the port city of Tabasco. The harbor being too shallow, *Potomac* did not participate in the engagement. Nonetheless, forty sailors and marines were sent from the ship under Stellwagen's command to participate in the invasion.

At the conclusion of the war the armed forces were returned to the States. Life in a peacetime navy returned to normal for all personnel, including Lieutenant Stellwagen. In 1854, Stellwagen began a second stint with the U.S. Coastal Survey, assigned to the New England area. While engaged in this activity, Stellwagen discovered a topographic feature extending across the mouth of Massachusetts Bay that had not been previously recorded. Stellwagen painstakingly mapped this bank and took sediment samples from the ocean floor. Alexander Bache, superintendent of the coastal survey, was so impressed with this work that he ordered the feature named "Stellwagen Bank" in honor of its discoverer. In 1855, Stellwagen was promoted to commander and returned to duty with the navy. In late 1858, Commander Stellwagen was assigned to command a string of lighthouses stretching from New Jersey to Metomkin Inlet in Virginia, holding this post until the outbreak of the Civil War.

The first war orders Secretary of the Navy Gideon Welles issued to Commander Stellwagen were to go to Baltimore where he was to buy old ships, weight them with excess ballast and tow them to the outer banks of North Carolina. Here Stellwagen was to scuttle the ships in the channels, blocking shipping in the Carolina inlets. Commander Stellwagen purchased twenty-two schooners and had them towed to the outer banks by two steamers in August. The plan was slowed by weather and the attacks on Forts Hatteras and Clark on August 27. Stellwagen was also required to use his ships to transport two regiments of New York troops under the command of Major General Benjamin Butler. Delays allowed increased Confederate naval presence in the area that made Stellwagen's mission even more difficult. Yet, in spite of the dangers presented by the weather and the enemy, the task was completed.

As this effort came to an end, Stellwagen demanded Admiral Louis M. Goldsborough, commander of U.S. Navy forces in the area, to transfer him to another assignment. In response, Stellwagen was granted a transfer to the Brooklyn Navy Yard where he took command of the nine-gun steamer USS *Mercedita*. This ship was a merchantman purchased by the federal government at the outset of the war for conversion to a warship. This assignment proved to be both the high as well as the low point of Stellwagen's service during the Civil War.

Mercedita was assigned to the Gulf Blockading Squadron and arrived on post on January 3, 1862. She quickly saw action, chasing two blockade runners, forcing their grounding and subsequent burning on the fifth. In March, *Mercedita* was assigned to guard the inlets at Apalachicola, Florida, where, on the twenty-first, she fired on and destroyed Battery Saint Vincent that had guarded the harbor. In early April, Stellwagen led crews in boats from *Mercedita* and USS *Sagamore* ashore, capturing Apalachicola, its harbor and all stock in port at the time. In the ensuing months *Mercedita* captured the blockade runners *Bermuda*, *Victoria* and *Ida* before being ordered to New York for repairs on July 28. While at New York, Commander Stellwagen was notified of his promotion to captain.

The *Mercedita* then reported to the coast of South Carolina where she was reassigned to the South Atlantic Blockading Squadron. She patrolled the area around Charleston Harbor. On the night of January 31, 1863, the rams CSS *Palmetto State* and CSS *Chicora* emerged from Charleston Harbor aiming to attack *Mercedita* and USS *Keystone State*. Lookouts on *Mercedita* spotted an attacker in the night and attempted to contact the oncoming ship but to no avail. When a second attempt to contact the ship went unanswered, Captain Stellwagen ordered his gunners to open fire. By this time it was too late and *Palmetto State* rammed *Mercedita*, firing one round from her forward rifled gun into the victim, severely damaging her steam engine. When Flag Officer Duncan N. Ingraham, commander of *Palmetto State*, inquired whether Stellwagen would surrender, the latter stated that he could put up no resistance as his engine had been disabled, and sent a boat with his executive officer, Lieutenant Commander Trevett Abbott, to discuss terms with Ingraham.

What then happened is a subject of controversy. Ingraham, impatient to proceed after other potential victims, didn't bother to take Commander Abbott aboard, instead directing Abbott, as he waited in his boat, to give verbal parole for his ship and crew. Agreeing that *Mercedita* and her crew would not fight until properly exchanged, Abbott returned to his crippled vessel. Officers and crew worked feverishly to repair the engine and hull damage, and *Mercedita* limped into the safety of Port Royal. After emergency repairs the ship made for New York for overhaul. Confederate authorities protested that *Mercedita* was a prize of war and that her crewmembers were prisoners under parole. Their protests were ignored. Captain Stellwagen asked for and received a court of inquiry to clear him of any accusation of dereliction of duty or of violation of the articles of war. The court cleared him of any responsibility and he was subsequently ordered to command USS *Constellation*, which was currently on duty in the Mediterranean. It is a matter of debate as to whether or not this was a punishment, since he was being assigned to an obsolete ship in a backwater of the war after commanding an active combat steamer on the blockade.

Captain Stellwagen relieved Commodore Thatcher as captain of *Constellation* on July 18, 1863. For this cruise, Captain Stellwagen employed his son, Thomas, as his personal secretary. After almost a year of sailing from port to port protecting American shipping and interests, Stellwagen was ordered to report with his ship for duty in the West Gulf Blockading Squadron in May of 1864. On the way, *Constellation* rescued the British merchant brig *Mersey*, which had been dismasted in a severe storm.

The *Constellation* arrived at Mobile, Alabama, on November 27, 1864, but was found to be unfit for blockade duty. Admiral Farragut ordered the ship to Pensacola Navy Yard for repairs. After completion of repairs and personal inspection by Farragut himself, the ship was ordered to Norfolk, since many enlistments of the crew were about to expire. On December 19, while en route, a blockade runner was spotted and fired upon. These shots were to be the only hostile fire given by *Constellation* during the war. The quarry disappeared over the horizon but the noise of the ship's guns alerted other ships in the area that eventually ran down the blockade runner. The *Constellation* arrived in Norfolk on Christmas Day where her boats were employed ferrying soldiers, sailors and marines wounded at the Battle of Fort Fisher to Norfolk hospitals. The ship was then taken out of commission and used as a receiving ship.

On February 15, 1865, Captain Stellwagen was assigned command of the ten-gun screw sloop USS *Pawnee* that was assigned to the South Atlantic Blockading Squadron. His order in this new command was to occupy a port in South Carolina, and was accomplished on February 23. Stellwagen remained in this command until he was granted his request for medical leave on April 24. Stellwagen never returned to duty, receiving approval for his request for retirement by the retirement board on Christmas Eve, 1865. His health steadily worsened until he died at Cape May, New Jersey, on July 15, 1866. Later his remains were returned to his hometown, Philadelphia.

Rear Admiral Henry K. Thatcher, USN
26 May 1806–5 April 1880

URING HER SERVICE IN THE Civil War, USS *Constellation* was commanded by two men: Captain Henry S. Stellwagen and Commodore Henry K. Thatcher. It is said that some men achieve greatness, some are born to greatness and some men have greatness thrust upon them. For Henry Thatcher, it can be said that the first two of these three statements apply.

On May 26, 1806, Lucy Flucker Knox Thatcher, wife of Ebenezer Thatcher gave birth to a son at her father's estate in Thomaston, Massachusetts (now part of Maine). While such happenings were commonplace, one of the players in this story was not a common man. The grandfather of the new child, on whose estate the child was born, was the great Revolutionary War hero and former United States secretary of war, Major General Henry Knox. The new child was named Henry Knox Thatcher, in honor of his grandfather.

Henry Thatcher was raised in Boston, attending several local schools. To continue in the family tradition, and possibly to capitalize on his relation to his famous grandfather, Henry applied for admission to the United States Military Academy at West Point, and was admitted in 1822. His stay at the academy was brief due to health problems that began soon after his arrival. He left the academy in November of that year to return home and convalesce. During this time at home, Thatcher applied to the navy, seeking appointment as a midshipman. In the days prior to the establishment of the United States Naval Academy at Annapolis, the entry and basic training level rank for those beginning in the officers' corps was midshipman. These newly created midshipmen were assigned to shipboard duty where their battle stations were amid ships, hence the title. The purpose of the midshipman's position was to learn seamanship and basic command in order to eventually qualify to take the examination for the rank of lieutenant.

Thatcher received his acting midshipman's warrant on March 4, 1823. Before reporting for duty, he formally resigned his position at West Point on April 3, 1823.

After a brief initial assignment at the Washington Navy Yard as an assistant to Commodore David Porter, Midshipman Thatcher was assigned to the USS *United States* in November 1823. The USS *United States* was the flagship of the Pacific Squadron commanded by

Commodore Isaac Hull. Therefore, in his first two assignments, the young midshipman was well positioned to ensure that his work was noticed by two of the most influential officers of the navy. At the age of seventeen, Midshipman Thatcher shipped out for the Pacific, not to return to the States until April 1827. As was the custom for officers returning from lengthy sea duty, he was granted an extended leave of absence until May 1828. He was then assigned to USS *Independence*, which was laid up in ordinary at the Boston Navy Yard; an assignment that allowed this Bostonian to remain close to home. After a two-year cruise aboard USS *Delaware* to the Mediterranean, Thatcher took and passed his examinations and was elevated to passed midshipman on March 23, 1829.

Soon Thatcher was shipped out for the West Indian Squadron in August 1830 as acting master (the period equivalent of a lieutenant, junior grade) of USS *Porpoise*. While on duty with the squadron, Thatcher was transferred to serve as acting master of the sloop USS *Erie*, returning to the States in October 1831. He was again granted leave of absence until November 1833. During this leave, two major events occurred in Thatcher's life. First, he married Susan Cony Croswell at Mercer, Maine, in December 1831. During their long marriage, the Thatchers had no children of their own, but did adopt a daughter, Susan. In February of 1833, the retiring board elevated Passed Midshipman Thatcher to the rank of lieutenant.

When Thatcher reported back for duty at Charlestown Navy Yard in Boston, he was assigned to the USS *Falmouth* for duty with the West Indian Squadron to further disrupt the slave trade while protecting American shipping. Following his return from the assignment, he was placed again on leave of absence through May of 1839, except for a five-month temporary assignment aboard his former command, USS *Erie* in the first half of 1838.

In May 1839, Lieutenant Thatcher was assigned to USS *Brandywine* for a two-year tour of duty in the Mediterranean. After a few months leave, Thatcher was ordered to Portland, Maine, to take command of the naval rendezvous. (A "rendezvous" was the period term for recruiting office or camp.) Lieutenant Thatcher held this position until August 1842, when he was again granted a few months leave. His next assignment was an important one in his career. In October 1842, he was made executive officer (second in command) of the ship of the line USS *Ohio*. Although this ship was old, obsolete and worthy only as a receiving ship (basically a floating barracks for the housing and training of new recruits), Thatcher was nonetheless second in charge of one of the largest ships in the fleet. Relieved of his duty after a year, he was assigned to other administrative duties at Charlestown before briefly being reassigned back to *Ohio* in mid-1847.

While many officers were gaining fame and commendation in the war with Mexico (1846–1848), Lieutenant Thatcher, among others, was tasked with maintaining the navy's ongoing responsibility to protect American shipping and other interests worldwide. As war raged in the Gulf of Mexico and along the Rio Grande, Thatcher was assigned to USS *Jamestown*, which was shipping out as Commodore William C. Bolton's flagship of the African Squadron in June 1847. After three years of cruising the coast of Africa attempting to interrupt the slave trade, and later being transferred to the Mediterranean, *Jamestown* returned in June 1850. After a brief leave, Lieutenant Thatcher was made inspector of the Charlestown Navy Yard, holding that position until March 1851. His next assignment would be a landmark in his career.

In March 1851, Thatcher was assigned to command USS *Relief*. After twenty-eight years in the navy, Thatcher had his first official command. This assignment was especially noticeable as *Relief* was the store-ship for the Brazil Squadron, which, next to the Pacific

Squadron, was the naval force stationed farthest from the installations on the east coast of the United States than any other. His job, as commander of the squadron's store-ship, was to run repeated supply missions from the States to the southern hemisphere in order to keep the ships of the squadron equipped with necessary supplies and ammunition.

Thatcher returned from his command in August 1852 and was granted several months of leave. After a brief stint as the commander of USS *Lexington* at Brooklyn Navy Yard in mid-1853, he was assigned as executive officer of the U.S. Naval Asylum (the old sailors' home) in Philadelphia in 1854. He captained a desk in Philadelphia until March of 1857. During this duty, the retirement board promoted Thatcher to commander on September 14, 1855. In April 1857, he was sent back to sea as the commander of USS *Decatur* with the Pacific Squadron. His ship was to patrol the west coasts of North and South America, protecting American interests and shipping until returning to Mare Island in August 1859.

With his next postings, Commander Thatcher employed his services in the first of several important roles that he filled in the Civil War. In November 1859, Thatcher was ordered to his hometown to serve as executive officer of the Charlestown Navy Yard. From the time that war erupted in April until he was reassigned in November of 1861, Commander Thatcher worked tirelessly to prepare every U.S. Navy ship in the area that was available for sea duty for the mission of destroying the Confederate Navy and commerce fleet. Then came the second of his important wartime duties.

Thatcher was ordered to the navy yard at Portsmouth, New Hampshire, to take command of the sloop of war *Constellation*, which had recently returned from two years of service on the African Station. Thatcher supervised the reconditioning and resupply of his ship and set sail for his new posting in the Mediterranean. With the urgency of the war at home, most of the foreign squadrons had been stripped of ships and *Constellation* was one of only four warships assigned to the European area in the early part of the conflict. Arriving at Gibraltar in April, Thatcher's *Constellation* joined USS *Kearsarge*, USS *Tuscorora* and USS *Ino* in blockading Raphael Semmes's CSS *Sumter* in port, resulting in her sale and abandonment at Algeciras. In July of that year, the retirement board elevated Commander Thatcher to commodore without first promoting him to captain. This was the second time in his career that he had passed over so many others higher than himself in seniority. The *Constellation* patrolled the Mediterranean protecting American interests and citizens in African Middle-Eastern hotspots while interrupting Confederate plans to take possession of ships.

In July 1863, the commodore was ordered to return to the States. While he may have missed the Mexican War, and essentially sat out the first part of this one, Thatcher would soon find himself in the thick of naval action for the balance of the war. In September 1863, he was sent to the North Atlantic Blockading Squadron in command of both the steam frigate USS *Colorado* and the First Division of the squadron. With the exception of a brief temporary reassignment to command store-ships in South Carolina, Commodore Thatcher held this command until January 1865. In the two assaults on Fort Fisher, North Carolina, in December 1864 and January 1865, Thatcher commanded the lead division of the squadrons. For his leadership during the January assault, Admiral David D. Porter singled out Thatcher for praise and elevated him to the rank of acting rear admiral.

Later that month Thatcher was ordered to proceed to the Gulf Coast to accept command of the West Gulf Blockading Squadron from the legendary Admiral David G. Farragut. Using USS *Portsmouth* (and later USS *Stocksdale*) as his flagship, Acting Rear Admiral Thatcher, in May 1865, coordinated the final attack on Mobile, Alabama, which resulted in the capture on May 10 of the Confederate naval squadron protecting the harbor. With

Mobile secured, Thatcher then proceeded to Galveston, Texas, where his fleet forced the surrender of that city and its defenses on June 2. With the war's end, the West Gulf Blockading Squadron and the East Gulf Blockading Squadron were combined into one Gulf Blockading Squadron under Thatcher's command. Employing USS *Estrella* as his flagship, he held this position until May of 1866.

The following July, the retirement board elevated Thatcher to the full rank of rear admiral and he was put in command of the North Pacific Squadron, which he commanded from his flagship USS *Vanderbilt* (and later USS *Pensacola*) until mid-1868 when the retirement board placed him on the retired list after forty-five years of faithful service. During his service in the Pacific, Admiral Thatcher was knighted by Hawaiian King Kamehameha.

After arriving back in the States, Admiral Thatcher served two years as "port admiral" at the naval station in Portsmouth until 1870. He retired to a home on Lake Street in the Winchester section of Boston and maintained a summer home in Nahant. During his retirement, he served as vice president of the Society of the Cincinnati in Massachusetts. This esteemed group consisted of descendent sons of officers who had served during the Revolution.

Rear Admiral Henry Knox Thatcher died of kidney disease at the Evans House in Boston on April 5, 1880. The secretary of the navy issued an official obituary order with instructions that thirteen guns be fired in honor of the passed hero with flags to be flown at half-mast. Admiral Thatcher joined a long list of American war heroes as he was laid to rest in Boston.

USS Constellation
1862–1865 Mediterranean Cruise
Commissioned Officers and Enlisted Servicemen

COMMISSIONED OFFICERS

NAME	RANK	REMARKS
Thatcher, Henry K.	Captain	Relieved in Spezia, Italy, on 07/18/1863
Stellwagen, Henry S.	Captain	Reported in Spezia, Italy, on 07/18/1863
Low, William W.	Lieutenant Commander	Relieved in Spezia, Italy, on 07/18/1863
Abbot, Trevett	Lieutenant Commander	Reported in Spezia, Italy, on 07/22/1863
Lowe, W.E.	Lieutenant	
Wallace, Rush R.	Lieutenant	
Messersmith, John S.	Surgeon	
Pangborn, Henry H.	Paymaster	
Mallett, Edward B.	Acting Master	
Allen, Abraham	Acting Master	
Kempton, Abner W.	Acting Master	
Clark, Stephen J.	Assistant Surgeon	
Ford, Robert O.	Second Lieutenant, USMC	
Backus, Sylvanus	Midshipman	
Blake, Charles F.	Midshipman	
Hinkley, Eugene B.	Captain's Clerk	Relieved in Spezia, Italy, on 07/19/1863
Stellwagen, Thomas C.	Captain's Clerk	Reported in Spezia, Italy, on 07/18/1863
Kay, Samuel W.	Paymaster's Clerk	
Langton, J.F.B.	Acting Boatswain	
Grainger, John R.	Acting Gunner	
Philbrick, Henry R.	Acting Carpenter	
Tatem, Samuel	Sailmaker	
Ryder, P.M.	Master's Mate	
Drew, George H.	Master's Mate	
Wilson, Matthew H.	Master's Mate	

Enlisted Navy

Ship #	Name	Enlistment	Rank	Remarks
26	Nelson, Munroe	10/30/1861	Ordinary Seaman	
27	Butler, C.W.	11/02/1861	Quarter Gunner	
28	Ripley, John	11/02/1861	Coxswain	
29	Phelps, Arthur	11/05/1861	Second Cabin Boy	
30	Rivers, George M.	09/27/1861	Ordinary Seaman	
31	Smith, George H.	11/05/1861	Seaman	
32	Nelson, John	11/08/1861	Quarter Master	
33	Weavler, John	11/12/1861	Seaman	
34	Cripps, Henry	11/14/1861	Captain of the Top	
35	Dunbar, Ansel	11/13/1861	Ordinary Seamen	
36	West, Henry	11/14/1861	Quarter Master	
37	Hughes, William	11/14/1861	Seaman	
38	Peabody, I.K.	11/05/1861	First Cabin Boy	
39	Mahoney, Thomas	11/13/1861	Seaman	
40	Evans, James	11/15/1861	Coxswain	
41	Hunter, John	11/22/1861	Boatswain's Mate	Appointed acting Boatswain
42	Gomez, Joseph	11/25/1861	Officer's Steward	
43	Wilson, Antonio	11/25/1861	Officer's Cook	
44	Fernandez, Joseph	11/27/1861	Landsman	Died at Genoa,
45	Humphries, John	11/28/1861	Landsman	
46	Frederickson, T.W.	11/29/1861	Ordinary Seaman	
47	Hawes, George L.	11/28/1861	Seaman	Transferred to hospital, N Y
48	Stephens, E.H.	12/02/1861	First Cabin Boy	
49	May, William	12/03/1861	Quarter Master	
50	Hyde, Jeremiah	11/07/1861	Seaman	
51	Wheeling, Matthew	12/07/1861	Seaman	
52	Haverty, John	11/07/1861	Landsman	
53	Fletcher, George	12/09/1861	Ordinary Seaman	
54	Burchstead, James	12/10/1861	Ordinary Seaman	
55	Moody, Nathan	12/10/1861	Armorer	
56	Rigley, Joseph	12/10/1861	Seaman	
57	James, Joseph	12/10/1861	Ordinary Seaman	
58	Brown, II, William	12/12/1861	Ordinary Seaman	
59	Gallagher, Daniel	12/12/1861	Ordinary Seaman	
60	Simmons, Isaac	12/12/1861	Landsman	
61	Francis, Joseph	12/13/1861	Landsman	
62	Oliver, Robert	12/12/1861	Seaman	
63	Johnston, Aling	12/13/1861	Seaman	
64	Clark, James	12/13/1861	Seaman	
65	Hubbert, Henry	12/12/1861	Ordinary Seaman	
66	Cunningham, Rufus	12/13/1861	Ordinary Seaman	
67	Burnes, J.H.	11/28/1861	Boatswain's Mate	
68	McFarland, Charles	12/14/1861	Landsman	
69	Leathers, George	12/13/1861	Landsman	
70	Brown, II, John	12/14/1861	Quarter Gunner	

Ship #	Name	Enlistment	Rank	Remarks
71	Leising, Jacob	12/16/1861	Seaman	
72	Fosc, Thomas	12/14/1861	Ordinary Seaman	
73	McCarthy, John	12/14/1861	Ordinary Seaman	
74	McDermott, John	12/16/1861	Landsman	
75	Hoff, Harry	12/16/1861	Landsman	
76	Miller, Edwin H.	12/16/1861	Quarter Gunner	Appointed acting Master's Mate
77	Campbell, John	12/17/1861	Captain of the F.C.	Lost at sea in 1862
78	Warner, Edward C.	12/16/1861	Ordinary Seaman	Deserted at Genoa,
79	Edwards, William	12/17/1861		Transferred to USS *Release*
80	Morgan, John	12/18/1861	Sailmaker's Mate	
81	Secundy, Carl	12/18/1861	Ordinary Seaman	
82	Remmington, James	12/18/1861	Ordinary Seaman	
83	Smith, William E.	12/18/1861	Landsman	
84	McHenry	12/18/1861	Ship's Corporal	
85	Low, Joseph W.	12/18/1861	Coxswain	
86	Brooks, John	12/18/1861	Seaman	
87	Luciena, George	12/18/1861	Seaman	Deserted at Naples, Italy
88	Raynes, Charles N.	12/19/1862	Coxswain	
89	Goskey, John	12/18/1861	Ordinary Seaman	
90	Reese, Henry	12/19/1861	Coxswain	
91	Hodgden, Thomas F.	11/19/1861	Ordinary Seaman	
92	Francis, Sylvester	12/19/1861	Landsman	
93	McFadden, William	12/19/1861	Ordinary Seaman	Deserted at Genoa, Italy
94	Buchanan, John	12/12/1861	Quarter Master	
95	Harrison, Alexander	12/21/1861	Seaman	Deserted at Cadiz, Spain
96	Black, Jeremiah	12/19/1861	Ordinary Seaman	
97	Joy, Henry F.	12/19/1861	Cooper	
98	Horen, John	12/21/1861	Ordinary Seaman	
99	Powers, William T.	12/21/1861	Seaman	
100	Mason, Joseph	12/24/1861	Seaman	
101	McKay, Henry	12/24/1861	Seaman	Deserted at Genoa, Italy
102	Johnston, Charles	12/24/1861	Seaman	
103	McIntire, John	12/24/1861	Boatswain's Mate	
104	Geyer, E.K.	12/24/1861	Quarter Master	
105	Spellman, Jeremiah	12/24/1861	Landsman	
106	Tibbitts, Samuel B.	12/24/1861	Ordinary Seaman	
107	King, William	12/24/1861	Ordinary Seaman	
108	VanTassell, Obediah	12/25/1861	Ordinary Seaman	
109	Bowman, John	12/24/1861	Seaman	
110	Russell, Thomas	12/24/1861	Seaman	
111	Carle, Robert	12/26/1861	Seaman	
112	Ellsworth, William	12/26/1861	Seaman	
113	Steine, Peter	12/28/1861	Seaman	
114	Price, William	12/28/1861	Seaman	
115	Preshaw, Joseph	12/28/1861	Seaman	
116	Lawson, James	12/30/1861	Captain of the Top	

Ship #	Name	Enlistment	Rank	Remarks
117	Leston, Frank	12/30/1861	Captain of the Top	
118	Champion, Christopher	12/31/1861	Ordinary Seaman	
119	Baker, L.W.	12/30/1861	Seaman	
120	Handren, M.E.	12/31/1861	Seaman	
121	Rain, Frederick	01/03/1862	Ordinary Seaman	
122	Wortman, George W.	01/02/1862	Landsman	Transferred to USS *Release*
123	Hustin, Lewis D.	01/02/1862	Ordinary Seaman	Deserted at Genoa, Italy
124	Hatch, F.C.	01/06/1862	Landsman	Transferred to navy yard, Portsmouth, N.H.
125	Wilson, Andrew	01/06/1862	Seaman	
126	White, John	01/17/1862	Seaman	
127	Arestrup, Alfred	01/06/1862	Quarter Gunner	
128	Callahan, James	01/24/1862	Ordinary Seaman	
129	Johnston, Peter	02/01/1862	Captain of the Forecastle	
130	Bates, John	02/01/1862	Seaman	
131	Christy, James	02/01/1862	Seaman	
132	Hagerty, Timothy	01/31/1862	Ordinary Seaman	
133	Cole, John R.	02/01/1862	Captain of the After Guard	
134	Baker, Hartwell	02/08/1862	Seaman	Transferred to hospital, N.Y.
135	Chase, George E.	02/04/1862	Seaman	
136	Rilley, Matthew	02/08/1862	Landsman	
137	Brady, Thomas	02/10/1862	Seaman	
138	Lemon, Thomas	02/08/1862	Seaman	
139	Moore, Charles	02/08/1862	Gunner's Mate	
140	Brown, James	02/08/1862	Seaman	
141	Brown, John	02/10/1862	Seaman	Deserted at Genoa, Italy
142	Judge, James W.	02/10/1862	Seaman	
143	Berryman, George	02/10/1862	Seaman	
144	Smith, Alvarado	02/10/1862	Ordinary Seaman	Deserted at Genoa, Italy
145	Grant, William	02/10/1862	Second Cabin Boy	
146	Lawrence, John	02/11/1862	Landsman	
147	Kimball, Thomas	02/10/1862	Landsman	
148	Hammenhirg, J.A.	02/10/1862	First Cabin Boy	
149	Johnston, Oloff	02/10/1862	Seaman	
150	Stevens, N.S.	02/11/1862	Captain of the Top	
151	Jones, Stephen	02/11/1862	Coxswain	Doing duty of Master's Mate at Rota, Spain
152	Driscoll, Thomas	02/11/1862	Landsman	
153	Bonit, Anthoine	02/11/1862	Landsman	Deserted at Portsmouth, N.H.
154	Griffiths, William	02/12/1862	Third Cabin Boy	
155	Graham, John	02/11/1862	Second Cabin Boy	
156	Jehanns, Alex	02/11/1862	Officer's Cook	Transferred to USS *Release*
157	Treadwell, H.P.	02/12/1862	Seaman	
158	Saunders, J.P.	02/10/1892	Second Cabin Boy	
159	McGilley, John	02/11/1862	Landsman	
160	Peter, James	02/14/1861	First Captain Boy	
161	Green, Hugh	02/13/1862	Landsman	
162	Ridler, Samuel	02/13/1862	First Cabin Boy	

SHIP #	NAME	ENLISTMENT	RANK	REMARKS
163	Baker, Elon G.	02/14/1862	Landsman	
164	Smith, Thomas U.	02/13/1862	Seaman	
165	Regan, Michael	02/15/1862	Ship's Corporal	
166	King, Oby	02/15/1862	Ordinary Seaman	Deserted at Genoa,
167	Kelly, Charles	02/14/1862	Ordinary Seaman	Transferred to hospital, N.Y.
168	Briggs, Joseph R.	02/15/1862	Seaman	
169	O'Donnell, John	02/10/1862	Coxswain	Deserted at Kittery, M.E.
170	Schenard, C.F.	02/17/1862	Ordinary Seaman	
171	McDonnell, Andrew	02/17/1862	Landsman	
172	Pray, Isaac C.	02/17/1862	Ordinary Seaman	
173	Nolan, Joseph	02/17/1862	Ordinary Seaman	
174	Sumner, Thomas C.	02/17/1862	Landsman	Transferred to hospital, Kittery, M.E.
175	Thompson, A.F.	02/17/1862	Captain of the Top	
176	Kulver, Ferdinand	02/17/1862	Ordinary Seaman	
177	Alurson, Peter	02/17/1862	Ordinary Seaman	
178	Peterson, Lars S.	02/19/1862	Coxswain	
179	McLaughlin, Patrick	02/17/1862	Seaman	
180	Nichols, John T.	02/15/1862	Landsman	
181	Hitchings, Marcus	02/18/1862	Ordinary Seaman	
182	Richards, Alonzo	02/18/1862	Landsman	
183	Lane, George W.	02/20/1862	Quarter Gunner	
184	Morgan, George W.	02/19/1862	Ordinary Seaman	Transferred to USS *Release*
185	Bennett, George C.	02/19/1862	Ordinary Seaman	
186	VanHornike, Amandus	02/19/1862	Ordinary Seaman	
187	Gallrap, Peter	02/20/1862	Landsman	Deserted at Genoa, Italy
188	Davis, Eben T.	02/18/1862	Seaman	
189	Giles, Charles	02/21/1862	Ordinary Seaman	
190	Jones, Robert	02/21/1862	Ordinary Seaman	Deserted at Palermo, Italy
191	McFadden, Robert	02/21/1862	Landsman	Transferred to USS *Release*
192	Coggen, A.F.	02/21/1862	Landsman	
193	Gallagher, Francis	02/11/1862	Landsman	
194	Anderson, Charles	02/11/1862	Quarter Gunner	
195	Matthew, Henry	02/13/1862	Landsman	
196	Dunning, Isaac	12/18/1861	Captain of the Top	Deserted at Genoa, Italy
197	Moffatt, Gaven	11/22/1861	Carpenter's Mate	
198	Allen, William	02/17/1862	Ordinary Seaman	
199	Faulk, Carl C.	02/20/1862	Ordinary Seaman	Deserted at Palermo, Italy
200	Brown, Charles	02/20/1862	Ordinary Seaman	
201	Wilson, Joseph	02/22/1862	Landsman	
202	Brown, William	02/22/1862	Landsman	
203	Ashport, Albert	02/22/1862	Landsman	
204	Lunan, Amos	02/24/1862	Landsman	
205	Ferguson, Daniel	12/24/1861	Seaman	
206	Clark, W.H.	02/10/1862	Seaman	
207	Mills, Willard A.	12/21/1861	Ordinary Seaman	
208	Mulligan, Robert	01/04/1862	Landsman	

Ship #	Name	Enlistment	Rank	Remarks
209	West, Jonah	01/07/1862	Ordinary Seaman	
210	Fortune, John	01/13/1862	Ordinary Seaman	
211	Dyer, Albert	02/08/1862	Ordinary Seaman	Discharged Dead at Naples, Italy
212	Nelson, Edwin	02/03/1862	Ordinary Seaman	
213	Jackson, Henry	01/03/1862	Ordinary Seaman	
214	Thrasher, E.W.	01/31/182	Landsman	
215	Crosby, Charles	02/03/1862	Ordinary Seaman	
216	Phelps, George W.	02/04/1862	Landsman	
217	Dugan, Daniel	02/05/1862	Ordinary Seaman	
218	Young, George A.	02/05/1862	Ordinary Seaman	Deserted at Portsmouth, N.H.
219	Gray, John	02/01/1862	Ordinary Seaman	
220	Wisner, James	02/06/1862	Ordinary Seaman	Transferred to hospital, Kittery, ME
221	Veazey, Charles U.	02/03/1862	Ordinary Seaman	
222	Conner, E.S.	02/03/1862	Ordinary Seaman	
223	Weldon, George W.	07/23/1862	Landsman	
224	Varnish, George P.	02/17/1862	Ship's Corporal	Deserted at Genoa, Italy
225	Stiles, Lewis C.	12/02/1861	Landsman	
226	Jones, Michael	01/17/1862	Second Cabin Boy	
227	Hurley, Patrick	01/16/1862	Second Cabin Boy	
228	Meader, Cornelius	01/16/1862	Second Cabin Boy	
229	Hodder, George	01/16/1862	Landsman	
230	Muchinore, John	02/06/1862	Landsman	
231	Rooney, Charles	01/13/1862	Seaman	
232	Turpie, Andrew	01/02/1862	Seaman	
233	Quanstram, G.V.	12/13/1861	Ordinary Seaman	
234	Barney, Orin	02/06/1862	Seaman	
235	Barnes, Emmet	02/06/1862	Landsman	
236	Place, Leonard	12/14/1861	Quarter Gunner	
237	Stevens, James W.	01/10/1862	Landsman	Transferred to hospital, N.Y.
238	Sullivan, John	02/01/1862	Landsman	
239	Littlefield, Jewett	01/10/1862	Landsman	
240	Lawson, E.W.	01/28/1862	Landsman	
241	Spinney, William	01/13/182	Landsman	
243	Johnson, George W.	01/17/1862	Landsman	
244	Littlefield, Joseph F.	01/10/1862	Ordinary Seaman	
245	Parks, John F.	01/16/1862	Boatswain's Mate	
246	Holland, Thomas U.	01/17/1862	Surgical Nurse	Deserted at Portsmouth, N.H.
247	Bellowes, C.D.	01/15/1862	Surgical Nurse	
248	Carter, Henry	01/17/1862	Seaman	
249	Butland, R.O.K.	01/28/1862	Landsman	
250	Clark, William W.	02/04/1862	Seaman	Died at Genoa, Italy
251	Wadsworth, A.A.	02/12/1862	Landsman	Discharged at Cadiz, Spain
252	Parody, Alfred	12/06/1862	Landsman	
253	Calef, D.R.	12/02/1862	Landsman	Deserted at Genoa, Italy
254	Stickney, M.L.	12/10/1861	Landsman	
255	Glenn, John W.	12/13/1861	Master at Arms	

Ship #	Name	Enlistment	Rank	Remarks
256	Lewis, John C.	12/12/1861	Landsman	
257	Bootman, John W.	12/16/1861	Ship's Cook	
258	Martin, Robert B.	12/30/1861	Ordinary Seaman	
259	Sargent, Charles	12/14/1861	Captain of the Hold	
260	Brown, Henry	12/20/1861	Boatswain's Mate	Deserted at Genoa, Italy
261	Rutland, John	12/26/1861	Seaman	
262	Manning, Augustus	12/12/1861	Seaman	
263	Peterson, Andrew	12/26/1861	Captain of the After Guard	
264	Safford, M.A.	12/26/1861	Yeoman	
265	Ridge, Thomas W.	03/04/1862	Surgical Nurse	
266	Buckley, James	05/30/1862	Ordinary Seaman	Deserted at Palermo, Italy
267	Sullivan, James	05/30/1862	Ordinary Seaman	Delivered up to captain of *Ocean Bird*
268	Giovanni, Borutt	06/03/1862	Landsman	Deserted at Genoa, Italy
269	Giovanni, Percerutti	06/10/1862	Landsman	Discharged at Genoa, Italy
270	Marinelli, Francisco	06/23/1862	Landsman	
271	Galletta, Ferdinando	07/01/1862	Officer's Cook	Discharged at Genoa, Italy
272	Bianco, Joseph L.	07/30/1862	Landsman	Discharged on survey at Genoa, Italy
273	Lucas, Peter	04/01/1862	Landsman	Special service at storehouse, Spezia, Italy
274	Portunato, Grolomo		Landsman	Special service at storehouse, Spezia, Italy
275	Coleman, George D.	04/01/1862	Third Cabin Boy	
276	Campagna, Ferdinand	04/07/1862	Landsman	Discharged at Messina, Italy
277	Vincenziana, Vincent	04/08/1862	Landsman	Discharged at Messina, Italy
278	Dart, Frederick	08/20/1862	Ordinary Seaman	
279	Wallace, James	08/20/1862	Landsman	
280	Gomez, Manuel	08/15/1862	Pilot	Entered on books, discharged order commodore
281	Riley, John	10/15/1862	Ordinary Seaman	
282	Lyon, William	10/15/1862	Ordinary Seaman	
283	Henison, William	10/15/1862	Ordinary Seaman	
284	Crissfulli, Vincenzo	08/22/1862	Landsman	Discharged at Genoa, Italy
285	Crisepille, Raffella	08/25/1862	Officer's Cook	Discharged at Genoa, Italy
286	Tyson, William	11/09/1862	Ordinary Seaman	
289	Hughes, Henry F.	11/26/1862	Ordinary Seaman	
290	O'Rouk, Michael	11/26/1862	Ordinary Seaman	
291	Simpson, William B.	11/26/1862	Ordinary Seaman	
292	Jones, William	11/26/1862	Ordinary Seaman	
293	Prescottm, George	11/26/1862	Ordinary Seaman	
294	Russell, John	11/26/1862	Ordinary Seaman	
295	Emanuel, Joseph	12/02/1862	Ordinary Seaman	
296	Olsen, Ivan J.	12/05/1862	Ordinary Seaman	
297	Melvin, George	12/10/1862	Ordinary Seaman	
298	Duffy, William	12/13/1862	Ordinary Seaman	
299	Hart, Ruben	12/15/1862	Seaman	
300	Percivle, William	12/16/1862	Ordinary Seaman	
301	Merca, Gaetaeno	12/17/1862	Landsman	Deserted at Genoa, Italy
302	Thompson, John	12/18/1862	Seaman	
303	Thompson, James (1st)	12/22/1862	Ordinary Seaman	

Ship #	Name	Enlistment	Rank	Remarks
304	Thompson, James (2nd)	12/22/1862	Ordinary Seaman	
305	Rose, William	12/24/1862	Quarter Master	
306	Stengert, Adolph	01/15/1863	Landsman	
307	Oliver, Peter	01/31/1863	Landsman	
308	Laughlin, John	02/10/1863	Second Cabin Boy	
309	Allen, Frederick	02/10/1863	Second Cabin Boy	
310	Lancuitte, Ferdinando	02/27/1863	Landsman	

ENLISTED MARINES

Ship #	Name	Enlistment	Rank	Remarks
2	Robbins, George W.	07/27/1859	Orderly Sergeant	
3	Wayland, Timothy	06/03/1861	Sergeant	
4	Clark, Thomas B.	10/25/1861	Corporal	
5	Whealan, Dennis	07/10/1858	Corporal	
6	Connolly, Patrick	12/20/1858	Corporal	
7	Hamilton, James	04/09/1859	Drummer	Deserted
8	McNamara, James	07/30/1858	Fifer	
9	Caulfield, George D.	08/29/1861	Private	
10	Carr, Daniel	09/18/1861	Private	
11	Curtis, Albert	09/10/1861	Private	
12	Davy, Charles	05/08/1861	Private	
13	Day, William	08/05/1861	Private	
14	Dolan, James	08/14/1861	Private	
15	Davis, John	10/02/1861	Private	
16	Edsall, Andrew J.	06/04/1859	Private	
17	Finigan, Christopher	05/18/1859	Private	
18	Fitzgerald, James	10/12/1861	Private	
19	Gallagher, Hugh	09/17/1859	Private	
20	Gaul, Michael	10/26/1861	Private	
21	Hurst, Thomas	05/23/1861	Private	
22	Hagan, Michael	05/24/1861	Private	
23	Humecks, Jacob D.	08/10/1859	Private	
24	Hart, James	08/05/1861	Private	
25	Hayden, William	04/20/1859	Private	
26	Jackson, William	05/08/1861	Private	
27	Kenny, Martin	08/17/1861	Private	
28	Littlefield, George	08/26/1861	Private	
29	Martin, Allen	06/15/1861	Private	
30	May, Peter	07/24/1861	Private	
31	Mahony, John	10/29/1861	Private	
32	O'Donnell, Hugh	09/30/1861	Private	
33	Page, Joseph A.	08/29/1861	Private	
34	Powers, Michael	10/03/1861	Private	
35	Regan, Dennis	01/12/1861	Private	
36	Strawser, Louis	08/06/1861	Private	
37	Smith, George W.	07/20/1859	Private	

Ship #	Name	Enlistment	Rank	Remarks
38	Sullivan, Daniel	10/16/1861	Private	
39	Slyne, John H.	08/29/1861	Private	
40	Slengert, Augustus	09/05/1861	Private	
41	Young, William	07/30/1859	Private	
42	McLeod, Alexander	08/16/1859	Private	
43	Burns, James	10/16/1861	Private	
44	Mullen, James	12/05/1861	Private	
45	Wood, Richard	11/23/1861	Drummer	

Notes

CHAPTER ONE NOTES

[1] Fort McClary and Fort Constitution were part of the Maine–New Hampshire defense system along the Piscataqua River. A salute was given by firing powder alone, and one gun would suffice. It is interesting to note that, though it was common practice, naval regulations forbid firing guns in salute from any ship to fort or vice versa.

[2] At the time of the Civil War, a yeoman was a staff petty officer responsible for virtually everything that came aboard as ship's stores, particularly in the boatswain's, carpenter's and sailmaker's departments. Any gunnery stores kept under his auspices were also his responsibility.

The rank has changed to an enlisted designation and today a yeoman is basically a ship's clerk, but during the war a yeoman served similarly to a present-day warrant officer.

[3] "Tricing up" meant tying a man by the thumbs and raising him up until he could only stand on tiptoe for a prescribed amount of time. Cords were also passed under the arms instead of using the thumbs. This was extremely painful and usually was done for several hours.

[4] The lowest deck of the ship, called the orlop (named for ancient times when oars were used at this level), was used, along with the open area between the fore and aft orlop decks, for storage. Large casks, shot, shell and gunpowder were kept in these areas to keep them as far below the waterline as possible. Variably one of the rooms on the orlop deck or an area just below the aft orlop deck was used for storing spirits (liquor) for medicinal use and/or personal use by the officers.

[5] The spar deck, also known as the weather deck, was the uppermost deck of the ship. Here the lines controlling the sails were made fast to rails with belaying pins along the side of the ship (pin rails) or to curving rails at the base of the masts (fife rails).

The area of the spar deck aft (to the rear) of the main mast is known as the quarterdeck. While in port the starboard side is reserved for the use of the commanding and executive officers or the officer of the deck, and the weather side is reserved while at sea. Normally considered "officers' country," the crew was usually mustered in this area for inspections and services.

[6] Usually staff petty officers would take their meals in the officers' wardroom located on the aft end of the berth deck. However, since Safford points out their nearly falling into the hold, it sounds as if they were messing in Safford's storeroom. His room was located on the forward orlop deck right next to the open area deep in the bottom of the ship known as the hold. The officers' ranks would entitle them to tables and chairs rather than the simple mess cloth of the enlisted men.

[7] Nettles, or knittles, are the halves of two adjoining yarns in a rope twisted together for pointing or grafting. They are also used for seizings or hammock clews (the woven lines on each end of a hammock).

[8] Since the captain's cabin occupies the entire aft end of the gun deck, and his cabin sits a good twenty feet or more above the waterline, the ship must have really been taking on severe water from above.

[9] "Horse" was sailor slang for any type of dried, salt-preserved meat.

[10] The USS Constellation carried forty-eight iron tanks capable of carrying twenty-eight thousand gallons of water. Due to the rust factor, it did not take long for the water to become tainted with iron oxide, which makes a reddish color.

[11] The CSS Sumter was the first Confederate warship, named for the Battle at Fort Sumter, which

opened the war with a Confederate victory on April 12, 1861. "Sumpter" is the spelling used by Safford, as was done by many of his contemporaries and even some people today but it has been corrected for the transposition of this diary.

[12] On the morning of November 1, 1755, one of the most powerful earthquakes ever recorded rocked central Portugal and western Spain.

[13] Each day the decks were hosed down and scraped to clean and whiten the wood. Sailors, usually on their knees, used rectangular stones about the size of a Bible for this sanding practice. The position of execution and the size of the stones explain the term of "holystoning."

[14] In 1860 the United States maintained 33 diplomatic posts and 282 consulates. John E. Harvey of Pennsylvania was appointed as the United States Minister Resident at Lisbon, Portugal, in 1861 and served in that post until 1869.

[15] Luis I (1838–1889) was King of Portugal from 1861 until his death in 1889.

[16] To commemorate his efforts to rebuild the city after the great earthquake of 1755, a statue was erected in the center of Commerce Square depicting King Josef I on horseback. Given the color of the equestrian statue, English sailors visiting the city dubbed this site "Black-Horse Square."

[17] "Rattling down" is a term explaining the adjustment, tarring and replacement of the shrouds or climbing ropes (called "ratlines" for the men who scurried up like a rat) that ran from the sides of the ship up to the tops of the masts. Despite the term, the lines are actually rattled *up*, that is starting at the bottom.

[18] The fighting actions Safford describes are exaggerated reports of the Battle of Shiloh on April 6 and 7, 1862. Out of approximately 65,000 Union troops and 44,000 Confederate troops engaged, the Union army suffered approximately 13,000 casualties and the Confederates approximately 10,500. This battle was the bloodiest in U.S. history until it was eclipsed by the Battle of Antietam the following September.

[19] The Escola Naval School still exists today and has a long history of Portuguese and Italian mariners who studied there.

[20] Lieutenant Commander William W. Low was the Executive Officer or second in command of the ship. Robert O. Ford was the lieutenant of marines and was responsible for all marine personnel on board. Surgeon John S. Messersmith had been in the navy since 1837 and would eventually become the medical director of the navy in 1871. Henry H. Pangborn was the purser, or paymaster, whose job was to supervise all the ship's accounts, supplies and payroll.

[21] There were numerous small engagements going on during the Peninsula Campaign of the U.S. Army of the Potomac, conducted by General George McClellan against the Confederate defenders led by General Joseph E. Johnston. It is unclear which battle Safford is referencing.

[22] Lieutenant of Marines Robert O'Neil Ford (1838–1913) was ordered to Portsmouth Navy Yard to assume command of the marine guard of the USS *Constellation* on November 18, 1861. Apparently Ford was a bit naive or ill suited for his position; Safford describes him as worthless. In his defense, the official duties of a marine officer on a ship were specific and very limited.

Little is known of Orderly Sergeant George W. Robbins (*c.* 1810–1866). As the reader progresses through this journal, he will read of many peculiarities and bizarre actions attributed to Robbins. While serving as orderly sergeant of the marine guard aboard USS *Portsmouth* in 1860, Robbins was the victim of a plot concocted by Corporal William Shuttleworth who attempted to convince one of the young marine musicians to complain to the captain that Robbins had tried to take sexual liberties with him. Instead the musician reported Shuttleworth to the captain. The corporal was court-martialed and removed from the service. Whether this was the cause or the result of imbalance on Robbins' part is not known.

[23] In the early 1850s, English hydraulic engineer William Armstrong revolutionized ordnance

design by creating a breech loading cannon that was forged not from a single piece of bored iron or steel, but from laying succeeding tubes of metal over a basic bore, relying on the heating and cooling of the process to provide strength to the composite barrel. The barrel was then rifled and the projectile was coated in lead to adhere to the grooves in the rifling.

Just prior to the Civil War, the Royal Army and the Royal Navy adopted the Armstrong system for field and naval artillery. The Armstrong gun failed to provide adequate punch against the ironclad ships that the navies of the world began constructing when the duel between the *Monitor* and the *Virginia* ushered out the age of the wooden warship. The technology of the time did not allow for construction of a breech mechanism for the gun that could withstand the large powder charges necessary to punch through armor. Nonetheless, Armstrong Guns continued in the service of the Crown into the 1890s.

[24] A standard practice in all military regulations is that officers do not fraternize with enlisted men. Had the officers been in uniform, the sergeant would never have made the offer. In fact, other than showing respect, the sergeant would have avoided any contact at all had he known their rank.

[25] Horatio J. Sprague, U.S. consul of Gibraltar, served as consular agent at Algeciras from 1855 to 1884.

[26] Singlesticks are wooden versions of cutlasses used to teach fencing movements without causing major harm to the participants. The cutlass was also called the broad sword or the saber in manuals of the time. All sailors who served guns were required to arm themselves with a waist belt carrying a pistol and cutlass. This was to have as many men as possible available in the event they would be needed to board an enemy vessel to take it by the force of small arms.

[27] The tower Safford refers to appears to be one of two churches dating from the twelfth and thirteenth centuries in the village of Porto Venere, a village on the Mediterranean coast south of Genoa.

[28] Since fresh water was always in limited supply aboard ship, it was reserved strictly for drinking and cooking purposes only. The men were required to use only salt water for cleaning and were even issued special soap that was designed for salt-water use. Only during rain showers were men sometimes given permission to enjoy the luxury to wash their clothes and themselves with rain water, since it did not diminish the ship's water supply.

[29] In the early hours of April 24, 1862, Admiral David Glasgow Farragut and his flagship, USS *Hartford*, successfully moved into the harbor area of the city of New Orleans and forced the Confederates to abandon their forts, now useless against the warships in the harbor. This gave the Union a strong foothold in taking back control of the Mississippi River.

[30] The Castel San Giorgio (St. George's Castle) is a thirteenth century fortress that overlooks the port city of La Spezia.

[31] Charles Lever (1806–1872) was one of the most successful novelists of his day. A native of Ireland, his popularity and commercial success rivaled that of Charles Dickens.

[32] Martin F. Tupper (1810–1889) was a British-born poet who was fortunate enough to have his work appreciated on a wide scale in his own lifetime. *Proverbial Philosophies* was a series of tracts published beginning in 1839 and, after a slow start, became popular reading in Britain and the United States in the 1850s. During this decade, tens of thousands of copies of this work were published in several languages. Although he had a total of thirty-nine volumes of work published between 1839 and 1876, *Proverbial Philosophies* is considered his signature piece.

The only prominent southerner to publicly attack the institution of slavery in the years immediately prior to the Civil War, Hinton Rowan Helper (1829–1909) published *The Impending Crisis of the South: How to Meet It* (1857). He attacked the institution for its exploitation of the Negro race and its effect on non-slaveholding southerners, both socially and economically. Helper's book rivaled *Uncle Tom's Cabin* for the furor it caused on both sides of the Mason-Dixon line. Although he was vehemently anti-slavery, he was not pro-black, writing three acrimoniously racist tracts advocating the deportation of blacks to Africa or Latin America.

[33] William T. Rice of Massachusetts was appointed by Abraham Lincoln to the post of U.S. consul at Spezia and served there from July 31, 1861 until 1874.

[34] In addition to making their own uniforms, sailors also made white work frocks. These pullover linen garments were of a simple pattern much like an eighteenth-century hunting shirt and allowed the men to do dirty work while sparing their good uniforms for inspections and liberty.

[35] All clothes were to be stenciled with the owner's name. This was usually done on the underside of the sailor collar on the frocks and on the waistband of the trousers. Any clothing found about the ship (marked or otherwise) was immediately taken and put into the "lucky bag." Later these clothes would be auctioned off to the crew. Of course, the original owner was responsible for his clothing and the cost of any missing items were subtracted from his pay.

[36] When iron ore was smelted in a blast furnace, the molten metal was directed into a channel called the "sow." Branch channels, or molds, hooked to the sow were called "pigs." When cooled, these somewhat rectangular blocks could be broken off the main channel and the pig iron could easily be transported to another furnace for re-melting to make products. Some of this pig iron still remains aboard the *Constellation* as ballast today.

[37] Tommaso, Prince of Savoy (1854–1931) was a member of the Italian royal family and held the title Duke of Genoa. At the time of the diary entry, he was eight years old.

[38] Safford is alluding to the fact that officers (who lived "further aft" in the rear of the ship on the berth deck in staterooms) were allowed to have liquor aboard and often abused the privilege. However, their drunkenness was usually punished by a mere confinement to quarters or a verbal reprimand as opposed to severe physical and/or financial punishments for enlisted men.

[39] Union General Nathaniel Banks was defeated by Confederate General Thomas "Stonewall" Jackson at the Battle of Winchester on May 25, 1862. This action allowed Jackson nearly full control of the Shenandoah Valley and served to build Jackson's growing reputation into legendary status.

[40] Although he never revealed the man's name, Safford related more of the story to his son Victor in later years. It seems that the deserter stole some civilian clothes belonging to Safford and was wearing them when he applied to serve as a mate of an American ship in port at Marseilles. As luck would have it, the mate was a fellow townsman of Safford and recognized the coat as one worn by Safford as an office coat in his home. Consequently, the deserter was found out and put under arrest.

[41] Federal gunboats defeated a Confederate river force in the last fleet action on the Mississippi River. Except for Vicksburg, the Mississippi River was now in Union hands. The news articles Safford mentions must be referring to General John Pope's capture of Island No. 10 and his subsequent moves against Confederate General Beauregard from the previous April, since Pope was, at that time, on his way east to command the newly created U.S. Army of Virginia.

[42] Unlike the British Navy, where benches and mess tables were suspended from the overhead for dining, American sailors spread a six-foot square painted piece of canvas on the deck called a mess cloth. The men sat upon the deck and used the cloth as a table. Thus originated the term three "square" meals a day.

CHAPTER TWO NOTES

[1] On June 17, 1862, General Braxton Bragg replaced General Pierre Gustave Toutant Beauregard as commander of the Western Department of the Confederate army. This change would allow Beauregard to recover his health after several maladies and would give Bragg a chance to show what change he could make with his new command. Bragg was never popular with his troops, being a severe disciplinarian, but the desertions that Safford suggests are more likely wishful thinking than reality.

[2] James H. Armsley of New York was appointed by President Lincoln to the post of U.S. consul at Naples on August 7, 1861. He served in that post until 1863.

[3] Every morning all hammocks were rolled lengthwise then tied with seven turns and doubled over to form a U-shape and tied again. They were then taken to the top deck and placed into the hammock rails on either side of the ship and covered with a tarp. (Pieces of cloth painted with each man's number were sewn to the hammock on the bend of the "U" to identify them.) Their placement here served to get them out of the way, give them a cursory airing and provide a small amount of protection from possible enemy fire.

[4] Newspaper accounts were probably reporting some results of what would become known as the "Seven Days Campaign," initiated by General Robert E. Lee in Virginia. After the wounding of General Joseph E. Johnston on May 31 at the Battle of Seven Pines, Lee was assigned to command the Confederate forces around Richmond. Beginning on June 25, Lee launched a series of attacks that steadily pushed McClellan's Union forces away from the Confederate capital, ending on July 1 with the Union forces at the southern end of the James peninsula. Safford's account could be for any one or a combination of these attacks.

[5] Luigi Monti of Massachusetts was appointed to the post of U.S. consul at Palermo on August 3, 1861, and served in that post until 1873.

[6] This account was false. In spite of numerous Confederate battle successes, no European promise to recognize the Confederate States of America as a sovereign nation ever came to pass.

[7] Since 1860, a civil war had been fought between the Maronite and Druse factions of Syria (which included present day Lebanon and was a part of the Ottoman Empire). Muslims had massacred Christians by the thousands and lives of many American missionaries throughout the Ottoman Empire were at risk. Commodore Thatcher was sailing for the trouble spot in order to protect American lives and interests as prescribed in his orders to show the flag.

[8] The editors were unable to identify from which of his works this passage was taken.

[9] Julius Bing of Washington, DC, was appointed by President Lincoln to the post of United States consul at Smyrna on September 30, 1861, and served in that post until 1864.

"Pasha" was a catch-all title for civil and military officers in the area now known as Turkey. Based on the diarist's description, it appears that they were meeting with the equivalent of a mayor of Smyrna or governor in the province in which Smyrna was located.

[10] Mehmet Reschid Pasha was the Turkish Governor General of the Smyrna area. One of the officers referred to was Captain Huseyin Bey, commander of the warship *Scheriff Numa*.

[11] Safford is referring to the Arabic water pipes known as hookahs. By filtering tobacco smoke through water, the smoke was greatly cooled and was more refreshing to the smoker. The air bubbles that appear in these pipes lead him to name them "hubble-bubbles."

[12] Generally, the side arms issued to the crew were .36 caliber, 1851 model Colt Navy revolvers, which fired six shots before needing reloading.

[13] Safford refers to the law abolishing the grog ration in the U.S. Navy as of September 1, 1862. Originally, every man was entitled to a ration of about one-eighth of a pint of grog daily, which was generally one part whiskey (rum in the Royal Navy) to five parts of water. In lieu of the ration a man could add five cents a day to his pay.

[14] A ladder consisting of rope rails and wooden rungs hanging from the ship's side.

[15] Jeremiah Augustus Johnson of Rhode Island was appointed to the post of United States consul at Beirut by President Buchanan on April 14, 1858.

[16] The abolition of the grog ration.

[17] On September 17, 1862 Union forces led by General George B. McClellan met Robert E. Lee's Confederate army along Antietam Creek near the Maryland town of Sharpsburg. Despite luck

at discovering the disposition of Lee's army prior to the fight, McClellan could not coordinate his assaults on the Confederate line and the battle broke down into three separate assaults, with Lee successfully countering each one. By dark, the U.S. had witnessed its bloodiest day in military history with more than 23,000 casualties strewn about the area. McClellan would remain commander until November, when he was replaced by Lincoln with General Ambrose P. Burnside. General Pope, who was defeated at Second Manassas the previous August, was transferred.

[18] This referral is in error and Fredericksburg, Virginia, was mistakenly identified by the foreign papers in place of the correct Frederick, Maryland.

[19] According to navy regulations, the rights of the accused are quite similar to the civilian courts as protected by the U.S. Constitution. The accused has the right to counsel, to face his accuser(s), to witnesses on his behalf and to cross-examine witnesses against him.

[20] Charleton H. Morgan of Kentucky was appointed to serve as United States consul at Messina by President Buchanan on September 21, 1859, and served until 1867.

[21] In later years Safford discovered that a woman who ran his hometown post office was intercepting his mail. It seems that this woman, who was older than Safford, held ideas of marriage toward him and felt that her scheme could work if she withheld his letters to his true sweetheart. Thus, many of his letters were destroyed or otherwise failed to reach their destination.

[22] A search of military records reveals no account of Edward Safford serving in the military at all. He was registered as a master's mate on a fishing vessel. However, his life was still in peril since civilian vessels at sea were at risk of capture or sinking by any enemy vessel that overtook them.

[23] Although minor skirmishing was taking place in the area around Centerville, Virginia, there was no such battle as Safford describes and again he was the victim of false newspaper accounts.

[24] On May 30, 1862, Corinth, Mississippi, fell to Union General Halleck after he had maneuvered Confederate General Beauregard into retreating. On October 3, building on seeming Confederate success in the East, Confederate Generals Earl Van Dorn and Sterling Price led their armies against the Union forces under General William Rosecrans. They failed to take the city and only succeeded in relieving pressure to other Confederate armies in Kentucky and Tennessee. The Union suffered 2,520 casualties and the Confederates 4,233.

[25] These are still more erroneous reports. General Breckenridge did not surrender and General Jackson still had six more months of life left to vex the Union Armies.

[26] The wooden cruisers CSS *Alabama* and CSS *Florida* were both loose at this time and preying on Union shipping. However, neither of these ships was an ironclad. Both were seeking out merchant ships and avoiding vessels of war.

[27] Another false report.

[28] This is yet another falsehood of the press. Lee was in Virginia, at the time threatened only by weak reconnaissance raids ordered by General McClellan.

[29] On October 8, 1862, the Battle of Perryville was fought along Chaplin Hills in Kentucky. Confederate General Bragg led his army of about sixteen thousand men against the defending thirty-seven thousand Union troops led by General Don Carlos Buell. Bragg achieved some success but realized that Buell's entire army was not engaged in the fight. Fearing he would be overwhelmed, he pulled back voluntarily to the anger of his troops and gave up whatever chance he might have had to continue his success. Buell allowed the Confederates to retreat unmolested. This inaction would eventually lead to Buell's replacement by Rosecrans.

[30] Raphael Semmes (1809–1877) was the most prominent naval officer of the Confederacy. He spent the years 1835–37 aboard the frigate *Constellation*. Later he moved up the ranks, becoming a commander before war caused him to resign his commission to cast his lot with the South. He became the commander of the very successful CSS *Sumter* and captained her to her great fame as

a Confederate raider. Later he was the first and only commander of the famous Confederate raider, CSS *Alabama*.

[31] On October 30, Napoleon III of France made overtures to Great Britain and Russia to put together a cooperative effort to mediate the war. However, no recognition was given to the Confederacy as a nation.

[32] Safford's reaction at this false report shows the disdain felt by the servicemen in regard to politics and the military. Politically-appointed General John Charles Fremont had resigned the previous June. In spite of lobbying efforts in behalf of this army explorer and former presidential candidate, Lincoln refused to reinstate the general.

[33] General Ambrose E. Burnside, who had replaced General McClellan in November 1862, moved his army on a new assault toward Richmond by moving his army rapidly to the Rappahannock River near the town of Fredericksburg, Virginia. Only a few thousand Confederates defended the town against close to 115,000 Federal soldiers. However, blunders caused the delay of bridging equipment and Burnside's army was stuck in place. Lee quickly moved troops to the town until he had nearly 78,000 building strong defensive positions on the high ground behind the city. A two-pronged assault was launched against the Confederate forces. By the end of the day on December 13, 1862, the Union forces had lost 13,000 soldiers and the Confederates 5,300. Fortunately for the Union army, Burnside was dissuaded from renewing the assault the next day and instead retreated his army through the town they had briefly held and recrossed the Rappahannock.

[34] Manning P. Waldron served in the 27th Maine Volunteer Infantry Regiment, which was mustered in for nine months service. He died of natural causes on December 3, 1862 in the regiment's camp on the site of what is now Arlington National Cemetery and Fort Myer, Virginia. Soldiers in the 27th who died in the service were embalmed and sent home financed by a subscription run by the men of the regiment. Waldron was interred in the First Baptist Church Cemetery in Kittery Point in a plot next to the Safford family lot where the diarist would join him in 1914.

[35] Mark Fenald Wentworth (1820–1897) and Moses Safford were next-door neighbors on what is now Wentworth Street in Kittery for many years after the war. Trained as a medical doctor, Wentworth organized the Kittery Artillery Company, Maine Militia and was appointed captain in 1854. The Kittery Artillery was called up to garrison Fort McClary at the outbreak of the war. An active recruiter, Wentworth was commissioned lieutenant colonel of the 27th Maine Volunteer Infantry (a nine months' regiment) on October 27, 1862, and was promoted to colonel on February 11, 1863. After voluntarily extending their service in the Washington defenses due to Lee's invasion, the regiment returned to Maine and mustered out in late July.

[36] Finally Safford receives a correct report as Burnside had, indeed, retreated across the Rappahannock. However, Lincoln had no love for McClellan and he would never be recalled.

CHAPTER THREE NOTES

[1] Due to the large number of crew aboard, there was not enough room for a full watch to sleep on the berth deck. Consequently hooks for hammocks were provided on the gun deck as well to accommodate those who did not fit on the berth deck.

[2] It is interesting to note that the casualty rates as reported by newspapers were initially low but grew as more accurate reports arrived. It is generally accepted that Burnside suffered about 13,000 casualties at Fredericksburg.

[3] A master-at-arms was a petty officer in charge of the ship's security. He functioned much as a police officer and handled all trouble-makers with his assistant, the ship's corporal. He was also considered to be the highest-ranking petty officer aboard.

[4] On December 29, 1862 the *Monitor* was towed by USS *Rhode Island* out of Hampton Roads,

Virginia to help in the attack on the forts along the Cape Fear River protecting the city of Wilmington, North Carolina. It was hoped that the *Monitor's* shallow draft would allow her to maneuver the shallow river in winter to get behind the forts. She ran into a storm on December 30, and by evening signaled for help and rescue operations were initiated. All but sixteen of her crew of sixty-two men were saved. The ship was lost on December 31, 1862.

[5] The Emancipation Proclamation declared that all slaves held then "in states in rebellion" were free. Those slaves residing in the four border states of Maryland, Delaware, Kentucky and Missouri were still legally in bondage. Lincoln excepted these four states for fear that freeing all the slaves might yet cause the desertion of these states to the Confederacy. Relatively few men in the Union army resigned in protest of this proclamation.

[6] This false report probably originated from the various efforts that were being made by Commanding General Grant, assisted by General Sherman, to take this Confederate fortress. At the time this report was received, Grant was trying to dig a canal to get at the city from another direction. This effort would fail as other past efforts had.

[7] The Battle of Murfreesboro, Tennessee, or Stones River, took place from December 31 to January 2.

General Bragg's Confederate forces managed to nearly rout Union General Rosecrans' troops when he struck on the thirty-first. Yet, the men in blue put up a dogged defense and managed to hold their own against repeated assaults. Eventually, Bragg decided to pull his men back to Shelbyville and Rosecrans elected not to pursue. Out of 41,400 Federal troops engaged, 12,906 were lost, compared to the Confederates', loss of 11,739 out of 34,739 engaged.

[8] Salted meat was kept in a huge barrel called a "harness cask." This term lent itself to the naming of salted meat as "salt horse."

[9] When the cook boiled meat, the top of the kettle would fill with the froth arising from the fat in the meat. This froth called slush was skimmed off of the water and put aside for sale to the crew. The sailors thought of this fatty, salty and slimy substance a luxury to spread on bread in lieu of butter (which was usually rancid). The money earned through these sales was used to support financial needs of the crew and was commonly called the "slush fund."

[10] "Scouse" is a name for sailor's hash, a much-desired meal. This punishment was designed to deny the means for making their favorite dish.

[11] Breechings are the thick lines or ropes that secure the gun to the walls of the ship. They are secured to the bulwarks (walls) of the ship then pass through a bracket on either side of the gun and through an open slot at the very back (breech) of the gun. These lines allow the recoil of the gun to be checked upon firing. Without such lines, the guns would recoil across the deck, which would cause severe damage and possible bodily injury.

[12] On January 11, 1863, U.S. Naval forces led by Admiral David Dixon Porter bombarded Fort Hindman in Arkansas. After several hours, the Confederate fort surrendered.

[13] Kate B. was Catherine C. Bellamy (1830–1907), whom Safford married in 1866.

[14] Safford was correct. USS *Brooklyn* survived to later participate in the taking of Mobile Bay, Alabama, in 1864.

[15] Edwin Harrison Miller was only a mate at the time but was acting in the role of a lieutenant. He did not attain this rank officially until December 1868. Thanks to descendants of Miller, the USS *Constellation* Museum now holds copies of the Civil War photographs taken of several of the crew in Italy.

[16] George P. Marsh of Vermont served as the United States Envoy Extraordinary and Minister Plenipotentiary at Turin from 1861 to 1862. The legation was relocated to Florence in 1865. David H. Wheeler of Iowa was appointed U.S. consul at Genoa on July 31, 1861, and served until 1866.

[17] Great Britain used any number of ruses to construct ships that were later sold to the Confederacy.

After the war, the "*Alabama* Claims" were settled in court with Great Britain making some restitution for the damage caused by *Alabama*, *Florida* and *Shenandoah*, all of which were built in Britain. Damage claims by other vessels manufactured in England were dropped.

[18] Thatcher need not have worried. The English were not building ironclads for the Mediterranean, nor were there any existing that could weather the Atlantic Ocean.

[19] On the evening of February 24, 1863, the USS *Indianola* was attacked by four Confederate vessels on the Mississippi River, including the recently captured *Queen of the West*. After being rammed at least seven times, and with his ship partially sunk, Lieutenant Commander George Brown surrendered. The Confederates spent the next day successfully raising *Indianola* to refit her as a Confederate vessel. On the night of February 26, a dark shape floated down the river and *Queen of the West* steamed away in fear while notifying *Indianola* of the danger. The Confederates sunk the ship rather than have her return to Union hands and fled. Later it was learned that the vessel was nothing more than an old coal barge the Union had rigged to look like an ironclad and had set forth as a joke.

[20] The *Constellation* carried sixteen eight-inch shell guns aboard. These are so named since they fire a fifty-two pound cast-iron ball that is eight inches in diameter. Each shell has a hollowed out chamber to carry a 1.84-pound charge of black powder. A wooden fuse is inserted through a hole in the ball and is designed so that it may be pierced to expose powder that is measured in calculated increments for detonation down range, usually at hundred-yard intervals. The fuse is preset and its lead covering is removed prior to it being placed in the barrel of the cannon. The initial ignition in the chamber burns the powder, which in turn lights the fuse. The fuse then burns down to the central powder charge in the ball while in flight. Ideally, the shell will hit or pierce the enemy vessel and the internal charge will then explode within the enemy vessel. For reasons unknown, *Constellation*'s fuses were not working properly and they were getting a near instantaneous explosion of the shell shortly after it left the gun. Thus, the crew was quite rattled and untrusting of their guns, which is not a good morale factor on a ship of war expecting to see action.

[21] On March 14, 1863, Admiral Farragut in the USS *Hartford* led his squadron of ships up the Mississippi to attempt to get north of Fort Hudson. The *Hartford* and *Albatross* made it through, but the rest of the fleet did not. USS *Mississippi* ran aground and suffered such severe fire that she was set on fire by her crew and abandoned, and subsequently she exploded.

[22] Safford gives no specifics on what he considered to be gains. At the time, Confederate cavalry was quite active in small skirmish actions in Kentucky, led by Confederate Generals John Hunt Morgan and Joseph Wheeler. However, their tactics were mostly hit-and-run, so no significant ground was taken.

[23] The church that Safford describes is the Church of Santa Maria. The organ contains three thousand pipes and was constructed in 1810. It exists to this day and is a tourist destination in Mao.

[24] H.B. Robinson of Pennsylvania was appointed American consul at Port Mahon on February 2, 1862 and served until 1869.

[25] On April 7, 1863, U.S. Admiral Samuel DuPont led his fleet into attack against Forts Moultrie and Sumter in Charleston Harbor. Although the forts were damaged considerably, their firepower far exceeded that of the Federal vessels and DuPont withdrew from this unsuccessful venture. He suffered five ships disabled and the following morning the ironclad USS *Keokuk* sank. Safford was wrong about the captures of *Alabama* and *Florida*, as they were both still very much active against Federal shipping.

[26] Inspection of the men was done by having each man walk from the ranks assembled on the aft spar deck past the inspecting officer. The man would hold his hat in his hands in front of him, walk down the deck, pass around the capstan and then return to his place in line. In this manner the officers

could observe the appearance of his uniform, his general state of health and his cleanliness. Most sailors dreaded this long lonely walk, with fears that some infraction might be found that could lead to punishment or loss of pay. Certainly, in the condition Safford describes these men after coming off liberty, such fears were far from groundless.

[27] Previously, on February 25, 1863, the British merchant ship *Peterhof* was seized by the USS *Vanderbilt* on the pretext that she was a blockade runner trying to get goods into the Confederacy via Mexico. The orders to the *Vanderbilt* were issued from Acting Rear Admiral Charles Wilkes aboard his flagship, USS *Wachusetts*, who had formerly won notoriety by seizing the British ship *Trent* on November 8, 1861. This seizure allowed Wilkes to be lauded by the United States, but denounced by the British and nearly caused the British to enter into war.

The British now demanded that *Peterhof* be returned. An international crisis was again narrowly avoided when U.S. courts ruled that U.S. ships had no right to stop any vessel going into a neutral port regardless of the ultimate destination of its cargo.

[28] Charles Whipple Pickering (1815–1888) was the captain of USS *Kearsarge* until he was relieved on April 8, 1863. Contrary to Safford's report, Pickering was a loyal Unionist and continued his U.S. service. He would later be the unfortunate captain of USS *Housatonic* during its attack and sinking by the Confederate submarine CSS *Hunley* in 1864.

[29] Safford was quite misinformed; not only was Port Hudson still not taken, but Vicksburg remained strongly in Confederate hands. Combined naval operations on the river by Admirals Porter and Farragut were being augmented by the army's success under the leadership of Ulysses S. Grant. However, the gains were slow and costly despite there being definite progress on the Union side.

[30] From Safford's account, the anchors were not properly hooked or "set" into a firm hold on the ocean floor. Consequently, the men had to use the ship's boats to tow or to "kedge" the anchor. This entails hauling the anchor with the ship's boats and then dropping it and pulling the line to the ship to drag the ship to the anchorage. This is an extremely demanding physical feat on the part of the crew. Despite the light remarks made by Safford, it appears the ship was in serious trouble and nearly lost. This dangerous situation makes the inebriation of the ship's officers all the more deplorable.

[31] Men who were found guilty of crimes aboard ship were listed for punishment duty. Since such crimes were permanently listed in the logbook in black ink, the list soon achieved the slang term "black list."

[32] Ships coming to join a squadron would pick up the mail from port for distribution to other ships known to be on station. When headed back to port the ships would, in turn, pick up mail from the stationed ships to send back to the states. Surprisingly, this method was quite reliable and fairly timely. Safford's accounts of home are received approximately ten days after their happening.

[33] U.S. General Joseph Hooker replaced Burnside as commander of the Army of the Potomac on January 25, 1863. Hooker did a masterful job of reorganizing the army and his troops were renewed in their hopes of finally gaining a general who could lead them to victory.

[34] Generally the men wore blue uniforms from October to May and switched to whites for the summer months. However, the uniform of the day was actually dictated by the captain. A square piece of tin was erected on the berth deck each morning with a rough drawing of a sailor. The color scheme depicted was the uniform the men were to wear that day. It could be a mixture of whites and blues, tops or bottoms. The uniform for inspection was always blues.

[35] Hooker had moved his army into Virginia and was pressing Lee's Army of Northern Virginia. Hooker sent a force to attack and take Fredericksburg while he moved the rest of his army to take on Lee. Lee assigned General Jubal Early to hold at Fredericksburg while he decided to meet Hooker head on, despite being greatly outnumbered (115,000 Union troops to 60,000 Confederate). Lee daringly held Hooker's army with just two divisions while Stonewall Jackson marched the rest of the

army west to strike the Federals on their right flank. After consuming most of the day of May 2 in marching, Jackson's men attacked just two hours before dusk and began rolling up the Union army's flank. Learning that the Federals had taken Fredericksburg and now threatened his rear, Lee was forced to send a force to cordon off these Union troops at Salem Church. When Lee redirected his attention to Chancellorsville, he learned that Hooker had withdrawn his army across the Rappahannock. The Confederates suffered nearly 14,000 casualties to the Union's 17,000.

[36] Commodore Edward Preble (1761–1807) was an American Revolutionary War hero who continued his service to the United States with distinction. He is credited with creating much of the fighting tradition of the U.S. Navy, and particularly for his influence on future naval heroes Stephen Decatur, William Bainbridge, Isaac Hull and David Porter who became affectionately known as "Preble's Boys."

[37] Hooker and Lee had both their armies in defensive positions in and around Fredericksburg; Lee was planning a second invasion of the North and had no ideas of retreat to Richmond.

The horror of men burning in underbrush is true and comes from the fighting at Chancellorsville where the wooded areas were known as "the wilderness." However, this horror would be repeated and become more publicly known the following year when both armies would meet again in this deadly wood.

[38] Two corps of Grant's army, led by Generals James B. McPherson and William T. Sherman, attacked the two Confederate brigades left behind by the retreating Confederate General Joseph Johnston at Jackson, Mississippi, on May 14. Fighting in a terrific rainstorm, the Union forces soon gained control of the city.

[39] Any group of men sharing mealtime duties as a group were called a mess. Usually these groups would contain from six to sixteen men. One or more men from each mess would take mess duties for a set period of time, usually a month. It was their job to secure all mess equipment for each meal, set it out and clean up afterward. They would go to the cook to select their meat and/or vegetable rations both before and after the cooking process. It was also their duty to use the mess funds contributed by each member to buy the necessary condiments and extras to round out their meals.

Safford's mess only included Glenn, the master-at-arms; Cox, the paymaster's steward (later called the paymaster's yeoman); Smith, at that time called the surgeon's steward (now the position of a warrant officer with the designation of pharmacist); and himself.

[40] Although dispatches from Commodore Thatcher (and later Captain Stellwagen) both refer to Page as the commander of the ship CSS *Southerner*, Commander Thomas Jefferson Page (1808–1899) never captained such vessel. Page, who resigned from the U.S. Navy in April 1861, to join the Confederacy, was sent to Europe to command the Confederate-purchased ironclad ram CSS *Stonewall* in January 1865.

Chapter Four Notes

[1] Surprisingly, Safford's news is fairly timely although still an exaggeration. Lee's Army of Northern Virginia had invaded the North in late June, but with about half as many troops as granted him by Safford. This invasion was to culminate in the famous battle of Gettysburg, which was beginning the very day Safford made this entry.

[2] Quite to the contrary, Lee was involved on that day in making a desperate assault on the Union lines in what would go down in history as "Pickett's Charge," named in honor of Confederate General George Pickett, the division commander in charge of the assault. This attack failed and gave the Union a victory, which finally seemed to turn the tide of war against the Confederacy.

[3] Safford's musings are quite poetic and ironic in light of the fact that American casualties—North and South—were indeed at that moment lying about the fields of Gettysburg hoping for aid. Estimates

of casualties run to 53,000 for this three-day battle, which ended in the evening of July 3, 1863.

[4] If Safford is quoting Thatcher correctly, it seems the commodore forgot his command of the store ship *Relief* from 1852 to 1854 as well as his command of the sloop-of-war *Decatur* from 1857 to 1859.

[5] Harpers Ferry was threatened by Lee's army but bypassed in their move north.

[6] Safford was unaware that U.S. General Joseph Hooker had been replaced shortly before the Battle of Gettysburg by General George Gordon Meade. He also did not know that Vicksburg had fallen to Union forces on July 4, 1863. His referral is to Confederate General Joseph E. Johnston, who failed to re-enforce Vicksburg prior to its fall. General James Ewell Brown "Jeb" Stuart, in charge of Lee's cavalry force, had indeed been defeated on the third day of the Gettysburg battle, signaling the end of the dominance of Confederate cavalry in the war.

[7] Safford was incorrect; the correct location was Frederick City, Maryland.

[8] For a change, this report is fairly correct.

[9] Lieutenant Commander Trevett Abbot had been in the navy since his commission as a midshipman in 1848. He had attained his rank as lieutenant commander on July 16, 1862, and became a commander in 1867. His career ended when he died of yellow fever on October 27, 1869, and was buried at sea.

[10] Once again Safford indicates that the naval regulations were not followed to the letter. According the naval regulations, "Cheers shall never be given as a compliment to any officer, or man, on joining a vessel of the Navy, or while attached to or being detached from her," yet Safford remarks that cheering was commonly done to acknowledge the crews' devotion to departing officers.

[11] A diligent search for such a vessel has, to date, been met with futility. There is a report that a wooden ship built with an iron frame was built in England with the idea to turn it over to the Confederates, but no confirmation has been found. There is a chance that the exploits of the CSS *Alabama* were being credited to this mystery vessel, but this is conjecture on the part of the editors.

[12] Once again, the news reports are grossly exaggerated. Confederate General James Longstreet went through the Gettysburg campaign unharmed and the numbers of captured artillery Safford gives are far too high. Confederate President Jefferson Davis never left Richmond during this campaign.

[13] When the act was put into effect on July 11, 1863, the first names for the draft were drawn in New York City. Now that anyone could be taken into the army, dissention grew, particularly with the feeling that newly freed blacks would be able to compete with immigrants for jobs. A massive riot broke out as rage at the government turned to prejudicial hatred for blacks. Eleven blacks, eight soldiers, two policemen and eighty-four rioters were killed, and approximately $1.5 million dollars of property damage was done.

[14] George W. Van Horn of Iowa was appointed U.S. consul at Marseilles on March 27, 1861, and served in that post until 1865.

[15] John Albro Little of Massachusetts was appointed U.S. consul at Barcelona on June 21, 1861, and served at that post until 1868.

[16] In order to take the city of Charleston, Federal troops landed on the southern end of Morris Island with the intention of taking Fort (Battery) Wagner on July 10. The next day a Federal assault on the fort was repulsed by heavy fire. On July 18, a second assault would attempt to take the fort, this time led by the gallant 54th Massachusetts, a black regiment.

[17] Safford's son, Victor, referred to this illness as Mediterranean fever, which was a common disability among soldiers in British garrisons throughout the Mediterranean. In the late 1880s its cause was found to be bacteria from goat's milk. Now known as brucellosis, or undulant fever, it can lead to heart failure and Safford was lucky to have pulled through. Today, antibiotics easily cure the malady.

[18] Amos Perry from Rhode Island, at that time was the U.S. minister at Tunis where he served from 1862 until 1867. However, Gustavus Koerner of Illinois was appointed by President Lincoln to the

post of Envoy Extraordinary and Minister Plenipotentiary at Madrid, Spain in August 1862 and served in that post until July 1864. Therefore, Perry must have been visiting Koerner and, consequently, *Constellation*.

[19] George Kent of Maine was appointed to the post of U.S. consul at Valencia on December 16, 1861, and served at that post until 1866.

[20] Since getting through the Federal blockade from Mobile, Alabama, on January 16, 1863, the CSS *Florida* had captured twenty-two prizes. John Newland Maffitt was her captain.

[21] This diary entry became extremely valuable to the restoration of the ship done in 1996. The only known existent images of the ship prior to 1870 were paintings done by Italian painter Thomaso de Simone in Naples in 1856. An examination of the paintings revealed no evidence of portholes and it was believed that these may have been added to the ship after the Civil War period. However, Safford's diary specifically mentions the ports several times and thus they were added to the present restoration of the ship.

[22] Realizing that assault by Federal infantry would overcome the garrison, General Beauregard ordered both Forts Wagner and Gregg to be abandoned. On September 6, the Confederate troops left the forts but Sumter and Charleston still held.

[23] Despite his good spelling and attention to detail, Safford is notorious for inaccuracies in names of people, ships and places. There never was such a ship in the U.S. Navy known as the *Aurora*. Instead, Low was sent to the *Octorara* (named for a creek in Pennsylvania after the Indian word for "running water").

[24] It is possible that Safford is referring to the British merchant ship *Juno*, which the *Kearsarge* engaged and searched. However, no contraband could be found on the suspicious ship and she was let go much to the regret of the U.S. sailors who had to endure the British sailors singing "Dixie."

[25] During the siege of Fort Wagner, the USS *Catskill* had been struck no less than sixty times. Captain George W. Rodgers was killed as Safford describes.

[26] This report is in error, since Fort Sumter and Charleston did not fall until February 1865.

[27] General Burnside was actively on campaign in charge of the Department of the Ohio. Here he would succeed in capturing Confederate cavalryman John Hunt Morgan and some of his men. Meanwhile General William B. Franklin, who had failed Burnside at Fredericksburg by not being aggressive, was active with Nathaniel Banks in the Red River campaign in Texas.

[28] As liberal as he appears in his accounts, it seems that Safford had a streak of prejudice when it came to Jews. It is also possible that he was a victim of a commonly accepted stereotype of the time, which associated all Jews with being stingy or dishonest in regard to monetary affairs.

[29] Safford was suffering from a very painful leg ulcer that had to be treated with laceration. One cause of such an ulcer is reduced mobility, which allows inadequate functioning of the calf muscle pump. It is possible that Safford was a victim of too much clerical work and lack of exercise. In any case, he was lucky that the surgery was successful.

[30] State Department records show no one by the name of Davidson serving at Spezia in 1863.

[31] George Harrington was the assistant secretary of the treasury until he was replaced by J. F. Hartley in 1865.

[32] The name Herman is incorrect, since it should be Heenan. As a sport, boxing experienced a growth of popularity in the 1840s and 1850s in America and Europe (predominantly Ireland and Britain). By the end of the 1850s, John Camel "Benicia Boy" Heenan, an Irish immigrant and resident of New York, rose to be the undisputed king of American boxing. Lacking serious competition at home, he traveled to England in search of new challengers, and arrived in England in 1860. Tom King, who learned to fight while serving in the Royal Navy, was the top man in the British boxing world. The two met in a contest held on December 8, 1863. After twenty-four rounds of a bloody contest,

King knocked out Heenan and claimed the title.

[33] Chattanooga, Tennessee, had become a refuge for Rosecrans' army after its defeat by Confederate General Bragg in September 1863. Bragg managed to control the surrounding hills and cut off the Union army's supply lines. When Rosecrans could not extricate himself from this situation, Ulysses Grant was put in charge. He managed to get a thin line of supply going and then ordered assaults on the Confederate positions. The Confederate army was pushed out of what appeared to be an impregnable position and General Bragg was relieved of his command.

[34] Safford is correct in his mistrust of the papers. Longstreet was on his way back to rejoin Lee and the Army of Northern Virginia. Confederate General John C. Breckenridge was also well and would soon become part of Jefferson Davis's cabinet. Both men would survive the war.

CHAPTER FIVE NOTES

[1] There are two possibilities for a Commodore Bell. One was Commodore Charles Heyer Bell (1798–1875), who happened to be the first captain of USS *Constellation* from 1855 to 1858. He became an acting rear admiral in July 1862 and was on the retired list as a rear admiral as of July 1866. However, more than likely the painting was of Commodore Henry Haywood Bell (1790?–1867), who had more combat experience and was fleet-captain of the Western Gulf Squadron during the taking of New Orleans.

Commodore Uriah Phillips Levy (1792–1862), one of the few Jewish members of the navy, led the fight for better working conditions for sailors, especially the abolishment of flogging. He was later instrumental in preserving Thomas Jefferson's home of Monticello. Commodore Elie A.F. La Valette (1790–1862) commanded USS *Congress* during the Mexican War and later, at various times, the Atlantic and African squadrons. He was also one of the first admirals appointed by President Lincoln.

[2] Charleston was under siege but still holding out against the Union attacks. CSS *Florida* managed to escape to sea despite the watchful eye of the USS *Kearsarge* when she slipped out of Brest, France, on February 10, after being laid up since August. *Florida* was now under command of First Lieutenant Charles W. Morris and very much afloat.

[3] Jusepe, José, or Giuseppe Ribera (1590–1652) was a Spanish baroque painter who studied in Valencia and Rome but who settled in then Spanish-possessed Naples. He achieved great popularity under the nickname of "Lo Spagnoletto" (little Spaniard).

[4] Acting Ensign William Brown had received his commission "without pay" on August 28, 1863. This system of giving a promotion in rank without the accompanying raise in pay is probably one of the reasons why his career was so short. He resigned from the service on June 16, 1865, with no further promotions.

[5] On February 1, 1864, Prussia and Austria declared war on Denmark. After only four days, Danish troops succumbed to enemy superiority. By October 30, 1864, Denmark was forced to sign a peace treaty giving up not only Holstein, but also Lauenborg and Schleswig or about one third of her territory.

[6] The holiday being celebrated was the birthday of King Willem III of the Netherlands, who was born on February 19, 1817. He became king in 1849 and would reign until his death on November 23, 1890.

[7] Charleston remained in Confederate hands and only minor Federal probes had been made at Mobile, Alabama.

[8] "Jimmy Legs" is a slang term for the master-at-arms. "Ironing" means putting handcuffs or restraining irons on malefactors.

[9] George G. Fogg of New Hampshire was appointed by President Lincoln to serve as U.S. minister to Switzerland in 1861 and he served at that post until 1865.

[10] Rush R. Wallace may have gone to the USS *Shenandoah*, but she was commanded by Captain Daniel B. Ridgely. *Shenandoah* was one of the many screw steamers in search of CSS *Florida*.

[11] Eugene B. Mallett was the navigation officer or master of the *Constellation*. He was from Maine, a Bath shipmaster and lifelong friend of the diarist.

[12] At the time the Pope was Blessed Pius IX (1846–1878) and very much alive.

[13] Once again Safford is the victim of a false report. Mobile would not fall until August.

[14] Safford is probably misinterpreting the change in the conscription laws. As of March 14, 1864, the navy and Marine Corps would finally receive conscripts. Formerly, only the army benefited from the draft and seamen were not counted in fulfilling a state's quota. Soldiers were induced to serve naval forces, particularly the riverine squadrons, throughout the war, but the army was never deliberately depleted to fill naval positions.

[15] Whenever the captain was received aboard during hours the colors were displayed; he was to receive honors by being piped aboard with a receiving line. However, at night he was to be met by a party of men carrying at least two lanterns to guide him to the officer of the deck for reception aboard. It was the duty of the sentinel to warn the officer of the deck of the approach of any officers of high rank well in advance so that proper reception could be made.

[16] Filibustering, or irregular efforts to capture territory through private military means, was quite popular during the 1850s. William Walker (1824–1860) was one American seeking to expand the land mass of the United States who made early efforts to secure lower California by leading a group of followers to establish the Republic of Senora. The combined failures of logistics, finances and loyal support led to failure in this enterprise. After several more failed expeditions into Central America, his men deserted him and he turned himself in to a British naval vessel. He was tried and shot on September 12, 1860.

[17] Makonite is most likely a misspelling of Maronite, which is a Lebanese Christian.

[18] Caught in a Confederate attack at Pleasant Hill, Banks' troops managed to turn the tide of battle and staged a counterattack. General Richard Taylor, commander of the Confederate forces, ordered a general withdrawal. Though having a clear victory, Banks also ordered a retreat to try to rejoin Admiral Porter's gunboats that were trying to support the Federal land invasion. Low water defeated Porter's attempts and both forces abandoned the operation as they worked desperately to extract themselves from this disastrous Red River campaign.

[19] State Department records do not list anyone holding the post of vice consul at Tunis in 1864. Amos Perry from Rhode Island was appointed U.S. consul at Tunis in 1862 and he served in that post until 1867.

[20] The Knights of the Order of St. John of Jerusalem (later Knights of Malta) was established in 1085 at the Hospital of St. John in Jerusalem as an order of monks attending the sick. Eventually they became a military order to defend crusader-held territory in the Holy Lands and to guard routes taken by religious pilgrims.

[21] The Turkish flag was flying over Egyptian land because the Mamelukes of Syria and Egypt were beaten by the Turks under Chaldiran in 1516—1517.

[22] Cleopatra's Needle was presented to the British by Mahommed Ali, Viceroy of Egypt in 1819, as a memorial to countrymen Nelson and Abercromby. It is quite likely that Moses Safford followed newspaper accounts of this engineering feat as closely as he had events transpiring at home during his time overseas.

[23] The United States did not post a consul to Jaffa during the Civil War period. It is likely that the person referred to by Safford is a local citizen retained by the U.S. government to tend to its interests in that city.

[24] Surgeon Messersmith was nearly fifty-five years of age at that time.

[25] According to State Department records, Albert Rhodes of Pennsylvania served as U.S. consul at Jerusalem from September 1863 to 1866. Lazarus S. Murad, whom Safford meets, appears to have been acting in an unofficial capacity for the consulate, as he was not appointed to the post of vice consul until May 13, 1865.

[26] A chibouque, or chibouk, is a long-stemmed Turkish pipe with a clay bowl.

CHAPTER SIX NOTES

[1] Lieutenant General Ulysses S. Grant elected to travel with the Army of the Potomac to pursue and destroy Lee's Army of Northern Virginia while General Sherman moved on to take Atlanta. The Army of the Potomac suffered tremendous casualties but rather than retreat as in the past, Grant moved the army steadily east and south to attack again and again. Lee's army was steadily rocked from one defensive position to another and by mid-June, Grant had sidled around Lee and was now attacking from the south at Petersburg.

[2] After nearly two years of raiding U.S. commerce, the raider CSS *Alabama* arrived at Cherbourg, France, and was granted permission to dock for a much-needed overhaul. Three days later USS *Kearsarge* arrived and patrolled the outer harbor waiting for the Confederate vessel to emerge. After repeated messages daring *Alabama* to come out and fight, Captain Raphael Semmes finally agreed and on June 19, 1864, the Confederate ship met the challenge. After nearly an hour of exchanging shots, despite *Alabama's* superior number fired, Union gunnery proved the more accurate and bested the Confederates as *Alabama* was reduced to a floating wreck.

[3] At this time, CSS *Florida* had lost her former captain, John N. Maffitt, due to illness and was now captained by Charles M. Morris. Although the ship was in need of extensive repairs and overhauling, she had resumed her raiding career quite successfully. Any number of ships could have been part of the encounter that Safford mentions.

[4] During a Turkish occupation of Greece the Parthenon was used as an ammunition dump. In 1687 the ammunition blew up, causing extensive damage to the building.

[5] Seventeen-year-old Prince William of Denmark (1845–1913) was endorsed as king by the English and accepted by the Greeks, since British influence would ensure the return of the Ionian Islands.

[6] Since the Austrians had recently been forced to cede territory and control through recent wars that led to Italian unity, and the wars were supported by the efforts of Italian patriots such as Garibaldi, the ship's band playing the Garibaldi March would have been received by them as an absolute insult.

[7] The *Constellation's* log indicates only that the ship's boy was put in the brig for "making a noise." The diary adds to the ship's entry, as one discovers that the boy was overcome with a religious hysteria—that he was "possessed." Efforts to calm the boy were in vain and he had to be removed from the ship in a straitjacket.

[8] The Republican convention was actually held in Baltimore on June 7 and 8. The Democratic Party held their convention in Chicago on August 29.

[9] At this time Confederate General Jubal Early was moving his army through the Shenandoah Valley and he would eventually threaten Washington, DC.

[10] Henry M. Canfield of Connecticut was appointed U.S. consul at Athens in January 1863. His offices were moved to Piraeus as of July 1, 1864. He served at this post until 1867.

[11] Grant had moved troops north of the James River to bring pressure upon Lee's defenses but Petersburg was far from falling. On July 30, after a long tunneling operation by Pennsylvania coal miners, the Union set off an explosion, creating a huge crater in the Confederate trench lines. The explosion was followed by an attack of Union troops to attempt to break through the trench lines. However, confusion reigned in the northern ranks and the Confederates rapidly rallied. Firing directly into approximately 15,000 Union invaders in the crater, the Confederates soon drove their enemy

back. The Union suffered about 4,000 casualties to the Confederates' 1,500.

[12] The rubber coats referred to were privately purchased by the officers and quite appropriate for men who merely stood on the quarterdeck to supervise the actions related to the sailing of the ship for protection against the rain and cold. The other men had no use for such heavy garments, which would hinder them in climbing to their tasks aloft. The entry serves to re-emphasize the believed superiority of officers to enlisted men and how quick and easy it was to put blame on the lower ranks.

[13] General John Bell Hood, who replaced Confederate General Joseph E. Johnston, staged a series of losing offensive attacks against Union General Sherman that served only to deplete the number of Confederate troops with severe casualties. By the end of July, Hood had retreated to the entrenchments around Atlanta itself. As Sherman used his infantry to destroy railroads and other supply routes, Hood realized he could no longer hold his position and on September 1, he ordered the evacuation of Atlanta. Confederate troops destroyed all military stores including factories, locomotives and railroad cars filled with ammunition. Sherman's army took the city the next day.

[14] On August 5, 1864, Admiral Farragut ordered his fleet into Mobile Bay, and pushed his way through Confederate torpedoes (mines), the narrow passage by Forts Gaines and Morgan, and found the dreaded Confederate ironclad CSS *Tennessee* easy to ram and rather vulnerable to Union shot. The *Tennessee* surrendered and the Union had a major victory with the capture of this key southern harbor.

[15] Edwin M. Stanton (1814–1869) replaced Simon Cameron as secretary of war in 1862. He remained in his position under Andrew Johnson, until the president removed him from office in 1867.

[16] T. Bigalow Lawrence was appointed United States consul general at Florence on March 27, 1861, and served in that post until 1869.

[17] The former raider CSS *Georgia* was captured by the USS *Niagara* on August 15 at Las Rocas. However, the *Georgia* had been decommissioned from Confederate service in May of 1864.

[18] Grant was extending the siege of Richmond and Petersburg westward by capturing the northern section of the Weldon railroad. Slowly but surely, Grant was stretching Lee's defenses more and more.

[19] The Knights of the Golden Circle, also known as Copperheads, were northerners who sympathized with the South. Their most renowned leader was Clement Vallandigham of Ohio. They were instrumental in getting former General George McClellan nominated for president in 1864. There is no evidence to support Safford's allegation that Grant was a member of this organization.

[20] John Hunt Morgan had led numerous raids that caused diversions of troops away from major campaign actions. In 1863 he led a raid across the Ohio River and, after effectually scaring the northern populace, was captured. Though he managed to escape and returned to the Confederacy, on September 4, 1864, he and his escort were caught by surprise in Greenville, Tennessee. While attempting to escape, Morgan was shot in the back and killed by Union cavalry trooper Andrew Campbell.

[21] For his efforts in assisting the *Mersey*, a grateful British government saw to it that Captain Stellwagen was given a certificate of appreciation and an engraved sword. The sword has an oversized gold-plated hilt and the scabbard is made of leather enclosed in blue velvet. That sword is currently on loan to the *Constellation* Museum from the Atwater-Kent Museum and belongs to the Pennsylvania Historical Society.

[22] The USS *Brooklyn* led the port column of wooden vessels into Mobile Bay while USS *Tecumseh* led the starboard column.

[23] On October 7, 1864, USS *Wachusett* sailed into the neutral port of Bahia, Brazil, where she discovered CSS *Florida* at anchor. At the insistence of U.S. Consul Thomas F. Wilson, Captain Collins decided to attack the enemy ship. The *Wachusett* slipped her cables and deliberately rammed *Florida*,

taking away her mizzen and main yards. The *Wachusett* then fired a broadside at point blank range. With only small arms to mount a defense, second in command Lieutenant Thomas K. Porter surrendered the *Florida*. The *Wachusett* towed the battered vessel to sea.

²⁴ Lincoln was, indeed, reelected. However, Farragut was never considered for secretary of the navy. Ben Butler, a politically appointed general, had fallen into great disfavor with the Lincoln administration due to his successive failures in coordinating his Army of the James with General Grant. Perhaps Safford's New England loyalty gave him hope of a northerner being put into high office.

²⁵ Franklin Buchanan (1800–1878) was taken prisoner when his ship, the ironclad ram CSS *Tennessee*, surrendered at Mobile Bay. He was later exchanged in February 1865.

²⁶ At the time Safford met Farragut aboard *Constellation*, Farragut was sixty-three years old.

²⁷ On January 12, 1861, Confederate troops took the surrender of the Pensacola Navy Yard, but failed in several attempts to take Fort Pickens which guarded the harbor. On September 2, attacking Union forces managed to burn the million-dollar dry dock and on September 14, Union marines attacked and burned the *Judah*. After several bombardments by the Union Navy in late 1861 and on January 1, 1862 and Union patrols, Confederate troops successfully evacuated the yard. Despite the yard's continuous use by the U.S. Navy through the following war years, efforts to restore the yard were at a minimum.

²⁸ Safford's fears were realized with the close of the war. The naval service, that had been so successfully integrated up through the Civil War, would now see the harsh face of discrimination come down solidly against African Americans. Where once black men served side by side with their brother white tars, now they would struggle to even gain admittance into what soon became an all-white navy. The trust that blacks had placed in their white compatriots for their future welfare proved false. In later years, blacks were recruited into the navy only as stewards or cooks, thus denying their former proven excellence as qualified seamen.

²⁹ General Benjamin Butler, in charge of one land force, and General Alfred H. Terry, leading an even larger land force, attempted a joint army-navy attack against Fort Fisher on January 13, 1865 (after the original plan in December 1864 was abandoned). Coordination became confused when the naval contingent attacked from the beach immediately upon the ships ceasing their firing from the sea, but the army failed to attack simultaneously as previously arranged. The naval force suffered large casualties and were repulsed. However, when the army did mount their assault, several attacks eventually wore down the Confederate garrison until the fort finally surrendered. The attackers lost 1,338 casualties and the defenders 1,500, which included 500 killed and wounded. The remaining Confederate army was soon overwhelmed and Wilmington fell into Union hands, thus cutting off another source of supply to the Confederacy.

³⁰ This was apparently week-old news by the time Safford learned of it and, with the capture of Savannah and the attack on Fort Fisher happening at the same time, this incident barely rated a news brief in some papers. According to the December 22, 1864 edition of the *Baltimore Sun*, the crew of the British Corvette HMS *Buzzard* made it a point while in port to aggressively insult men from the USS *Sabine*. The two groups met in a local theater where a brawl ensued that required the provost marshal's force to be called out. The newspaper makes no mention of fatalities.

CHAPTER SEVEN NOTES

¹ After Butler's fiasco in the failure to carry through the original attack plan on Fort Fisher, Grant had him removed from command. With his military career at an end, Butler dabbled in politics, serving in the House of Representatives, running for and being elected as governor of Massachusetts, and campaigning for president of the United States.

² The captain of a naval vessel making a capture was required to list all personnel involved,

including any vessel within signaling distance. The prize was then taken to a friendly harbor and there condemned and sold. All officers and enlisted men who took part in the capture were due for shares of the prize money. Any vessel within the prescribed signaling distance was also eligible for shares. Since *Constellation* was well over the horizon when the capture was made, she could not claim any part of the prize money.

[3] "Bounty men" were unscrupulous scam artists who would enlist under false names in several states to collect the bounty money (monetary rewards sometimes offered for enlisting) and then disappear to repeat the scam over and over again.

[4] Edward Everett (1794–1865) was famous as an outstanding orator of his time, most noted for his key note speech at the dedication of the national cemetery at Gettysburg on November 19, 1863.

[5] Safford's account is fairly accurate in regard to the sailors and marines returning to the fight. Recent research shows that the marines were unfairly blamed for the failure of the first attack and their role was far more prominent than originally believed. The magazine explosion casualty numbers are highly inflated. While a company of New York soldiers slept on the ground above the fort's powder magazine the night following the battle, a group of drunken sailors and marines wandered into the magazine with lit torches. The resulting explosion added another 104 killed and wounded to the U.S. casualties suffered that day.

[6] Captain J.M. Berrien, the former captain of USS *Monadnock*, at the time was commandant of the navy yard at Norfolk.

[7] Moses Safford liked John "Jack" Hunter very much. He always felt that if he had not become separated from Jack, the man would have received a permanent warrant as boatswain. All the officers including the captain greatly supported Hunter. However, he had a weakness for alcohol, which caused him to be reduced to the ranks again and spent most of the remainder of his naval career as a chief boatswain's mate.

Bibliography

Belknap, Captain Reginald R., USN. *Routine Book*. Annapolis, MD: U.S. Naval Institute, 1918.

Biesty, Stephen and Richard Platt. *Cross Sections Man-Of-War*. New York: Dorling Kindersley, 1993.

Blake, Nicholas and Richard Lawrence. *The Illustrated Companion to Nelson's Navy*. London: Stackpole Books, 1999.

Bockmiller, Stephen R. *The United States Marine Corps Aboard the USS Constellation, 1855–1868*. Westminster, MD: Opera House, Inc. 1999.

Bockmiller, Stephen R. and Lawrence J. Bopp. *USS Constellation: An Illustrated History*. Charleston, SC: Arcadia Publishing, 2000.

Bolster, W. Jeffrey. *Black Jacks*. Cambridge: Harvard University Press, 1997.

Bopp, Lawrence J. *Sailor Life Aboard the* USS Constellation, *1855–1868*. Westminster, MD: Opera House, Inc., 2000.

Callahan, Edward W. *List of Officers of the Navy of the United States and of the Marine Corps From 1775 to 1900*. Philadelphia: L.R. Hamersly & Co., 1901.

Campbell, R. Thomas. *Sea Hawk of the Confederacy*. Shippensburg, PA: Burd Street Press, 2000.

Canney, Donald L. *Lincoln's Navy: The Ships, Men and Organization, 1861–65*. Annapolis, MD: Naval Institute Press, 1998.

Chapelle, Howard I. *The American Sailing Navy: The Ships and Their Development*. New York: Konecky & Konecky, 1949.

"Cleopatra's Needle." The *Illustrated London News*, March 10, 1877.

Cogar, William B. *Dictionary of Admirals of the U.S. Navy*, Vols. 1 and 2. Annapolis, MD: Naval Institute Press, 1996.

Corbesier, A.J. *Principles of Squad Instruction for the Broadsword*. Pennsylvania: J.B. Lippincott & Co., 1869.

Dana, Richard Henry, Jr. *The Seaman's Friend: A Treatise on Practical Seamanship*. Mineola, NY: Dover Publications, Inc., 1997.

Deck logs, USS *Constellation* 1855–1865, RG 45.

Fagg, Charlie. (Staff of Bluebeard's Castle Resort.) Telephone interview with authors, April 3, 2002.

Faust, Patricia, ed. *Historical Times Illustrated Encyclopedia of the Civil War*. New York: Harper & Row, 1986.

Green, A. Wilson. "The Battle of Fredericksburg, 1862." (Fredericksburg and Spotsylvania National Military Park, National Park Service training booklet.)

Harland, John. *Seamanship in the Age of Sail*. Annapolis: Naval Institute Press, 1985.

Hearn, Chester. *Admiral David Dixon Porter*. Annapolis, MD: Naval Institute Press, 1996.

————. *Admiral David Glasgow Farragut: The Civil War Years*. Annapolis, MD: Naval Institute Press, 1998.

————. *Naval Battles of the Civil War*. San Diego, CA: Salamander Books Ltd., 2000.

Houston, Henry C. *The 32nd Maine Regiment of Infantry Volunteers: An Historical Sketch*. Portland, ME: Southwick Brothers, 1903.

Illustrated Atlas of The Civil War. Echoes of Glory. Alexandria, VA: Time Life Books, 1991.

"Ironmaking." National Parks Brochure. (GPO 28-2-612/20158, 1991.)

Johnson, Caleb. "Lincoln's 1863 Thanksgiving Proclamation." Lincoln Collection, Library of America Series.

Kunitz, Stanley J., ed. *British Authors of the 19th Century*. NY: The H.W. Wilson Company, 1936.

Labaree, Benjamin W., William M. Fowler, John B. Hattendorf, Jeffrey J. Safford, Edward Slaon and Andrew W. German. *America and the Sea: A Maritime History*. Mystic, CT: Mystic Seaport Museum, 1998.

Langley, Harold D. "The Sailor's Life," *Fighting For Time*. The Image of War: 1861-1865, Vol. 4. ed. William C. Davis. Garden City, NY: Doubleday, 1981.

Lever, Darcy. *The Young Sea Officer's Sheet Anchor: or a Key to the Leading of Rigging and to Practical Seamanship*. Mineola, NY: Dover Publications, Inc., 1998.

Long, E.B. *The Civil War Day By Day: An Almanac 1861–1865*. New York: DaCapo Press, 1971.

Lord, Francis. *They Fought For the Union*. New York: Bonanza Books, 1980.

Luce, Lieutenant Commander. S.B., USN. *Seamanship: Compiled From Various Authorities and Illustrated with Numerous Original and Select Designs For the Use of the United States Naval Academy*. NY: D. Van Nostrand, 1877.

Mack, William P. and Royal W. Connell. *Naval Ceremonies, Customs, and Traditions*. Annapolis, MD: Naval Institute Press, 1980.

Marvel, William. *The Alabama & the Kearsarge: The Sailor's Civil War*. Chapel Hill: The University of North Carolina Press, 1996.

Marvel, William, ed. *The Monitor Chronicles*. New York: The Mariner's Museum, Simon & Schuster, 2000.

McPherson, James M. *Battle Cry of Freedom*. New York: Ballentine Books, 1988.

Miller, Francis Trevelyan, ed. *The Navies*. The Photographic History of the Civil War, Vol. 6.. New York: Castle Books, 1906. Reprinted in 1957.

Musicant, Ivan. *Divided Waters: The Naval History of the Civil War*. Edison, NJ: Castle Books, 2000.

Muster Rolls, U.S. Navy Ships 1862–1865, RG 24.

Naval Historical Center Official Website. http://www.history.navy.mil/index.html.

O'Connell, Kim. "The 54th Massachusetts and the Assault on Fort Wagner." Northstar Productions, 1997.

Official Records of the Union and Confederate Navies in the War of the Rebellion. 30 vols.. plus index, Washington, 1896.

Olmstead, Edwin, Wayne C. Stark and Spencer Tucker. *The Big Guns: Civil War Siege, Seacoast, and Naval Cannon*. Bloomfield, Ontario: Museum Restoration Service, 1997.

Pack, James. *Nelson's Blood*. Annapolis, MD: Naval Institute Press, 1982.

Parker, Captain William D., USMCR. *A Concise History of the United States Marine Corps, 1775–1969*. Washington: Historical Division, U.S. Marine Corps, 1970.

Porter, Admiral David Dixon USN. *The Naval History of the Civil War*. New York: Sherman Publishing Co., 1886. Reprinted, Mineola, NY: Dover Publications, 1998.

Priest, William L. *Swear Like a Trooper*. Charlottesville, VA: Rockbridge Publishing, 2000.

Regulations for the Government of the United States Navy. Washington: Government Printing Office, 1865.

Ringle, Dennis J. *Life in Mr. Lincoln's Navy*. Annapolis, MD: Naval Institute Press, 1998.

Roberts, James B. and Alexander G. Skutt. *The Boxing Register*. Ithaca, NY: McBrooks Press, 1997.

Rogers, John G. *Origin of Sea Terms*. Mystic, CT: Mystic Seaport Museum, Inc. 1985.

Rye, Scott. *Men & Ships of the Civil War*. Stamford, CT: Longmeadow Press, 1995.

Safford, Moses. *Personal Diary 1907–1910*. Unpublished manuscript in possession of Joseph W.P. Frost, Kittery, ME.

Safford, Victor. *A Cruise in an Old Frigate prefaced by An Autobiography of the Diarist.* Boston: Unpublished, 1933.

Scharf, J. Thomas. *History of the Confederate States Navy: From Its Organization to the Surrender of Its Last Vessel.* New York: Gramercy Books, 1887, reprinted in 1996.

Silverstone, Paul H. *Civil War Navies: 1855–1883.* Annapolis, MD: naval Institute Press, 2001.

Simpson, Lieutenant Edward USN. *A Treatise on Ordnance and Naval Gunnery, Compiled and Arranged as a Text Book for the U.S. Naval Academy.* New York: D. Van Nostrand, Public Printers, 1862. Located in Navy Library, Rare Book Collection, U.S. Historical Center, Washington Navy Yard, Washington, DC.

Smith, Yvonne Brault. *John Haley Bellamy, Carver of Eagles.* Hampton, NY: Portsmouth Maine Society, 1982.

Stackpole, Everett S. *Old Kittery and Her Families.* Somersworth, ME: New England History Press, 1981.

Still, William N., John M. Taylor and Norman C. Delaney. *Raiders and Blockaders: The American Civil War Afloat.* Washington: Brassey's, 1998.

Stone, Lieutenant Colonel James M. *The History of the 27th Maine Volunteer Infantry.* Portland, ME: The Thurston Print, 1895.

Sullivan, David M. *The United States Marine Corps in the Civil War.* 4 vols. Shippensburg, PA: White Mane Publishing Co., 1997.

Symonds, Craig L. *Confederate Admiral: The Life and Wars of Franklin Buchanan.* Annapolis, MD: Naval Institute Press, 1999.

Taunt, Lieutenant. Emory H. USN. *Young Sailor's Assistant.* Washington: Bureau of Equipment and Recruitment, 1883.

Taylor, Hohn M. *Confederate Raider: Raphael Semmes of the Alabama.* Washington: Brassey's, 1994.

Todd, Frederick P. *American Military Equipage 1851–1872,* Vol. 3. Westbrook, CT: The Company of Military Historians, 1978.

Toucy, Isaac. *Report of the Secretary of the Navy, 1858.* Washington, DC: A Naval Historical Foundation Publication series 2, No. 21. Spring 1977.

Tucker, Spencer C. *Handbook of 19th Century Naval Warfare.* Annapolis, MD: Naval Institute Press, 2000.

U.S. Navy Department, Naval History Division. *Civil War Naval Chronology 1861–1865.* Washington, DC: Government Printing Office, 1971.

U.S. Navy Department, Naval History Division. *Dictionary of American Naval Fighting Ships,* Vols. 1–5. Washington, DC: Government Printing Office, 1970.

U.S. Navy Department. *Ordnance Instructions for the United States Navy, Relating to the Preparation of Vessels of War for Battle: to the Duties of Officers and Others When at Quarters: to Ordnance Stores, and to Gunnery,* Second Edition. Washington, DC: George W. Bowman, Public Printer, 1860. NARA, RG 45.

Valle, James E. *Rocks and Shoals.* Annapolis, MD: Naval institute Press, 1980.

War of the Rebellion, The: A Compilation of the Official Records of the Union and Confederate Armies. 70 vols. in 128 parts and atlas. Washington, 1880–1901.

"War That Never Was, The." *Military Images,* Vol. 23, No.2, September/October, 2001.

Wegner, Dana M. *Fouled Anchors: the Constellation Question Answered.* Bethesda, MD: David Taylor Research Center, 1991.

Who Was Who in American History, the Military. Chicago: Marquis Who's Who, Inc., 1975.

Wideman, John C. *Naval Warfare: Courage and Combat on the Water.* Civil War Chronicles. New York: MetroBooks, 1997.

Williams, Glenn F. USS *Constellation: A Short History of the Last All-Sail Warship Built by the U.S. Navy*. Virginia Beach, VA: The Donning Company, 2000.

———. "The Many Tasks of Uncle Sam's Webfeet." *America's Civil War*, Vol. 15, No. 1, 2002.

Willis, J.L.M., ed. *Old Eliot: A Quarterly Magazine of the History and Biography of the Upper Parish of Kittery, Now Eliot*. Vol. 7. Eliot, ME: Historical Press, 1906.

Windas, Cedric W. *Traditions of the Navy*. Annapolis: MD: Leeward publications, Inc., 1978.

Winslow, Richard E., III. *Constructing the Munitions of War: The Portsmouth Navy Yard Confronts the Confederacy, 1861–1865*. Portsmouth, NH: Portsmouth Marine Society, 1995.

Winter, Frederick R. *U.S. Naval Handguns, 1808–1911*. Lincoln, RI: Andrew Mowbray Incorporated, 1990.

Zabecki, Colonel David T. *American Artillery and the Medal of Honor*. Bennington, VT: Merriam Press, 1997.

Index

Symbols

100th Regiment of Foot (Brit) 222
27th Maine Volunteer Infantry Regiment 87, 94
2nd Maine Cavalry 283
32 Pounder Gun 25, 271

A

Abbott, Phillips & Co. 278
Abbott, Trevett 329
Acre, City of 222, 241
Acropolis 248, 250, 251, 252
Act of Congress 61
Adams Express 290
Aegean Sea 62
African Squadron 12, 16, 332
Agawam, USS 298
Age of Reason 109
Alabama, CSS 11, 79, 85, 100, 112, 246
Alexandretta, Turkey 66
Alexandria, Egypt 161, 223, 224, 225, 227, 241, 242, 258
Algeciras, Spain 35, 36, 37, 115, 116, 152, 153, 154, 269, 333
Algiers 160, 161
Allen, Stillman B. 13, 15, 299
Almonecan, Spain 150
Ameen, Moustafa 63
Ancelini 163
Anderson, Charles (Cocky) 49, 163, 164, 167, 199, 205
Andrea Doria theater 102
Anglo Saxon, SS (steamer) 118
Annapolis, MD 299, 331
Antietam, Battle of 66
Anti Gozo 255
Aqua Sola 91, 100, 102
Archer, SS (schooner) 137
Armstrong, William 37
Armstrong Guns 37, 159
Articles of War 44, 69, 272, 329

B

Askalan 227
Athens, Greece 248, 249, 250, 251, 252, 253, 254, 255
Atlanta, SS (bark) 286
Azores 21, 24, 79, 154, 271

Bacchus, Sylvanius 282
Bahia, Brazil 277
Balearic Islands 39, 106
Baltic, USS 290
Baltimore, MD 11, 67, 70, 254, 294, 298, 299, 325, 326, 328, 381
Barcelona, Spain 143, 144, 152, 158
Bartolini, Augusto 143
Basseria 95, 96, 97, 102
Bath, ME 192
Bay of Fundy 137
Bay of Naples 170, 171, 180, 186, 194
Beauregard, Pierre G.T. 33, 51
Bedouins 211, 216, 218
Beirut 62, 63, 64, 65, 66, 67, 68, 241, 242, 243, 244, 245, 246, 247, 248
Bell, Charles H. 181
Bell, Henry H. 294
Bellamy, Catherine C. 323
Bellamy, John H. 299, 323
Bellows, Charles D. 263
Bennett, George C. 124, 184, 185, 282
Bermuda 275, 281
Berth Deck 23, 25, 32, 65, 73, 89, 100, 110, 112, 116, 117, 118, 132, 136, 145, 146, 153, 160, 161, 166, 205, 213, 266, 267, 270, 288, 326
Bethany 232, 233
Bethlehem 231, 232
Bey, Huseyin 211
Big Bethel, VA 33
Black-Horse Square 29
Blake, Charles F. 118
Blenheim, CSS 299
blockade runner 279, 284, 285, 286, 287, 295, 329, 330
Blue Beard's Castle 278
boat drill 42, 72, 104, 220
Bordeaux, France 279

About the Authors

A proud Baltimorean, Lawrence Bopp is retired after a combined thirty-two years of teaching English, reading and history in the Baltimore City and Baltimore County School systems. He is a graduate of the University of Baltimore with a master's degree from Loyola College. Larry has been a Civil War re-enactor since 1967 and has appeared in several films including *Glory*, *Gettysburg* and numerous NPS productions. He is the founder of the 4th North Carolina, CSA, Inc., and the co-founder of Ship's Company, Inc., that has been serving USS *Constellation* since 1981. Larry spends his retirement researching the Civil War Navy and is currently occupied with the United States Marine Corps Historical Company in researching the history of Marine Corps uniforms. He resides in the Catonsville community with his wife, Katie.

A Baltimore native and graduate of Towson State University, Stephen Bockmiller is a member of the USS *Constellation* Museum Advisory Board and volunteers on the ship, coordinating living history programming pertaining to the U.S. Marine Corps in the Civil War. Steve is a former National Park Service ranger, and is employed in the public sector in the land use development field in three jurisdictions in Maryland and West Virginia. He and his wife Stefania reside in a pre-Civil War log home in Western Maryland.

Stephen Bockmiller is the author of *The United States Marine Corps Aboard the USS* Constellation, *1855–1868*; Larry Bopp is the author of *Sailor Life on the USS* Constellation, *1855–1868* and they have co-authored the book, *USS* Constellation: *An Illustrated History*.